PENGUIN BOOKS

THE PENGUIN CLASSIC
BABY NAME BOOK

Carol McD. Wallace is the author of twenty books, ranging in subject from children's manners to Victorian collectibles. Two of these were bestselling baby name books, *20,001 Names for Baby* and *The Greatest Baby Name Book Ever*. Also published by Penguin is *All Dressed in White: The Irresistible Rise of the American Wedding*. Wallace lives in New York City with her family.

THE PENGUIN

CLASSIC BABY NAME BOOK

Carol McD. Wallace

Previously published
under the name Grace Hamlin

PENGUIN BOOKS

PENGUIN BOOKS

Published by the Penguin Group

Penguin Group (USA) Inc., 375 Hudson Street,
New York, New York 10014, U.S.A.
Penguin Books Ltd, 80 Strand, London WC2R 0RL, England
Penguin Books Australia Ltd, 250 Camberwell Road,
Camberwell, Victoria 3124, Australia
Penguin Books Canada Ltd, 10 Alcorn Avenue,
Toronto, Ontario, Canada M4V 3B2
Penguin Books India (P) Ltd, 11 Community Centre,
Panchsheel Park, New Delhi – 110 017, India
Penguin Books (N.Z.) Ltd, Cnr Rosedale and Airborne Roads,
Albany, Auckland, New Zealand
Penguin Books (South Africa) (Pty) Ltd, 24 Sturdee Avenue,
Rosebank, Johannesburg 2196, South Africa

Penguin Books Ltd, Registered Offices:
80 Strand, London WC2R 0RL, England

First published under the name Grace Hamlin in Penguin Books 2001
Published in Penguin Books 2004

1   3   5   7   9   10   8   6   4   2

LIBRARY OF CONGRESS CATALOGING IN PUBLICATION DATA
Wallace, Carol McD.
The Penguin classic baby name book / Carol McD. Wallace.
p. cm.
Includes index.
ISBN 0 14 10.0152 6 (pbk.)
ISBN 0 14 20.0470 7 (pbk.)
1. Names, Personal—Dictionaries.   2. Characters and
characteristics in literature—Dictionaries.   I. Title.
CS2377 .H344 2001
929.4'4—dc21   00-065231

Printed in the United States of America
Set in Sabon
Designed by Bonni Leone

With enduring love
to my classically named sons,
William and Timothy

ACKNOWLEDGMENTS

To an even greater extent than usual, I owe this project to the good offices of my agent, Lynn Seligman. Kathryn Court, Caroline White, Barbara Campo, and everyone I came into contact with at Penguin made it a joy to work on. My greatest debt, however, is to the authors of the Penguin Classics, whose characters made such wonderful company while I was writing this book.

CONTENTS

INTRODUCTION

*"We heard of poor Charming Handy's death the tenth of
September."*
"Was his name Charming?" I asked.
*"His mother named him," Abram said, "with a name that
she had picked out of Novel's works."*

—Elizabeth Stoddard, *The Morgesons*

It's a time-honored solution to the expectant parent's quest for a
baby's name. Literature was the obvious place to look for inspiration before the invention of the baby name book, so parents
have named children "out of Novel's works" for hundreds of
years. And for hundreds of years before the development of the
novel, they turned to other literary sources (epic poetry, legends, the Bible) for help in choosing names. In fact, literature and
drama have long represented the widest world available to the
average man or woman. Where better, then, to look for names
than in classic literature?

The classics, by their very definition, offer staying power. They
feature names that have been around for hundreds of years. No
upstart inventions, no phonetic variations, but stalwart, time-
honored choices like Henry and Catherine and Isabel. They also
feature names from different cultures. Every part of the world
from classical Greece to Chaucerian England to prerevolutionary

Russia has produced landmarks of literature, including epic poetry, historical chronicles, letters, criticism, drama, and fiction, and names ranging from Cassandra to Rodion. The names in this book are drawn from the editions published as the Penguin Classics, which offer a comprehensive overview of world literature.

The works consulted, however, were only those of literary invention. This book concerns *characters,* not historic figures. The line, of course, is fuzzy—Macbeth actually lived in Scotland in the eleventh century. Nevertheless, the character invented by Shakespeare eclipses the scanty facts. His name is here. On the other hand, of all the major characters thronging the Penguin Classics (excluding the Twentieth-Century Classics), not one is named Victoria. So that name is missing from this book, despite the great flowering of the English novel during Queen Victoria's reign.

In fact, there are a number of fairly subjective exclusions, and inclusions as well. This book does not contain every name of every character in literature. Some of them are linguistically too far from English to be likely choices for Western parents. (There are thus few names from Asian or Norse sources, for instance.) On the other hand, some characters, especially in Greek sources, have names that sound odd to the anglophone ear, and are profoundly unpleasant to boot. Yet you'll find them here: all three of the Greek Furies—Alecto, Megaera, and Tisiphone—are listed. Why? They are so important to many of the Greek tragedies that they virtually petitioned for inclusion. Not all of these names are actually usable for a child, I have to admit—but who would deny the Kindly Ones? In fact, long after your baby is walking, this book can serve as a swift reference to the principal characters of world literature.

Yet in spite of the breadth of the possibilities and my impulse toward inclusion (sometimes at the expense of practicality), this book is heavily weighted toward the novels of the nineteenth century. This is so for a number of reasons. First, the fiction of that era is expansive. *Great Expectations,* one of Dickens's more compressed novels, runs longer than five hundred pages, while most of the other Dickens titles are over nine hundred. A long book means a big cast of characters. What's more, Victorian novelists tended to be extremely prolific. Thomas Hardy wrote fourteen novels, Henry James twenty. Add the works of Dickens, Trollope, and Balzac, and you have hundreds of characters right there.

Perhaps even more to the point, however, is the way these authors used names, and the names they chose. Broadly, two naming traditions predominate in literature. Some authors (and some periods) lean toward a kind of allegorical naming; the name highlights an attribute. Edmund Spenser's *The Faerie Queen* is full of allusive names like Una (unity) and Charissa (charity). Yet Spenser's contemporary, Shakespeare, relied more heavily on naturalistic names: names that were plausible for real people in the admittedly exotic settings of his plays—Viola, Antonio, Rosalind. Allegorical choices like Touchstone or Bottom are usually restricted to Shakespeare's lesser characters.

European writers employed both naming systems, but as the novel developed through the eighteenth and nineteenth centuries, the naturalistic style predominated. For instance, though Dickens and Trollope persisted in their use of allusive names until the 1860s and '70s, their principal characters usually bore the names of people you might have met on the streets of London. For potential parents, the names drawn from these authors' books are more likely to appeal in a practical sense than the attribute names employed by other writers; hence their predominance in this book.

Allusion did not vanish in the nineteenth century, however; it merely took the appearance of naturalism. Authors like Hardy, Dostoyevsky, and Henry James took care to choose names for their characters that incorporated ideas the authors had about them. Critics talk about Dostoyevsky's "psychonyms," for instance: the three Karamazov brothers bear names that point to their preoccupations. Dmitri, whose name harks back to Demeter, the earth goddess, is the carnal, matter-bound son; Alyosha, whose name comes from the Greek Alexander ("defender of mankind," i.e., Christ, in this interpretation), is the spiritual one. Authors of the nineteenth century also played with the literary baggage accompanying some names. In *The Wild Ass's Skin*, Balzac with utter lack of subtlety names his angelic-looking protagonist Raphaël, after one of the archangels, while one of the miracles of James's art is that he manages to make his psycho-nyms like "Christopher Newman" plausible as real names. It is often these layers of literary association that draw parents to names from classic books. For hundreds of years readers have found their favorite characters admirable, compelling, challeng-ing, memorable. A name from literature can be both a compli-ment to that character and an inspiration to a child.

USING THIS BOOK

Although some baby name books present their selections in innovative ways, this book proceeds in the conventional manner with an alphabetic list of given names, divided by gender. The main entry gives the most common form of the name (Catherine, for instance) in boldface, followed by its source and a simple definition. Variants, especially those that occur in other works, are also listed in boldface type. Some historical background may be included, especially if it might have influenced a writer to choose that name for a character. The body of each entry describes the character who has borne the name in literature—or the characters, if there are more than one. It's particularly exciting to see how early literary use of a name informs the later use, as with Arthur, a name that cannot be used without invoking England's legendary king.

Foreign names present special issues. If the name appears in the Penguin Classics in a foreign but not an English form, that is how it is listed. Spelling follows the spelling in the book where the name appears. This leads to some inconsistency with Russian names, as translators use different methods to approach Russian pronunciation, and include or ignore patronymics, nicknames, and inflected surnames. I have included simple pronunciation for names that seemed to require it.

I have also included quotations about specific characters throughout the book, as well as boxes with irresistible tidbits of information that readers may find entertaining. Finally, names are indexed by author and title at the back of the book.

This book contains nearly two thousand names, many fewer than most of the encylopedic collections of baby names available. But with each name comes a story, a history, a character—a wonderful legacy to share with your new child.

BOYS' NAMES

AARON *(Hebrew, "raised up, elevated")* Shakespeare's tragedy *Titus Andronicus* is a notorious bloodbath, featuring twelve murders and countless gruesome atrocities. Aaron, the Moorish (read black) slave and lover of Tamora, queen of the Goths, is a deep-dyed villain, both whimsical and cruel. In George Eliot's *Silas Marner*, Aaron Winthrop is a minor character, the young gardener who will eventually marry the heroine Eppie. In sharp contrast to the squire's sons Dunstan and Godfrey, his aristocratic contemporaries in the book, Aaron is an honest, hardworking, contented man. His name points up the disparity: by the mid-nineteenth century the educated classes had turned to older English names with a Norman influence. Rural families still used the Old Testament names that had been familiar for several hundred years.

> *His name was Abel, and all his life he had been known as able Abe.* —ANTHONY TROLLOPE, *THE PRIME MINISTER*

ABEL *(Hebrew, "breath")* Anthony Trollope used this unusual name for Abel Wharton, the eminent barrister and father of Everett and Emily, in *The Prime Minister*. He is a stern widower, "a man of whom men were generally afraid." Resonances of Cain and Abel are nonexistent here: Mr. Wharton is anything but a victim. Charles Dickens may have intended to invoke the biblical brothers, however, with Abel Magwitch, the terrifying convict in

Great Expectations. As a child, Pip rescues Magwitch, saving his life. From that point on, the two are secretly linked, as Magwitch is finally the source of Pip's "expectations." Pip's journey to manhood includes finally accepting Magwitch's large role in his life.

ABNER *(Hebrew, "my father is light")* Thomas Hardy's *A Laodicean* focuses on the tension between the past and the present, as headstrong heiress Paula Power falls in love with the architect she has hired to renovate Stancy Castle to a "romantic and historical" state. Abner Power, her uncle and an engineer, meddles with her romance.

ABRAHAM *(Hebrew, "father of the multitude")* Though naturalism is not the point of Henry Fielding's *Joseph Andrews,* his curate Abraham Adams is somewhat plausibly named—Old Testament names were still used in well-to-do families in the eighteenth century. The curate of the Booby Hall parish, Adams is classically educated but perfectly ignorant in the ways of the world. Though he travels to London to try to sell his sermons to a publisher, for instance, he neglects to bring them with him. The alliteration of his name and its jingling five-syllable rhythm are somehow innately comical rather than patriarchal. On the other hand, Bram Stoker's Abraham Van Helsing is everything one could want in a father figure. Imposing, oracular, and wise, he is the Dutch doctor in *Dracula* who understands the ways of vampires, and insists on driving a stake through the heart of Lucy Westenra to rescue her from being Undead. The author's name—Bram—just happens to be derived from Abraham.

ABSALOM *(Hebrew, "father is peace")* In the Old Testament, Absalom is the beautiful son of King David who is captured and killed by enemies when his hair is caught on a tree as he rides under it. Geoffrey Chaucer's Absalom (or **Absolon**) in "The Miller's Tale" has curly hair, which might have rung a bell with the biblically literate readers of *The Canterbury Tales.* This young man, however, is merely a parish clerk with a crush on the nubile Alison that rouses the suspicions of her husband John.

ACHILLES *(Greek place-name)* The great hero of Homer's *The Iliad,* Achilles is the son of the sea goddess Thetis and the human Peleus. Thetis dipped him into the River Styx to render him immortal, but forgot to wet the back of the heel where she held him. It was thus the only vulnerable part of his body, and we still refer to both the literal Achilles tendon and the metaphorical Achilles' heel. Achilles is the Greeks' greatest soldier during the Trojan War, though until Book 19 of *The Iliad* he refuses to fight, having squabbled with Agamemnon over possession of a female captive. He finally stops sulking and enters the fray, killing the Trojan hero Hector and dragging his body three times around the walls of Troy. It is Paris, Hector's brother, who shoots Achilles in his vulnerable heel with an arrow, finally killing him. In Euripides' *Iphigenia in Aulis,* Achilles is slightly incongruously embroiled in a romance. Euripides portrays him as a warrior eager to get to Troy and join battle. Agamemnon, however, has been told by an oracle that his daughter Iphigenia must be sacrificed to attract favorable winds to speed the fleet to Troy. Agamemnon, to placate his restive troops and spare his daughter, claims that she is betrothed to the great warrior Achilles. In Euripides' version of the tale, Iphigenia agrees to the sacrifice to let the men get on with their war. (Jean Racine, in a seventeenth-century rewrite, finesses the sacrifice and lets her survive.)

ACTAEON *(ak tay' on; Greek, "from Attica")* The grandson of Cadmus, king of Thebes, and, according to Ovid's *Metamorphoses,* an object lesson in avoiding the wrath of the gods. Out hunting one day, young Actaeon mistakenly happened on the virginal goddess Diana as she bathed in a stream. In fury that she had been seen naked, she turned him into a stag. His own pack of hunting dogs tore him to shreds.

ADAM *(Hebrew, "reddish, red earth")* George Eliot's *Adam Bede,* set in 1799, sought to portray the emotional and moral lives of simple rural characters who had been ignored by fiction up to that point. Adam Bede (the last name is also significant, conjuring up Old English images of almshouse residents or even the ancient church historian) is a tall, handsome, morally upright man who rises from the status of carpenter to land agent in the course of the narrative. He falls in love with the flighty Hetty Sorrel, and her tragic career softens his somewhat rigid morality. Robert Louis Stevenson probably had the word "adamant" in mind when he named a law lord Adam in his last, unfinished novel, *Weir of Hermiston*. Scholars speculate that the "hanging judge" Adam Weir is based in a profound way on Stevenson's own uncommunicative father—"He did not try to be loved, he did not care to be; it is probable the very thought of it was a stranger to his mind." In Henry James's last novel, *The Golden Bowl*, Adam Verver is a wealthy American connoisseur, father of the heroine Maggie Verver, and the most straightforward character in a deeply complex book. For James, the name may have had connotations of something primal, even primitive—Adam as the first man in the Bible.

ADMETUS (*Greek, meaning unknown*) In Euripides' play *Alcestis*, Admetus is king of Thessaly. The Fates have agreed that he must die young, but Apollo intervenes, decreeing that if someone will agree to die in his place, he may live. His friends and relatives all refuse, but his wife Alcestis volunteers, and meets her death in the first scene of the piece. Since the play is a comedy, she is later brought back to life.

ADOLPHUS (*German, "noble wolf"*) Though George Eliot names a clergyman Adolphus Irwine in *Adam Bede,* it is Anthony Trollope's characters who lay the strongest claim to the name. In *The Small House at Allington*, Adolphus Crosbie is "a swell," as the heroine Lily Dale puts it. She is gently mocking him, in her sardonic style, and goes on to dub him "Apollo," but when she gets to know him better she falls in love with him and the two get engaged. Crosbie, however, is just what she had first thought him, a "swell," a handsome, charming, and arrogant dandy. He is also unprincipled, and two weeks after leaving Lily's home, he becomes engaged to the proud thirty-year-old spinster Lady Alexandrina de Courcy. In this book, the name brings a notion of something finicky and overwrought to the character, but Adolphus Longstaff in _The Duke's Children_ and _The Way We Live Now_ is something of a fool. His nickname of "Dolly" marks him as a figure of fun. Yet in Trollope's evenhanded way (few characters are wholly good or wholly bad), it is Dolly Longstaff who unwittingly brings down the swindler Augustus Melmotte in the latter book.

The French form of the name is **Adolphe,** the title of a novel by Benjamin Constant. Adolphe is the callow protagonist—emphatically _not_ a hero—of this narrative written in 1816. Traveling in Germany to round out his education, he falls in with the aristocratic society of a small principality and soon sets out to seduce Ellénore, the mistress of a count. The novel details the uneven course of the love affair, which bores Adolphe once Ellénore is his responsibility.

ADONIS (_Greek, meaning unknown_) In Ovid's _Metamorphoses,_ Adonis is the son of Myrrha by her father, and a heartbreakingly beautiful youth: "Even Jealousy personified would have praised his beauty." Venus falls in love with him, and warns him to beware the boars that inhabit the woods where he likes to ramble. He doesn't heed her warning, and is gored to death. As he dies, Venus comes upon him and decrees that his body be turned into an anemone, the beautiful but fragile and short-lived flower with petals the color of blood.

AEGEUS (ay gee' us; _Greek, "a goatskin shield" or "protection"_) In Greek myth, Aegeus is the father of Theseus, who went with the youths of Athens to Crete to fight the Minotaur as part of a tribute exacted by King Minos. Aegeus instructed Theseus to equip his ships with black sails as well as white. If he came home triumphant over the Minotaur, he was supposed to hoist the white sails. He forgot this important instruction and when Aegeus saw the black sails come into sight, he threw himself off the headland into the sea—the Aegean sea thereafter.

AENEAS (ay nee' as; _Latin from Greek, "to praise"_) Aeneas is the wandering hero of Virgil's _Aeneid_ whose primary characteristic is *pietas,* or devotion to his duty, to his family, and to the gods, as well as submission to his fate, which was, ultimately, to found the city of Rome. Thus he sometimes performs odious actions like abandoning the besotted Dido, queen of Carthage, with whom he has spent a year of love. Unlike the more monolithic Greek heroes, he is psychologically complex. Not so his namesake Aeneas Manston in Thomas Hardy's *Desperate Remedies*—this Aeneas is a deep-dyed villain. Hardy enjoyed allusive names. The heroine of the novel is **Cytherea**, another name for Venus. She was named after an early love of her father's who turns out to be—gasp!—the mother of Aeneas Manston. Victorian readers would not have needed to be told that the legendary Aeneas was the son of Venus.

AGAMEMNON *(Greek, meaning unknown)* Supreme commander of the Greek forces during the Trojan War. His brother Menelaus, as Helen's husband, was the wronged party. Furthermore, as king of Mycenae and commander of the largest contingent of the assembled Greek army, Agamemnon had ample military reasons for leading the troops. His position was not without its perils, though. Euripides' tragedy *Iphigenia in Aulis* (reworked by Jean Racine in the seventeenth century) focuses on Agamemnon's crisis when the army is stranded in Aulis by contrary winds. An oracle proclaims that his daughter Iphigenia must be sacrificed to attract favorable winds. Euripides has Iphigenia engaged to Achilles, a situation that tightens the tension between the two great warriors. When Agamemnon finally returns home from Troy, he finds that his wife Clytemnestra is the mistress of Aegisthus. She murders Agamemnon in his bath, paving the way for further violence as the curse of the house of Atreus is worked out.

AHAB *(Hebrew, "uncle")* The name of the famous captain of the *Pequod* in Herman Melville's *Moby-Dick*. It's not entirely clear that this is his first name: the first mate Starbuck, for instance, is known by his last name. Yet the Old Testament king Ahab seems to be the precedent here. Melville makes Captain Ahab's hubris clear, calling him "a grand, ungodly, god-like man." He is, of course, seeking the white whale to get revenge for the loss of his leg, and in his quest (a mad inversion of a knightly quest) flouts every rule of religion and humanity.

> So giant Ajax marched, that bulwark of the Achaeans—
> a grim smile curling below his dark shaggy brows,
> under his legs' power taking immense strides,
> shaking his spear high, its long shadow trailing.
> —HOMER, *THE ILIAD*

AJAX *(Greek, "alas")* Another hero from the Trojan War and the *Iliad,* Ajax was the king of Salamis. Physically daunting and courageous, he was the greatest of the Greek warriors after Achilles. He was so proud of his prowess that when the dead Hector's armor was awarded to Odysseus instead of to him, he stabbed himself in mortification.

ALADDIN *(Arabic, "height of the faith")* One of the most famous characters in *Tales from the Thousand and One Nights,* Aladdin is the lazy and mischievous son of the tailor Mustafa. He manages to get himself shut into a cave by a magician, rubs a lamp, and is rewarded when a genie pops out.

> *"I like you very well, Alan, but your ways are not my ways, and they're not God's."*
> —ROBERT LOUIS STEVENSON, *KIDNAPPED*

ALAN *(Gaelic, meaning unclear; "rock" is often proposed)* Also **Allan, Allen.** Robert Louis Stevenson created the unforgettable Alan Breck in *Kidnapped.* A Highland Scot, a fervent Protestant at a time when religion mattered a great deal, he is short in stature, a dandy, and very proud. "His eyes were unusually light and had a kind of dancing madness in them that was both engaging and alarming." He and the hero David Balfour, on the run together, explore the limits of trust and loyalty. Dickens uses Allan for the altruistic young Dr. Woodcourt in *Bleak House*. In spite of his mother's social pretensions he is attracted to the modest, sweet, and self-effacing Esther Summerson. Wilkie Collins's sensational *Armadale* features four characters called Allan Armadale, whose relationships are entwined through two generations. The novel is mostly concerned with the fate of young, trusting, impulsive Allan Armadale, the heir to a fortune—and his mixed-race double, who goes by the name of Ozias Midwinter.

> *My mother had a woman's romantic objection to my father's homely Christian name [Matthew]. I was christened Allan, after the name of a wealthy cousin of my father's—the late Allan Armadale—who possessed estates in our neighbourhood.* —WILKIE COLLINS, ARMADALE

ALBERT *(French from German, "noble, bright or brilliant")* Though Queen Victoria's 1840 marriage to Prince Albert of Saxe-Coburg-Gotha inspired many parents, English authors steered clear of the name during the nineteenth century. It may have had too many strong connotations to accommodate a character. Alexandre Dumas named a secondary character Albert Morcerf in *The Count of Monte Cristo*—he is the son of the hero's lifelong enemy. And in Goethe's *The Sorrows of Young Werther*, Albert is the prosaic, steady, suitable fiancé of Lotte, Werther's beloved.

ALEXANDER *(Greek, "defender of men")* Also **Alec, Alex.** Alexander the Great's military exploits give this name a resonance that writers have occasionally exploited. (Dante, by the way, placed the great warrior in the seventh circle of Hell, being boiled in blood with the rest of "The Violent.") Thomas Hardy may well have had Alexander's bullying nature in mind when he created Alec D'Urberville, Tess's downfall. A cocky young man of means, he seduces Tess and makes her pregnant. Later, after Alec has become a preacher (an excellent outlet for his domineering personality), Tess goes back to him, a decision that leads to tragedy. For some of the characters in *A Tale of Two Cities,* Dickens needed names that could cross the English Channel with impunity: hence **Alexandre**, for Dr. Manette, the famous prisoner of the Bastille. He is liberated and brought to England, where he is rehabilitated and lives peacefully with his daughter Lucie. But in times of stress, he reverts to his prison identity and returns to making shoes, as he had done in prison.

Alexander also crosses over easily to the Russian language (often as **Aleksander** or **Aleksandr**) and has, furthermore, links to the imperial family: by the 1890s, when Chekhov wrote *Uncle Vania,* Russia had had three tsars named Alexander. In that play, Alexandre Serebriakov is the elderly, egotistical hanger-on of the estate that Uncle Vania manages, and a man who sees the world solely through the prism of his own needs. In *The Three Sisters,* Alexandr Vershinin is an officer in the local army brigade, and the receptacle of Masha Prozorov Kulygin's romantic dreams.

For the two men in Anna Karenina's life, Leo Tolstoy chose **Alexei** (also **Alexey** or **Aleksey**), a shorter variant of Alexander. Karenin, the sober, intellectual husband, is always referred to as Alexei Alexandrovich (to emphasize the legitimacy of his familial ties to Anna?), while the dashing lover is known simply as Vronsky. In *The Brothers Karamazov,* written just a few years later, Dostoyevsky names the youngest of the three brothers **Aleksey**, but he is generally known as **Alyosha**, a diminutive form. He is the brother who represents the religious and the redemptive side of mankind.

Another set of nicknames, **Sandy** and **Sasha**, are based on the middle syllable of **Alexander**. George du Maurier's *Trilby* includes a Sandy M'Allister as a broadly drawn Scottish laird spending a few youthful years painting in Paris. He speaks terrible French and specializes in canvases of Spanish toreadors, though he's never seen a bullfight. **Sasha**, the Russian nickname for Alexander, is

GERMAN NAMES

One of the peculiarities of the German language is the portmanteau word. When confronted with a new concept, German, rather than turning to other languages for a cognate form, will simply link two of its own words to create a new one. Hence *baumwolle,* or "tree wool," for "cotton."

English resists this tendency. Two nouns placed side by side do not coexist happily until a grammatical relationship has been established between them, even if that relationship is implied. An umbrella stand is a stand *for* umbrellas; "umbrella" modifies "stand."

Many of our English names come from German sources. They can often be broken down into elements that frequently recur in other names: *bert,* for instance, means "bright," while *adal* or *edel* means "high" or "noble." So **Albert,** translated strictly, means "noble bright." **William** means "will helmet" and **Frederick** means "peace rule."

Some name books finesse these awkward definitions by modifying one of the elements. **Albert,** for instance, is sometimes defined as "noble brightness." Other books insert punctuation ("will/helmet") for instance, which expresses the loose linkage of concepts. I have tried to leave these definitions alone, in all their awkwardness. Even in cases when changing the order may produce a more graceful definition, I have left the clumsy formation because amateur etymologists may enjoy tracking the various elements that German uses, like building blocks, to create meaning. "Bright intelligence" sounds better than "intelligence bright" (the name is **Hubert**), but devotees of language may enjoy making the connection between the *bert* ending and the meaning of "bright" or "shining" that occurs so often in these German names.

used for both genders. In Chekhov's short story "The Fiancée," Sasha is Alexander Timofeyevich, a distant relative of the affianced Nadya. Cultured and artistic, he opens Nadya's eyes to the limited life her projected marriage would bring her. She breaks her engagement and goes off to get an education because of him.

> "*Because Alexei—I am speaking of Alexei Alexandrovich (such a strange, terrible fate, that they are both Alexei, isn't it?)—Alexei would not refuse me. I should forget, he would forgive.*"
> —LEO TOLSTOY, *ANNA KARENINA*

ALFONSO (*Spanish from Old German, "prepared for battle"*) Lord Byron used this name for a somewhat stock character, the fifty-year-old husband of his Don Juan's first sexual conquest (twenty-three-year-old Doña Julia). Alfonso was a royal name in Spain, and thus not unduly exotic. In a case like this, where the character is less a person than a concept, a remarkable name can be overpowering. A variant is **Alonso,** the given name of the nobleman who imagines himself into Cervantes's Don Quixote after reading too many novels of chivalry. In Shakespeare's *The Tempest,* Alonso is the shipwrecked king of Naples and father of Ferdinand. He once plotted with Antonio and Sebastian to drive Prospero from his rights as duke of Milan, but his treachery is petty compared to theirs. His chief concern on Prospero's island is the safety of his son Ferdinand, whom he believes has drowned.

ALFRED (*Old English, "elf counsel"*) Alfred Jingle of *The Pickwick Papers* is one of Charles Dickens's earliest fictional creations. His first name is perfectly commonplace, especially for the early Victorian era, but his last name, like those of so many Pickwickian characters, is ridiculous. He is a rascal, a strolling actor for whom deception is instinctive. Ultimately, he and Pickwick are thrown together enough by the meandering plot to have substantial influence on each other. In George Gissing's *New Grub*

Street, the name retains the early Victorian air, but since Gissing wrote in the 1880s, the character is, naturally, an older man. Alfred Yule's jolly last name belies his nature. He is a bitter and exhausted writer, worn down by the difficulty of the writer's trade. Trollope uses a Latinized variant, **Alured,** for a character in *The Prime Minister.* Sir Alured Wharton, baronet, is the head of the Wharton family, a stiff-necked conservative full of family pride.

ALI *(Arabic, "exalted")* In *Tales from the Thousand and One Nights,* Ali Baba is the woodcutter who witnesses the forty thieves opening their magical cave with the charm "Open Sesame." With the help of his slave Morgiana he makes the treasure his own.

ALVARO *(Spanish from Old English, "elf army")* Leopoldo Alas's *La Regenta* is Spain's answer to the naturalistic novels of nineteenth-century France. It takes place in the provincial town of Vetusta and concerns the lonely young matron Ana Ozores Quintana. Married to a kindly but impotent older man, Ana becomes the prey of Vetusta's rake, Alvaro Mesia. He pursues her for the pleasure of the conquest, but after killing her husband in a duel, he decamps, leaving Ana alone to face the opprobrium of the townspeople.

AMASA *(Hebrew, "burdened")* In "Benito Cereno" (1856), Herman Melville adapted the story of a naive American sea captain from a published nonfiction account, and kept the captain's name as well. As told by Melville, Amasa Delano's encounter with a Spanish slaving ship under the command of rebellious slaves is a tale of innocence reluctantly recognizing evil, or an encounter between the New World and the Old.

AMBROSIUS *(Latin, "immortal")* The English form is **Ambrose,** but in *Idylls of the King* Tennyson chooses the more antique-sounding form for the monk to whom Sir Percival tells the story of the Holy Grail. The poet may use the name to refer to the immortality of Percival's deeds.

AMERIGO *(Italian from Old German, "home power" or "home rule")* In Henry James's last novel, *The Golden Bowl*, Prince Amerigo is the elegant young sprig of a decadent Roman family who marries the American heiress Maggie Verver. Her money permits him to continue his life of elegance and ease, as well as his love affair with her old friend Charlotte Stant. Some emphasis is laid on Amerigo Vespucci's discovery of America and Prince Amerigo's discovery of "the Americans."

> *Maggie happened to learn ... that one of the Prince's baptismal names ... was Amerigo: which ... was the name, four hundred year ago, or whenever, of the pushing man who followed, across the sea, in the wake of Columbus and succeeded, where Columbus had failed, in becoming godfather, or name-father, to the new Continent, so that the thought of any connection with him can even now thrill our artless breasts.* —HENRY JAMES, THE GOLDEN BOWL

AMOS *(Hebrew, "borne")* An Old Testament prophet. George Eliot's first published fiction, *Scenes of Clerical Life*, includes a tale called "The Sad Fortunes of the Rev. Amos Barton." Barton is an evangelical-minded curate whose parishioners despise him both for his theology and because he is not a gentleman. He is also poor, and burdened with many children. Eliot is unsparing in her portrayal of his courage and his unhappiness.

ANASTASIUS *(Greek, "resurrection")* A minor character in James's *Princess Casamassima*, Anastasius Vetch is the violinist in a second-rate orchestra whose financial gift permits protagonist Hyacinth Robinson to go to Europe. There, the young man discovers all the cultural refinements that his modest upbringing did not include. Since Hyacinth is an anarchist, committed to overthrowing the world that produced these refinements, this development is tragic for him. As Henry James was careful about names, and Anastasius is a very unusual choice, one wonders if irony is intended.

ANATOLY *(Greek, "from Anatolia, from the East")* Anatoly Kuragin is one of the least admirable characters in the throng crowding Tolstoy's *War and Peace*. A dissolute rake, he seduces Natasha Rostova though she is engaged to Prince Andrei Bolkonsky. He even arranges a false marriage ceremony to allay her qualms. He and the rest of the unscrupulous Kuragin family stand for the corruption in Russian aristocratic society.

> *He had been called Andy by the late Sir Florian, and, though every one else about the place called him Mr. Gowran, Lady Eustace . . . called him Andy.*
> —ANTHONY TROLLOPE, THE EUSTACE DIAMONDS

ANDREW *(Greek, "manly, masculine")* In Shakespeare's *Twelfth Night*, Sir Andrew Aguecheek is a comical character, one of Olivia's suitors who postures as a rake but is actually a simpleton. He is bested in a duel with Sebastian. Wilkie Collins named a character Andrew Vanstone in his early novel *No Name*. He is a conventional English gentleman who had the misfortune to marry injudiciously when very young. Thus his two daughters, carefully brought up to believe in the security of their prosperous life, find out when he dies that they are illegitimate. Saint Andrew the Apostle is the patron saint of Scotland, so the name is favored there, and Anthony Trollope took advantage of this fact in *The Eustace Diamonds* to call the bailiff of Portray Castle Andrew Gowran. Portray is the castle in Scotland owned by Lizzie Eustace. Gowran is "an honest, domineering, hard-working, intelligent Scotchman" and Lizzie Eustace is a gold-digging rogue. Their mutual loathing provides some of the best comedy in the book.

The Russian form of the name is **Andrei** or **Andrey,** and it appears frequently in the Russian works among the Penguin Classics. One of the most notable examples is Prince Andrei Bolkonsky in Tolstoy's *War and Peace.* An intellectual and a spiritual seeker, he is entangled in a marriage to a woman less intelligent than he, and joins the army as a kind of escape. In Chekhov's grim story "Ward 6," the protagonist is Andrey Yefimych Ragin. A reform-minded doctor, he takes up a post at a provincial mental hospital but, worn down by the bureaucratic impossibility of improving medical service, has a breakdown. He ends up as a patient in his own hospital.

ANGELO *(Latin, "angel")* A name that has been primarily used in Latin countries. In Shakespeare's *The Comedy of Errors,* set in the Mediterranean city of Ephesus, Angelo is a goldsmith, a secondary character. In *Measure for Measure,* however, Angelo is the deputy to Duke Vincentio of Vienna. Handed the reins of government in the ruler's absence, Angelo turns out to be a severe and hypocritical ruler. He revives an old law that forbids fornication, while plotting that very sin (with a nun, no less) himself.

The English form of the name, **Angel,** is rarely seen outside literature, but Angel Clare of Thomas Hardy's *Tess of the D'Urbervilles* is memorable, if only for his association with the unforgettable Tess. If Tess is ruled by her passions, Angel, the son of a minister, lives by theory. He marries Tess but abandons her when she confesses her prior relationship with Alec D'Urberville. He eventually arrives at a more humane point of view and forgives Tess, but too late.

ANSELME *(Old German, "god helmet")* One of the rare benign characters in Balzac's Parisian novels, Anselme Popinot of *César Birotteau* is a clever, pious, redheaded youth, the nephew of Birotteau's predecessor in the Queen of Roses perfume concern. He is Birotteau's clerk, and deeply in love with Birotteau's innocent young daughter Césarine.

> *Anselme Popinot was a little fellow and club-footed,—an infirmity bestowed by fate on Lord Byron, Walter Scott, and Monsieur de Talleyrand, that others so afflicted might suffer no discouragement.*
>
> —HONORÉ DE BALZAC, *CÉSAR BIROTTEAU*

ANTHONY *(Latin clan name, possibly meaning "of great value")* Sir Anthony Absolute, a character in Sheridan's *The Rivals,* is an ambitious baronet who wishes to marry his eligible son Jack to Lydia Languish. In this play about deception, his delusions about his own character stand out, for he believes himself to be a gentle, sweet-tempered man, surrounded by hotheads. Dickens uses the nickname **Tony** in *The Pickwick Papers*: Tony Weller is the irresponsible coachman, father of Pickwick's valet Sam. Under the influence of the benign Pickwick, the son grows closer to his irrepressible father.

The Mediterranean form of the name is **Antonio,** used by Shakespeare for several characters. In *The Two Gentlemen of Verona,* Antonio is the father of one of the men of the title, while in *The Merchant of Venice,* he is the merchant in question. Overextended financially, he goes with his friend Bassanio to secure a loan for the latter from the moneylender Shylock. Shylock requires no financial guarantees, but insists that the loan be backed by the promise of one pound of Antonio's flesh if it is not repaid on time. *The Tempest*'s Antonio is Prospero's brother, the true villain of the piece, who usurped the magician's place as duke of Milan.

APOLLO *(Greek, meaning unknown)* Apollo is one of the twelve Olympian deities, also known as Phoebus; it is his carriage that brings the sun each day. He and his twin sister Diana (Artemis) are the offspring of Jupiter (Zeus) and Leto, a Titaness. Music, archery, and healing are his special concerns (he taught the Muses to sing), and the Delphic Oracle speaks with his voice. His love life, however, is less successful than those of some of his relatives, and Ovid's

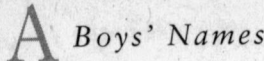

Metamorphoses tells several tales of maidens, nymphs, or youths who resisted Apollo—to their distinct disadvantage.

ARAMIS *(French, meaning unknown)* Aramis is the pseudonym of one of the Three Musketeers, in Alexandre Dumas's book of that name. Francophones may detect a similarity to *amour* or "love" in the name, which would be appropriate, for Aramis is the handsome, courtly dandy who constantly proclaims his intention to become a priest, and just as constantly defers priesthood in favor of his amours.

ARCHIBALD *(Old German, "famous, brave")* Robert Louis Stevenson was working on the novel *Weir of Hermiston* when he died. It concerns a stern Scottish judge, Adam Weir, and his rebellious son Archie. The latter is a quiet only child, handsome, reserved, and lonely: "You're a friend of Archie Weir's?" a character is asked, and the reply is, "I know Weir, but I never met Archie." Since scholars concur that the father is based on Stevenson's own father, it's fair to speculate that Archie is in some elementary way an alter ego for Stevenson himself.

ARES *(Greek, meaning unknown)* The god of war, one of the legitimate offspring of Zeus and his wife Hera, and the least popular of the twelve Olympians. (He is known as Mars in the Roman pantheon.) His children by Aphrodite include Eros and his nasty sons Phobos (which means "fear," as in "phobia") and Deimos (or "terror"). He allied himself with the Trojans in the Trojan War, but was defeated (as always) by Athena and her protégés, the Greeks.

ARIEL *(Hebrew, "lion of God")* Shakespeare may have chosen this name more for its connotations than for its literal meaning, for Ariel is the "airy Spirit" who assists Prospero in *The Tempest*. Intelligent, mischievous, and mercurial, he resents his bondage to Prospero, yet joins in Prospero's schemes with zest.

ARJUNA *(Sanskrit, "sinless")* The *Bhagavad Gita* is one section of the immense Hindu epic, *The Mahabharata*. In it, Arjuna, one of the five Kaurava brothers, refuses to fight at the battle of Kurukshetra. Krishna takes him in hand and counsels him through this pacifist crisis.

ARKADY *(Russian from Greek, "from Arcadia")* Arcadia was an area in southwestern Greece, and a fourth-century bishop named Arkadios is honored in Eastern Rite churches. In Turgenev's *Fathers and Sons,* Arkady Nikolayevich Kirsanov is the genteel landowner's son, admirer and sidekick of the revolutionary Barsanov. Dostoyevsky, in *Crime and Punishment,* puts the name to very different use: Arkady Ivanovich Svidrigailov is the child-molesting criminal who loves Raskolnikov's sister Dunya. He believes that her love can redeem him, and when he finally realizes that he appalls her, he commits suicide. Possible echoes of Arcadia (once a name for Paradise) or even archangels could only be ironic here.

> *"My name is Arkady Nikolayevich Kirsanov, and I don't do anything."*
> —IVAN TURGENEV, *FATHERS AND SONS*

ARMAND *(French from German, "army man")* In Balzac's tale "The Duchess of Langeais," Armand de Montriveau is indeed a man of the army—a hero of Napoleon's forces who lands in brittle, sophisticated Paris like a bird of prey, fascinating and unpredictable. "Terse of speech, like a hermit or a savage, his shyness was thought to be haughtiness, and people were greatly taken with it. He was something strange and great." The proud, coquettish duchess of Langeais allows him to fall in love with her and a titanic battle of wills results, with a tragic outcome.

ARSENY *(Russian from Greek, "manlike, male")* The name of one of the Desert Fathers of early Christianity. Prince Arseny Lvov, in *Anna Karenina,* is the husband of Natalie Lvov, one of three sisters, of whom Kitty and Dolly are the other two.

ARTHUR *(Origin unclear, though scholars have linked it to a Celtic word meaning "bear" and an Irish word meaning "rock")* An actual military hero named Arthur appears in documents recounting a sixth-century battle in Britain. Legend, of course, goes on from there. Works ranging from *Sir Gawain and the Green Knight* to Mark Twain's *A Connecticut Yankee in King Arthur's Court* include Camelot's king as a principal character. Spenser's *The Faerie Queen* mentions not only Arthur the king, who appears as a splendid figure in jeweled armor with a diamond shield, but also a knight called **Artegall**, "the equal of Arthur," who represents justice. Along with his imposing wife Britomart he founds the royal line of English kings. Literary treatments of the mythical King Arthur tend to focus on different aspects of his character—in *Sir Gawain and the Green Knight,* for example, he is a boy king at a feast, awaiting the telling of a marvelous tale. Mark Twain tweaks the king into a theatrical monarch who always wants to be the center of attention.

Of course Twain is building on a hundred years of debunking the Arthur myth, or at least deglamorizing the name. The trend goes back to one of the first American Gothic novels, *Edgar Huntly, Or, Memoirs of a Sleep-Walker,* Charles Brockden Brown's phantasmagoric epistolary novel that features Arthur Wiatte as the evil twin of a kind landowner. (A rake, a gambler, a highwayman, transported to the New World for his crimes, he is a complete villain.) Then we have the unheroic protagonist of Edgar Allan Poe's *The Narrative of Arthur Gordon Pym of Nantucket,* another tale that bridges reality and fantasy. A stowaway on a mercantile ship, he passively survives a visit to the core of the earth where all the inhabitants are jet black, and cannibals to boot. Anne Brontë's *The Tenant of Wildfell Hall* concerns a woman escaping from a dissipated, alcoholic husband named Arthur—"I am tired out with his injustice, his selfishness and hopeless depravity," she says.

Arthur Dimmesdale, in Hawthorne's *The Scarlet Letter,* is the timid minister who fathered Hester Prynne's illegitimate child. As she has an "A" on her clothes to mark her adultery, he has one on the skin of his chest—and it's not a monogram. George Eliot's

Arthur Donnithorne, the young squire's son in *Adam Bede,* is another cowardly Arthur, though not strictly an adulterer since neither he nor his seducee, Hetty Sorrel, is married.

By the mid-nineteenth century, Arthur was actually being used with frequency in the real world; Queen Victoria's seventh child, born in 1850, was Prince Arthur. Anthony Trollope's Arthur Fletcher, in *The Prime Minister,* may reflect this trend. By 1874, this was a plausible name for an upper-class English landowner. But Trollope restores some of the luster to the name by making Fletcher rich, handsome, kind, and brave. Not only is he unhappy in love—he even confesses to his pain.

ARVERAGUS *(Latin)* Possibly invented by Geoffrey Chaucer for a character in *The Canterbury Tales,* constructed around the second syllable *ver,* which means "true." He is a knight in "The Franklin's Tale," husband of the Breton lady Dorigen, who is courted strenuously by a neighbor. Hoping to get rid of him, she tells him she will be his only when the cliffs of the Brittany coast disappear. The would-be seducer, Aurelius, finds a magician who makes the cliffs vanish and Arveragus, insistent that Dorigen be true to her word, sends his wife next door. Aurelius, impressed by the way the husband honors his wife's vow, sends Dorigen back untouched.

ASTOLFO *(Italian, meaning unknown)* Probably a creation of Ariosto's for one of the legion of characters in his epic poem *Orlando Furioso.* He is the son of King Otto of England, a cousin of Orlando and Rinaldo, and the fortunate possessor of a magical horn that makes everyone who hears it immobile with terror. In the course of his adventures Astolfo falls afoul of an enchantress and is turned into a myrtle bush.

ATHOS *(Greek place-name)* Mount Athos, on a peninsula in northeastern Greece, is inhabited solely by monks. Alexandre Dumas makes it plain that the Three Musketeers' snappy names are merely pseudonyms, and that Athos was "obviously a great nobleman." It later transpires that he is the Count de la Fère. He is the most reserved of the three men, intellectual, laconic, and verging on the misanthropic. His pseudonym may purposely refer to the ascetic life on Mount Athos.

AUGUSTUS *(Latin clan name meaning "honorable, worthy of respect")* The English word "august" comes from the same source. It has never been considered a truly English name, which is why it works so effectively for the Continental swindler Augustus Melmotte of Anthony Trollope's sardonic *The Way We Live Now*. Melmotte epitomizes everything that Trollope found suspect in the world of the late nineteenth century, from the immense power of the new financial industries to the erosion of gentlemanly values like honesty, loyalty, and modesty. Edith Wharton shortens the name to **Gus** for the businessman whose financial assistance compromises Lily Bart's reputation in *The House of Mirth*. Gus Trenor is a sharply observed example of the crude, money-obsessed New Yorkers whom Mrs. Wharton found so distasteful.

In France, **Auguste** is a more common option. Edgar Allan Poe's detective Auguste Dupin is the forerunner of later brilliant observers like Sherlock Holmes and Hercule Poirot. In Balzac's "Ferragus," collected in *History of the Thirteen*, Auguste de Maulincour is "a man of gentle melancholy, and spiritual in love" who becomes enamored of the virtuous bourgeoise Clémence Desmarets, and turns into a nineteenth-century stalker. He falls afoul of a cabal of criminals, of whom the leader is Clémence's father, and begins to collect mysterious injuries and illnesses.

The diminutive form of the name, **Augustine**, owes its fame to the great fourth-century saint, whose teaching and writing had a profound effect on early Christianity. Harriet Beecher Stowe calls the enlightened slave owner in *Uncle Tom's Cabin* Augustine St. Clare, a name that is linguistically plausible for a man from New Orleans. But for theological adepts (like Stowe, whose brother was one of the great preachers of his era) it may have deeper resonance. St. Clare treats his slaves well and fairly, on some level acknowledging their humanity—yet he wholeheartedly defends slavery. Saint Augustine's *Confessions* make clear his ambivalence about giving up the joys of the flesh, writing at one point, "O God, make me chaste—but not yet."

Spoken English contracts Augustine to **Austin.** Henry James consistently exploits the connotations of his characters' names, and "austere" is the word that springs to mind when it comes to Austin Sloper, the distant father of Catherine Sloper in *Washington Square.* His lifelong disappointment in his daughter has a devastating effect on her romantic and emotional fate.

> *Auguste had lost the only faculty that makes us live—memory.* —HONORÉ DE BALZAC, "FERRAGUS"

BACCHUS *(Greek mythology name)* Bacchus was one of Jupiter's children, a god of wine who was worshipped in ecstatic rites. He is also known as **Dionysos,** a name that took firmer root in the European naming vocabulary.

BAIARDO *(Italian from Latin, "reddish brown")* The name of a legendary horse. In Ariosto's *Orlando Furioso,* which built on many existing myths, Baiardo was given by Charlemagne to his nephew Rinaldo when the latter was knighted. He is as intelligent as a human, uncannily swift, and loyal to Rinaldo. In French forms of the legend, he is known as **Bayard.**

> *Baldassare was exacting, and had got stranger as he got older: he was constantly scrutinising Tito's mind to see whether it answered to his own exaggerated expectations.*
> —GEORGE ELIOT, ROMOLA

BALTHAZAR *(Greek, "God save the king")* Also occurs as Balthasar. In Shakespeare's *The Comedy of Errors,* a farce involving two sets of identical twins, Balthazar is a minor character, a merchant. The Italian form of the name is **Baldassare.** In George Eliot's *Romola,* Baldassare Calvo is the scholar who has raised the young Greek Tito Melema. When pirates capture Baldassare as the two sail across the Mediterranean, Tito fails to redeem this father figure from slavery. Later, Baldassare turns up in Florence and Tito, by then in a position of power, repudiates his former protector.

BANQUO *(Meaning unknown)* A name that appears in early genealogies of Scottish kings as well as in Shakespeare's *Macbeth,* where Banquo is the thane of Lochnaber and the first victim of Macbeth's plotting. His ghost, which appears at a banquet to Macbeth alone, is one of the most effective dramatic devices in the play.

BARDO *(Italian, meaning unknown)* Bardo de Bardi is Romola's father in George Eliot's novel of that name. A blind scholar and scion of an illustrious family, he has raised Romola to help him in his studies as a replacement for a scapegrace son, but because of her feminine "weakness" Romola can never completely please him. Eliot, no mean scholar herself, is surprisingly gentle with his narrow point of view.

BARNABY *(Hebrew, "son of consolation")* Barnaby Rudge is one of Dickens's historical novels, set during the 1780s when anti-Catholic riots swept across England. Half-witted but good-natured Barnaby is one of Dickens's more picturesque creations; he has long red hair, pale skin, dresses only in green, and carries a raven named Grip on his back. He gets involved in the riots and is sentenced to death, but his friends get him released.

BARNES *(English place-name)* William Thackeray set *The Newcomes* in the 1820s and '30s, focusing on the segment of London society where commerce met the aristocracy. Barnes Newcome (later Sir Barnes Newcome, M.P.) is the snobbish, grasping, cold-hearted head of the banking house of Hobson Brothers. His name is his aristocratic mother's maiden name.

BARRINGTON *(English place-name)* In upper-class England, as in the United States, last names are often co-opted as first names, especially out of respect to a wealthy branch of the family. One of the recurring characters in Trollope's Palliser novels is Liberal politician Barrington Erle. He exerts a great deal of behind-the-scenes influence without ever achieving high office. His blood ties to many of the great Whig families contrast sharply with Phineas Finn's constant task of creating and maintaining such ties.

BARTHOLOMEW (*Aramaic, "son of Talmai"—which in turn means "furrow" or "hill"*) He was one of the twelve Apostles. Dickens uses the name to comic effect in *Bleak House* for Bart Smallweed, the tiny, grasping, monkeylike law clerk brought up by his poisonous, penny-pinching grandparents. In *The Barber of Seville* Beaumarchais adapts the name to a more Spanish-sounding form, **Bartholo.** He is Rosine's guardian, and in Figaro's words, "a stoutish, shortish, oldish, greyish, cunning, smarmy, posing, nosing, peeping, prying, creeping, whining, snivelling sort of man." English names include a number of offshoots like Bartlett, Bartow, and **Bartley,** the name of one of the less attractive characters in William Dean Howells's *A Modern Instance.* Bartley Hubbard is a bright but lazy journalist who is happy to use his talents in the service of the muckraking penny-dreadful papers. (Lest readers ignore his moral degradation, he also gets fat.) To hammer home the point of his weakness, Howells gives him a best friend with an upstanding character—and initials of B.H.

BASIL (*Greek, "like a king"*) In Oscar Wilde's *The Picture of Dorian Gray,* Basil Hallward is the portrait painter who creates the image of Gray. He admires Gray very warmly and wants to protect him from the sensual, corrupting viewpoint of Lord Henry Wotton. In this fable of the sensual versus the moral life, Basil Hallward claims the moral part, declaring that "love is more wonderful than art." Henry James works on an herbal theme with the names in *The Bostonians;* in addition to his heroine, Verena (Verbena) Tarrant, he has her great friend Olive Chancellor and her would-be protector, Basil Ransom. Ransom is a knight-errant of sorts, a tall, handsome lawyer from Mississippi whose adventures in post–Civil War Boston strain his chivalric Southern sensibilities. Verena, as a beautiful young orator in the women's rights movement, is personally alluring and ideologically appalling to him.

The Russian cognate is **Vassily**, also spelled **Vasily** or **Vasili**. In Tolstoy's *War and Peace,* Prince Vasili Kuragin represents everything that is shallow, hypocritical, and corrupt about St. Petersburg society. He is the father of the faithless Hélène, whom he maneuvers into marriage with naive Pierre Bezuhov. All of life, to him, is a battle for social or financial advantage. Lest the reader miss his hypocrisy, Tolstoy gives him a facial muscle that twitches only when he is alone, to emphasize how his civilized demeanor masks corruption.

BASSANIO *(Origin unknown)* A name used by Shakespeare in *The Merchant of Venice,* possibly invented for the purpose. Bassanio is a wealthy young blade who loves the fair Portia. Having squandered his fortune, he now needs money to carry out his courtship. He approaches his friend Antonio, the merchant of the title, for a loan, and Antonio's cash-flow problems send the two men to the moneylender Shylock.

BEALE *(English from French, "handsome")* A version of *beau.* Certainly appropriate for Beale Farange, the handsome, well-dressed, well-mannered father of Maisie in Henry James's *What Maisie Knew.* Unfortunately his moral beauty doesn't match the physical. Maisie, witnessing his easy shifts of romantic loyalty, suffers as she learns all too much about the vagaries of adult love lives.

> *Beale Farange had natural decorations, a kind of costume in his vast fair beard, burnished like a gold breastplate, and in the eternal glitter of the teeth that his long moustache had been trained not to hide and that gave him, in every possible situation, the look of the joy of life.*
> —HENRY JAMES, *WHAT MAISIE KNEW*

BEDIVERE *(English, meaning unknown)* According to the most popular Arthurian legend, there were twelve knights of the Round Table, mirroring the twelve Apostles. Yet the count varies from version to version of the tale: Malory's *Le Morte D'Arthur,* for instance, comes up with over a hundred. Bedivere is usually included as one of the number, however select. He was one of the handful of knights who survived the final battle against Mordred. He tossed the magical sword Excalibur back into the lake whence it had come, and witnessed Arthur's translation to Avalon.

BEN *(Diminutive, usually of* Benjamin: *Hebrew, "son")* Names drawn from the Old Testament were much more widespread in nineteenth-century America than in England at the time. Thus, Ben was a perfectly reasonable name for Ben Halleck, the moral mirror of Bartley Hubbard in William Dean Howells's *A Modern Instance.* (It could even have been short for a truly exotic name like Benoni.) He is a loyal friend to the drunkard Hubbard, loaning him money, even moving to Uruguay when he realizes that he loves his friend's wife. Not surprisingly, he becomes a minister. Robert Louis Stevenson's *Treasure Island* is set in the latter half of the eighteenth century, when Ben, or Benjamin, would have been an unpretentious, modest name—ideal for "poor Ben Gunn," the crazy castaway Jim Hawkins encounters on the island of Hispaniola.

BENEDICK *(Latin, "blessed")* The more common form of the name is **Benedict.** Shakespeare's *Much Ado About Nothing* follows the reluctant surrender to romance of the hardened bachelor Benedick. Having sworn to avoid marriage, he overhears his friends discussing how much Beatrice loves him. His tune changes remarkably quickly to "No; the world must be peopled. When I said I would die a bachelor, I did not think I should live till I were married."

The Spanish version of the name is **Benito.** Herman Melville's tale "Benito Cereno" (in *Billy Budd and Other Stories*) contrasts the straightforward, occasionally naive New World with the passivity and decay of the Old World. Benito Cereno is the Spanish captain of a slave ship who is being held captive by his "servant" Babo after a slave rebellion, when an American ship hails him. The name may also allude darkly to the Catholic Church, whose power often unnerved nineteenth-century Americans.

BENTLEY *(English, "meadow of the bent grasses")* Another last name used as a first name, and in Dickens's *Great Expectations,* that means pretension. Bentley Drummle is the only "gentleman" living with Mr. Pocket, Pip's tutor. But his status is entirely superficial, a matter of money and accent rather than character. He is actually a boor, and though he is deemed well-bred enough to be worthy of the fair Estella, he betrays his true nature by abusing her once they are married.

BENVOLIO *(Latin, "well wishing")* In *Romeo and Juliet,* Benvolio is one of Romeo's sidekicks. He serves as audience to Romeo's lovesick poetry, and defends Romeo to the Prince after Romeo has killed Tybalt.

BEOWULF *(Swedish, meaning unknown)* The hero of the eponymous Old English epic is a prince of the Geats in southern Sweden. He rescues the neighboring Danes from the depredations of the monster Grendel, wrestling with him bare-handed. He accomplishes further Herculean feats in the course of the tale, finally dying an old man after fifty years of ruling Geatland.

BEPPO *(Italian diminutive of* Giuseppe/Joseph: *Hebrew, "Jehovah makes greater")* The eponymous central character in a cynical little narrative poem by Lord Byron. He is the swarthy, solid husband of a Venetian lady named Laura. He has been absent for many years, presumed kidnapped by Turks, and he returns to Venice dressed very convincingly as one of the same. Though Laura consoled herself with a Venetian count in his absence, she swiftly rearranges her loyalties once Beppo reappears.

BERCILAK *(Gaelic, "churl")* The fourteenth-century poem *Sir Gawain and the Green Knight* recounts the encounter between Gawain, King Arthur's nephew, and the supernatural Green Knight, unmasked in the end as Sir Bercilak. A key element is Gawain's temptation at the hands of Bercilak's beautiful young wife—whom Bercilak forgives in the end.

BERNARD *(Old German, "bear brave")* A classic Anthony Trollope character who excites compassion without much liking, Bernard Dale of *The Small House at Allington* is the nephew of the squire. Squire Dale would like his niece Bell to marry Bernard, and is willing to give Bell a generous dowry to make such a match feasible. But Bernard is practical and dry—charmless in fact—and Bell refuses his suit.

> *There was a great deal of sound, common sense about Bernard Dale.*
> —ANTHONY TROLLOPE, *THE SMALL HOUSE AT ALLINGTON*

BERTIE *(Old German, "bright")* Most commonly a nickname for **Albert.** For Trollope, it is a pet name for the slightly ridiculous **Ethelbert.** No one calls Bertie Stanhope by his full name, however. He is a member of the rather louche clerical family, the Stanhopes, in *Barchester Towers,* and his unconventional clothes and long curly hair create quite a stir in the cathedral close of Barchester. He has converted, lightheartedly, to both Catholicism and Judaism, and is trolling for a rich wife. When *Barchester Towers* was written, in 1855–57, Queen Victoria's eldest son, Prince Albert, was reaching young manhood. Despite an excellent education, he seemed inclined to womanize, and was certainly a dandy. He was also known as Bertie.

BERTRAM *(Old German, "bright raven")* Bertram, the Count of Roussillon in *All's Well That Ends Well,* is to modern eyes one of Shakespeare's less attractive comic heroes. Beloved by the estimable Helena, he refuses at first to marry her because of her low rank. Under pressure from his king, he relents, but abandons her before the match is consummated. Helena manages to win him back via trickery that involves Bertram's seduction and abandonment of a putative virgin—Helena herself, in disguise.

BILL *(Diminutive of* **William**: *Old German, "will helmet")* For much of the eighteenth and nineteenth centuries in England, Bill was a lower-class name. Men named **William** abound in literary high society but the Bills are to be found as pirate captains (Bill Flint in Stevenson's *Treasure Island*) or as outright brutes (Bill Sikes in Dickens's *Oliver Twist*). Dickens even goes so far as to dehumanize Bill Sikes, frequently comparing him to an animal. Herman Melville's Billy Budd, too, is a common sailor. But far from being a criminal, he is a creature of primordial beauty and innocence. He combines a kind of ethereal good looks with a strapping build and a speech impediment—when upset, he stammers so badly as to be incomprehensible. Thus he can't defend himself when caught up in the toils of evil, and ends up being hanged from the yardarm of his ship—"crucified," as Melville puts it.

In George du Maurier's *Trilby*, written at the very end of the nineteenth century, **Billee** is a nickname for a very different kind of man. William Bagot is a well-to-do, well-connected art student in Paris, and the name, with its connotations of crudity, is facetious, since he is a supremely refined man. Small, slender, dandyish, and sensitive, he becomes a great painter and dies young, in despair after the love of his life dies.

BJORN *(Scandinavian, "bear")* A Norwegian chieftain's son in the twelfth-century *Egil's Saga*. He is outlawed in his own country for carrying off the fair Thora Lace-Cuff, so he migrates to the Shetland Islands and thence to Iceland. The saga provides a glimpse of an almost unimaginably harsh world where to be known as a bear is a great compliment.

BOB *(Diminutive of* **Robert**: *Old German, "renown bright")* A jaunty, informal nickname, used by Charles Dickens for two engaging characters. *The Pickwick Papers'* Bob Sawyer is a young medical student on a spree, warm and impulsive and given to wild behavior. Bob Cratchit, in *A Christmas Carol,* is an endlessly forgiving clerk, loyal to his employer even when he is treated most cruelly.

BONAPARTE *(French from Italian, meaning unknown)* The last name of the famous French emperor, adopted for his own purposes by the scoundrel Bonaparte Blenkins in Olive Schreiner's *The Story of an African Farm*. He claims, to the naive inhabitants of the farm where he settles, that he is descended from Napoleon himself. However what he really seems to have in common with the Corsican adventurer is a ruthless eye for opportunity.

BORIS *(Slavic, "conflict, battle")* Anton Chekhov's *The Seagull* is full of conflict between its intimately linked characters. Boris Trigorin, a successful writer of light commercial fiction, is the lover of middle-aged actress Irena Arkadina Trepliov. His relationship with her is largely passive until he falls in love with the young actress Nina Zaryechnaia, who is loved in turn by Madame Arkadina's son Konstantin. Tears, disillusion, pregnancy, and suicide ensue.

BORS *(Old English, meaning unknown)* According to Malory's *Le Morte D'Arthur*, one of only three knights of the Round Table who was privileged to see the Holy Grail. Not only did a knight have to be a great fighter, he also had to be religiously pure to see the Grail. Lancelot was disqualified because of his love affair with Guinevere, Gawain because he valued the knightly code above his Christian duty. Legend has Bors ending up as a hermit.

BRIAN *(Unknown origin, possibly Irish Gaelic)* A tenth-century Irish king was named Brian. In Sir Walter Scott's hands, it is the name of a Norman knight, Sir Brian de Bois-Guilbert, one of the villains of *Ivanhoe*. Sir Brian is violent, brutal, and cruel to women, most particularly to one of the heroines, Rebecca. In one of the climaxes of the book, Sir Brian and Ivanhoe are supposed to fight in a trial by combat to prove that Rebecca is (or is not) a witch. In 1819, when the book was written, the good guys always won—Sir Brian was dead before Ivanhoe's lance touched him.

BURGO *(Origin unknown)* Possibly invented by Anthony Trollope, as an analog to the Scottish Mungo. Ever the naturalist,

Trollope is not given to making up names, but the rakish, dashing aura of this one perfectly suits the character. He is a handsome, kind, desperately charming man of middle age who, though related to half the British aristocracy, has no money. In *Can You Forgive Her?* he dangles after the impetuous Lady Glencora Palliser, encouraging her to leave her dull husband and run away with him. His is a kind of Lucifer figure, beautiful but doomed to self-destruction.

> *No more handsome man than Burgo Fitzgerald lived in his days...* —ANTHONY TROLLOPE, *CAN YOU FORGIVE HER?*

BUTE *(Scottish place-name)* The Isle of Bute is a small island off the wild west coast of Scotland near Glasgow. Bute is the youngest of the three aristocratic Crawley brothers in Thackeray's *Vanity Fair*. The amoral heroine, Becky Sharp, marries his elder brother, Rawdon. The names, while plausible, are also caricatures of the upper-class predilection for using last names, however inappropriate, as Christian names. Despite the violent sound of his name (reminiscent of "brute"), Bute Crawley is a clergyman with seven children and a penny-pinching wife.

CADMUS *(Greek, meaning unknown)* In Greek myth Cadmus, a prince of Phoenicia, was the brother of Europa, and was sent off to find her after Zeus in the shape of an ox spirited her away. Cadmus ended up settling in an area north of Athens where he killed a dragon sacred to Ares and sowed its teeth in the ground. Armed men sprang up, and promptly took to battling each other until only five were left alive. They were the original citizens of the city of Thebes, which Cadmus founded. His wife was Harmonia, and they had five children, among them Semele and Polydorus, whose descendants included Oedipus and his terrifying family. Cadmus and Harmonia eventually turned into serpents. He is also immortalized in the Table of Elements as Cd, or cadmium.

> *Cadmus wandered over the whole world: for who can lay his hands on what Jove has stolen away?*
> —OVID, *METAMORPHOSES*

CAIN *(Hebrew, "spear")* According to the Bible, Cain was the first murderer, killing his brother Abel. Thomas Hardy, who chose his characters' names with great attention to allusions, created a rustic laborer named Cain Ball in *Far from the Madding Crowd*. The anecdote about how he got his name demonstrates what an insular community he lives in—thus dramatizing the effect on it of the flamboyant heroine, Bathsheba Everdene.

> *"How did Cain come by such a name?" asked Bathsheba.*
>
> *"Oh, you see, mem, his pore mother, not being a Scripture-read woman, made a mistake at his christening, thinking 'twas Abel killed Cain, and called em Cain, meaning Abel all the time. The parson put it right, but 'twas too late, for the name could never be got rid of in the parish. 'Tis very unfortunate for the boy. . . . We soften it down as much as we can, and call him Cainy."*
>
> —THOMAS HARDY, *FAR FROM THE MADDING CROWD*

CALEB *(Hebrew, "dog" or "brave, courageous")* An Old Testament name of the kind that survived in rural areas of England long after the Puritan anti-Catholic fervor made saints' names unacceptable. George Eliot, whose *Middlemarch* is a sociological document as well as a novel, would certainly have known that. Caleb Garth ("garth" is a Middle English word for a small yard) is the honest, hardworking, self-sacrificing land agent whose family provides a strong contrast to the Middlemarch citizens with greater social pretensions.

CALIBAN *(Origin unknown)* In Shakespeare's *The Tempest,* Caliban is "a savage and deformed Slave" to Prospero. He is unrepentantly lazy, greedy, and nasty. In Act I he attempts to rape Miranda and shows no remorse. Yet recent interpretations of the play have gone a long way to regenerate Caliban's reputation. Some characters see him as an outright monster, yet he is given some of the most beautiful poetry in the play, including the speech that begins, "Be not afeared: the isle is full of noises,/Sounds and sweet airs that give delight and hurt not."

CAMILLE *(Latin, meaning unknown)* In anglophone countries this is usually a girl's name, but on the Continent boys were sometimes named after the sixteenth-century Italian Saint Camillus, the founder of an order of priests and lay brothers called the Servants of the Sick. Émile Zola may have referred to him in naming Camille Raquin, the frail, spoiled young husband of Thérèse in *Thérèse Raquin*. Because of his poor health he has almost no education, and he has relied all his life on his mother to solve every problem for him—including finding him a wife in his cousin Thérèse. He is much too feeble to consummate the marriage, and when a real man enters the Raquins' lives, Thérèse falls hard for him.

In Shakespeare's comedy *The Winter's Tale*, which nominally takes place in Sicily, one of King Leontes's courtiers is named **Camillo.** He staunchly attempts to limit the damage done by his ruler's jealous paranoia, and is rewarded, in the end, with a happy marriage to a similarly courageous and loyal character.

> *Saved from death, Camille had grown up, but was left badly shaken by the repeated assaults of pain his body had sustained. His growth had been retarded and he was now small and weedy. His skinny limbs moved slowly as though they were tired out.* —ÉMILE ZOLA, *THÉRÈSE RAQUIN*

CANDIDE *(French, "without guile, ingenuous")* The eponymous hero of Voltaire's novel, which is subtitled *The Optimist*. Candide undergoes appalling adventures (including condemnation by the Inquisition and attendance at the disastrous 1755 earthquake in Lisbon), yet maintains that "all is for the best in this best of all possible worlds."

CARLOS see **CHARLES**

CASPAR *(Possibly from Persian, "treasure guardian")* A variant of **Jasper**. Caspar Goodwood is the stalwart American courtier of Isabel Archer in Henry James's *The Portrait of a Lady*. He pursues her indefatigably, but she finds his aggressive masculinity distasteful, even threatening. In the final scene of the book, James says (ambiguously), "She believed just then that to let him take her in his arms would be the next best thing to her dying."

CASSIO *(Italian from Latin, "vain")* The precedent is possibly Cassius, the Roman general who plotted against Julius Caesar. Shakespeare's play about that conspiracy was written in 1599. In *Othello*, which was produced around 1604, Cassio is an extremely handsome Florentine soldier whom Othello promotes over Iago's head, thus sparking the plot that ends in tragedy. Though this is actually the character's last name (his first name, implausible for an Italian, is Michael), it is how he is commonly known, and most of the other characters are designated by single names like **Othello** and **Iago**.

CEDRIC *(Origin disputed)* Some scholars suggest Old English, "leader in battle," while others hark back to a pair of Welsh names meaning "loved one" or "bounty, favor/pattern, vision." Possibly Sir Walter Scott, whose antiquarian research broke ground in his day, transposed a pair of letters and created Cedric instead of Cerdic (who was a king of the West Saxons). *Ivanhoe*, the 1819 novel in which Cedric the Saxon appears, was so popular that the name entered public consciousness regardless of its historical legitimacy. Cedric the Saxon's great goal is to expel the Normans from England. His son Wilfred of Ivanhoe falls in love with the fair Rowena, Cedric's ward, who is destined for a match with Athelstane, a powerful Saxon lord. Several obnoxious Norman knights threaten Cedric's plans and Ivanhoe, naturally, has to save the day.

CÉLESTIN *(French from Latin, "heavenly")* The highly unsuitable first name, if taken literally, of the fat nouveau-riche former perfumer Crevel in Balzac's *Cousin Bette*. Balzac says about Crevel that "he wore the aureole of complacency achieved by wealthy, self-made, retired shopkeepers." His bright yellow gloves represent his utter vulgarity.

CÉSAR *(Italian from Latin, a clan name that may mean "hairy")* Generally taken to mean "emperor," for the Roman title (as in Julius Caesar) and the cognates "kaiser" and "tsar." César Birotteau, in Balzac's eponymous novel, is one of the author's more likeable protagonists—Balzac even refers to him as "the gentle and modest peasant." He is a perfumer who, having become rich by selling "Double Paste of Sultans" and "Carminative Balm," has been elected deputy mayor of Paris. He has been bitten hard by ambition and gotten involved in real estate speculation—the kind of enterprise that usually ends badly for gentle peasants in Balzac's novels. In Aphra Behn's scandalous seventeenth-century *roman à clef, Love-Letters Between a Nobleman and His Sister,* **Cesario** is the pseudonym for the Duke of Monmouth, Charles II's illegitimate son. A Protestant, he laid claim to the throne of England in place of his uncle James II. His loyal supporter Lord Grey is the "nobleman" of the title, who actually did seduce his own sister-in-law, identified in the book as **Silvia** but Lady Henrietta Berkeley in real life. Fictionally, Cesario seduces Silvia's sister Mertilla. This is also the name Viola uses in *Twelfth Night* when she is disguised as a man.

> *"Yes! You shall be rich, richissime, or I'll renounce my name of César!"* —HONORÉ DE BALZAC, *CÉSAR BIROTTEAU*

CHAD *(Origin unclear; possibly Old English, "ready for battle")* Also **Chadd.** Saint Chad was a seventh-century English bishop, but the name has been most widely used in America. Henry James calls the callow traveler of *The Ambassadors* Chad Newsome. He is on a Grand Tour of Europe, in flight from the textile mills of Woollett, Massachusetts, and his domineering mama. The pleasures of the Old World that he is sampling include love with an older, married woman.

CHARLES *(Old English, "man")* From the same root as "churl." Very widely used in both French and English literature, as befits a name that has long been a staple in both cultures. The Reverend Charles Primrose is the title character in Oliver Goldsmith's 1766 novel *The Vicar of Wakefield.* A generous, unworldly, and optimistic clergyman, he and his family submit cheerfully to a string of misfortunes. Jane Austen also used Charles several times for principal characters. *Persuasion,* her last novel, features both Charles Hayter, an unpretentious curate, and his cousin Charles Musgrove. The latter is married to the heroine Anne Elliot's sister Mary, who finds his bluff insensitivity as much of a trial as his inferior social status. The handsome, rich, well-bred, and charming Mr. Bingley, tenant of Netherfield Park in *Pride and Prejudice,* is also named Charles, though he is rarely called by his first name.

Balzac's *Eugénie Grandet* is the tale of a young provincial heiress who has been raised by a miser. A simple, warmhearted girl, she falls in love with her dandified Parisian cousin Charles Grandet, and freely gives him her dowry of six thousand francs in gold coins when she discovers he is penniless. But Charles is not as strong a character as his cousin, and after several years abroad in the slave trade, he forgets Eugénie and marries for a title. One of fiction's more unfortunate characters, Flaubert's *Monsieur* Bovary, is also called Charles. Vulgar and insensitive, something of a buffoon, he nevertheless dearly loves his high-strung Emma and sticks with her through all of the trouble she gets herself into. A contrast is the saintly Bishop of Digne, Charles François Bienvenu Myriel, in Victor Hugo's *Les Misérables*. His kindness to Jean Valjean inspires the hero to good deeds for the rest of the (very long) novel.

Another saintly Charles is Charles Darnay of Dickens's *A Tale of Two Cities*. The heir to the evil Marquis de St. Evrémonde, he lives in England as a humble tutor and returns to revolution-torn France only to save an old employee. He is, alas, cast into the shade for readers by his sardonic and self-destructive double, Sydney Carton. Both men fall in love with the heroine, Lucie Manette, but—this being after all a Dickens novel—the man with the clean résumé gets her.

The Spanish version of the name, **Carlos,** appears in Balzac's *A Harlot High and Low*. The arch-villain Jacques Collin, also known (in *Old Goriot*) as Vautrin, has disguised himself as a Spanish cleric called Carlos Herrera. He brings Lucien de Rubempré back to Paris and masterminds Lucien's renewed assault on high society. He is clever, subtle, and pitiless.

CHARON (ka' ron; *Greek, meaning unknown*) In Greek myth, the boatman who ferries the dead across the River Styx. Dante, in Canto III of the *Inferno*, describes him as "that sour/Infernal ferryman of the livid wash," with red-rimmed eyes and shaggy white hair. He appears in a lighter guise in Aristophanes' *The Frogs*, bargaining hard with Dionysos, who wants to get into Hades for his own purposes.

CHÉRUBIN (kay roo banh'; *French, "cherub"*) In Beaumarchais's *The Marriage of Figaro*, Chérubin is the Count's page, a lecherous little soul. He chases after a servant girl yet all along loves his godmother, the Countess Almaviva. In Mozart's sublime opera of the same title—the form of the story most familiar today—the role of Cherubino is traditionally sung by a woman.

CHINGACHGOOK (*Delaware Indian, "great serpent"*) The noble, dignified Indian, chief of the nearly extinct Mohican tribe, in James Fenimore Cooper's *The Last of the Mohicans*. He is Natty Bumppo's great friend, and has forest skills that eclipse even Natty's. (His Native American name refers to his stealth.) He also appears in other installments of the "Leatherstocking Tales," *The Pathfinder* and *The Pioneers*, where he is also known as "Indian John."

CHRISTIAN (*Greek, "anointed"*) A follower of the Christian faith. John Bunyan's *The Pilgrim's Progress* (1684) is an allegory that follows the protagonist, Christian, from the City of Destruction to the Celestial City. He is Everyman, carrying a heavy sack on his back that contains his sorrows and sins.

CHRISTOPHER (*Greek, "bearing Christ"*) A name that, without ever being truly fashionable, was familiar in the English-speaking world from the seventeenth century onward. Anthony Trollope uses it for the resolutely old-fashioned Squire Dale in *The Small House at Allington*. He is a gruff but good-hearted, crusty, and conservative old man whose family feeling prompts him to loan a house to his deceased brother's family. "His thoughts were ever gentler than his words, and his heart softer than any exponent of his heart that he was able to put forth."

Trollope tended to a generally naturalistic use of names for his main characters, while Thomas Hardy was more elaborately allusive. In the early novel *A Pair of Blue Eyes,* the Reverend Christopher Swancourt is the snobbish Cornish parson, father of the heroine Elfride. He disapproves deeply of her romance with the young architect Stephen Smith, a mere mason's son, whose blunt name contrasts with Swancourt's more aristocratic one. Presumably, as a cleric, he does "bear Christ" in his heart. Hardy's *The Hand of Ethelberta* includes among its characters Christopher Julian, a musician of good family who once loved Ethelberta but could not afford to marry her. He falls in love with her sister Picotee, whose social ambitions are more limited.

Christopher Newman, the hero of Henry James's *The American,* conjures up Christopher Columbus, for he is an explorer in reverse. He is the New Man visiting the Old World, and what he finds there (most especially the lovely widow Claire de Cintré, who loves but will not marry him) enchants and baffles him. Alessandro Manzoni, in *The Betrothed,* uses **Cristoforo,** the Italian form, in the most literal way for a pious monk, Fra Cristoforo. He stands in contrast to several other clerical characters who lack his moral strength. Having once killed a man in a duel, he is constantly aware of sin, and thus humble. On several occasions he helps the beleaguered betrothed couple.

An old nickname for Christopher is **Kit,** used into the early nineteenth century. Maria Edgeworth's *Castle Rackrent,* a sardonic look at several generations of Irish landlords, features Sir Kit Rackrent as the greatest wastrel of all of them. Though personable and kind to his inferiors, he sees his estate only as a source of income, and handles it with complete irresponsibility. He is killed in a duel, after seducing another man's wife.

CLARENCE *(Latin clan name, or possibly "shining, illuminated")* Mark Twain uses Clarence in *A Connecticut Yankee in King Arthur's Court.* His intent seems to be sardonic; the character is a young page whom the hero, Hank Morgan, tries to enlist in his reforming efforts. The name apparently stands for effete aristocracy in Twain's hands. In historic terms, Clarence is a royal dukedom, bestowed at the pleasure of the monarch on one of his (or her) children. Twain's use of the name is also anachronistic: it appears to have been coined in the fourteenth century, some eight hundred years after Arthur's putative reign.

THE DUKES OF CLARENCE

The name **Clarence** comes from the Latin, but its fame comes from the royal dukedom of Clarence. Other royal dukedoms are York, Kent, Gloucester, and Sussex, and if the title is not currently occupied (Sussex is open at the moment), a monarch may bestow it upon one of his or her children. The dukedom of Clarence has been somewhat unlucky, however. The fifteenth-century holder of the title got caught up in the tail end of the Wars of the Roses, and was thrown into the Tower of London after being arrested for treason. According to legend, he was "drowned in a butt of Malmsey," or a barrel of sweet wine.

The title was not used again until the late eighteenth century, when George III's third son assumed it. He came to the throne as William IV and reigned for seven years, affectionately known as "Silly Billy." His open liaison with a married actress contributed to the raffish reputation of the royal family at the time.

Edward VII's eldest son, Albert Victor, was the next Duke of Clarence. Born prematurely and weighing just over three pounds, he never quite caught up. Physically, mentally, and morally frail, he died in 1892. A popular (if far-fetched) theory holds that Jack the Ripper, the mysterious killer of London prostitutes, was actually the Duke of Clarence.

The title has not been used since.

CLAUDIUS *(Latin clan name, "lame")* Also **Claude.** History and culture together have endowed this name with remarkable connotations. The famous emperor Claudius I, Caligula's nephew, set aside his son Britannicus and proclaimed his stepson Nero as his successor. (He was poisoned by his wife Agrippina for his pains.) Themes of usurpation are taken up in *Hamlet,* where Claudius reigns as king, having had his brother poisoned. Henry James may have had these notions of displacement in mind for Sir Claude in *What Maisie Knew.* He is the handsome, kindly second husband of Ida Farange, who takes Maisie into account more thoroughly than either of her parents ever did. Yet ultimately, he betrays Maisie by transferring his affections from her mother to her stepmother (the governess originally hired by, then married by, her father). Victor Hugo doesn't bother much with literary allusion for *Nôtre-Dame of Paris,* but he does hit the irony pretty hard. The villain Claude Frollo, archdeacon of the cathedral, is not lame as his first name suggests, but physically whole. Yet morally, he is a wreck—what a contrast to the saintly hunchback Quasimodo ("half-made")! Frollo takes Esmeralda prisoner, demands that she become his mistress, and ultimately delivers her to the mob to be hanged. Crippled, indeed!

Shakespeare, however, uses the Italian form of the name, **Claudio,** with no regard for subtext. His Claudios, in *Much Ado About Nothing* and *Measure for Measure,* are fairly conventional young men, whose greatest problems concern their romantic lives.

CLEMENT *(Latin, "merciful")* As the conventions of fiction took shape in the seventeenth and eighteenth centuries, the attribute name became a staple way to identify characters. Fanny Burney, when she wrote *Evelina* in 1778, turned that tradition on its head with Sir Clement Willoughby, for he is anything but mild to the poor heroine. As a sheltered young girl in the fashionable world without wise parental guidance, Evelina is at the mercy of a resolute rake like Sir Clement.

A hundred years later, Thomas Hardy took Clement more literally for *The Return of the Native.* The "native" of the title is

Clement Yeobright, better known as **Clym** in his home village of Egdon. He returns from Paris to open a school. The passionate, beautiful Eustacia Vye marries him, hoping to be rescued from Egdon, but Clym stays put, with tragic consequences. A sensitive, dreamy thinker, he ends up as an itinerant preacher, thinking mercifully, perhaps, about his headstrong late wife.

CLIFFORD (*English place-name, "ford near sloping ground"*) It has long been an upper-class tradition in both England and America to use last names as first names, especially to mark a significant financial gain brought by a woman into a marriage. Thus, a name like Clifford was probably once a maiden name. Family piety would have kept it as a first name for generations. In Nathaniel Hawthorne's *The House of the Seven Gables,* a name is not all that Clifford Pyncheon inherits. Rather, he falls heir to the curse that follows the Pyncheon family and their house. As an individual, he is unintimidating: handsome, refined, sweet, and ruined by thirty years of imprisonment. He has the nature of a selfish child. Henry James was well aware of Hawthorne's work, and Clifford Wentworth in *The Europeans* may be a kind of *hommage,* for his character is somewhat similar to Clifford Pyncheon's. Charming, handsome, but weak, he is the sybarite of his upright family and is temporarily intoxicated by the presence of his exotic cousin Eugenia. Intoxication, in fact, is his primary problem, and by the end of the comedy he has regained his senses.

> *Not to speak it harshly or scornfully, it seemed Clifford's nature to be a sybarite.*
> —NATHANIEL HAWTHORNE, *THE HOUSE OF THE SEVEN GABLES*

CLIVE (*English place-name, "cliff"*) Scholars suggest that Thackeray's use of Clive for the hero of *The Newcomes* promoted the name's use. In his novel, Clive is the young son of an officer in the Indian army who could have named the boy after eighteenth-century military hero Robert Clive, known as "Clive of India." Clive Newcome is a handsome, kind, but faintly spineless young man who, on the strength of an aptitude for drawing, becomes an artist. He loves his cousin Ethel Newcome but is not permitted to marry her, because she, as a wealthy beauty, is destined for an aristocratic mate.

CONNALLY *(Derived from a Gaelic phoneme meaning "high")* In Maria Edgeworth's *Castle Rackrent,* a pointed tale about several generations of feckless Irish landlords, Sir Connally Rackrent, known as **Condy,** is the last of his line to occupy the castle. Like his ancestor Sir Patrick, he dies of drink.

CONRAD *(Old German, "courageous counsel")* Conrad is the title character of Byron's poem "The Corsair," a noble, mysterious pirate chieftain and the very prototype of the Byronic hero: "That man of loneliness and mystery,/Scarce seen to smile, and seldom heard to sigh." However hackneyed the concept may be, in Byron's exceptionally skilled hands the character himself takes on alluring life. Shakespeare's *Much Ado About Nothing* features a secondary character named **Conrade,** an unusual form of the name. Conrade is a follower of Don John, the bastard brother of the prince of Aragon.

> *Unlike the heroes of each ancient race,*
> *Demons in act, but Gods at least in face,*
> *In Conrad's form seems little to admire*
> *Though his dark eyebrow shades a glance of fire.*
> —GEORGE GORDON, LORD BYRON, "THE CORSAIR"

CORIN *(Latin, "javelin")* Shakespeare's *As You Like It* takes a group of aristocrats including Celia and Rosalind into the Forest of Arden, where Corin is one of the rustic inhabitants. He is practical and capable, finding them shelter and sheep so they may become "shepherds" with a little more verisimilitude.

CORNELIUS *(Latin clan name, "horn")* In Christopher Marlowe's *Dr. Faustus,* Cornelius is one of the two magicians who help Dr. Faustus strike his bargain with the Devil. Unlike the title character, he has some scruples about the power of magic. His name reflects a Latinizing fashion current among educated Germans in the sixteenth century.

CREON *(Greek, meaning unknown)* There are two kings named Creon in Greek myth. One, the king of Corinth, appears in Euripides' tragedy *Medea* as the father of Jason's new wife—the one he leaves Medea for. He is easily confused with the king of Thebes, Jocasta's brother. Though honorable, he is terribly harsh, sentencing Oedipus and Jocasta's daughter Antigone to be buried alive in Sophocles' famous tragedy *Antigone.*

CUTHBERT *(Old English, "famous, bright")* A seventh-century bishop of the name was beloved in northern England. Sir Walter Scott uses his name for a strictly Protestant servant in *Old Mortality,* which covers the violent sectarian strife of the late seventeenth century in Scotland. Thomas Hardy takes advantage of the aura of sanctity in the name for Cuthbert Clare, one of Angel Clare's clergy-bound brothers in *Tess of the D'Urbervilles.*

DAMIAN *(Greek, meaning unclear; possibly "taming")* The name also resembles the Greek word for "spirit," which closely resembles the English "demon." In *The Canterbury Tales,* "The Merchant's Tale" is a story of an older man who marries a young woman and is cuckolded. The husband is January, the wife May, and the young man who persuades her to stray is called Damian, possibly in the sense of "spirit." The names of Thomas Hardy's principal characters are almost always freighted with meaning, so **Damon** Wildeve of *The Return of the Native* may be intended to recall a daemon/demon. He is a failed engineer who now keeps a tavern (ominously named "The Quiet Woman"). Although engaged to Thomasin Yeobright, he longs for that very unquiet woman, Eustacia Vye, and he has the personal charms to achieve his goal. Hardy says, "The grace of his movement was singular; it was the pantomimic expression of a lady-killing career." In this case, all too literally.

DANAOS *(da nay' ohs; Greek, meaning unknown)* The legendary grandson of Zeus and Io, brother of Aegyptus. Danaos had fifty daughters, whom Aegyptus wanted to match up with his sons. They murdered their husbands on their wedding nights. This bloodshed is the subject of Aeschylus's *The Suppliants.*

DANIEL *(Hebrew, "God is my judge")* The same name in French and in English. Honoré de Balzac, in his *Lost Illusions,* creates Daniel d'Arthez, a generous, honest novelist who takes Lucien Chardon under his wing in Paris. D'Arthez is a member of the group called the Cénacle, to whom he introduces Lucien. All hardworking men of genuine genius, they represent the narrow path of artistic integrity from which Lucien so readily strays. Daniel even rewrites Lucien's novel for him. Henry James creates a similarly sacrificial Daniel in *The Portrait of a Lady:* Daniel Touchett is Isabel Archer's uncle, and the man whose money permits her to stay in Europe and choose her future. Charles Dickens was less attentive to the nuances of given names than James, and his last names or nicknames tend to be more expressive. This is certainly the case with Daniel Quilp, the evil dwarf of *The Old Curiosity Shop*. His outsized appetites, his lust for little Nell, and his vitality are memorable, but he is usually known by his last name.

Another memorable Daniel of Victorian literature is Daniel Deronda, in George Eliot's eponymous novel. The handsome, intelligent, serious young Daniel has been brought up by an English baronet as the very flower of the British upper class. But he finds out that he is actually Jewish, and his earnest struggle to reconcile his two worlds provides the heart of the drama.

DARIUS *(Greek, "rich, royal")* The name of a great king of Persia, who ruled from 521 to around 485 B.C. He appears, as a ghost, in Aeschylus's play *The Persians,* which deals with the Greek defeat of the Persians at Salamis under the command of his son Xerxes.

D'ARTAGNAN *(French place-name)* The main protagonist of Dumas's *The Three Musketeers*. He is a Gascon, embodying the traditional characteristics of men from Gascony: he is proud, hot-tempered, obstinate, and short. Dumas even compares him to Don Quixote in his relentless grip on various causes. When he first arrives in Paris he manages to offend, serially, three members of the elite corps of musketeers. He is challenged to three duels which he schedules, with a certain élan, at hourly intervals that very afternoon. Naturally his proposed opponents are Athos, Porthos, and Aramis.

DAVID *(Hebrew, "beloved, dear")* The patron saint of Wales bore the name of the Old Testament king, and King David of Scotland was also revered as a saint. As a royal name and a saint's name,

David was used consistently through the Middle Ages and beyond, and its very familiarity repels specific connotations. The variety of ways in which authors have used the name confirms this notion. Balzac, for instance, creates a naive and honest inventor, David Séchard, as Lucien Chardon's best friend from the provinces in *Lost Illusions*. David Copperfield, the hero of Dickens's novel, is also in some ways naive, and as poor a judge of character as Séchard. Robert Louis Stevenson's David Balfour, though only eighteen, is much warier than either of the Balzac or Dickens heroes—which is a good thing, considering the adventures he undergoes in *Kidnapped*. David Gamut, the New England choirmaster accompanying the Munro girls in James Fenimore Cooper's *The Last of the Mohicans,* also has adventures, yet he is the very opposite of a good traveler; not only are his mannerisms irritating but he bursts into song often, prompting the Indians to think him crazy. Mark Twain's Pudd'nhead Wilson's real name is David, and he turns out to be less crazy than his neighbors of twenty-three years think him. His hobby of collecting fingerprints, long considered part of his eccentricity, permits him to solve a serious crime.

> *Generous souls make poor business men. David was one of those shy and sensitive people who shrink from argument.*
> —HONORÉ DE BALZAC, *LOST ILLUSIONS*

DECIMUS (*Latin, "tenth"*) The character of the Reverend Decimus Brock in Wilkie Collins's *Armadale* may owe a bit of inspiration to Trollope's Septimus Harding, who had appeared twenty years earlier in *The Warden*. Certainly this kind of Latin name, only plausible in a very large family, turned up in High Church clerical families in Victorian English literature. "Brock" is also an Old English term for a badger, and Decimus Brock, in the course of *Armadale,* shows badgerlike tenacity as he labors to protect innocent Allan Armadale from a plot with its roots in the past.

Boys' Names

DEMETRIUS *(Greek, "follower of Demeter")* Demeter is the earth goddess, known to the Romans as Ceres. Since Shakespeare's *A Midsummer Night's Dream* is set in Greece, the names chosen by the playwright support the conceit. Demetrius is one of a pair of frustrated lovers—he loves Hermia, to whom he is betrothed, but Helena is in love with him.

Far more important in literature is the Russian cognate **Dmitri** or **Dmitry**. The Bulgarian student Dmitri Insarov in Turgenev's 1859 *On the Eve* is a brooding revolutionary whose goal is to liberate Bulgaria from the Turks. His eruption into the calm, prosperous, stagnant world of the Stahovs has tragic consequences. Equally tragic—though infinitely less clear-cut—is the effect of Dmitri Dmitrich Gurov, the protagonist of Chekhov's famous story "Lady with Lapdog." A persistent womanizer, he is incapable of emotion until he falls disastrously in love with Anna, the lady of the title.

It is Dostoyevsky, though, who appropriates Dmitri with all the force of his immense energy. In *Crime and Punishment*, Dmitri Razumikhin is a friend of Raskolnikov's and thus serves as a kind of marker—if such a sane, reasonable man can maintain affection for the outrageous protagonist, Raskolnikov must have redeeming features. Dostoyevsky was as consistent in creating nuanced names as Henry James. The name Dmitri is linked with earthly characteristics, and in the trinity created by the legitimate Karamazov brothers, the eldest, Dmitri, is the most earthbound. Ruled by his passions, Dmitri most closely resembles the brutal and depraved Fyodor Pavlovich, the Karamazov father (who bears the author's own name). When accused of his father's murder, he refuses to defend himself, hoping that punishment will redeem him.

DESMOND *(Irish, "from south Munster")* Elizabeth Stoddard's *The Morgesons* is narrated by quirky Cassandra Morgeson, whose strong sexual reaction to Desmond Somers is especially striking, given the repressed atmosphere of small-town Massachusetts that pervades the novel. Desmond, the elder brother of Cassandra's friend Ben, is strikingly handsome and moody, and has a serious drinking problem. He goes off to Spain in an effort to control his alcoholism, demonstrating a courage that Cassandra approves.

> *"Desmond is a violent, tyrannical, sensual man; his perceptions are his pulses. That he is handsome, clever, resolute, and sings well, I can admit; but no more."*
> —ELIZABETH STODDARD, *THE MORGESONS*

DICK see **RICHARD**

DIEGO see **JAMES**

DIGGORY *(Old English; meaning obscure, but probably relates to a ditch or a dike)* An uncannily apt name for the "reddleman" in Thomas Hardy's *The Return of the Native*. His job involves dealing in red ochre, a pigment obtained from the earth and used to mark sheep. Diggory Venn is an elusive presence. His skin is reddened by his trade, which obscures not only his features but even his benevolent nature. Ultimately he functions as a kind of guardian angel to his beloved Thomasin.

DIONYSOS *(Greek, "twice-born")* Also **Dionysus.** The legendary god of the vine, known in Roman mythology as Bacchus. He is the son of Zeus and the human Semele, daughter of Cadmus. When Zeus appeared to her in his flaming glory she became overwhelmed and died, but Dionysos, with whom she was pregnant, was saved and sewn into Zeus's thigh, whence he was born a second time. He gradually replaced Hestia as an object of worship, and one of the elements of Euripides' play *The Bacchae* is resistance to the gradual spread of his ritual. It involved ecstatic processions, dancing, and orgies, very threatening to the status quo. Our modern name **Dennis** means "follower of Dionysos."

DIRK *(Old German, "people rule")* The root is actually **Dietrich.** However, a dirk is also the term for a long dagger or short sword traditionally carried in Scotland, and it is this sense of the name that Edgar Allan Poe invokes in *The Narrative of Arthur Gordon Pym of Nantucket.* Dirk Peters is the short, dark, hairy sailor who proves to be the narrator's salvation. (His last name clearly alludes to the Apostle Peter.) His physical strength and overall know-how keep Arthur safe from shipwreck, starvation, and capture by demonic black cannibals in the alternate world the travelers discover *inside* the continent of Antarctica.

DONALD *(Scottish Gaelic, "world mighty")* An archetypal Scots name, perhaps more familiar in its patronymic form, **McDonald**. Sir Walter Scott uses it in *Waverley* for a secondary character, the colorful sheep-stealing bandit Donald Bean Lean, whose loyalty to Bonnie Prince Charlie and the Jacobite cause is unshakable. Donald Farfrae, in Thomas Hardy's *The Mayor of Casterbridge*, is almost comically aptly named. He presents a challenge to Mayor Michael Henchard's power, supplanting and becoming, if not "world mighty," at least "Casterbridge mighty." His last name indicates that he is "far from" his origins. His rational, calculating, unemotional approach to life triumphs over Michael Henchard's emotional, impulsive self-destruction.

> *In social intercourse, these familiar friends of his habitually and instinctively allowed for him, as for a child or some other lawless thing, exacting no strict obedience to conventional rules, and hardly noticing his eccentricities enough to pardon them. There was an undefinable characteristic about Donatello, that set him outside of rules.*
>
> —NATHANIEL HAWTHORNE, *THE MARBLE FAUN*

DONATELLO *(Italian diminutive, "given")* The name of the brilliant Florentine sculptor of the Renaissance. In Nathaniel Hawthorne's *The Marble Faun,* Donatello is a young Italian man who resembles a faun. He is in love with a young American woman, Miriam, who has a mysterious past. At her unspoken behest, he commits a serious crime, which Miriam later regrets desperately. He may represent European influence on Miriam and her friends, but his involvement with them actually results in his loss of innocence rather than that of the Americans.

DORIAN *(Greek, "from Doris")* Sparta was the center of the Dorian branch of the Greek nation, known for its harsh laws, severe dress, and stern style of architecture. Dorian Gray, the protagonist of Oscar Wilde's *The Picture of Dorian Gray*, leans toward the very opposite pole of civilization. In fact, after his portrait is enchanted, his whole life involves gratifying the senses, even to the extent of debauchery. The portrait, of course, ages in a closet, bearing the brunt of Dorian's dissolution.

DROMIO *(Origin unclear)* The Greek word *dromos* means "course" or "racecourse." The twin brothers named Dromio in Shakespeare's *The Comedy of Errors* are servants to the twin brothers Antipholus. Much of the merriment of the play comes from their energy and the confusion surrounding their frequently mistaken identities.

DUNCAN *(Scottish Gaelic, "brown battler")* The Duncan whom Macbeth kills in Shakespeare's play is a historic character who was killed by one of his generals, Macbeth, around A.D. 1040. This precedent has little resonance in James Fenimore Cooper's *The Last of the Mohicans*, where Major Duncan Heyward is the English soldier escorting the Munro sisters to their father at Fort William Henry. He is handsome, brave, and conventional, at an utter loss in the American wilderness, and thus stands in contrast to Natty Bumppo.

DUNSTAN *(English place-name, "brown stone")* One of the early archbishops of Canterbury, Saint Dunstan is credited with inventing the coronation rite for King Edgar that serves as the basis for English coronations today. In George Eliot's *Silas Marner*, Dunstan is one of two sons of Squire Cass. His consciously "antique" name would have been fashionable in the upper class of that era, as would **Godfrey**, his brother's name. Dunstan (affectionately known as "Dunsey") is a reprobate, a gambler who loses a sum of money his father gave his brother. He steals Silas Marner's gold, setting off the process that results in that character's redemption.

EBENEZER *(Hebrew, "rock of aid")* Readers who can't name any other Dickens character still know the name of Ebenezer Scrooge, the miser of *A Christmas Carol.* Possibly Robert Louis Stevenson was playing on this familiarity with the name of Ebenezer Balfour in *Kidnapped.* He is the hero David Balfour's uncle, "a mean, stooping, narrow-shouldered, clay-faced creature" and the heir in penny-pinching to Scrooge. He has David kidnapped in order to lay claim to the estate that David rightfully owns.

EDGAR *(Old English, "prosperous spear")* In historic terms, Edgar was a king of the English in the tenth century. His reign was remembered as a kind of golden age and he was called "the Peaceful." Whether or not Shakespeare knew about this precedent, Edgar in *King Lear* is one of the very few loyal or peaceful characters. The son of the earl of Gloucester, he is ousted by his brother Edmund and joins his father in exile. A later use of Edgar continues the mild-mannered theme. Readers of Emily Brontë's *Wuthering Heights* always remember Cathy and Heathcliff, but Cathy was actually married to Edgar Linton—the blond, blue-eyed, gentle, and civilized antithesis to Heathcliff. An American use of the name dates from 1799 in Charles Brockden Brown's *Edgar Huntly.* The narrator, by walking in his sleep, makes a number of disturbing discoveries about his Pennsylvania neighbors that eventually involve murder.

EDMUND *(Old English, "prosperous protector")* Like **Edgar,** the name of a very early English king (the grandson of Edgar, in fact). Also used by Shakespeare for a character in *King Lear;* Edmund is the illegitimate and evil son of Gloucester, who works to disinherit his brother Edgar. Jane Austen uses the name in a more benign way for Edmund Bertram, the second son of Sir Thomas Bertram in *Mansfield Park*. He is kind to his poor cousin Fanny Price, and after a flirtation with the worldly Mary Crawford, becomes engaged to Fanny. George Gissing, in *The Odd Women*, engages in a bit of the allusive naming so popular among other nineteenth-century novelists. Edmund Widdowson is the wealthy older man who literally becomes Monica Madden's "prosperous protector" by marrying her. In this study of late Victorian women, Monica, the only wife, is no better off than her unmarried, "odd" sisters. Widdowson believes that a woman's sphere is the home and that her husband should make decisions for her—protection that amounts to imprisonment.

The French form is **Edmond,** and Alexandre Dumas has no such axe to grind with Edmond Dantès in *The Count of Monte Cristo*. Dantès, in fact, sheds his name partway into the book. Ultimately he becomes not a sailor, not a prisoner in the Château d'If, not even the protégé of a wealthy priest, but the mysterious Count of Monte Cristo, bent on revenge against the people who plotted to imprison him in the first place.

> *"What a change you have made in my life, Edmund! How much I have to thank you for!"*
> —GEORGE GISSING, *THE ODD WOMEN*

EDWARD *(Old English, "rich defender")* A classic English name given fame not only by a saint and several kings, but even by two sainted kings of England (Edward the Confessor and Edward the Martyr). Queen Victoria's eldest son, who assumed the throne in 1901 as Edward VII, was christened Albert Edward. And while the name was used very extensively by Victorian novelists, most of those characters are known to this day by their last names. Sir Walter Scott wrote the first of the "Waverley" novels in 1814, and the central character, whose adventures with the Jacobins in Scotland form the basis for the novel, is named Edward. Jane Austen also used the name prominently, for Edward Ferrars of *Sense and Sensibility*. Possibly the least charming of her heroes, he is the would-be clergyman who depends on his proud mother's financial support. Though he loves Elinor ("sense"), he is helplessly entangled in a relationship with the vulgar Lucy Steele. In contrast with Willoughby, the lover of Marianne ("sensibility"), Edward Ferrars is a dull stick.

Edward Ferrars is often referred to by his first and last names, but many other fictional Edwards of the nineteenth century are known simply by their last names. Who could have said, for instance, that the brooding Mr. Rochester of Charlotte Brontë's *Jane Eyre* was called Edward? In fact, the Brontë sisters used the name several times. In Charlotte's first novel, *The Professor,* the narrator's elder brother is an Edward. He is a harsh mill owner in the north of England who resents his younger brother's excellent education and social opportunities. Anne Brontë's *Agnes Grey,* another novel about a governess, features Edward Weston as the love interest. Somewhat predictably, he is a curate in a parish near where Agnes Grey works, and though he is neither handsome nor rich nor especially charming, his sterling features—honesty, kindness, loyalty—show through. Much less attractive is another clerical Edward, Mr. Casaubon of George Eliot's *Middlemarch.* He is a dry pedant whom the high-spirited Dorothea Brooke sees, romantically, as a glorious project. She will be his helpmeet, and the production of his great work on the mythology of the world will become her raison d'être. He sees her as a socially presentable source of unpaid labor. Fortunately for Dorothea, he dies halfway through the book, leaving her a financially comfortable widow. George Eliot used the name again in *The Mill on the Floss,* for the quarrelsome, hotheaded father of Maggie and Tom Tulliver, whose business troubles result in the family's loss of Dorlcote Mill. Finally, Robert Louis Stevenson's terrifying Mr. Hyde is an Edward. He represents the evil side of man: "Tales came out of the man's cruelty, at once so callous and violent, of his vile life, of his strange associates, of the hatred that seemed to have surrounded his career."

Johann Wolfgang von Goethe often used names with a French flavor, though of course he wrote in German. Thus, the form of Edward he uses in *Elective Affinities* is **Eduard.** In fact, the rich middle-aged baron was originally named **Otto,** like his great friend the Captain, but he relinquished that name so that his friend could use it. The novel is an early example of stories about rich married people with too little to do and too much romantic temptation to relieve their boredom. In this case, Eduard's downfall is his wife's foster daughter Ottilie.

> *Edward Ferrars was not recommended to their good opinion by any peculiar graces of person or address.*
> —JANE AUSTEN, *SENSE AND SENSIBILITY*

EDWIN *(Old English, "wealthy friend")* Charles Dickens's last novel, *The Mystery of Edwin Drood,* was left unfinished at Dickens's death. The portion of the manuscript he wrote sketched out a projected marriage between the two orphans Edwin Drood and Rosa Bud, who have known each other since childhood. Shortly before they are to be wed, Edwin disappears, and what remains of the novel does not explain how or why. Another character is arrested for his murder, but released because there is no body. In point of fact Edwin is more interesting in absentia than he was alive. George Gissing wrote about the cutthroat values of the modern literary world in *New Grub Street,* and Edwin Reardon is one of the casualties. Though he has shown some literary talent, he has a socially ambitious wife to support. She is incapable of understanding the creative process, but leaves him when he takes a lowly job as a clerk to support her. Yet when she receives a substantial inheritance and offers to support him while he returns to writing, he refuses out of pride.

EGIL *(ay' gill; Scandinavian, "point, edge")* The hero of a thirteenth-century Icelandic epic that harks back to the ninth and tenth centuries. Egil, larger than life, is a Viking, a poet, a sorcerer, and a murderer. Though he is swarthy and ugly, he is a very compelling character because of his vitality.

EJLERT *(eye' lert; Scandinavian, "hard point")* In Henrik Ibsen's *Hedda Gabler,* Ejlert Lovberg is Hedda's rejected suitor whom she cannot quite relinquish. Under the influence of her friend Thea, Ejlert has published one book and written another one. Hedda cannot abide this evidence of his productivity (or her friend Thea's benign influence), so she provokes him into an evening's worth of self-destructive activity that ends in suicide.

ELMER *(Old English, "noble famous")* One of the Old English names that survived the Norman Conquest and were revived in the nineteenth century. For some reason Elmer was much more popular in the United States than in Britain, and Edith Wharton's Elmer Moffatt, in *The Custom of the Country,* could only be an American. He is the fiercely ambitious New Man who ultimately demonstrates that he is Undine Spragg's true soul mate: "Undine was perfectly aware that he was a vulgar over-dressed man . . . and was conscious that he stirred the fibres of a self she had forgotten but had not ceased to understand."

EPHRAIM *(Hebrew, "productive, fertile")* An Old Testament name that was revived among certain Protestant Scots known as Covenanters. Those great chroniclers of Scotland Sir Walter Scott and Robert Louis Stevenson both used the name for minor characters. In Scott's *Old Mortality,* Ephraim MacBriar is a fanatical young religious partisan, while Ephraim McKellar, in Stevenson's *The Master of Ballantrae,* is the narrator. He has served as steward for the Durie family and is a frank partisan of the younger son Henry, rather than of the sinister James, the Master of the title.

ERNEST *(Old English, "sincere, truthful")* Charles Dickens chose this name for Monsieur Defarge, the wineshop keeper of the Faubourg St. Antoine in *A Tale of Two Cities,* and husband of the virago Thérèse Defarge. In Samuel Butler's *The Way of All*

Flesh, the name is used for Ernest Pontifex, the unfortunate misfit of a clergyman who struggles against his father's harsh requirements that he conform to the standards of the upper middle class. Here, it is an attribute name as well as a fitting selection for a man of his caste.

ETEOCLES (ee tee oh' klees; *Greek, meaning unknown*) A character in Aeschylus's *Seven Against Thebes* and Euripides' *The Phoenician Women*. He and Polyneices are twin sons of Oedipus and Jocasta who were supposed to serve alternate years as king of Thebes. Eteocles refused to give way to his brother Polyneices, sparking a war in which both brothers were killed.

ETHAN (*Hebrew, "strength, firmness"*) Edith Wharton's *Ethan Frome* is the short, bleak tale of a poor Massachusetts farmer's fleeting grasp on happiness. A sensitive but taciturn soul, Frome is shackled to his querulous older cousin Zeena in a bitter marriage. When her young and lively orphaned cousin Mattie Silver joins the household, a startling vision of emotional and intellectual intimacy appears to Ethan—all too briefly.

> *If you know the post-office you must have seen Ethan Frome drive up to it, drop the reins on his hollow-backed bay and drag himself across the brick pavement to the white colonnade: and you must have asked who he was.*
> —EDITH WHARTON, *ETHAN FROME*

ETHELBERT see **BERTIE**

EUGÈNE (euh zhehn'; *French from Greek, "well-born"*) A name that is virtually owned by Balzac's great creation, Eugène de Rastignac. Though Balzac wrote around ninety books and invented more than two thousand characters, Rastignac is in many ways the quintessential Balzacian hero, a handsome young provincial who comes to Paris to live on his wits and grapples with the fluid forces of post-Napoleonic society. He is, as his name proclaims, "well born," coming from decayed provincial aristocracy (unlike Lucien Chardon, he really deserves his *particule*). In *Old Goriot,* he is a law student, but as Balzac's "Human Comedy" progresses, he becomes a financier and bon vivant. He also differs from Lucien Chardon in that he possesses the basic ruthlessness that Parisian success requires. Scholars suggest that Rastignac is in profound ways an alter ego for Balzac himself.

Eugene is also used heavily in Russia in the form **Yevgeny** (*yev gay' nee*) or **Evgeny.** Alexander Pushkin's 1833 verse novel *Eugene Onegin* introduces the first "superfluous man"—a rich, handsome, educated man for whom Russian society provides no opportunities. His estates can be run successfully without him; he shuns the hypocrisy of politics—only hedonism is left, so he flirts and duels. Yevgeny Barsanov, in Ivan Turgenev's *Fathers and Sons,* is a medical researcher staying at the home of his aristocratic friend Arkady Kirsanov. He is considered by some critics to be the first Bolshevik because his response to the inequities in Russian society is to yearn for revolution. Turgenev wrote of him, "I conceived him as a sombre figure . . . powerful, nasty, honest, but doomed to destruction because he still stands only in the gateway to the future."

EUMAEUS (yoo may' uhs; *Greek, meaning unknown*) In *The Odyssey,* Eumaeus is the faithful swineherd who welcomes Odysseus home to Ithaka. Alone of the people left behind, Eumaeus recognizes the hero, and extends hospitality without requiring proof of his identity.

EVANDER (eh van' der; *Greek, "good man"*) Virgil's *Aeneid* is both an adventure story and the background to the founding of the city of Rome. Evander is one of the minor characters, a wise man who lives in Pallanteum, the Italian site where Rome must rise. He becomes a kind of father figure for Aeneas, imparting his rustic wisdom and politician's insight.

EVERARD (*Old English, "boar hard"*) Everard and its variants, Everett and Everell, fall into the large category of men's first

ENGLISH LAST NAMES

A significant number of first names (usually male) in English were originally last names. It has long been a custom in both England and America for families to give a boy baby, as a first name, his mother's maiden name. In Thackeray's *The Newcomes,* for instance, Thomas Newcome's wife is Sophia Hobson, and his eldest son is called Hobson.

Last names in English tend to fall into a few clear categories. Their function, of course, is to distinguish among members of a growing population. First are the names that describe the quality of a person, like **Everard** ("boar hard"). These are often Germanic names, though sometimes physical description (**White, Brown**) is recognizably English. Occupation names are another big group. Many of these pertain to the trade in wool, which was England's great industry in the thirteenth century, when last names became officially hereditary. **Weaver, Shepherd, Tailor,** and **Smith** are typical of this period. Still another category is place-names, which tend to be Old English and refer to features of a landscape, like **Linton** ("flax settlement"). Finally, there are genealogical names. In England, they end with *son*, like **Richardson** or **Johnson.** In Scotland, they start with *Mac* or *Mc*, like **McDonald.** The Norman French version is *Fitz*, as in **Fitzwilliam,** and the Irish form is *O'*, like **O'Dowd.**

names that are transferred from last names. In George Gissing's *The Odd Women,* Everard Barfoot is a well-to-do man-about-town who finds himself attracted to the self-sufficient Rhoda Nunn. Gissing does not tailor names to characters as explicitly as some of his contemporaries, but the "hardness" the name alludes to may apply to his attitude toward women's independence. For Trollope, unless he is being whimsical, the origins of names are less important than their social suitability, and Everett Wharton in *The Prime Minister* is a perfectly appropriate name for the son of an eminent barrister. Everett is one of Trollope's young men-about-town who gamble and flirt and make dangerous friends but can't settle down to a career. When Catharine Maria Sedgwick wrote *Hope Leslie* in 1824, her subject was, in part, the stultifying nature of the Puritan colony of Boston. Everell Fletcher, with his refined, Anglocentric name (instead of the name of an Old Testament prophet), comes to Massachusetts tainted by his taste for luxury and frivolity, not to mention the Church of England. He is also impetuous enough to get engaged to a young Puritan lady who would probably have done better to choose a reliable Jeremiah or Habbakuk.

> *Everett Wharton was a trouble to his father.*
> —ANTHONY TROLLOPE, *THE PRIME MINISTER*

EZEKIEL *(Hebrew, "strength of Jehovah")* Nineteenth-century English authors often found American men's first names deeply comical, and Trollope plays with this cultural difference in *The Duke's Children*. Ezekiel Boncassen is the wealthy American scholar whose daughter Isabel is much sought after in the drawing rooms of London. At the time when this most cynical of Trollope's novels was written, American women with potentially huge dowries were traveling to England in search of aristocratic husbands. Many of them came of unsophisticated, even crude families, but Ezekiel Boncassen is a refined and appealing character.

EZRA *(Hebrew, "help, aid")* By the third quarter of the nineteenth century, the names of the Old Testament prophets were found in a few groups, including modest rural families with non-Anglican allegiances, and Jews. We don't find out much about Ezra Jennings's past, in reading Wilkie Collins's *The Moonstone*—his present is all too startling. His name, though, marks him as coming from the lower classes. He is the bizarre-looking, opium-addicted medical practitioner who provides an important clue to the mystery of the disappearing "moonstone," a gigantic diamond. George Eliot used Ezra as a Jewish name in her carefully researched *Daniel Deronda*. It is, in fact, the name of two men, one an East End jeweler and one the visionary biblical scholar who chooses Daniel Deronda as his spiritual heir.

FABRIZIO *(Italian from Latin, "worker, fabricator")* Stendhal, an author who knew quite a bit about inventing characters—in the Napoleonic era, when invention of self could be a heroic feat—created two protean young men in Julien Sorel of *Scarlet and Black* and Fabrizio del Dongo of *The Charterhouse of Parma*. The latter's name even refers to the fabricating process. He is a handsome young nobleman, a great admirer of Napoleon, whose great promise culminates in nothing more than a series of abortive love affairs. The charterhouse referred to in the title is the monastery where he finally ends his days.

> "... if anybody talks sense I can follow him; but Felix talks so wild, and contradicts his mother."
> —GEORGE ELIOT, *FELIX HOLT: THE RADICAL*

FELIX *(Latin, "happy")* The hero of George Eliot's least-known novel is the eponymous Felix Holt—the subtitle dubs him "The Radical." He is a working-class hero, a "shaggy-headed, large-eyed, strong-limbed person" who has disruptive ideas about the social order. In Anthony Trollope's *The Way We Live Now,* Felix Carbury is a classic upper-class wastrel: cynical, handsome, and expensive. Neither Trollope nor Eliot exploits the literal sense of the name, but Henry James, in *The Europeans,* makes the most of it. Felix Young is the European-raised cousin of the Massachusetts Wentworth family. He and his sister Eugenia, a German baroness, have arrived in provincial Massachusetts to visit their rich relatives with an eye to bettering their own precarious financial situation. Felix accepts his sister's schemes without any moral qualms.

> *Felix was not a young man who troubled himself greatly about anything—least of all about the conditions of enjoyment.*
> —HENRY JAMES, THE EUROPEANS

The name is the same in French, though pronounced *fay leex´*, and Victor Hugo uses it in much the same way that Henry James does. In *Les Misérables,* Félix Tholomyes is Fantine's lover, a balding, thirty-year-old jester who refuses to take their love seriously: "To him, it was an affair; to her, it was a passion." Honoré de Balzac's Félix Grandet, on the other hand, is anything but happy-go-lucky. The miser father of Eugénie Grandet in the novel of the same name, he and his family live in near squalor despite his immense wealth. Balzac's other name for him is "Avarice"—a far cry from felicity.

A more Latinate form of the name is **Felician** or **Felicien.** Henry Wadsworth Longfellow, working hard in "Evangeline" to evoke a French Canadian milieu, calls the priest of Grand Pré Father Felician. He becomes the guardian of Evangeline in her wanderings, pointing her toward moral happiness: "Sorrow and silence are strong, and patient endurance is godlike"—a truly Victorian recipe for woman's fulfillment.

FERDINAND *(Old German, "travel courage" or "peace courage")*
A name more familiar on the Continent than in England; the king of Spain who sent Columbus to America was King Ferdinand. Shakespeare, in *Love's Labour's Lost,* written some hundred years later, invented a king of Navarre named Ferdinand who vows, with three of his courtiers, to avoid women and concentrate on intellectual pursuits for three years. Naturally no sooner is the oath taken than four ravishing ladies appear at the court

and severely test the resolution of the king and his fellow scholars. Ferdinand, the prince of Naples in *The Tempest*, is also subjected to a test; Prospero requires that he pile up a thousand logs before he may woo Miranda. He patiently accomplishes the task and gratefully claims his bride.

In Miguel de Cervantes's *Don Quixote*, few of the characters encountered by the hero have much in the way of individuality; this is certainly true of Ferdinand, the young man who serves as Dorothea's love interest. Anthony Trollope uses the name in *The Prime Minister:* "Ferdinand Lopez was not an honest man or a good man." Trollope was very suspicious of foreigners who seemed to him to be corrupting the great old British social system, and in his novels creates several foreign rogues who take advantage of British naiveté; Lopez is one of these, a soft-spoken, plausible reprobate. Trollope is xenophobic enough to refer slightingly to Lopez's foreign looks, but he is also honest enough to mirror the xenophobia in English society.

> *Physically, Ferdinand was a tall, slender young man, with a good figure and adaptive manners, which enabled him to take, on occasion, the key-note of the various societies in which he found himself.*
>
> —HONORÉ DE BALZAC, *CÉSAR BIROTTEAU*

Honoré de Balzac's *César Birotteau* examines the social conditions in postrevolutionary Paris. One of the characters who is in a position to benefit most from the fluidity of society is Ferdinand du Tillet, Birotteau's clerk. Energetic, unscrupulous, and ambitious, he rises above his past and makes himself into a figure of society, using seed money borrowed from Birotteau as the foundation for financial speculation. Ferdinand is sometimes contracted into **Fernand**, the form used by Alexandre Dumas for Fernand Morcerf, a secondary character in *The Count of Monte Cristo*. His big mistake is to marry his cousin Mercédès, the young woman whom Edmond

Dantès loves. Years later, when he has become a general (in the supremely fluid world of Napoleonic Paris), Dantès comes back as the Count of the title—and gets his revenge.

FERGUS (*Gaelic, "best choice"*) Virtually an ethnic Scottish name, and Sir Walter Scott uses it thus in *Waverley* for clan chieftain Fergus MacIvor. It is he who lures the protagonist Edward Waverley into joining the Jacobite rebellion. He plays heavily on the "Highland virtues" of warmth and hospitality, but in truth his support for Bonnie Prince Charlie is quite calculated. Anne Brontë also uses the name for a secondary character in *The Tenant of Wildfell Hall*. Fergus Markham, a good-natured, boisterous farmer's son, is the younger brother of the narrator Gilbert. The latter has delusions of grandeur and fancies himself superior to his bumpkin brother.

FERMIN (*Spanish, "strong"*) A saint's name in Spain—the famous running of the bulls in Pamplona is carried out in his honor. In Leopoldo Alas's *La Regenta*, Fermin De Pas is the cleric to whom the hard-pressed Ana Ozores turns for comfort when her marriage turns out to be a disaster. Father Fermin is anything but strong in the faith, for he falls in love with Ana and ultimately refuses her forgiveness for her sins.

FESTUS (*Latin, "joyous, festive"*) *The Trumpet-Major* is one of Thomas Hardy's pastoral novels, set in deeply rural England at the time of the Napoleonic war. Festus Derriman is a secondary character, the nephew of the small neighborhood squire. A big, bluff, arrogant drunkard, he woos the pretty Anne Garland, but without success. Hardy says of Festus that "his disposition divided naturally into two, the boastful and the cantankerous."

FIGARO (*Italian, meaning unknown*) The character so familiar to the public from Rossini's *The Barber of Seville* and Mozart's *The Marriage of Figaro* first appeared in Beaumarchais's plays of the same titles. He is a classic scoundrel, the servant more canny than his aristocratic master. His wit at the expense of his social superiors was considered revolutionary when the plays first appeared.

> *"Ah! Figaro! My friend! You shall be my guardian angel, my liberator, my guiding spirit."*
> —PIERRE-AUGUSTIN CARON DE BEAUMARCHAIS,
> *THE BARBER OF SEVILLE*

FITZWILLIAM *(Middle English, "son of William")* Jane Austen never claimed for herself wide powers of invention, and her genius is such that this limitation is rarely perceptible. Yet her selection of names is hardly wide-ranging. Of course most of her male characters are generally known by their last names: Mr. Bingley, Willoughby, Colonel Brandon, and of course Mr. Darcy of *Pride and Prejudice*. It's hard to imagine Elizabeth Bennet ever calling him "Fitzwilliam," but the name does smack of the upper class, emphasizing the discrepancy between her social standing and his.

FLORIAN *(Latin, "in bloom")* Sir Florian Eustace is not a living character in Anthony Trollope's *The Eustace Diamonds*, but he is referred to frequently. His widow, the grasping, amoral Lizzie, invokes his memory (often with crocodile tears) when she conceives it may help her, while the Eustace family attorneys do much the same, though dry-eyed. Trollope makes plain that Sir Florian was "vicious," but draws a discreet veil over the nature of the vice. A variant form from the same root is **Florizel,** the name of the prince of Bohemia in Shakespeare's *The Winter's Tale*. He and his beloved Perdita fall into the classic—and somewhat vacant—mold of many Shakespearean lovers. Their youth and good breeding and good looks constitute their characters. An interesting historical note, however, is that the actress Mary Robinson, who played Perdita in a London production of 1779, became the mistress of the very young Prince of Wales. When he finally ascended to the throne as George IV in 1820, after years of being regent for his deranged father, it was easy to forget that he had once been affectionately known as "Prince Florizel."

OLD ENGLISH, MIDDLE ENGLISH

English is something of a mongrel language, exhibiting traits from its several parents. The history of the words we use is the history of the island northwest of Europe and of its successive rulers.

Two thousand years ago England was Britain and its people were Celtic. (The Celtic tongue survives in Gaelic, Welsh, and Breton, the language indigenous to Brittany.) The Romans came in A.D. 43 but their architecture endured better than their language. Hadrian's Wall still stands, but Old English is primarily Germanic, the language brought by Angles, Saxons, Jutes, and Friesians beginning in around A.D. 400.

Middle English, which scholars date from about 1100, mixes in Norman French, which of course has Latin roots. William the Conqueror brought with him nobles and priests to administer this new country, and in short order, French was the language of power. The lilting Middle English of *The Canterbury Tales,* written at the end of the fourteenth century, owes a great deal to French. The word particle *Fitz,* which occurs in a number of male names (and surnames), means "son of" and comes from the French word *fils,* or "son." The name **Fitzwilliam** is thus a classic artifact of Middle English: a Germanic name with a French prefix.

FRANCIS *(Latin, "Frenchman")* Originally a name denoting a place of origin: the kingdom of the Franks evolved into what is now France. The name had a great vogue in the nineteenth century, and men named Francis or **Frank** appear in many of the English novels of that era. Charlotte Brontë even has a **François** in *The Professor;* he is the proprietor of the pension where the protagonist first works in Brussels. Charlotte Brontë herself spent several years at a boarding school in Brussels where she carefully observed the naming patterns of educated Belgians.

There is much less American use of the name; one of the few American Francises is the protagonist Francis Carwin of Charles Brockden Brown's *Wieland: Memoirs of Carwin the Biloquist.* One of the earliest novels to be published in America, it is a Gothic tale involving madness, haunting, and attempted murder. Francis Carwin's ability to throw his voice—"biloquist" is the contemporaneous term for what we call ventriloquism—moves the plot along in several places, while contributing to the general air of mystery.

William Thackeray assigns the name to two generations of Viscounts Castlewood in *The History of Henry Esmond.* The eponymous hero of this ironic bildungsroman is actually the heir to the title rather than his (apparently legitimate) brother Francis, a boisterous, hard-drinking, womanizing gambler. The latter's son, called Frank to distinguish him from his father, is a handsome, easygoing aristocrat.

As the nineteenth century wore on, Frank became the normal usage and Francis took on a slightly formal air. In this guise it is very suitable for Trollope's somewhat intimidating Dean Arabin, who first appears in *Barchester Towers.* He is a brilliant clergyman, worldly and efficient, who is nevertheless humble: "a droll, odd, humorous, energetic, conscientious man," as Trollope puts it. Francis and Frank are used interchangeably for the unsettling Sergeant York in Hardy's *Far from the Madding Crowd.* Naturally it is the women who call him by his pet name—and it is the women whom York damages. First Fanny Robin gets pregnant by him, then he marries Bathsheba Everdene and squanders her money.

Hardy, ever alert to names, probably calls York "Frank" ironically, referring to the quality of openness and honesty so prized in Victorian men—a quality signally lacking in the charming and improvident York. (It is also missing from Frank Vanstone, another feckless young man in Wilkie Collins's *No Name.*) Trollope is less concerned with the psychological baggage of his names, yet that connotation of disclosure lingers around his characters. Trollope, in fact, almost owns the name Frank, in that he used it for three very important characters. First there is Frank Gresham of Greshambury, who appears in *Doctor Thorne*. Francis, his father, is the squire of Greshambury, beset with financial problems and a hypochondriac, aristocratic wife. Frank's problems are largely romantic, for he loves the penniless Mary Thorne. Trollope's next Frank still qualifies as "manly," but "frank" is a tougher call. He is Frank Greystock, cousin of the duplicitous Lizzie Eustace in *The Eustace Diamonds*, who—in the guise of relying on him for legal help—attempts to ensnare him romantically. Though he is engaged to the modest governess Lucy Morris, his definition of "legal help" is elastic enough to include canoodling with his "client." Finally, in *The Duke's Children*, Trollope creates another young hero in the penniless Cornishman Frank Tregear. He is the love interest of Lady Mary Palliser, daughter of the Duke of Omnium. Though marriage with Frank Tregear is a major social step downward for Lady Mary, Trollope makes him handsome, intelligent, principled—a very appealing suitor in every sense except the worldly ones.

A name that has been in use as long as Francis often spawns diminutives like **Franklin**. Though more familiar as a last name, it was also used as a first name, as in Wilkie Collins's *The Moonstone*. Franklin Blake is the male romantic lead, a handsome, charming dilettante whose involvement in the affair of the gigantic diamond focuses his attentions in a way that nothing else has.

FREDERICK *(Old German, "peace rule")* An old name that was widely used throughout Europe: Frederick I, the king of Germany and the Holy Roman emperor (1152–1190) was known as "Barbarossa" for his red beard. Like a few other standard masculine names (**Charles, Edward**), Frederick is virtually neutral. No famous saint or sinner has attached associations to the name, and its meaning is both obscure and abstract, making Frederick something of a blank slate. Jane Austen used it for Captain Wentworth in her last novel, *Persuasion,* and though the somewhat world-weary sailor is one of her more alluring heroes, men's first names matter very little in Austen's books. The narrator of Henry

James's *Daisy Miller* is Frederick Winterbourne, but again, detachment and coldness (note the wintry last name) are the point of his character. In *The Tenant of Wildfell Hall*, Anne Brontë calls the squire of the hall Frederick Lawrence, but he is little more than a mechanism in the plot, the reason for the mysterious Helen Graham to be in the neighborhood. One of Trollope's more entertaining minor characters is Lord Fawn, the timid peer who courts several of Trollope's rich and strong-minded heroines in *The Eustace Diamonds* and actually, to his consternation, gets engaged to Lizzie Eustace. His many loving sisters call him Frederick.

In French, the name is **Frédéric,** as in Gustave Flaubert's *A Sentimental Education.* Frédéric Moreau is that staple of the nineteenth-century French novel, a young man from the provinces determined to take Paris by storm. He regards himself as a romantic hero and Flaubert is determined to bring him back to earth in this novel of disillusionment. Though banker Frédéric Nucingen of Honoré de Balzac's Paris novels is German, he uses the French spelling for his name, the better to fit into aristocratic society. He appears extensively in *A Harlot High and Low,* making a fool of himself over Esther Gobseck. Some scholars believe that Balzac based the character in part on German banker Jacob de Rothschild.

The Italian version of the name, **Federigo,** is used for a virtuous cardinal, Federigo Borromeo, in Alessandro Manzoni's *The Betrothed,* and the German version, **Friedrich,** appears in Louisa May Alcott's *Little Women,* for another virtuous character. He is Friedrich Bhaer, also called **Fritz,** the German professor who finally wins Jo March's heart by his wisdom and patience.

FYODOR see **THEODORE**

GABRIEL *(Hebrew, "hero of God")* In Christian, Jewish, and Muslim scripture Gabriel is an archangel. Christians believe that Gabriel announced to the Virgin Mary that she was to bear God's son, so the name is frequently associated with bringing news. For instance, Robert Louis Stevenson brings a minor character into *Dr. Jekyll and Mr. Hyde*—a lawyer with extensive information about Jekyll. His name, pointedly, is Gabriel Utterson. Henry James also has a Gabriel bringing a message in *The Tragic Muse;* Gabriel Nash is the aesthete who persuades Nick Dormer to abandon a conventional career in politics and chance his arm as a painter. Even Sir Walter Scott, not much given to joking names, puts an unctuous preacher named Gabriel Kettledrummle in *Old Mortality.*

The two memorable Gabriels in nineteenth-century fiction, however, belong to Wilkie Collins and Thomas Hardy. The former is the principal narrator of *The Moonstone*, Gabriel Betteredge. He is the steward of Lady Verinder, well positioned to observe the entire saga of the gigantic diamond and its effect on numerous characters. His detached but affectionate observation of the various personalities earns the reader's affection as well. In *Far from the Madding Crowd*, Gabriel Oak is one of the men who woos the headstrong Bathsheba Everdene. Because he is merely a shepherd, she cannot at first take him seriously, but his persistence and reliability (like oak?) finally win her over.

The Russian form of the name is **Gavril** or **Gavrila,** and Dostoyevsky uses it for a minor character in *The Idiot*. Gavrila Ardalionovich Ivolgin, known as Ganya, is secretary to General Yepanchin. An ambitious man with an eye to the main chance, he, like so many other characters, has had dealings with the alluring Nastasya Barashkov. Dostoyevsky took great care in choosing his names, so it is possible that Gavrila represents ("announces") the crude, worldly point of view in St. Petersburg society.

GAIUS *(Latin, "rejoicing")* Most of the names in John Bunyan's *The Pilgrim's Progress* are either biblical or straightforward attribute names—Mercy, Christian, and so on. Gaius, however, is a disciple who keeps an inn that pilgrims may stop at between the valley of the Shadow of Death and the metropolis full of temptation known as Vanity Fair.

GALAHAD *(Old English, meaning unknown)* Later versions of the Arthurian legends were overlaid with explicitly Christian themes, among them the quest to see the Holy Grail. In the most elaborate form of the myth, the Grail is the vessel used by Christ to administer communion at the Last Supper, brought to England by Joseph of Arimathea. Those few knights of the Round Table who were both physically strong and morally beyond reproach were privileged to see the Grail. In Sir Thomas Malory's *Le Morte D'Arthur*, Galahad was one of them.

GARETH *(Old English, meaning unknown)* In the Arthur legends, the youngest son of King Lot and Queen Morgause of Orkney. He was desperately eager to join his brother Gawain at Arthur's Round Table but his mother was loath to let him go, so she made him promise to work in the kitchen at Camelot for a year in the hope that he would be disillusioned by the lack of glamour. Kay, Arthur's steward, teased him by calling him "beau mains" because his hands were so large. Tennyson devoted a segment of *Idylls of the King* to Gareth and his courtship of Lynette.

GAVROCHE *(French, "bold, nasty youth")* In *Les Misérables*, the names chosen by certain of the characters for their children add to the reader's negative opinion of them. Scorn is particularly lavished on the grasping, pretentious Thénardiers' selections of names for their children. Gavroche, the youngest boy, is cast out to live on his own in Paris despite his parents' having a Paris home where his sisters live with them. He becomes, perforce, a street urchin, with a descriptive name.

GAWAIN *(Welsh, "white falcon")* In the Arthurian legends, Gawain is a nephew of King Arthur's; Arthur's sister Morgause married King Lot of Orkney and had three sons, Gawain, Gaheris, and Gareth. Gawain is one of the brave and virtuous knights who seek the Holy Grail, but he fails in his quest, unlike Galahad, because he bases his behavior on the code of chivalry rather than on biblical precepts. In Thomas Malory's *Le Morte D'Arthur,* Gawain is killed by Lancelot in the mayhem after Lancelot rescues Guinevere from being burned at the stake for adultery. He also figures in a later work, the fourteenth-century *Sir Gawain and the Green Knight,* an allegorical epic of courtly life.

GEOFFREY see **JEFFREY**

GEORGE *(Greek, "farmer")* The historical Saint George was a Roman soldier who was martyred in the fourth century. Those Christian soldiers the Crusaders found him an appealing figure and by the fourteenth century he was patron saint of England. In popular legend he killed a dragon (the Devil, of course) and this is how he appears in Edmund Spenser's *The Faerie Queen.* The work is an extended allegory and its hero Saint George is the perfect Christian knight—a model Englishman, perhaps? By the time **George** reappears in English literature as the name of a major character, it has lost much of its supernatural luster, possibly at the hands of the distinctly human Hanoverian kings of England. In fact, in Oliver Goldsmith's *The Vicar of Wakefield* (published in 1766, early in the reign of George III), the narrator states pragmatically, "Our eldest son was named George, after his uncle, who left us ten thousand pounds."

Jane Austen uses the name twice, both times for important characters who are more generally known as "Mr." The first is the dashing rogue George Wickham in *Pride and Prejudice,* who flirts

JANE AUSTEN'S HEROES

In her major novels, Jane Austen created some of the best-loved characters in English literature. Many a well-read woman has built a few daydreams around Mr. Bingley or Captain Wentworth.

Yet in part because of the formality of the era in which Miss Austen was writing, we often scarcely know the first names of these alluring men. Colonel Brandon, for example, Marianne's successful suitor in *Sense and Sensibility*, doesn't seem to have one. In an era when a wife addressed her husband as "Mr. Bennet," who would call him anything else? In fact, the male characters seem to be handled with an extra degree of deference and formality. While women are referred to by their first names, this is rarely the case for men.

This may be why Austen expended little effort on the names of her heroes. In any event, there is considerable overlap between the names of the six Austen brothers and the seven Austen heroes.

Brothers	Heroes
George	George Knightley, *Emma*
Edward	Edward Ferrars, *Sense and Sensibility*
Henry	Henry Tilney, *Northanger Abbey*
Charles	Charles Bingley, *Pride and Prejudice*
James	Edmund Bertram, *Mansfield Park*
Francis	Fitzwilliam Darcy, *Pride and Prejudice*
	Frederick Wentworth, *Persuasion*

with both of the elder Bennet girls and then shockingly elopes with their sixteen-year-old sister Lydia. The other is Mr. Knightley of *Emma*, who seems almost a father figure to Emma until he is suddenly a successful suitor. Austen had a brother named George, and perhaps her use of the name refers to him. When

William Thackeray wrote *Vanity Fair* in the 1840s he named two principal characters George. One is the reprehensible rake George Osborne, whom sweet Amelia Sedley marries, to her ultimate regret. The other is the dissolute Lord Steyne. His given names are George Augustus, the same as George II and George IV, and in this book written early in Victoria's reign they may refer to the dissolute nature of the latter king. Even Anthony Trollope created a pair of rakish Georges. One, Lord George deBruce Carruthers in *The Eustace Diamonds,* seems a close relative to Thackeray's Lord Steyne: he is a vice-ridden aristocrat who is drawn to the headstrong amoral heroine. George Vavasor, in *Can You Forgive Her?,* is a more complete character. He is a selfish, tempestuous young man who loves his first cousin, Alice Vavasor. He borrows money from her to run for Parliament, unsuccessfully, and becomes terrifyingly violent.

American society doesn't usually include rakes, and the most important George in the American past is George Washington, so it is hardly surprising that the two Georges in Harriet Beecher Stowe's *Uncle Tom's Cabin* are very different from their English contemporaries. They are in a way mirrors of each other. George Harris is the husband of the slave Eliza, and like her, he is intelligent and talented. George Shelby is the son of the man who originally owned Uncle Tom. As a youth he taught Uncle Tom to read, and upon Tom's death, swears to do his utmost to end slavery. In Edith Wharton's *The Reef,* George Darrow is an American diplomat who believes he has finally found the love of his life in Anna Leath, until the repercussions of a casual seduction wreak havoc with his plans.

A Scottish variant of George is **Geordie,** and the name is even used informally to denote a Scot. In Sir Walter Scott's *The Heart of Midlothian,* George Staunton is yet another rake, a handsome, clergyman's son who has seduced and abandoned two women by the time he impregnates Effie Deans. He goes by the name of Geordie Robertson during a portion of the novel when he is caught up with a gang of criminals.

Though the name George has cognate forms in other European languages—**Giorgio, Jorge, Gyorgy,** or **Jorgen**—it was not widely used outside England. One exception is the nonentity George Tesman, husband of Hedda in Ibsen's *Hedda Gabler*. He is an abstracted, pedantic scholar whom Hedda has apparently married for security and social position. As the play begins, the Tesmans have just returned from their honeymoon and Hedda is already bored with George. Perhaps one of the rakish Georges of English literature would have suited her better.

> *George Vavasor has the name, at least, of being very wild.*
> —ANTHONY TROLLOPE, *CAN YOU FORGIVE HER?*

GERAINT *(jay ranh'; Greek, "old man")* From the same root as "geriatric." Tennyson's *Idylls of the King* includes a section called "Geraint and Enid." Geraint is a Round Table knight who is particularly disturbed by Guinevere's faithlessness. He is deeply in love with his wife Enid and begins to withdraw from his knightly responsibilities the better to keep watch over her. He eventually puts Enid through a test of loyalty that would break most marriages.

Géronte, a French name from the same root, is used for a stock character in baroque French drama, an old man. Molière took this stereotype a bit further for the miserly Géronte in *The Scoundrel Scapin* and the authoritarian father of Lucinde in *The Doctor in Spite of Himself.*

GERALD *(Old German, "spear ruler")* In *The Duke's Children,* Anthony Trollope names the younger Palliser son Lord Gerald. In this last of the Palliser novels, Plantagenet Palliser, the Duke of Omnium, is plagued by children who do not conform to his ideas of propriety. Lord Gerald, rather conventionally, gets in trouble by gambling.

GERARD *(Old German, "spear brave")* Another Trollope character; this time he is Gerard Maule of *Phineas Redux,* a charming ne'er-do-well who would be characterized today as "passive." He cares only about fox hunting, and is in love with Adelaide Palliser, but can barely raise the energy to propose to her, let alone to determine how he might support her. Work, of course, is out of the question—it would interfere with his hunting. An archaic German form of the name is **Geert.** Theodor Fontane uses it for Baron von Instetten, the punctilious, aristocratic diplomat whom Effi's parents choose as a husband for her in *Effi Briest.* The fact that he is of her parents' generation makes real communication between the couple unlikely. When Effi has an affair, he feels duty-bound to fight a duel with the man who cuckolded him.

GERASIM *(Russian, "honored")* In Russian literature of the nineteenth century, vernacular names are usually reserved for serfs and peasants, since the upper classes used Western European names by preference. The Gerasim in Tolstoy's "The Death of Ivan Ilyich" is no exception, and (this being a Tolstoy work) he is an idealized model of the Russian peasant. The meaning of the name is surely no accident, for Gerasim is the kind, simple, empathetic servant who ministers to Ivan Ilyich throughout his illness and whose deep faith allows him to accept death as part of life.

GIAFAR see **JA'AFAR**

GILBERT *(Old German, "promise bright")* An unusual name both in life and literature. Anne Brontë uses it for the narrator of *The Tenant of Wildfell Hall,* and it seems rather refined for the character, a young farmer who is full of romantic notions and finds himself drawn to the mysterious main character, Helen Graham. Vain and obtuse about other people, he convinces himself that she is attracted to him. A more famous literary Gilbert is the connoisseur Gilbert Osmond in *The Portrait of a Lady* by Henry James. Isabel Archer, beautiful, spirited, and rich, chooses to marry him rather than one of her more conventional suitors. To Osmond, Isabel is merely part of his collection: the perfect wife, to go along with the perfect Ming vase. Better yet, her money will support his lifestyle and she gives him cover for his long-standing affair with Madame Merle. In Jamesian terms, this is deep-dyed evil.

> *"Never, Gilbert, put me to the painful necessity of repeating what I have just now said to you," she earnestly added, giving me her hand in serious kindness. How sweet, how musical my own name sounded in her mouth!*
> —ANNE BRONTË, *THE TENANT OF WILDFELL HALL*

GIOCONDO *(Italian from Latin, "cheerful")* In Ariosto's *Orlando Furioso*, Giocondo is a knight of surpassing beauty. He catches his wife in adultery and witnesses King Astolfo's wife cheating on her husband. Giocondo and Astolfo then go off together to try to fathom the faithlessness of womankind. They ultimately share a girl, Fiammetta, who manages to cheat on both of them simultaneously by bringing a third man into bed with them when she thinks they are sleeping.

> *Wherever there was a table with a committee of ladies sitting round it in council, there was Mr. Godfrey at the bottom of the board, keeping the temper of the committee and leading the dear creatures along the thorny ways of business.*
> —WILKIE COLLINS, *THE MOONSTONE*

GODFREY *(Old German, "God peace")* In three very different Victorian novels, **Godfrey** is quite clearly a class marker: Godfrey, in the nineteenth century, was a resoundingly upper-class name. In George Eliot's *Silas Marner*, Godfrey Cass is the elder son of the squire (his brother, also in antiquarian mode, is called Dunstan). He is a reprobate, secretly married to a barmaid with a drug habit who bears his child. He serves initially as a contrast to the rustic but honest Silas. Wilkie Collins uses the name for Godfrey Ablewhite, the barrister cousin in *The Moonstone*. Tall, handsome, and self-satisfied, he is the mainstay of several charities and adored by the ladies who staff them. Henry James's Godfrey, Captain Sholto of *The Princess Casamassima*, is a nonentity: "He was nothing whatever in himself and had no character or merit save by tradition, reflexion, imitation, superstition" of the upper class. He is thus the antithesis of the lower-class protagonist.

GRAHAM *(Old English, "gray village")* Generally used as a last name or occasionally as a first name in Scotland. Graham Bretton in Charlotte Brontë's *Villette* is actually named John Graham. The heroine Lucy Snowe knows him in his youth as Graham, but he later appears in her Brussels life as "Dr. John." Lucy, although reserved and detached, is far from being the conventional Victorian heroine and is attracted to Graham, who overlooks her recessive merits.

GRATIEN *(grah tyehn′; French from Latin* Gratian, *possibly a clan name. May refer to thankfulness.)* One of Honoré de Balzac's more ingenious inventions is Gratien Henri Victor Jean-Joseph Bourignard, who appears throughout the Human Comedy in as many guises as he has names. He is a protean figure of villainy, the leader of a group called the Dévorants. A loyal and secretive order of criminals, they dominate Balzac's invented Paris. Gratien Bourignard (also known as Ferragus, a ceremonial name) is naturally handsome and compelling. It is worth noting that an Emperor Gratian ruled over Britain, Spain, and what was then Gaul in the fourth century A.D.

GREGORY *(Greek, "alert, keeping watch")* The saint known as Gregory the Great was the first pope of that name. He was tremendously influential in the formation of the medieval church, and Gregorian chant was introduced during his papacy (590–604). Anthony Trollope uses his name more for alliteration than allusion—Sir Gregory Grogram is one of the minor recurring characters in the political novels. He is a Liberal politician who holds various posts in various books. In *The Story of an African Farm,* Olive Schreiner uses the name for Gregory Rose, who, unlike Trollope's Sir Gregory, is a realistic character. He is the tenant farmer on half of the farm in South Africa that the novel is concerned with. Full of self-pity and ultimately self-absorbed, he falls in love serially with Em, then Lyndall, the two young women who live on the farm.

The Scandinavian version of Gregory is **Gregers,** and Ibsen uses it for the self-righteous Gregers Werle in Ibsen's *The Wild Duck.* In a blundering effort to right his father's moral wrongs, he tries to force Hjalmar Ekdal to face the deceptions on which his life is based, with tragic results. The Russian cognate, **Grigory,** appears several times in Chekhov's short stories, often as a name for modest men overwhelmed by their circumstances. The bleakest of these tales is probably "Grief," narrated from the point of view of wood-turner Grigory Petrov, who drives his wife to the hospital during a snowstorm. She dies en route, he gets frostbite in his arms and legs, and is treated with contempt by the hospital staff. Mikhail Lermontov's Grigory Pechorin, in *A Hero of Our Time,* predates Grigory Petrov by some forty years but he is no more cheerful. His view of the universe is colored by the fact that it holds nothing for him. Though handsome, rich, intelligent, and aristocratic, he realizes that, at the age of twenty-five, he has used up the options for such a man in Russian society. Uninterested in a military or government post, he can only consult his own pleasure, which results in a career of debauchery and cruelty. His catchphrase is, "I prefer to doubt everything."

GRIFFIN *(Middle English from Greek, "having a hooked nose")* The griffin is a mythical creature, half eagle and half lion, that appears most often in heraldic settings. Ludovico Ariosto uses the Italian cognate **Grifone** for one of the Christian warriors in *Orlando Furioso.* Like most of the principal characters, Grifone undergoes adventures both military and logistical (worldwide travel having been so unreliable in the early Renaissance). Anthony Trollope's use of the name for Sir Griffin Tewett in *The Eustace Diamonds* tips us off to the fact that the man's aristocratic provenance is his only merit—and a dubious one at that. He is "a fair, frail young man, with a bad eye, and a weak mouth, and a thin hand, who was fond of liqueurs," and the American heiress Lucinda Roanoke goes mad rather than marry him.

GUNTHER *(Scandinavian, "warrior")* The Nibelungenlied is a German epic poem dating back to the twelfth century and based in part on Scandinavian myths. Richard Wagner adapted the epic quite loosely for his *Ring* cycle of operas. Gunther is the senior king of Burgundy, smooth, diplomatic, and not as physically strong as the superhero Siegfried. He even needs Siegfried's help to woo and bed Queen Brunhild of Iceland.

GURTH *(Possibly Middle English, "to encircle")* An example of Sir Walter Scott's enthusiastic scholarship, Gurth is a rustic swineherd in *Ivanhoe,* later chosen by the hero as squire despite his lack of breeding. Was Gurth a genuine Anglo-Saxon name, or did the author invent it?

> *"What is your Christian name?" Mr. Longdon asked.*
> *Vanderbank felt of a sudden most guilty—as if his answer could only impute extravagance to the lady. "My Christian name"—he blushed it out—"is Gustavus."*
> *His friend took a droll, conscious leap. "And she calls you Gussy?"* —HENRY JAMES, THE AWKWARD AGE

GUSTAVUS *(Scandinavian, "God's staff")* Also **Gustave** or **Gustav.** Used to comic effect by Anthony Trollope in *Phineas Finn.* Lord Boreham is the staid, sensible son of Lady Baldock, who serves as chaperone to the rich and headstrong Violet Effingham. Trollope often uses these Latinized Germanic names to denote stuffiness and pretension; in case readers miss the point (Lord *Boreham?* How could they?), Gustavus's sister is called Augusta. The name is similarly ludicrous in Henry James's *The Awkward*

Age, but James gives it to a more or less sympathetic character. Gustavus Vanderbank is a hard-working young government employee who has been Mrs. Brookenham's admirer. Young Nanda Brookenham, however, is in love with him. Straitlaced Mr. Longdon sizes up the situation and offers to give Nanda a dowry if Vanderbank will propose to her—but Vanderbank feels he can't accept what would amount to charity, or even a bribe.

GUYON *(French variant of* Guy, *meaning unknown)* Guyon is the hero of Book Two of Edmund Spenser's *The Faerie Queen.* Allegorical and highly schematic, the work includes few characters who are not emblematic. Sir Guyon represents Temperance, and he travels with Palmer, a pilgrim, on his quest for revenge against the sorceress Acrasia.

HABBAKUK *(Hebrew, "embrace")* A minor Old Testament prophet, whose name Sir Walter Scott uses for one of the most fanatical of the Covenant preachers in his *Old Mortality*. The novel, set in the late seventeenth century, handles the conflict between Catholics and Protestants (also known as Covenanters) in Scotland. Scott may have been a little overenthusiastic giving the Covenanters Old Testament names; their real-life counterparts were more likely to have commonplace names like James or William. Habbakuk Mucklewrath bears a strong resemblance to the mad King Lear. ("Muckle" is a Middle English word meaning "much.")

> *"Am not I Habbakuk Mucklewrath, whose name is changed to Magor-Missabib, because I am made a terror unto myself and unto all that are around me?"*
> —SIR WALTER SCOTT, OLD MORTALITY

HADES *(Greek, "invisible, unseen")* In Greek myth, the deity of the underworld, known in Roman versions as Pluto. His most famous deed, recounted in Ovid's *Metamorphoses*, is the kidnapping of his beautiful young niece Persephone and the subsequent creation of the seasons. He is generally a rather gloomy fellow.

HAGEN *(German from Scandinavian, "chosen son" or "of the highest race")* In the *Nibelungenlied*, the source of Wagner's *Ring* cycle of operas, Hagen is the crafty retainer to Gunther, the senior king of Burgundy. Jealous of the hero Siegfried, he tricks Kriemhild (Siegfried's wife) into revealing the location of Siegfried's one vulnerable spot. (Like Achilles, he was bathed in magical liquid: in his case, the blood of a dragon, and a leaf stuck to his skin left that one place unprotected.) Hagen then kills Siegfried and tosses the Nibelung treasure into the Rhine.

HAMLET *(Scandinavian, "foolish, dim-witted")* The name may also mean "small village," a term that's still current today. Shakespeare seems, however, to have taken the name of his melancholy Dane from a play based on a ninth-century saga about a prince called "Amleth." Hamlet is, of course, the young introvert whose father was killed by his uncle Claudius. He sees ghosts and feigns madness and agonizes about how to respond to his uncle's depredations.

HAROLD *(Old English, "army strength" or "army ruler")* When Lord Byron wrote *Childe Harold's Pilgrimage,* the name for his hero was of little account—he toyed with the notion of naming the narrator Burun. The character, inasmuch as a character separate from the poet exists, is an observant and sensitive young man who is exiled from home after endless debauchery.

Childe Harold was published in 1812. By the Victorian era, Harold was a well-used name among the educated classes who embraced the antiquarian revival. (The king of England who was defeated by William the Conqueror was Harold.) In George Eliot's *Felix Holt: The Radical,* Harold Transome is a rich, handsome, vain, and materialistic young man who cannot be bothered to show his mother any kindness. His despicable character, for Eliot, is but a manifestation of his class affiliation. Anthony Trollope also created a Harold he disapproved of. In *Framley Parsonage,* Harold Smith is a hardworking Member of Parliament: "laborious, well-informed, and, on the whole, honest; but he was conceited, long-winded, and pompous." His very name is forgettable. The memorable Harold of Victorian fiction was one of Charles Dickens's creations. Harold Skimpole is not one of the principal characters in *Bleak House,* but a friend of John Jarndyce's who lives at Bleak House. He is utterly charming and perfectly irresponsible, especially in regard to money.

> *"The butterflies are free. Mankind will surely not deny to Harold Skimpole what it concedes to the butterflies!"*
> —CHARLES DICKENS, *BLEAK HOUSE*

HAROUN *(hah roon': Arabic, "exalted")* The English cognate is **Aaron,** which comes from a similar Hebrew word. Haroun al-Rashid was the fifth caliph of Baghdad, also known as "Aaron the Upright." He was a great patron of the arts and brought Hindu doctors to Baghdad to found hospitals. He appears in great splendor in *Tales from the Thousand and One Nights.*

HARPAGON *(French, "miser, skinflint")* The Greek word *harpage* means "hook" and the Latin form means "grappling iron." It seems likely that when Molière sought to create a name for the title character in *The Miser,* he used the classical terms to create a sense of a man hanging onto his money. The character's name—for he is a fabulously memorable skinflint—probably entered the vernacular.

HASSAN *(Arabic, "handsome")* In Lord Byron's "The Giaour," the title character is an infidel (i.e., a Christian) who seduces the fair Leila in the Turk Hassan's seraglio. Hassan has her put to death for this infidelity and the Giaour then kills Hassan in revenge.

HEATHCLIFF *(English, "cliff with heather")* The riveting anti-hero of Emily Brontë's *Wuthering Heights.* A gypsy boy picked up in a Liverpool slum, he was raised with the Earnshaws as charity. He is a one-name celebrity—as the housekeeper Mrs. Dean says, Heathcliff "was the name of [an Earnshaw] son who died in childhood, and it has served him ever since, both for Christian and surname." Cathy Earnshaw is his true soul mate but she later marries neighbor Edgar Linton, dooming both herself and Heathcliff (and the unregarded Linton) to misery. Charlotte Brontë had the best words for her sister's famous creation: "He stands unredeemed, never once swerving in his arrow-straight course to perdition."

> *In the end [Madame Hulot] came to treat her Hector as a mother treats a spoiled child.*
> —HONORÉ DE BALZAC, *COUSIN BETTE*

HECTOR (*Greek, "defends, holds fast"*) Hector is the great Trojan hero in Homer's *Iliad*. He is a prince, son of Priam and Hecuba, and the commander of the Trojan forces. Although his name has come to mean "to browbeat," he is one of the more humane of all the swaggering, blustering military heroes Homer portrays. When he dies, Troy falls.

Balzac's Hector Hulot could not present a more pointed contrast as he appears in *Cousin Bette*. Like his namesake, he is a career soldier, but in Balzac's post-Napleonic world, that career provided disillusionment above all. Hulot takes refuge in the pursuit of women while his wife—the true hero—indulges his vanity and squandering of the family funds.

HENRY (*Old German, "home ruler"*) The eight Henrys on the throne of England brought this name to such common use that it is virtually neutral. Most of the many writers who have used it have attached it to educated characters, but Thomas Hardy does create a rustic "Henery" in *Far from the Madding Crowd*. Jane Austen, whose repertoire of masculine names was limited, wrote three important Henrys into her books. One—Emma Woodhouse's father in *Emma*—is weak and ineffectual. Henry Crawford in *Mansfield Park* is a plausible, charming rogue. And Henry Tilney of *Northanger Abbey* is a kindly clergyman. It is worth mentioning that one of Jane Austen's six brothers was named Henry.

Lord Henry Wotton is the man who corrupts Oscar Wilde's Dorian Gray. The name of Stevenson's Dr. Jekyll is Henry. So is that of the boy who narrates Stephen Crane's *The Red Badge of Courage.* Even the narrator of *A Connecticut Yankee in King Arthur's Court* is named Henry, though of course Mark Twain calls him "Hank" to demonstrate how informal and American he is. William Thackeray's *The History of Henry Esmond* is the tale of a young Henry raised among aristocrats in the eighteenth century, while Benjamin Disraeli's *Coningsby* is the tale of a young Henry raised among aristocrats in the nineteenth. (There are few other points of similarity between the books.) The Grantly family, that mainstay of Trollope's Barchester novels, includes a son named Henry who becomes very important in *The Last Chronicle of Barset.*

The name, in its French form **Henri,** is a good deal less common in French literature, though Balzac's Henri de Marsay does make frequent appearances in the Parisian novels of *The Human Comedy.* He appears first in "The Girl with the Golden Eyes," when Balzac lays bare his entire story. The illegitimate son of the English Lord Dudley, de Marsay is "a young man as beautiful as the day itself, dressed with taste, easy of manner" and possessing "a heart of bronze, a brain of steel." While seducing Paquita, the girl of the title, he calls himself Adolphe—possibly in reference to the hero of Benjamin Constant's novel.

> He always signed his name "Henery"—strenuously insisting upon that spelling, and if any passing schoolmaster ventured to remark that the second "e" was superfluous and old-fashioned, he received the reply that "H-e-n-e-r-y" was the name he was christened and the name he would stick to—in the tone of one to whom orthographical differences were matters which had a great deal to do with personal character.
> —THOMAS HARDY, *FAR FROM THE MADDING CROWD*

HEPHAESTUS *(Greek, meaning unknown)* Also **Hephaestos.** Known in Roman mythology as **Vulcan,** Hephaestus is the metal-worker of the gods. He is a tremendously skilled craftsman but surly as well as hideous and crippled to boot (from the time his father Zeus hurled him off Mount Olympus). His mother Hera managed to get him married to the beautiful Aphrodite, but she, like the prom queen shackled to a grease monkey, cheats on him whenever possible.

HERACLES *(Greek, meaning unknown)* In Roman myth and later, he is known as **Hercules,** and some Greek sources spell the name **Herakles.** He is the son of Zeus by a human woman, and from his crib demonstrated superhuman strength. His great enemy was always Zeus's official wife Hera, who sent snakes to kill him as an infant and later drove him mad. He is most famous for performing the Twelve Labors (hence our common phrase "a Herculean feat"). They included cleaning out the Augean stables and capturing the three-headed dog Cerberus. Euripides wrote tragedies about his madness *(Mad Heracles)* and the later persecution of his family *(The Children of Heracles).* He also appears in Aristophanes' *The Frogs* when Dionysos requests his advice on getting into Hades. (Dionysos eventually puts on a lion skin and pretends he's the hero.) In *Metamorphoses,* Ovid tells of Hercules' marriage and death in some detail.

HERBERT *(Old German, "army bright")* Classic Victorian name used by Dickens for the stalwart Herbert Pocket in *Great Expectations.* He is the son of the tutor who is supposed to turn Pip into a gentleman. Pip, in his snobbery, undervalues Herbert at first but eventually appreciates his merit.

HERMES *(Greek, meaning unsure but possibly "pillar")* The quicksilver messenger of the gods, known in Roman myth as **Mercury.** He is the son of Zeus and Maia. Homer, in *The Odyssey,* calls him "the guide and giant-killer Hermes." He is supposed to have invented the lyre, and to shepherd souls on their way down to Hades.

HILARION *(French from Greek, "cheerful")* In Émile Zola's stark *The Earth*, Hilarion is the pathetic grandson of harridan and matriarch Marianne. He is "simple," harelipped, and crippled, and his sister Palmyre (the elaborate names are ironic) has to support him out of her meager earnings.

HINDLEY *(Old English, "meadow of the deer")* The Earnshaw son in Emily Brontë's *Wuthering Heights*, and Heathcliff's lifelong enemy. Once he owns Wuthering Heights he treats Heathcliff as a servant and persecutes him. He becomes a tyrannical drunk later on, and loses the property to Heathcliff by gambling.

HIPPOLYTUS *(Greek, alluding to horses)* In myth and in Euripides' eponymous play, Hippolytus is the son of Theseus by the queen of the Amazons. He is devoted to hunting and to Artemis, neglecting his duties toward Aphrodite. She, in revenge, causes his stepmother Phaedra to fall in love with him. Two deaths later his grieving father is without both son and wife. Jean Racine turned the tale into the tragedy *Phaedra*.

HIRAM *(Hebrew, possibly "very noble")* An Old Testament name of the kind that denoted rural or country (as opposed to "county") people in Victorian England. In Charlotte Brontë's *Shirley*, Hiram Yorke is a practical, unsentimental Yorkshire mill owner.

HJALMAR *(Old Norse, "army helmet")* The protagonist of Henrik Ibsen's *The Wild Duck* is Hjalmar Ekdal, a lazy, self-absorbed but contented man who finds in the course of the play that his contentment is based on deception. The tragedy that ensues only offers him greater opportunity for self-dramatization and self-pity.

HONORÉ *(French, "honored")* George Washington Cable's *The Grandissimes* focuses on race relations in New Orleans during the early nineteenth century. His protagonists are half brothers, both named Honoré Grandissime—but the elder is an "f.m.c.," or "free man of color." The novel traces their parallel careers as men of means but strikingly unequal social status. The younger Honoré, legitimate and white, is the head of the family while his elder brother can never be anything but marginal.

HORACE *(Latin clan name, possibly indicating something to do with time or "hours")* The Latinate form is **Horatio,** which was more commonly used as a given name in past centuries. Hamlet's loyal sidekick Horatio represents rational man in the morass of emotion other characters experience. Horace Bianchon, the reliable physician in Balzac's *The Human Comedy,* can also be said to represent reason. Legend has it that on his deathbed the author called for Bianchon.

HROTHGAR *(Scandinavian, meaning unknown)* In the Anglo-Saxon saga *Beowulf,* which dates from as early as the eighth century, Hrothgar is king of the Danes. It is his court that is ravaged by the monster Grendel. He is just, wise, generous—a good king, but incapable of exterminating the horrifying threat to his kingdom that Grendel represents.

HUBERT *(Old English, "intelligence bright")* In Geoffrey Chaucer's *Canterbury Tales,* the Friar is named Hubert. He is a very lax cleric, a cheat and a charlatan who is far too well-acquainted with all the barmaids along the journey. It seems likely that he preys on the women who confess to him and he certainly fails to practice charity.

HUCKLEBERRY *(English, name of the fruit)* In Mark Twain's *The Adventures of Tom Sawyer,* Huck Finn appears as a town outcast, not a middle-class boy like Tom but the son of the town drunk. He is unregenerately lazy and perfectly resistant to education. Eight years later, *The Adventures of Huckleberry Finn* follows Huck on his journey down the Mississippi River with Jim the runaway slave. Huck turns out to be a true gentleman, generous and loyal, though resolutely opposed to the conventions of society.

HUGH *(Old English, "intelligence")* Henry James's tale "The Figure in the Carpet" is about a literary critic who becomes obsessed by the work of writer Hugh Vereker. Vereker (remember, his name means "mind" or "intellect") has told the critic that his literary output contains a secret that nobody has understood. George Eliot uses an earlier form of the name, **Hugo,** for the kindly baronet Sir Hugo Mallinger in *Daniel Deronda*. The archetype of the conservative English gentleman, he raises Daniel from childhood because he once loved Daniel's mother.

> *There was irony in the words, for it is a remarkable fact that even at the age of ten Hyacinth Robinson was ironic.*
> —HENRY JAMES, THE PRINCESS CASAMASSIMA

HYACINTH *(Greek, plant name)* Ovid, in *Metamorphoses,* tells the story of Hyacinthus, the beautiful boy beloved by Apollo. The god accidentally killed Hyacinthus with a throw of the discus, and in his mourning, caused blossoms to grow from the ground where drops of blood had stained it—"a flower brighter than Tyrian purple grew up and took on the shape of a lily." The French form **Hyacinthe** *(ee ah sahnt´)* has been used with some consistency, possibly out of tribute to several martyrs named Hyacinth. Thus the bearded, unkempt character known as "Jesus Christ" to his family in Zola's *The Earth* was really christened Hyacinthe. (His nickname refers to his pointed beard rather than to his character.)

Henry James picks up several of these threads in *The Princess Casamassima*. His hero, Hyacinth Robinson, is the illegitimate son of a French prostitute and an English nobleman. He is raised by a seamstress and gets drawn into a group of violent revolutionaries, but not before he has his eyes opened to the refinements of civilization by the princess of the title. The irony is that he has pledged himself to destroy the world that he feels is his true home. As his name signals from the start, he ends up a martyr.

ILYA *(Russian variant of* Elias: *Hebrew, "the Lord is God")* The central character of Ivan Goncharov's *Oblomov* is the young landowner Ilya Ilyich Oblomov. He personifies apathy. He spends his life in bathrobe and slippers, loses his estate, and finally marries his landlady to ensure peace and quiet. He embodies the slothful nature of mankind, though Russian critics have also seen his indolence as induced by the structure of Russian society.

ION *(Greek, "first met")* In Greek legend and Euripides' drama *Ion,* Creusa is the daughter of King Erechtheus of Athens. Her husband Xuthus has no children, but she was raped by Apollo and Ion is their child, raised by the priestesses at Delphi. Xuthus goes to the oracle at Delphi and is told that the first person he will meet on leaving is his child. That person is the youth Ion. Eventually in legend (though not in the play) he becomes king of Athens and founder of the Ionian race. Ions in atomic science have nothing to do with him, but the Ionic column can be traced back to the civilization that bears his name.

ISAAC *(Hebrew, "laughter")* Sir Walter Scott, that assiduous researcher, always made sure his characters had plausible names. Prior to the Reformation, Old Testament names were virtually unknown among Christians (Isaac was the name of the son whom Abraham was prepared to sacrifice in Genesis). Christians also did not lend money because of a religious ordinance that forbade them to charge interest. In *Ivanhoe,* set in the early Middle Ages, Isaac of York is a Jewish moneylender. He loans armor to the young hero, allowing him to subdue the nasty Norman knights.

ISHMAEL *(Hebrew, "the Lord will hear")* "Call me Ishmael," commands the narrator of Melville's *Moby-Dick* at the beginning of the story. What readers of his era would probably have known was that the biblical Ishmael was an outcast, the son of Abraham by the servant maid Hagar. Upon the birth of the legitimate son Isaac, Ishmael was sent away. Legend has it that the Arab people are descended from his twelve sons. Melville's Ishmael is perhaps an outcast from society, but by his own choice. His telling of the tale of the whale often reveals an unexpectedly tender and humorous outlook.

ISIDORE *(Greek, "gift of Isis")* Isis is the Egyptian goddess whom the Greeks identified with the goddess of nature. The name would not have survived into general European use without the cult of several Saints Isidore. In Wilkie Collins's *The Woman in White,* Count Isidore Ottavio Baldassare Fosco is the magnetic yet repulsive villain. He is immensely fat and immensely charming; gentle, yet merciless; kind to animals, yet capable of murder.

ISRAEL *(Hebrew, sometimes translated as "wrestling with the Lord")* This is the name God gave Jacob after his three-day bout with the angels in Genesis. Robert Louis Stevenson, while always careful to assign his characters appropriate names, doesn't usually bother with the game of allusion that Hardy, James, and Dostoyevsky so enjoyed. Yet in *Treasure Island* he calls a sailor Israel Hands—as in a "hand" on board ship. The first name may refer to some moral struggle in the young man, who turns out to be one of the craftier pirates. It is certainly the kind of name a working-class man would have had in the eighteenth century, when the book is set.

IVAN see **JOHN**

JA'AFAR *(Arabic, "stream")* Also **Giaffar, Jafar.** In *Tales from the Thousand and One Nights*, Ja'afar is vizier or councilor to Haroun al-Rashid, the fifth caliph of Arabia. The historic Ja'afar ibn-Abi-Talib carried a banner bearing the Muslim legend "Paradise" at the Battle of Mota. He lost both hands in the fighting, but continued to hold the banner high with his stumps until he received a mortal wound.

JACK see **JOHN**

JACOB *(Hebrew, "he takes by the heel, he supplants")* Charles Dickens didn't bother with literary allusions in his names; most of the time he simply invented them, often tinkering with sounds and syllables until they achieved the effect he sought. When Scrooge sees Jacob Marley's ghost in *A Christmas Carol*, though, there may be echoes of the biblical Jacob wrestling with angels. Marley is at any rate a deeply disconcerting—and life-changing— vision. When Trollope names his stationer Jacob Bunce in *Phineas Finn*, the allusions are historical. Bunce is Finn's landlord, and he harbors revolutionary tendencies. In fact, he gets himself arrested at a demonstration about the Reform Bill. Trollope is no doubt counting on his reading public to remember that many of the most ardent French revolutionaries, like Danton and Robespierre, were known as Jacobins.

In Italian the name is rendered as **Jacopo** *(yah' coh poh)* and Alexandre Dumas uses it slightly comically in *The Count of Monte Cristo*. Jacopo is the classic sidekick, who meets Edmond Dantès, the count of the title, on a smuggling ship. The count hires him and turns him into a manservant, but he doesn't make a convincing upper-class valet. The Russian form of the name is **Yakov.** The protagonist of Chekhov's tragic tale "Rothschild's Fiddle" is a small-town coffin-maker called Yakov. He can't support himself by building coffins, and when he gets ill, he builds his own casket and wills his valuable violin to the town's Jewish fiddler.

JAFFREY see **JEFFREY**

JAMES *(Hebrew, "he takes by the heel, he supplants")* From the same root as **Jacob,** only Latinized. In nineteenth-century England, this was an unremarkable upper-class name, as borne, for instance, by Sir James Chettam in George Eliot's *Middlemarch.* Sir James is the conservative English landowner who is drawn to Dorothea at the beginning but ultimately finds her intimidating and marries her gentler sister Celia. Dickens used the name twice, both times for rakes. James Harthouse in *Hard Times* flirts with poor, miserable Louisa Bounderby and leads her astray from married life, while James Steerforth, David Copperfield's headlong young friend, outright seduces Emily Peggoty and dies in a shipwreck.

   Robert Louis Stevenson rings a change on this theme with his James Durie, the Master of Ballantrae in the eponymous novel. Set in eighteenth-century Scotland, it deals with a character whom Stevenson called "an *Incubus.*" Is he the Devil? It seems possible. He possesses all the destructive charm of Lucifer, and he cannot be killed, though his brother, sorely tried, attempts the deed several times.

   The French form of the name, **Jacques** *(zhahk)*, used to have the connotation of "a French peasant." "Jacques Bonhomme" was "your average Joe." In Dickens's *A Tale of Two Cities,* for instance, all of the revolutionaries in the Defarge wineshop call themselves Jacques. Denis Diderot's *Jacques the Fatalist and His Master* is narrated by Jacques, a servant, telling his master a monstrously digressive account of his amorous adventures. Finally Balzac, in *The Human Comedy,* gives us Jacques Collin, or

Jacques Vautrin, the arch-villain of post-Napoleonic France who takes on different identities in different books. Unlike Gratien Bourignard, known as Ferragus, Collin/Vautrin works alone and is wholly human. The mutability of his persona is his great advantage. Shakespeare used a slight variant of the name, **Jaques** *(jay' kwees)*, for one of the characters in *As You Like It*. He is an aristocrat exiled to the forest, known as "the melancholy fool." He is the one who utters the famous "All the world's a stage,/And all the men and women merely players" speech.

A common informal nickname for James is **Jim**. That informality has significance that may elude readers in our relaxed age, but it does indicate that a Jim is not all that a James would be. For instance, the narrator of Stevenson's *Treasure Island* is Jim Hawkins, a resourceful, courageous boy—but still, a boy. In Twain's *The Adventures of Huckleberry Finn,* Jim is the runaway slave whom Huck befriends. Jim has sterling human values: loyalty, sensitivity, kindness. But he doesn't even have a last name. Finally, Henry James puts a Jim in *The Ambassadors*. In the formality of the European setting, in a novel whose plot turns on choosing Europe over the United States, Jim Pocock is an American businessman on a spree, "small and fat and constantly facetious."

Iago *(ee ah' goh)* is one of the Spanish forms of James. It may surprise some *Othello* fans to realize that Santiago is one of the most revered saints in Spain. Legend has this Apostle spreading the gospel to Spain, and his church at Compostela was one of the major pilgrimage sites of the medieval church. The villain of Shakespeare's play persuades his commander that Desdemona is unfaithful. Some scholars suggest that he is jealous because the young soldier Cassio was promoted over him; other critics, however, ascribe his behavior to "motiveless malignancy." **Diego**, another Spanish cognate of James, is probably derived through Iago. Pierre Corneille's 1637 play *Le Cid* is an adaptation of a Spanish epic akin to the Roland story. It deals with the exploits of a warrior, Rodrigo, who fought both for and against the Moors in Spain in the eleventh century. In Corneille's version Don Diego is his father, an honorable, dignified man who points out to his son that "love's but a pleasure; duty's a command."

JANUARY (*English month name*) In Chaucer's *Canterbury Tales* this is an attribute name. January is the knight in "The Merchant's Tale" who at age sixty marries a young wife and is cuckolded by her. There is no logical reason, though, why **May** (the wife's name) should have entered common use while January remains schematic.

JARVIS (*English variant of* Gervase, *meaning unknown*) "Jarvey" is obsolete English slang for a hackney coach or its driver. In Dickens's *A Tale of Two Cities*, we first meet Jarvis Lorry in a stagecoach. Coincidence? Probably. Lorry, after all, is a staid, cautious banker, the man of business for the Manette family, which is so deeply affected by the French Revolution. There is nothing remotely jaunty or freewheeling about him.

JASON (*Greek version of* **Joshua**: *Hebrew, "Jehovah is salvation"*) In Greek myth Jason is the young man who captured the Golden Fleece and brought it home to Iolcus. Euripides, in *Medea*, is far less interested in that heroic deed than in Jason's callous treatment of Medea. After he married her and she used her sorcery on his behalf, he dumped her for another woman. He lost the favor of the gods, lost the throne of Corinth, and wandered Greece as an outcast. Chaucer, in "The Legend of Good Women" section of *Love Visions*, also has harsh words for Jason.

Reference to betrayal may be behind the name of Jason Quirk of Maria Edgeworth's *Castle Rackrent*. He is the son of the Irish steward on an Anglo-Irish estate, and he gets uppity, taking over some mortgages and claiming portions of the ancestral estate as his own when the Rackrents can no longer meet payments.

> *False Jason quested on, and peace found never,*
> *For longing through his lustful appetite*
> *To have fine women was his whole delight.*
> —GEOFFREY CHAUCER, "THE LEGEND OF GOOD WOMEN"

JASPER *(English mineral name)* The hero of James Fenimore Cooper's *The Pathfinder* is called Jasper Western, a name that conjures stony cliffs and open spaces and every desirable kind of American ruggedness. He is a Great Lakes waterman (a trade requiring immense skill) and a friend of Natty Bumppo's as well as Natty's rival for the love of the fair Mabel Dunham. Ultimately Natty's forestry skills can't compete with Jasper's looks and potential for civilization—Jasper ends up as a merchant in New York City, surely a more appealing métier to the prospective bride.

In Victorian England, Jasper was not a hero's name but more likely a villain's. Jasper Milvain (note the connotations of that last name: "vain" and perhaps "mal" as in the French word for evil) in George Gissing's *New Grub Street* is a cynical hack of a writer who thrives in the superficial literary environment that so appalled the author.

JEFFREY *(Old German; meaning unclear, but refers to "peace")* Also spelled **Geoffrey** and **Jeoffry**. The visionary eighteenth-century poet Christopher Smart (who composed much of his work in an insane asylum) believed that every creature worshiped God by fulfilling his nature completely. Thus his long fragment "Jubilate Agno" is full of creatures like cuttlefish and mice, praising God by being what they are. Included is Smart's cat Jeoffry, weaving around the poet's ankles and purring.

Nathaniel Hawthorne uses an unusual form of the name, **Jaffrey**, for a sinister character in *The House of the Seven Gables*. Judge Jaffrey Pyncheon is a rich relative of old Hepzibah Pyncheon who lives in the house of the title. He has a sinister hold on her and on her fragile brother Clifford. Hawthorne makes it clear that Jaffrey is a last name from a previous generation, transferred to first-name use. Anthony Trollope writes a Jeffrey Palliser into *Can You Forgive Her?* He is the heir presumptive of the dukedom of Omnium. That is to say, if Plantagenet Palliser and his wife Lady Glencora do not produce a son, Jeffrey Palliser will ultimately be duke. In the meantime he is "a poor, embarrassed man, without prospects" and with an income of only six hundred pounds a year. He is, in other words, a nonentity whom fate could elevate into a very important man.

> For I will consider my cat Jeoffry.
> For he is the servant of the Living God duly and daily serving him.
> For at the first glance of the glory of God in the East he worships in his way.
> For this is done by wreathing his body seven times around with elegant quickness.
>
> —CHRISTOPHER SMART, "JUBILATE AGNO"

JEREMIAH *(Hebrew, "the Lord raises up")* One of Charles Dickens's great comic characters is Jerry Cruncher in *A Tale of Two Cities*. His given name is Jeremiah but his affability and informality render him **Jerry**. He calls himself "an honest tradesman" and sometimes "a resurrection-man." He takes pride in what he views as his craft, which is robbing graves to sell the bodies to medical students. Far less benign is Jeremiah Flintwich in *Little Dorrit*. The sadistic manservant for secretive Mrs. Clennam, he has spent years covering up a sinister secret and bullies his wife by giving her "doses" of medicine that gives her nightmares.

JOB *(johb; Hebrew, "the afflicted one")* In the Bible, Job is the man upon whom misfortunes rain down, yet whose faith is steadfast. Elizabeth Gaskell, writing in the nineteenth century, could be sure that to her readers, the name bore connotations of patience under suffering. In *Mary Barton,* Job Legh is a workman in a fabric mill. The working conditions are extremely harsh, but, unlike several other characters, he is not tempted toward violence in protest.

JOCELYN *(Old German, meaning unclear)* A name that was once used for both men and women. The protagonist of Thomas

PURITAN NAMES

In Catholic England before the seventeenth century, naming sources were limited. In addition to family names, the Calendar of Saints provided most of the inspiration for parents. The Reformation and the rise of Puritanism, however, changed those habits radically.

Saints, for one thing, were taboo. In the Puritan view, man's relationship to God was direct; there was no need for mediation by a saint. The Bible, too, was newly available to worshipers, translated into the vernacular and read and studied with enthusiasm. And the Old Testament provided a rich source for naming inspiration. Hence names like **Abel, Jeremiah, Jacob,** and **Caleb,** exotic-sounding Hebrew names that became familiar to English families who had previously known only **John** and **Henry** and their like.

The Old Testament names, once introduced, were very popular and endured well into the nineteenth century. The authors of that era, eager to reflect the world they lived in, often used these names for their characters. It becomes clear that these Puritan names frequently serve as class markers. The establishment in England usually adhered to the Church of England, so upper-class characters tend to have Norman or Latin or German names. Methodist and Presbyterian churches were more likely to be filled with working folk, and they were the ones with the Hebrew names. In George Eliot's *Silas Marner,* for instance, the squire's sons are **Godfrey** and **Dunstan,** two old names, while the villagers are **Silas** and **Aaron** and **Eppie** (short for Hephzibah).

Hardy's *The Well-Beloved* is Jocelyn Pierston, a sculptor who has a dream of the ideal woman. He finds her in successive generations of women on the small island where he grew up. Unfortunately, his vision of the ideal prevents him from really connecting with the actual.

JOHN *(Hebrew, "Jehovah is gracious")* In some literary hands, John is Everyman, the character who makes choices we too might make. Dr. Faustus, in Christopher Marlowe's play about that compelling figure, is a brilliant scholar named John (or **Johan**) Faustus. He sells his soul to the Devil in exchange for twenty-four years of unfettered self-indulgence free of all human constraints or considerations. Shakespeare's Don John, in *Much Ado About Nothing,* is an outright villain. The bastard brother of the prince of Arragon, he is vindictive and jealous, and nearly derails Claudio's romance with Hero. Another John with murky morals is the dark character in Herman Melville's "Billy Budd." John Claggart contrasts with the innocent Billy in numerous ways, but most of all in his "spider-like" personality. He pursues and finally ruins Billy, who is provoked enough to kill him. Robert Louis Stevenson often preferred to roll good and bad into one character, like Long John Silver in *Treasure Island.* The fatherless Jim Hawkins is completely taken in by Silver's avuncular charm, and his confusing shifts of allegiance fool the reader too. Stevenson used the name with some frequency in his short stories, almost as if he couldn't be bothered to invent more elaborate names for some of his characters. In Jane Austen's *Sense and Sensibility,* three characters are called John, including the alluring rogue Willoughby— but then, Austen's range of male names is very small.

For generations, this was one of the most common masculine names in Christian countries, probably because of the importance of two saints. John the Baptist was the saint who predicted Jesus' arrival and baptized him in the River Jordan, while John the Evangelist was nominally the author of the fourth Gospel. To date, twenty-three popes have chosen to be called John (not counting the two John Pauls). England's lone King John is famous for having been forced by his barons to sign Magna Carta in 1215.

Other writers have used John to set off a last name. When the reader meets Mr. Jarndyce, a party to the famous lawsuit of *Jarndyce* v. *Jarndyce* in Dickens's *Bleak House,* it's clear that the man, John, kindly and generous, is subsidiary to his role as party to an interminable lawsuit. In his unfinished *The Mystery of Edwin Drood,* Dickens named the sinister, opium-addicted choirmaster John Jasper, evoking the evil that the name **Jasper** often indicated in English Victorian novels. Henry James names his characters with great care, so what are we to make of John Marcher, the protagonist of the tale "The Beast in the Jungle"? Is this John another Everyman figure? Or should we focus on him marching toward his obscure but fearful destiny? (He finds out that his destiny is missing life completely: exactly the opposite of what happened to Johan Faustus.)

Anthony Trollope created hundreds of characters in his fiction-writing career, and he, too, named them carefully. John Eames of *The Small House at Allington* is "a hobbledehoy"—a callow country boy working in London as a clerk, in love with a woman of a higher class and entangled with a lower-class vixen. But during the course of the novel John grows, and Trollope marks that growth by changing his name. He starts out as "Johnny" to everyone, from his mother to his office colleagues. But as he becomes a man, everyone starts calling him John. Another important character in the Trollope novels is John Bold of *The Warden*. Here, Trollope harks back to the biblical. It was John the Baptist who forecast the coming of Christ, and John the Evangelist who told of his deeds. It is John Bold, the reforming radical, who tells Barchester how wrongly its church is ordered, and who precipitates great changes. The tie to John the Baptist, perhaps, is zeal.

Jack is the familiar nickname for John, but, perhaps because of its informality, it has not been used much in literature through the nineteenth century. The Artful Dodger of Dickens's *Oliver Twist* is actually named Jack Dawkins, but this charming rogue is generally known by his title rather than his name. Stephen Crane's story "The Bride Comes to Yellow Sky" depicts a completely different world from Victorian London. Yellow Sky is a small town in Texas and Jack Potter is its marshal. He is bringing his (nameless) bride home, and is concerned about whether the community will accept him in his role as husband.

The French form of the name is **Jean** and the dominant character of that name in French fiction is the towering Jean Valjean, Victor Hugo's Christlike figure at the center of *Les Misérables*. He takes on a number of identities as the novel careers through the landscape of post-Napoleonic France but his struggle is always for liberation from his criminal past. His last name, Valjean, incorporates a syllable from the French verb *valoir*, which means "to be worth," or worthy.

The enduring Spanish character of this name (**Juan** in that language) is, of course, Don Juan, the prototypical libertine. Molière's *Don Juan* is a comedy, albeit one with grim overtones, and the rake himself is a dashing, selfish aristocrat. It took Lord Byron to put a human face on the rake, though the face does closely resemble his own. (Or his womanizing father's; curiously, Byron's father's first name was John.) The spoiled son of a libertine aristocrat, Don Juan is exiled at age sixteen for his affair with a neighboring lady. His further adventures take him to Greece, to a seraglio in Constantinople, to the Russian court of Catherine the Great, and thence to England. The narrative thread gets very thin at times as the poet intrudes himself. Benito Pérez Galdós is a nineteenth-century Spanish author working in the realistic tradition of Balzac. *Fortunata and Jacinta* follows the stories of two women who are both in love with the same man, handsome, charming Juanito Santa Cruz. Jacinta is his respectable, loving wife and Fortunata the woman of the streets who bewitches him. The diminutive *ito* at the end of his name hints that, as he is a seducer without the stature of Don Juan, he is also essentially childish.

In Russian, John becomes **Ivan**, and it is similarly prominent in Russian literature. For one thing, one of Dostoyevsky's Brothers Karamazov is called Ivan. Scholars suggest that the three brothers represent the three facets of life—earthly, intellectual, and spiritual—and their names reflect their dispositions. Ivan is the brilliant, rationalistic one, coldly intellectual, questioning especially religious faith (does that make him an anti-Evangelist?). A less tortured view of life is found in Tolstoy's story "The Death of Ivan Ilyich." The protagonist is an ordinary man, a law-abiding bureaucrat, whose illness and death bring him to a new level of humanity. The Russian habit of playing with names turns Ivan, affectionately, into **Vanya** or **Vania**, as in *Uncle Vania*, one of Anton Chekhov's plays. Ivan Voinitsky has for twenty-five years managed the estate that belonged to his deceased sister, for the benefit of her widower, scholar Alexandr Serebriakov. He has always believed that he was promoting the lifework of a worthy man, but when Serebriakov arrives at the estate, he reveals himself to be deeply selfish and mediocre. He proposes selling the estate, thus nullifying Vania's lifework. In his disillusionment, Vania realizes, "I have not lived! I have not lived!"

JONAS *(Hebrew, "pigeon")* A version of **Jonah.** One of the pleasures of reading Dickens is that his villains are as desperately bad as his heroines are desperately sweet. Jonas Chuzzlewit, nephew of Martin in *Martin Chuzzlewit,* is a deep-dyed blackguard. He tries to poison his father; murders the con man Montague Tigg; makes his wife Mercy's life a misery to her; and finally commits suicide, which was a disgraceful act in Dickens's era.

JONATHAN *(Hebrew, "gift of Jehovah")* Bram Stoker's *Dracula* is structured in a complex way, with multiple narrators and excerpts from letters and diaries. The overall narrator is the observant, rational solicitor Jonathan Harker, whose very resistance to belief in Dracula makes the tale of the vampire all the more convincing.

> *Agathe hoped for wonders from Philippe, but expected nothing from Joseph.*
> —HONORÉ DE BALZAC, *THE BLACK SHEEP*

JOSEPH *(Hebrew, "Jehovah adds")* In the book of Genesis, Joseph is one of the younger sons of Jacob and much cherished by his father. He shares a number of characteristics with Joseph Andrews, hero of Henry Fielding's eponymous novel. Both Josephs are comely, honest, and chaste. Both are displaced from their families. And both, as household servants, are subject to what could be called sexual harassment from the boss's wife. What's more, both Josephs prevail in a harsh world, largely because of their honesty.

USING A FIRST NAME

One of the more puzzling aspects of Victorian manners to modern readers is the importance placed on the use of the first name. Anthony Trollope managed to write an entire novel *(He Knew He Was Right)* about a man who nearly loses his sanity because an old family friend calls his wife "Emily" after her marriage.

The use of a first name among adults was a badge of intimacy. Male characters, even fast friends, tended to call each other by their last names. Women were more free with first names, but reaching that stage of closeness in a friendship was a distinct event, never something to take for granted. And when a single man called a single woman by a first name, it was usually a sign that he intended something warmer still. Trollope's novels are full of moments when intimacy is established or refused or even unexpectedly maintained. Lily Dale, for instance, continues to call John Eames "John" long after she refuses to marry him, in both *The Small House at Allington* and *The Last Chronicle of Barset.* By doing so, she is paying him a significant compliment.

William Thackeray's Jos Sedley in *Vanity Fair* has none of Joseph Andrews's character. He is a plump, conceited, social-climbing middle-class dandy, too cowardly to fight against Napoleon and too lazy to support his family, which is his clear duty. He is a perfect consort for the conniving Becky Sharp. In *The Eustace Diamonds,* Anthony Trollope gives Lizzie Eustace (his own conniving heroine) a smarmy Joseph as a consort as well. The Reverend Joseph Emilius actually outdoes Lizzie and Becky in manipulation. He parades as a charismatic preacher—but is he a preacher at all? He wants to marry the rich widow Lady Eustace—but does he have a wife back in Hungary? Trollope, piling on the odium, calls him a "fawning, pawing, creeping, black-browed rascal" and Lizzie almost deserves him.

The form of the name does not change in French, but the pronunciation does, to *zhoh zeff'*. Balzac uses the underappreciated-younger-son theme in his novel *The Black Sheep*. Philippe is the handsome elder son, the dashing soldier and apple of his mother's eye—who turns out to be an unregenerate gambler and thief. Joseph, the original black sheep, is a late-blooming portrait painter who stands by his mother and supports her financially while Philippe steals from both of them. In later novels of *The Human Comedy,* Joseph Bridau is a well-established portrait painter in Paris.

Shortened, of course, Joseph becomes **Joe,** as in Joe Gargery, the amiable blacksmith of Dickens's *Great Expectations*. He is warm, affectionate, and loyal, and Pip's snobbishness toward him reveals the hidden shallows in the hero's character. Shortened even more, Joseph becomes **Jo,** the name of the street-sweeping boy in *Bleak House*. Possibly the most pathetic character in a book where the competition is stiff, Jo is as poor and ignorant and hopeless as a human being could be.

> *Name, Jo. Nothing else that he knows on. Don't know that everybody has two names. Never heerd of sich a think. Don't even know that Jo is short for a longer name. Thinks it long enough for* him. He *don't find no fault with it. Spell it? No. He* can't *spell it.* —CHARLES DICKENS, *BLEAK HOUSE*

JOSHUA (*Hebrew, "Jehovah is salvation"*) Thomas Hardy's *The Mayor of Casterbridge* is the story of the domineering Michael Henchard and his career in the town of Casterbridge. Joshua Jopp is a minor character, a former employee of Henchard's who has long resented him. When Henchard's mistakes start to catch up with him, Jopp seizes the opportunity to further wreck his reputation.

JOSIAH (*Hebrew, "the Lord supports"*) If there was ever a character who needed support from the Lord it is Josiah Crawley, a proud and unworldly minister in Anthony Trollope's Barchester novels. He appears in *Framley Parsonage* as a very poor cleric, "a strict, stern, unpleasant man" who will not accept help from his lifelong friend Francis Arabin. Trollope manages to make Josiah sympathetic by stressing his sincerity and the eagerness of his faith. *The Last Chronicle of Barset* centers on a misunderstanding that results in his being accused of theft. The ensuing fuss and its effect on his reputation nearly drive him mad. Josiah Bounderby in Dickens's *Hard Times* is not a fully rounded character like Crawley. Rather, he represents the heedless, crass side of capitalism as it manifests itself in Coketown, Dickens's industrial nightmare. Bounderby's devotion to numbers and hard facts makes him a cruel boss and a worse husband to Louisa Gradgrind.

JOURDAIN *(French version of* Jordan: *Hebrew, "descending")* The name of the title character in Molière's comedy *The Would-Be Gentleman*. Although Molière often used the elaborate invented names conventional in baroque drama, Jourdain is a relentlessly plain, unadorned, real-life name. The character is nouveau riche and desperate to climb into the upper class despite the fact that his parents were tradesmen. He falls into the hands of an unscrupulous aristocrat who makes a fool of him while relieving him of significant sums of money.

JOVE see **JUPITER**

JUDE *(Hebrew, "praise")* In Thomas Hardy's novels a name is seldom simply a name, though most do function naturalistically as well as on a metaphoric level. Jude Fawley, of *Jude the Obscure,* is a dreamy, bookish country boy who, with the token encouragement of a schoolmaster, dreams of going to university. He sets himself on a course of disciplined reading and saving money, but reckons without the effects of his hormones. First the crude Arabella, then his cousin Sue Bridehead, interfere with his plans. Amateur hagiographers might remember at this point that Saint Jude is traditionally the patron of lost causes.

JULIAN *(Latin clan name possibly meaning "bearded")* This is, by a slight margin, the most common of a group of names that includes **Julius** as well as the French **Julien** *(zhool yeh´)* and **Jules** *(zhool´)*. The hero of Edward Bellamy's utopian novel *Looking Backward: 2000–1887* is Julian West, a neurasthenic young Bostonian who lives on inherited money. He has himself hypnotized to treat his insomnia and wakens in the year 2000, finding it a much-improved collectivist society. Some irony may be intended in his name since Saint Julian the Hospitaller was a wealthy young man who gave up his goods and cared for his fellow man. Many versions of his tale exist and scholars tend to doubt his historic existence, but Flaubert's "The Legend of St. Julian" spells out the classic outlines: rich young man loves hunting; mistakenly kills his parents; becomes a ferryman in penance; carries a leper across the river; the leper is Christ, who forgives him.

The French form of the name is Julien, as in Julien Sorel, hero of Stendhal's *Scarlet and Black*. He is the ultimate egoist, seeing life only through the lens of his own ambitions. A striver from the provinces, he yearns above all for success. The scarlet and black of the title represent the military and the church, two traditional means of advancement for the bourgeoisie. In the wake of Napoleon's defeat the church holds out more promise, even though Julien's greatest gift is his seductive appeal to women. It is also, ultimately, his downfall. Guy de Maupassant's poignant novel *A Woman's Life* may be based in part on de Maupassant's own mother's life. Young Jeanne de Vauds, fresh from convent school, is married to Julien, Vicomte de Lamare, knowing little about him but madly in love. He has wed her largely for her money, and seduces her maid within days of the wedding. He is brusque, uncommunicative, and perpetually unfaithful to her.

Jules appears less prominently as the name of a kindly, lucky banker in Honoré de Balzac's *The Human Comedy*. In the tale "Ferragus" he is the patient husband of Clémence Desmarets, perfectly content with his lovely wife until the aristocratic Auguste de Maulincour becomes enamored of her. His obsession makes Desmarets suspicious, though Clémence is perfectly innocent.

Julius Klesmer in George Eliot's *Daniel Deronda* is the musician retained by the hugely wealthy Arrowpoint family to teach their daughter Catherine and to perform occasionally for their guests. His first name evokes his Continental background, while "Klesmer" (also the name of a kind of Jewish folk music) refers both to his calling and to the Jewish theme of the novel. Scholars suggest he may be based in part on Franz Liszt. He has a strong, magnetic personality, but his genius somehow justifies it: "The rankest affectation he could have shown would have been to look diffident and demure."

> *Suddenly she asked: "What is your Christian name?"*
> *"Julien," he replied; "Didn't you know?"*
> *She did not answer, thinking: "How often I shall repeat that name!"* —GUY DE MAUPASSANT, A WOMAN'S LIFE

JUPITER *(Latin, meaning unknown)* The name of the chief god of the Olympic pantheon, in its Roman version. Also known as **Jove** and, to the Greeks, as **Zeus**, Jupiter is the son of the Titan Cronus and the earth goddess Rhea. He is married to his sister Juno but chronically unfaithful to her. He courts human women and nymphs in various forms—as a shower of gold, as a bull, as a swan—and has many children by them. When angered, he throws thunderbolts from the sky. In Virgil's *Aeneid,* which was written as a background history of the Roman Empire, he insists that Aeneas leave Dido, the queen of Carthage, in order to found Rome. Nineteenth-century Americans often gave their slaves classical names. In Edgar Allan Poe's short story "The Gold Bug," only the slave Jupiter (practical common sense incarnate) resists the obsession that destroys the narrator.

KAY *(Welsh version of* Gaius: *Latin, "rejoice")* Not a girl's name and not related in any way to **Katherine**. In the Arthurian legends Kay is the son of Sir Ector, and thus Arthur's foster brother. Despite Arthur's unremitting kindness to him—he makes Kay his steward, a position of great importance—Kay harbors a chip on his shoulder and resents his glamorous foster brother. In Mark Twain's sardonic *A Connecticut Yankee in King Arthur's Court,* he appears as Sir Kay the Seneschal, who captures Hank Morgan upon his appearance in sixth-century Britain.

KENYON *(Meaning unknown, possibly Irish Gaelic, "fair-haired")* Commonly a last name. *The Marble Faun* by Nathaniel Hawthorne follows three young Americans and one Italian in nineteenth-century Rome. Kenyon is a young sculptor. Detached, rationalistic, he is more observer than participant in the emotional entanglements of his friends and may be a stand-in for Hawthorne himself.

KIT see **CHRISTOPHER**

KONSTANTIN *(Russian from Latin, "holding fast")* The Western spelling is **Constantine**. Constantine the Great was a Roman emperor in the fourth century A.D. He tolerated Christianity and moved the capital of the Roman Empire east, to what had formerly been Byzantium. In Tolstoy's *Anna Karenina,* Prince Konstantin Levin is the idealized aristocrat. He husbands his estate carefully and shares proceeds with his workers; he is also utterly faithful to his wife Kitty. Some scholars suggest that Levin represents Tolstoy's best hope for Russia's future. Poor Konstantin Trepliov in Chekhov's *The Seagull* represents nothing so positive. He is the sensitive playwright son of the monstrously egotistical actress Arkadina. Desperate for her approval, he is doomed to frustration.

LAERTES *(Meaning unknown)* In Shakespeare's *Hamlet,* the man of action contrasting with Hamlet's own inaction. He is Ophelia's brother, the son of Polonius, and his quest for revenge upon Ophelia's death ends with his own death, and Hamlet's.

LAIUS *(Greek, meaning unknown)* King of Thebes and father of Oedipus in various tellings of the Oedipus myths such as Aeschylus's *Seven Against Thebes.* An oracle told him that he would be killed by his own son, so when his wife Jocasta had a son, he ordered that the child's feet be maimed with a spike and the child be left on a mountainside to die. Oedipus was found and raised by a shepherd, and later, meeting Laius, killed him in an argument. Some translations spell the name **Laios.**

LAMBERT *(Old German, "bright land")* Probably a Belgian name originally, owing its usage to the cult of a Belgian martyr of the seventh century. In Henry James's *The Ambassadors,* however, the connotations rather are of lambs to the slaughter. Lambert Strether (invoking "tether"?) is the middle-aged bachelor sent to Europe by Mrs. Newsome to retrieve her errant son Chad. This is the heroic quest Strether must carry out before he is permitted to marry Mrs. Newsome. Chad, however, engages Strether's sympathy, and Europe awakens long-dormant longings in him. He returns empty-handed to Woollett, Massachusetts, after telling Chad, "Live all you can; it's a mistake not to."

LAMBRO *(Meaning unknown)* Lord Byron may have invented this name as a plausibly foreign-sounding choice that would fit easily into the meter of his epic poem *Don Juan.* Lambro is the fierce Greek sailor who, because his country is in thrall to the Turks, preys on the commerce of all Mediterranean countries. (Logic is apparently not a necessity to a pirate.) Don Juan falls in love with his daughter Haidée and when Lambro discovers them in an amorous situation, she dies of shock.

LAMORACK *(Meaning unknown)* Also **Lamorak**. One of the more destructive figures in Thomas Malory's *Le Morte D'Arthur*. He is the son of King Pellinore and brother of the stainless Percival, but the lover of Queen Morgause. He reveals the adultery of Tristram and Yseult, and is killed by Gawain, Morgause's son.

LANCELOT *(Meaning unknown)* Also known as **Launcelot**. Possibly the most disruptive knight of the Round Table, but a fighter of tremendous prowess. He was raised by Vivian, the enchantress of the lake, hence his nickname, "Lancelot du Lac." Though he is Arthur's favorite, he cannot resist his love for Guinevere. Their adultery sows the seeds of Camelot's destruction.

LANVAL *(Meaning unknown)* The name is almost an anagram for "Avalon," the island where the dead King Arthur rests. In *The Lais of Marie de France,* a collection of twelfth-century tales from Brittany, Lanval is an unpopular knight of the Round Table: "Because of his valor, generosity, beauty and prowess, many were envious of him." In a dream he encounters a beautiful, magical woman who gives him a fortune and sleeps with him, on the condition of secrecy. When Queen Guinevere casts a lustful eye his way and he rebuffs her, it takes his dream lady to rescue him from the consequences.

LATINUS *(Latin, "of Latium")* In *The Aeneid,* Latium is the area of Italy where Aeneas is destined to found an empire. King Latinus is its ruler, but he is too old and too set in his ways to resist Aeneas's new regime. Aeneas marries his daughter Lavinia.

LAWRENCE *(Latin, "from Laurentium")* Charles Dickens often pairs a naturalistic first name with a descriptive last name, as in Lawrence Boythorn, a minor character in *Bleak House.* An old friend of John Jarndyce's, he is a vehement sixty-year-old, "incapable . . . of anything on a limited scale." He goes crashing and thrashing through the novel like a large, good-natured boy armed with a heavy stick. Edith Wharton's Lawrence Selden, in *The House of Mirth,* is Boythorn's opposite, a man of restraint and sensibility who holds himself aloof from life. Unfortunately, it is largely his influence, combined with his lack of engagement, that spoils Lily Bart's schemes for self-preservation. Anthony Trollope uses an alternate spelling, **Laurence,** for Phineas Finn's experienced but unreliable Parliamentary mentor in the Palliser novels, Laurence Fitzgibbon. Like Finn, Fitzgibbon is Irish, but from an aristocratic family. He is more emphatically Irish than Phineas, but his brogue would have been irritating in a character who is "onstage" as much as Phineas.

Confusingly enough, Shakespeare calls the friar in *Romeo and Juliet* (set, after all, in Verona), Friar Laurence. Yet in *The Merchant of Venice* he adopts the Italian form of the name, **Lorenzo,** for the young Christian who elopes with Shylock's daughter Jessica. The name is sometimes shortened to **Renzo** as in Alessandro Manzoni's *The Betrothed.* An honest, upright young worker in a silk mill, he is engaged to the beautiful and pious Lucia. The pair are separated by the machinations of aristocrat Don Rodrigo, who wants to seduce the virginal Lucia. Renzo remains faithful to Lucia and even manages to forgive Don Rodrigo on the latter's deathbed. In France the name is **Laurent,** which Émile Zola uses in *Thérèse Raquin.* Passive invalid Camille Raquin meets an old school friend shortly after the Raquin family moves to Paris, and Camille invites Laurent to visit the family. Alas, this intensely masculine and selfish man promptly seduces Thérèse, and the affair between the two heats up into an obsession. Laurent kills Camille to get him out of the way, but the affair goes sour.

LEANDER (*Greek, "lion man"*) In Greek myth, Leander is the heroic youth who so loves his girlfriend Hero that he swims the Hellespont to be with her. Molière uses the name twice, in *The Doctor in Spite of Himself* and *That Scoundrel Scapin.* The two young men called **Léandre** are both primarily lovers who encounter difficulties.

LEAR *(Meaning unknown)* The title character of Shakespeare's *King Lear*. His lazy attempt to divide his kingdom fairly among his three daughters unleashes tragedy. He is based on a king in Geoffrey of Monmouth's twelfth-century document *The History of the Kings of England*. It is not, by modern standards, strictly history.

LEICESTER (lehs´ ter; *English, name of a county*) The first name of the proud Lincolnshire baronet Sir Leicester Dedlock in Dickens's *Bleak House*. This use of a place-name instead of a Christian name serves to dehumanize him as well as to invoke the upperclass habit of using naming to broadcast bloodlines. The bombastic Lawrence Boythorn is a neighbor of the Dedlocks and is involved in a kind of border quarrel with them. He says, "It is morally impossible that his name can be Sir Leicester. It must be Sir Lucifer." Yet Sir Leicester is in fact kind and loyal to his wife, even after he learns that she has betrayed him.

LEMUEL *(Hebrew, "belonging to God")* The narrator of Jonathan Swift's satiric *Gulliver's Travels* is Lemuel Gulliver. He is an early example of an unreliable narrator, who undergoes fantastic journeys to the lands of Lilliput, Brobdingnag, Laputa, and Houyhnhnmland. The creatures he meets are tiny, then large, then equine—in the end, he goes mad.

LÉON (lay aw´; *French from Latin, "lion"*) The usual English forms are **Leo** or **Leonard**, though Shakespeare uses **Leonato** (for Beatrice's father, the governor of Messina in *Much Ado About Nothing*) and **Leontes** (for the jealous king of Sicilia in *The Winter's Tale*). In Gustave Flaubert's *Madame Bovary*, Léon Dupuis is one of the men with whom Emma commits adultery. She meets him as a law clerk in Yonville, and is drawn to his cultured tastes; later in the novel, they begin a full-fledged affair, meeting weekly in Rouen, but Léon is no help to Emma when she needs him. There is nothing lionlike about him. Nor is Leonid Gayev of Anton Chekhov's *The Cherry Orchard* an especially courageous character. (**Leonid**, pronounced *lay´ oh nihd,* is the Russian form of the name.) He is the brother of Madame Ranevskaya, who owns the estate with the cherry orchard. In this drama of a fading aristocracy's inability to cope with a new world, Gayev is one of the incompetents. Educated, genteel, but impractical and idle, he cannot pull himself together to greet the future constructively. Prince Leo Myshkin, the central character of Fyodor Dostoyevsky's *The Idiot,* is another Russian man poorly adapted to deal with reality. He is blond, handsome, and aristocratic, but fatally flawed, not only by epilepsy but also by his innocence and naiveté. His venture into St. Petersburg society is disruptive to the characters he meets and causes him to literally lose his mind. Scholars have described Myshkin as a "holy fool," a character whose subnormal mental processes earn him protection by God. But in this case, heavenly intervention fails to materialize.

Elizabeth Gaskell's *Ruth* is the sympathetic tale of a good and naive girl who is seduced and abandoned by a rich man. Her son Leonard is a bright and happy young boy, not tainted in the least by his unpromising conception.

> *"What made you wish to call him Leonard, Ruth?"* asked Miss Benson.
> *"It was my mother's father's name; and she used to tell me about him, and his goodness, and I thought if Leonard could be like him. . ."*
> —ELIZABETH GASKELL, *RUTH*

LINTON *(Old English, "settlement of flax")* Emily Brontë employs some strategic naming for *Wuthering Heights*. The rough-hewn, untamed hero is Heathcliff while the more civilized, town-bred neighbors are the Linton family. The name sounds tame, little, like a small bird in a cage (a linnet, perhaps?). Although the central love affair of the novel is between Cathy and Heathcliff, it only occupies the first part of the book. Heathcliff marries Isabella Linton and, after her death, promotes a match between their son,

Linton Heathcliff, and his cousin Cathy Linton. Linton is peevish, spoiled, petulant, and sickly, and he dies not long after his marriage.

> *There was nothing royal about Louis Philippe Scatcherd but his name.* —ANTHONY TROLLOPE, DOCTOR THORNE

LOUIS *(French version of* Ludwig: *Old German, "famous warrior")* The name of eighteen kings of France—a point not lost on Émile Zola, who calls his peasant patriarch in *The Earth* Louis Fouan. As the novel opens he is on the verge of dividing his little kingdom among his three children. Comparisons to Lear are on the mark.

The name does not change in English, though it may be pronounced and spelled **Lewis.** In Charlotte's Brontë's *Shirley,* the headstrong and beautiful heiress Shirley Keeldar somewhat implausibly falls in love with Louis Moore. Though perfectly deserving—he is a well-meaning, intelligent young man who has been forced by financial reversals to work as a tutor—he lacks glamour. Louis Moore, Brontë explains, is half Belgian, hence his francophone name. Louis Philippe Scatcherd, of Anthony Trollope's *Doctor Thorne,* is one hundred percent English. The wastrel alcoholic son of railway contractor Sir Robert Scatcherd, he tries unsuccessfully to court his cousin Mary Thorne. His comical name refers to the king of France who reigned between 1830 and 1848. One of Trollope's most psychologically vulnerable characters, Louis Trevelyan of *He Knew He Was Right,* is a rich young man who marries a penniless young lady, Emily Rowley. Trevelyan is handsome, intelligent—and somewhat at the mercy of his imagination, for he soon comes to believe that his wife is unfaithful to him. The evidence is merely that an old family friend continues to call her "Emily" (rather than the more conventional "Mrs. Trevelyan") after her marriage.

A more antique version of the name, more closely related to the

> ## TROLLOPE ON ROYALISTS
>
> Anthony Trollope has a reputation as a "cozy" author, one whose works are as reassuring as a warm blanket and a cup of tea. Yet he had his dyspeptic side. He was especially alert to pretension in any form, as he demonstrated very clearly in *Doctor Thorne*, one of the Barsetshire novels. One of the characters is Louis Philippe Scatcherd, the bumptious son of nouveau riche Roger Scatcherd. As Trollope explains the son's name:
>
> *Yes, he was christened Louis Philippe, after the King of the French. If one wishes to look out in the world for royal nomenclature, to find children who have been christened after kings and queens, or the uncles and aunts of kings and queens, the search should be made in the families of democrats. None have so servile a deference for the very nail-parings of royalty; none feel so wondering an awe at the exaltation of a crowned head; none are so anxious to secure to themselves some shred or fragment that has been consecrated by the royal touch.*

root **Ludwig,** is the unusual **Ludovic.** Trollope gives this name to the pleasant, kindly young aristocrat Lord Lufton in *Framley Parsonage*. He is one in a long line of Lords Lufton—the very peculiarity of his name attests to it—and his widowed mother takes his social position very seriously. She wants a grand wife for him and believes that he will accede to her will rather than marry the modest Lucy Robarts.

The Spanish form of the name is **Luis,** and Molière uses it for the father of his Don Juan. In this telling of the libertine's story, Don Luis is a respectable man, deeply ashamed of his son's propensities. (In Byron's version, Don Juan's father—named Don José—is a rake himself.)

> *Nothing could be more reasonable than Ludovic.*
> —ANTHONY TROLLOPE, *FRAMLEY PARSONAGE*

LUCIEN *(loo syeh'; French, "light")* The protagonist of Honoré de Balzac's *Lost Illusions* is a character we meet over and over again in French fiction of the nineteenth century: the gifted young man from the provinces who goes to Paris in search of his destiny. Lucien Chardon's gifts are his poetic talent and his extraordinary male beauty. The former, nurtured by hard work, could have made his success in Paris, but he chooses to exploit his looks and charm instead. Ultimately, he is neither disciplined nor ruthless enough to prevail, and he comes spectacularly to grief. Like Lucifer, he falls from the heavens. *A Harlot High and Low* depicts Lucien's renewed assault on the peaks of Parisian society, backed by the evil genius of Jacques Vautrin.

Shakespeare's plays with foreign settings feature characters with foreign names, of course, and while some of his female characters' names have been co-opted into everyday use, the male names often remain unusual. Since *The Taming of the Shrew* takes place in Padua, Shakespeare uses the Italian **Lucentio** for Bianca's most earnest suitor. With the help of his servants he manages to woo Bianca while pretending to be her "tutor."

Edith Wharton's bleak novel *Summer* portrays the limited world of rural Massachusetts. When Lucius Harney arrives in North Dormer, he brings a beam of light into young Charity Royall's life. Even the Latinate form of his name, **Lucius**, sets him apart from the North Dormer natives and speaks of a wider world Charity can't even imagine.

LUKE *(Latin, "from Lucanus")* The name of one of the four evangelists, yet never as widely used as **Matthew, Mark,** or **John.** In *Rachel Ray*, Luke Rowan is one of the genre that Trollope portrayed so well, the callow young man. He is handsome, has polished social manners and good intentions, but "he was conceited, prone to sarcasm, sometimes cynical, and perhaps sometimes affected." The characters in *Rachel Ray* are all more or less rustic, and there is something homespun in the name Luke that indicates he is no sprig of nobility. Luke Larkin in Horatio Alger Jr.'s *Struggling Upward* is, similarly, a young man from the middle class. Ambivalence about his heroes is not Alger's style, however—Larkin is honest, hardworking, loyal, and forgiving.

The French form of the name is **Luc** *(lewk)*. In Victor Hugo's *Les Misérables,* Marius Pontmercy, Cosette's love interest, comes from a loyal royalist family. His grandfather, Luc-Esprit Gillenormand, is a crusty old gentleman with eighteenth-century ideas. (The hyphenated form of his name, in which "Esprit" refers to the Holy Ghost of the Catholic faith, identifies his old family allegiances.) He is horrified by Marius's liberal tendencies.

LYSANDER *(Greek; meaning unclear, but* andros *means "man")*
It is Shakespeare's conceit that *A Midsummer Night's Dream* takes place in ancient Greece, so one of the two love-stricken young men is called Lysander. It is also the name of a fourth-century (B.C.) Spartan naval commander.

MACBETH *(Scottish Gaelic, "son of Beth")* Central figure in Shakespeare's tragedy *Macbeth*. He is the thane of Glamis, a position of nobility and command under King Duncan. When the famous witches prophesy that he will be king of Scotland, his ambition is fired and a chain of plotting and murder set off; his first victim is the king. Theatrical lore holds that the play is unlucky, and actors often refuse to refer to it by name, calling it "the Scottish play" instead. It is based on historical records of a real Macbeth who died around 1058 after seventeen years on the throne.

MACDUFF *(Scottish Gaelic, "son of the swarthy one")* One portion of the witches' prophesy is that Macbeth cannot be defeated by any man born of a woman. His friend Macduff, thane of Fife, is appalled by his crimes and journeys to England to join the army led by Duncan's son Malcolm. Macduff, who was born by cesarean section, does ultimately kill Macbeth.

MALACHI *(Hebrew, "messenger")* An alternate spelling is **Malachy**, the form used by the Irish bishop St. Malachy. In Trollope, one of Phineas Finn's hurdles in his quest for worldly power is that he is a Catholic in a country that often regarded the Roman church with suspicion. He gets his faith from his father, Dr. Malachi Finn, a hardworking, practical man who has five daughters to raise besides Phineas. Though he supports Phineas financially through the latter's Parliamentary campaign, he is sharply aware of his son's failings.

MALCOLM *(Scottish Gaelic, "follower of Saint Columba")* Columba was an immensely influential sixth-century Irish missionary. Malcolm is a historical figure, the son of the King Duncan murdered by Macbeth. In Shakespeare's play he travels to England to raise an army and avenges his father by retaking the throne.

MALVOLIO *(Italian, "wishing ill")* From the same source as "malevolent." Shakespeare's *Twelfth Night* nominally takes place in Illyria, the coast of Italy and former Yugoslavia sometimes known as Dalmatia. It was really a kind of never-never land, which may explain how the characters have such mismatched names. Some—Orsino, Viola, Malvolio—are exotic while others—Sebastian, Toby, Andrew—are standard English. Malvolio is a prissy, pompous fool, the steward of the countess Olivia, who fancies himself as a romantic match for his mistress. A highly comical subplot of the play involves his comeuppance at the hand of a conspiracy of other secondary characters.

MANDRICARDO *(Italian, probably from an Old German name containing elements that mean "man," "rule," and "hard")* In Ariosto's *Orlando Furioso* Mandricardo is the king of Tartary in central Asia and thus a pagan. He travels to France to avenge the death of his father Agrican. He possesses Hector's armor by virtue of his fighting prowess but he has vowed to win Orlando's sword and will use none other. Naturally he is defeated by a Christian hero, Ruggiero.

MANFRED *(Old German, "man peace")* The title of a narrative poem by Lord Byron. Manfred is a Faust-like character who, in the fastness of his Alpine castle (the poem dates from 1817, squarely during the Romantic movement), conjures wizards, witches, and other supernatural creatures in the search for all knowledge. What made the poem a scandal was that Manfred also summoned the Eastern goddess Astarte who was, as they said in those days, "most improper." Her incestuous relations with her fellow deities reminded readers of Byron's famous love for his half sister. Once again, he succeeded in being the real hero of his poem.

MARIUS *(Latin, clan name related to Mars)* In the throng of characters populating Hugo's *Les Misérables*, few are as attractive as young lawyer Marius Pontmercy. An aristocrat by birth and a liberal by conviction, he resembles Hugo in some ways. His love affair with Cosette is fairly conventional but his prejudice against ex-convict Jean Valjean rescues him from insipidity.

MARK *(Latin, "warlike")* Despite the martial precedent set by Roman general Mark Anthony, the literal meaning of the name is generally overlaid by its association with one of the authors of the Gospels. In Trollope's *Framley Parsonage*, Mark Robarts is anything but warlike. Rather, he is an extremely successful young cleric. He is vicar of Framley, a parish that brings in a good income, and also has a remunerative post at the cathedral in Barchester. But success has come to him very young and he handles it poorly, moving in a fast social set and getting into debt. In "The Author of 'Beltraffio,'" Henry James makes use of the gospel associations. The author in question is a man named Mark Ambient, and his book, *Beltraffio*, promotes the aesthetic life at the expense of "real life." Ambient even suggests that real life (the ambient life?) is but a shadow of the life of the aesthete. Alas, the aesthete must live in a real family, and Mrs. Ambient's philistine point of view provides the conflict in the tale. **Marcus** is the Latin form of the name.

MARS *(Latin mythology name)* Mars is the Roman name for the Greek Ares, the god of war. One of the legitimate sons of Jupiter and Juno, he is a problem child because he loves conflict for its own sake. This makes him all too ready to sow discord at his whim. Ironically, considering his poor reputation on Mount Olympus, Mars's name lives on in words like "martial" as well as names like **Mark** and **Marcus**. The same cannot be said for the peace-loving Minerva or even for Jupiter.

MARTIN *(Latin, "warlike")* This name tends also to be associated with the story of Saint Martin of Tours, a fourth-century French bishop famous for having divided his cloak with a beggar whom he perceived to be Christ. His feast day of November 11 and the numerous churches named for him in England made his name familiar, but it seems unlikely that Charles Dickens had him in mind when he named Martin Chuzzlewit. The eponymous novel features two men of the name. The elder is a wealthy, ailing old man. Devotees of Victorian novels know what comes next: jockeying for position over who will benefit from his will. The logical legatee is Chuzzlewit's namesake grandson, but he is in bad odor, having fallen in love with his grandfather's pretty paid companion. He is disowned and various unsavory relatives gather. Meanwhile young Martin, the hero of the tale, gets cured of his arrogance and selfishness by hard times in America.

MATTHEW (*Hebrew, "the Lord's gift"*) Traditionally the author of the first Gospel. John Bunyan's *The Pilgrim's Progress,* written in the seventeenth century, is an allegory rather than a novel and the characters' names are highly schematic. Thus, the eldest son of the pilgrim Christian and his wife Christiana is called Matthew. Nathaniel Hawthorne's *The House of the Seven Gables,* though set in the mid-nineteenth century, includes action from the seventeenth century in which a character named Matthew Maule is important. He is the original builder of the house, but he was hanged as a wizard in 1690, cursing the Pyncheon family and its descendants.

By the Victorian era in England, Matthew is a fairly lower-class name. Dickens's *Bleak House* features a charming character named Matthew Bagnet, a wholesome, cheerful proprietor of a London music shop who plays the bassoon—and resembles it, too. In George Eliot's *Felix Holt: The Radical,* the lawyer Matthew Jermyn is stigmatized as "one of your educated low-bred fellows." Of course his crime is more than merely presumption; he has also embezzled money from an estate entrusted to him.

Sometimes the popularity of a name is demonstrated by the number of last names it has generated, like Matthews or **Matthewson.** In Charlotte Brontë's *Shirley,* a novel about industrialization in north Yorkshire, the minister Matthewson Helstone is a harsh opponent of what he sees as mill workers' insubordination. The hard connotations of his last name are no accident.

MAURICE *(Latin, "swarthy, Moorish")* A name with connotations of ancient gentility, whose literal meaning was more or less lost. In Sir Walter Scott's *Ivanhoe*, Sir Maurice de Bracy is a Norman knight—in this story, the enemy. He kidnaps the heroine Rowena, which is bad enough; but he does it disguised as the peerless hero Robin Hood, which puts him beneath reproach. In Anthony Trollope's *Phineas Redux*, Maurice Maule is not exactly beneath reproach, but he comes in for plenty of it. The inimitable Madame Max Goesler refers to him as "a battered old beau about London, selfish and civil, pleasant and penniless." What Trollope can't forgive is his dismissal of responsibility to his son Gerard, who would like to marry but lacks the money.

An Anglicized spelling is **Morris**, the last name of a family very prominent in New York history (Lewis Morris signed the Declaration of Independence). Henry James's *Washington Square* is a glance back at the Old New York of his youth, when the upper class still lived in Washington Square and the social options for a young lady were strictly limited. Morris Townsend, the idle, handsome socialite who courts Catherine Sloper, has a strictly Old New York name that adds, in a subtle way, to the claustrophobia of the novella.

MAX *(Latin, "greatest")* This has traditionally been a shortened version of various forms of **Maximus** such as **Maximilian, Maximiliano, Maxim** or **Maxime,** even **Maxence.** The evil genius of Honoré de Balzac's *The Black Sheep* is Maxence Gilet, a handsome, calculating former soldier. Most of the characters in his provincial town are under his thumb for one disreputable reason or another. Balzac created another character with a similar name, Maxime de Trailles, who is a much more polished article. One of the crowd of young men about Paris in *Old Goriot, Cousin Bette,* and *A Harlot High and Low,* de Trailles is a count. Coming from the aristocracy, he is enviable to strivers like Lucien Chardon and Eugène de Rastignac, but his morals are no more pure than theirs.

In George Eliot's *Felix Holt: The Radical*, Maximus Debarry is also an aristocrat. But where the radical reformer is the hero, the man with a name going back to Roman times can hardly be expected to shine. In fact, he is barely flesh and blood at all, simply a representation of the outdated aristocratic interests in the neighborhood. Benito Pérez Galdós also plays on the grandiosity of the name with Maximiliano Rubin in *Fortunata and Jacinta*. The name recalls the glory of Austria's Emperor Maximilian, but the character known to his family (and the readers) as Maxi is physically feeble and unprepossessing. He manages to marry the splendid Fortunata, but within days of their marriage she is back in the arms of Juanito Santa Cruz.

One of the unsettling features of Mikhail Lermontov's sardonic *A Hero of Our Time* is its use of several narrators. One of these is Maxim Maximych, a battered older soldier who relates part of Grigory Pechorin's actions involving a Cossack girl in the Caucasus. He is emotionally unsophisticated and cannot grasp the extent of Pechorin's alienation.

> *Maynard Gilfil's love was of a kind to make him prefer being tormented by Caterina to any pleasure, apart from her, which the most benevolent magician could have devised for him.* —GEORGE ELIOT, SCENES OF CLERICAL LIFE

MAYNARD (*Old German, "hard strength"*) The second of three stories in George Eliot's *Scenes of Clerical Life* is called "Mr. Gilfil's Love Story." It recounts the painful and frustrating love of the Reverend Maynard Gilfil for a brilliant Italian girl. She loves Anthony Wybrow, the nephew and heir of the aristocratic family that brought her up, and Gilfil is the family's ward, destined for the church. When Wybrow marries a rich girl, Caterina marries Gilfil in her disappointment, but she dies not long after their wedding. Gilfil cherishes a broken heart for the rest of his days.

MEDORO (*Meaning unknown; may come from Greek, meaning "gift"*) In Ariosto's *Orlando Furioso*, Angelica is the proud, beautiful princess of Cathay (or China). Though pursued hotly by many of the pagan heroes in this epic, she ultimately falls for the Moorish soldier Medoro. He is wounded while searching for the body of his leader, Prince Dardinello, in order to bury it. Angelica finds him dying and falls in love with him, admiring both his physical beauty and his loyalty.

MENELAUS *(men uh lay´ us; Greek, meaning unknown)* A key figure in two interlocking elements of classic Greek literature, the works of Homer on the one hand, and the tragedies of the house of Atreus on the other. Menelaus is the brother of Agamemnon and the husband of Helen. In *The Iliad* he is king of Sparta, and the unlucky guy on whose behalf the Trojan War is fought. In *The Odyssey*, he is restored to his luxurious palace and treats Odysseus's son Telemachus with great hospitality. Euripides drags him through more emotional fuss, however. He appears in no fewer than five of Euripides' dramas, usually as a supporting character, though in *Helen* the dramatist sends him to Egypt on his way home to Sparta with his recaptured wife. Considering his brother Agamemnon's fate, however, Menelaus looks fortunate to be out of the spotlight.

MENTOR *(Greek, meaning unknown)* Telemachus's tutor in *The Odyssey*; the trusted friend to whom Odysseus had confided his household upon leaving for the Trojan War. The name has come to mean a wise guide to a younger person.

MERCURY *(Latin mythology name)* The Roman name for the Greek god Hermes. He is the son of Zeus and Maia, and a trickster. Plucky, full of swagger, he is an even finer musician than Apollo, and much less reliable. The word "mercurial" to describe a temperament comes from his name. He is also, as befits the gods' messenger, speedy, wearing winged sandals and a winged helmet. *Webster's Third International Dictionary* suggests that the element mercury got its name "from the comparison of the mobility of the metal to the fleet-footedness of the god." It seems likely that Shakespeare had this source in mind when he came up with the name **Mercutio** for Romeo's quick-witted friend in *Romeo and Juliet*. He is full of mockery and zest, and delivers several very showy speeches, including one of the great valedictories in drama.

MERLIN *(Latin from Welsh, "sea hill")* The name of the wizard in the Arthurian legends. Geoffrey of Monmouth's *History of the Kings of Britain* has him constructing Stonehenge and putting Uther Pendragon in Igraine's bed to conceive Arthur. Malory's *Le Morte D'Arthur* portrays Merlin as more of a mentor to Arthur. Powerful as a sorcerer, he is nonetheless vulnerable to the wiles of Vivian, the Lady of the Lake, who imprisons him in a tower in perpetuity.

Mark Twain's *A Connecticut Yankee in King Arthur's Court* stresses Merlin's vulnerability to nineteenth-century technology. The Yankee, Hank Morgan, comes up with practical solutions to a number of problems like the repair of a "holy well." Merlin has the last laugh, though, putting Morgan under a spell that makes him sleep thirteen hundred years.

MERTON *(Middle English, "lake settlement")* Also the name of an Oxford college, which gives it intellectual connotations just right for Merton Densher in Henry James's *The Wings of the Dove*. A handsome, clever, penniless young journalist, he is in love with equally penniless Kate Croy. When she suggests that he pay court to the mortally ill heiress Milly Theale (the "dove" of the title) he participates in the plot, but discovers his own scruples.

MICHAEL *(Hebrew, "who is like the Lord")* In the Bible, Michael is a dragon-slaying archangel, and Christian art often portrays him with a sword. In Shakespeare's *Othello* the handsome young soldier Cassio's first name is Michael, but he is more often referred to as simply Cassio. Michael is a common anglophone first name and the casual way it us used for minor characters in Victorian novels suggests it had little connotational baggage. Michael Millward in Anne Brontë's *The Tenant of Wildfell Hall* is the narrow-minded Church of England vicar. Sir Michael Audley, in *Lady Audley's Secret* by Mary Elizabeth Braddon, is a tall, handsome country gentleman who marries a conniving governess in his late middle age. Thomas Hardy did not name characters lightly, however, so perhaps readers should be alerted to the fierce might of the archangel in considering Michael Henchard, the title character in *The Mayor of Casterbridge*. From his origins as a hay-trusser, Henchard has risen to be a prosperous grain merchant and mayor of the town. But his strong will and poor judgment, not to mention his susceptibility to alcohol, lead him into some terrible mistakes and ultimately a tragic, lonely death.

Saint Michael, or in French, **Michel,** was much venerated in France, making the name also a standard there. In Émile Zola's *The Earth,* Michel is the hapless younger brother of Louis, the peasant patriarch. He feels himself ill-used in terms of the inheritance he does not receive.

In Russia, where the name is **Mikhail,** folk stories add another level of meaning. In Nikolai Gogol's *Dead Souls* we are told that the bear in Russian fairy tales is often called Mikhail. Landowner Mikhail Sobakevich, none too subtly, physically resembles a bear and has some of its cunning, too. The protagonist Pavel Chichikov visits his estate on his quest to buy "dead souls," but Sobakevich drives a hard bargain. Mikhail Astrov is the country doctor near the estate of Anton Chekhov's *Uncle Vania.* As disaffected as the other characters, he drinks too much, lusts after another man's wife, and generally prefers trees to people anyway.

MILES *(Latin, "soldier")* In 1535 an English monk named Miles Coverdale published an English translation of the Bible, thus providing one of the essential elements for the establishment of the Protestant Church of England. By assigning this name to the narrator of *The Blithedale Romance,* Nathaniel Hawthorne introduces the notion that his narrator is the witness to the dawning of a new order in the commune at Blithedale. Yet Hawthorne's Coverdale, a New England poet, finds the utopian Blithedale full of complex human relationships, and leaves disillusioned. Mark Twain refers obliquely to the literal meaning of Miles in *The Prince and the Pauper,* set in 1547. Miles Hendon is the raffish nobleman who serves as Edward VI's protector while the young king is on his own in London.

The Turn of the Screw is Henry James's most deeply enigmatic piece of fiction, in part because two of its main characters are charming, intelligent, beautiful children. The ten-year-old boy is Miles, and in spite of his apparently excellent behavior he has been expelled from school for using reprehensible language. He claims not to be able to see the ghosts that the governess sees, but certain aspects of his behavior are inexplicable. Interpretations vary: Is he deeply corrupt? Is there sexual tension between him and the governess? Does he even die at the end?

MILTON *(Old English, "mill town")* A last name turned into a first name. Nineteenth-century English visitors to the United States found American naming habits entertaining. The use of a middle initial (or numerals or "Jr." after names) was considered particularly side-splitting, as was the use of a last name as a first name. This criticism hardly seems fair, since it is a British habit as well (and Britons do very well in the silly-name stakes). Still, Milton K. Rogers could only be an American. In fact, he is the cunning, dishonest former business partner of Silas Lapham in William Dean Howells's *The Rise of Silas Lapham*. Rogers, in fact, ruins Silas financially, unintentionally saving him—from a moral point of view, that is.

MISAIL *(Slavonic, probably a variant of* **Michael:** *Hebrew, "who is like the Lord")* In Chekhov's short story "My Life," Misail Poloznev is the idealistic narrator. Naive, a little dull, he insists on forgoing the perquisites of his educated class and becoming a manual laborer. He and his wife do not benefit at all from this choice; rather, they are consistently robbed and cheated by the crafty peasants into whose milieu they have interjected themselves.

MONTAGUE *(French, "pointed mountain")* Also **Montagu.** Montague Tigg is one of the least attractive of the broad array of dubious characters portrayed in Charles Dickens's *Martin Chuzzlewit*. A con man, Montague Tigg is a flashy dresser who reverses his names and somehow becomes a bigwig in the "Anglo Bengalee Disinterested Loan and Life Assurance Company." He is murdered by Jonas Chuzzlewit. This is also the last name of that famous lover, Romeo.

MORDRED *(Middle English, meaning unknown)* The Welsh tales known as *The Mabinogion* are one source of the Arthurian legends, and a character called **Medrawd** occurs in them. Sir Thomas Malory's *Le Morte D'Arthur* calls him **Mordred**. By Malory's time, of course, English was influenced heavily by French and Mordred's name may have been affected; the French word for "bite" is *mordre* and "murder" is a cognate. In Tennyson's *The Idylls of the King* he is **Modred**. By any name, he's an ugly customer. Depending on the version, he is the son or nephew (or both) of King Arthur, and a traitor. In Malory's version he tries to usurp the throne and marry Guinevere in Arthur's absence; in Tennyson's, he exposes Guinevere's adultery with Lancelot. Either way, Mordred sows the seeds that destroy Camelot.

MORTEN *(Scandinavian, "settlement on the moor")* Henrik Ibsen's *A Public Enemy* pits idealistic Thomas Stockmann against his fellow townspeople and members of his family. He believes that the public baths for which his town is famous are actually poisoning people, and proposes closing them. His father-in-law, Morten Kiil, has bought stock in the baths and takes no interest in anyone's health. His pocketbook is his sole concern.

MOSES *(Hebrew, meaning unclear; possibly "savior," possibly "child")* Moses Primrose is the second son of the unlucky Reverend Charles Primrose in Oliver Goldsmith's *The Vicar of Wakefield*. His name has to have been a comic invention. For one thing, "Moses Primrose" simply sounds funny. What's more, Old Testament names were very sparingly used among educated English families in the eighteenth century. Finally, Moses is beautifully plain compared to the Primrose daughters' names, **Olivia** and **Sophia**. Moses' great contribution to the Primrose family's financial rescue is going to a fair to sell a horse and coming back with a gross of green glass spectacles instead of cash.

MURTAGH *(Irish Gaelic, "sea warrior")* In Maria Edgeworth's sardonic *Castle Rackrent*, Sir Murtagh Rackrent is one in a succession of terrible landlords who squeeze the maximum possible money from a poorly maintained agricultural estate, penalizing tenant farmers in the process. The term "rackrent" (as in torturing someone on the rack) meant to extract nearly the full annual value of a property in rent. Sir Murtagh, heir to Sir Patrick, is a miser who uses his legal training to squeeze the tenantry even further. In his avarice and cruelty he is a portrait of the worst Irish landlords.

NARCISSUS *(Greek, "daffodil")* The son of the nymph Liriope, so handsome that he attracted myriad admirers, among them the nymph Echo. He scorned her advances cruelly and she wasted into nothing but her voice. He was punished by falling in love with his own reflection in a pool of water. Ovid, in *Metamorphoses,* says that even "when he was received into the abode of the dead, he kept looking at himself in the waters of the Styx." His body vanished and in its stead grew up "a flower with a circle of white petals round a yellow centre."

> *Narcissus had played with her affections, treating her as he had previously treated other spirits of the waters and the woods, and his male admirers too.* —OVID, METAMORPHOSES

NATHANIEL *(Hebrew, "God has given")* Also **Nathanael.** The name of one of the Apostles but not a saint's name. A variation is **Nathan.** Nathaniel Winkle is one of the earliest characters Charles Dickens created, and the most inept member of the Pickwick Club in *The Pickwick Papers.* Anthony Trollope's Nathaniel Sowerby of *Framley Parsonage* is his contemporary, for he is fifty at the time of the novel, and thus was born around 1810. He could be considered Nathaniel Winkle perfected, for some of Winkle's imaginary skills (as a horseman, for instance) Sowerby possesses in reality. He is also deeply in debt: "It was believed he could not live in England out of jail but for his protection as a member of Parliament."

Fiction's most memorable Nathaniel, however, is Natty Bumppo of James Fenimore Cooper's "Leatherstocking Tales." Cooper introduces him as a crafty old woodsman in *The Pioneers*. *The Last of the Mohicans* explains his background (he is European Christian raised among Native Americans) and centers on his relationship with Chingachgook, the Mohican of the title. In *The Pathfinder* (one of Bumppo's nicknames, along with "Hawkeye") Cooper delves more deeply into Natty's emotional history; he falls in love and actually proposes to the beautiful Mabel Dunham. But she turns him down—Cooper has long since made clear that he is not only odd-looking but also barely civilized. The prototypical American hero can hardly be shackled by domesticity. Finally, *The Deerslayer,* written last of the "Leatherstocking" books, goes back and discusses his first warpath and the formation of his moral code, which is as strict as that of any Puritan.

NEPTUNE *(Latin mythology name)* The Roman god of the sea, who corresponds to the Greek Poseidon. He and Zeus and Hades are brothers who divided the realms: Zeus got the air, Hades the earth, and Poseidon/Neptune the sea. With his trident he creates earthquakes, and he can be vengeful when offended.

NESTOR *(Greek, meaning unknown)* The eldest warrior present at the Trojan War, Nestor is the ruler of Pylos, a kingdom next to Achaea. In *The Iliad* he frequently proffers long-winded advice based on his extensive experience of war. In *The Odyssey,* where he is often referred to as "Nestor, breaker of horses," he is handled with similar respect. An old friend of Odysseus, he gives Telemachus an eyewitness account of the end of the Trojan War.

NEVILLE *(French, "new town")* In Charles Dickens's unfinished *The Mystery of Edwin Drood,* Neville Landless is one of a pair of twins who arrive in the small town of Cloisterham and get entangled with Edwin Drood and the sinister organist John Jasper. Neville detests Drood on meeting him, and Jasper manages to get him arrested for Drood's murder—but he is released, since there is no evidence that Drood is actually dead.

NEWLAND *(English place-name)* Though Edith Wharton explains protagonist Newland Archer's name in *The Age of Innocence* (his mother was a Newland), its connotations are still significant. It is, after all, a new land Archer perceives in the place of Old New York, once he has fallen under Ellen Olenska's spell.

> *What was or was not "the thing" played a part as important in Newland Archer's New York as the inscrutable totems that had ruled the destinies of his forefathers thousands of years ago.* —EDITH WHARTON, *THE AGE OF INNOCENCE*

NICHOLAS *(Greek, "victory people")* Also **Nick.** The famous saint who is recognized as Santa Claus in the United States left only the vaguest concrete history. Legends about him include his bringing back to life three children drowned in a tub of brine. This was never a royal name in England or France, which may account for its somewhat scanty use in those countries. In "The Miller's Tale," one of Chaucer's *Canterbury Tales,* Nicholas is a poor but enterprising scholar who loves music and women. He especially loves his landlord's fair young wife Alison. His scheming does end up with him in Alison's bed, but he gets branded on the buttocks when he is discovered. Similarly buffoonish is Nick Bottom, the weaver in *A Midsummer Night's Dream* who is adorned with the head of an ass. Nicholas Bulstrode in George Eliot's *Middlemarch* is a bumptious banker with a secret in his past. He uses his evangelical faith to bully the people around him. Nicholas Dormer of Henry James's *The Tragic Muse* is the "dreamy" politician son of an eminent diplomat and an ambitious mama. His family expects him to marry his rich cousin and forge ahead in a political career but he hankers after the calling of a painter. The most memorable Nicholas of Victorian literature is certainly Charles Dickens's creation, Nicholas Nickleby. Dickens does not usually bother with literary allusion in his names, preferring to tinker with their sounds in order to freight them with meaning.

Possibly in this case he also had an eye to the name's literal meaning, for Nicholas Nickleby does end up victorious. He is a noble, brave, and loyal young man, the sole financial support of his mother and sister. His adventures at the grim school Dotheboys Hall, and later in the Crummles's acting troupe, serve to set off his heroic qualities.

Nicholas—in the Russian form, **Nikolai** or **Nikolay**—is a royal name in Russia. What's more, Saint Nicholas is greatly venerated in the Eastern Rite churches. It is no surprise, then, that Russian writers use the name extensively. In Ivan Turgenev's *On the Eve*, Nikolai Stahov is a retired army officer with a rich wife and limited intelligence. He keeps a mistress who refers to him as a "simpleton," and lards his speech with French phrases, an affectation of the Russian upper classes. Nikolai Kirsanov of *Fathers and Sons* is a different stamp of man. A genuine liberal, he has freed the hundred serfs that work his five thousand acres—only to find that, liberated, they now take advantage of him. He adores music and his son Arkady, and is warmly hospitable to Arkady's revolutionary friend Yevgeny Barsanov. Anton Chekhov's great gallery of the bored and disaffected includes many characters named Nikolai. The drama *Ivanov* concerns the exhausted and bankrupt landowner Nikolai Ivanov. His wife dies of tuberculosis, he loves the young daughter of his neighbor, but he is too weary and disillusioned to start a new life with her. The protagonist (certainly no hero) of "A Boring Story" is Nikolai Stepanovich, a highly esteemed academic. Despite his successes he looks back with despair on a life of missed emotional connections. A common nickname for Nikolai is **Nikita**. Ordinarily characters in Russian literature are known by their full first names or their first names and patronymics; use of a diminutive signals either affection and intimacy implied on the reader's part, or else a gap in social standing (or sometimes both). In Chekhov's story "Ward 6," the ward's caretaker is called Nikita. A retired soldier, he is, in Chekhov's words, "one of those simple-minded, intolerant, obtuse people." The nickname emphasizes his humble station in this case.

Nikolai is also an important name in several of Leo Tolstoy's works. Nikolai Levin, in *Anna Karenina,* is the gravely ill brother of Konstantin Levin. His tranquil acceptance of death helps his brother accept it as part of the cycle of life. *War and Peace* features two significant characters named Nikolai. One is Prince Nikolai Bolkonsky, a controlling and selfish aristocrat who meddles in his adult children's lives with drastic consequences. Count Nikolai Rostov is a more engaging creation, a passionate, dashing soldier who embraces war and worships the tsar. His experiences of battle mature him and he ultimately becomes a practical husband and successful landowner.

Nikolai Stavrogin is the central character of Fyodor Dostoyevsky's *The Devils*, a portrayal of early revolutionary movements in Russia. Stavrogin is a brilliant but disaffected young nobleman who toys with crime and debauchery as well as nihilist political sentiments. He gets involved with a dangerous revolutionary group, and when bloodshed ensues, ends by committing suicide.

> *Nick was often mystifying—it was his only fault.*
> —HENRY JAMES, *THE TRAGIC MUSE*

NICODEMUS *(Greek, "people's victory")* Nicodemus Boffin of Dickens's *Our Mutual Friend* is informally known as "Noddy." He is a dustman, and was originally a servant of John Harmon. He is also Harmon's residuary legatee, since Harmon's son John has been missing for fourteen years. Boffin pretends to be a miser, but he is actually nursing the fortune for the eventual return of the young Harmon, and happily hands it over.

NILS *(Scandinavian version of* Neil: *Gaelic, "champion")*. In Henrik Ibsen's *A Doll's House* Nils Krogstad looks at first like a conventional villain, threatening the unstable Nora with exposure of a forgery. Yet he is redeemed; he withdraws his accusation, thus restoring the possibility that Nora and her morally upright husband Torvald may repair their marriage.

NIMROD *(Hebrew, "we shall rise up")* In the Old Testament, Nimrod is recorded as "a mighty hunter before the Lord." Dante places him with the Giants in the Inferno, and Christopher Smart invokes him in his long poem of praise, "Jubilate Agno."

NOAH *(Hebrew, meaning unclear)* The biblical Noah was selected by God in the Old Testament to survive a flood because of his righteousness. Noah Claypole, a minor character in Charles Dickens's *Oliver Twist,* does not answer to this description. An orphan who works at the undertaker's where Oliver is apprenticed, he demonstrates the aggression and selfishness that might help Oliver to make his way in the world but that Dickens can't really approve of.

NOEL *(French, "Christmas")* Wilkie Collins's *No Name* is a novel about two privileged girls, Norah and Magdalen Vanstone, who are suddenly orphaned and find themselves illegitimate to boot. Their cousin Noel thus inherits their father's whole fortune, which he refuses to share with them. Collins calls him "a frail, flaxen-haired, self-satisfied little man." There is perhaps a suggestion of effeminacy here: Collins stresses his fussiness and lack of vitality. Certainly in that era the English idea of masculinity did not include French names.

OBADIAH *(Hebrew, "servant of God")* Anthony Trollope has great fun with the "servant of God" in *Barchester Towers,* Obadiah Slope. His defects are numerous, for he is a self-serving, arrogant, power-hungry clergyman. As if his character flaws weren't enough, Trollope also makes him physically repulsive, with reddish, greasy hair and a complexion like bad beef. To crown the reader's enjoyment, the author then pits Slope against the detestable bishop's wife Mrs. Proudie, in a titanic struggle for domination of Barchester church politics.

OBERON *(Old German, "noble bearlike")* The king of the fairies in Shakespeare's *A Midsummer Night's Dream.* He is all-powerful, like Zeus, and, like Zeus, jealous of his wife. It is his love potion that causes her to fall in love with the ignominious Bottom. Another form of the name is **Auberon.**

OCTAVIO *(Latin, "eighth")* Used in literature as an identifier, but not really as a naturalistic name. In Molière's *That Scoundrel Scapin,* a lovesick young man (who has no other characteristics) is called Octavio. In Aphra Behn's *Love-Letters Between a Nobleman and His Sister,* many of the characters are thin disguises for real people, and the names (**Cesario, Philander**) make no gesture toward realism. Octavio is one of Silvia's many lovers after she is debauched by Philander.

ODYSSEUS *(Greek mythology name)* The legendary hero of Homer's *Odyssey,* also a towering figure in *The Iliad* who is also known as **Ulysses.** He is the king of Ithaka, a crafty and resourceful warrior. Physically huge, brave, skilled at combat, he is above all a persuasive leader. In *The Odyssey* Homer calls him "the man of twists and turns," and stresses his crafty nature. It takes suspicion and deception to get Odysseus home from Troy to Ithaka, especially with Poseidon plotting against him—ultimately, of course, he prevails, but his wiles are essential to his success.

OEDIPUS *(Greek, "swollen feet")* In Greek myth Oedipus is the son of Laius and Jocasta, the king and queen of Thebes. His father was told by an oracle that he would be killed by his son, so when Jocasta bore Oedipus he had a spike put through the baby's feet and had the child exposed on a hillside. There is no evading the Fates, however: Oedipus was reared to adulthood and, meeting his father on a road one day, killed him after an argument. He went to Thebes and married Jocasta, unaware that she was his mother. Only after famine struck Thebes years later did the blind seer Tiresias reveal to Oedipus his identity, upon which his sons banished him, he blinded himself, and his daughter Antigone went into exile with him. This legend provided fodder most notably for Sophocles, whose *Antigone, Oedipus the King,* and *Oedipus at Colonus* explore different aspects of the tragedy. Throughout all this misery, Oedipus demonstrates great dignity.

OLAF *(Scandinavian, "ancestor")* A royal name in Norway. The tenth-century King Olaf who brought Christianity to Norway was canonized. The *Laxdaela Saga* recounts a century and a half of Icelandic history and centers on a willful woman named Gudrun. Her great love Kjartan is the son of Olaf the Peacock, a sophisticated, well-traveled chieftain in a time and place when a voyage to Norway was a great adventure. Another form of the name is **Olav.**

OLIVER *(Meaning disputed; possibly Latin, "olive tree," possibly Old German "elf host," possibly related to* **Olaf***)* The French version is **Olivier** *(oh lee vee ay')*. He appears as a sidekick to Roland/Orlando in the Roland legends, where he is a moderating influence on the hotheaded Roland. In *The Song of Roland,* it is

Olivier who urges Roland to blow his famous ivory horn to summon the army when Roland's troops are ambushed by Saracens in the mountain pass of Roncesvalles. In Ariosto's *Orlando Furioso*, Oliver is an ally of Orlando and an important member of the Christian forces who eventually defeat the pagans. Shakespeare's *As You Like It*, a pastoral comedy, also includes an Orlando and an Oliver, but they are brothers. Oliver is the jealous elder who has plotted to undermine Orlando. Once in the Forest of Arden, however, when Orlando saves his life, he changes his ways.

The pathetic Victorian orphan Oliver Twist (in Dickens's novel of the same title) has little in common with either of his literary predecessors. All of nine years old when the novel opens, he is sold to an undertaker and runs away to London where he falls in with a gang of juvenile thieves led by the magnetic criminal Fagin. His last name refers in part to the twists and turns of his fate, which finally brings him prosperity and affection.

> *Oliver Twist's ninth birthday found him a pale thin child, somewhat diminutive in stature, and decidedly small in circumference.* —CHARLES DICKENS, *OLIVER TWIST*

ORESTES *(Greek, "man of the mountain")* Which Greek character has the most tragic existence: Oedipus or Orestes? It's a difficult choice. Orestes, the son of Agamemnon and Clytemnestra, is merely working out a curse placed on his family (the Atrides, or descendants of Atreus) by his great-uncle Thyestes. Clytemnestra becomes the mistress of Aegisthus while Agamemnon is at the Trojan War. When her husband comes home she kills him. Orestes, encouraged by his sister Electra, then kills Clytemnestra and her lover Aegisthus. He is hounded by the Furies afterward. Orestes' plight was so dramatically compelling that he appears in more Greek plays than any other character. Euripides wrote a drama called *Electra* while Aeschylus's trilogy—*Agamemnon, The Libation Bearers,* and *The Eumenides*—is known as "the Oresteia."

ORGON *(French, meaning unknown)* The names in Molière's plays frequently conform to a convention setting them apart from legitimate baptismal names. In this case the *org* phoneme may refer to *orgueil*, the French word for pride. In *Tartuffe*, Orgon is the rich fool whom the hypocrite Tartuffe victimizes. The stubborn, self-deceiving buffoon is a classic Molière type.

ORLANDO *(Italian from Old German, "fame land")* Also known as **Roland**, and hero of epics such as *The Song of Roland* and Ariosto's *Orlando Furioso*. Roland/Orlando is Charlemagne's nephew and a paladin of France. In Ariosto's version he is no mere type, but an individual: rash, impulsive, courageous, loyal, straightforward, uncalculating. He is madly in love with the pagan princess Angelica and when he finds evidence of her love for the soldier Medoro, loses his senses. Ariosto's epic is sometimes divided into two parts: *Orlando Inamorato* ("Orlando in Love") and *Orlando Furioso* ("Orlando Mad"). He does regain his senses in the second half of the epic. Dante places him with the "Defenders of the Faith" in the *Paradiso*.

Shakespeare's Orlando, in *As You Like It*, presents a different facet of the romantic hero. He is the brave, gentle hero who has been cheated of his birthright by his elder brother Oliver. (Their father's name is Sir Rowland, suggesting that Shakespeare knew the outlines of the Roland/Orlando legend.) He is madly in love with Rosalind and writes poems to her, hanging them on trees throughout the Forest of Arden.

Anthony Trollope then picks up this name redolent of high romance, and subverts it by giving it to two bureaucrats. Orlando Hittaway is the chairman of the Board of Civil Appeals in *The Eustace Diamonds* and a dullard beyond compare. Sir Orlando Drought, a minor character in several of the political novels, has the temerity to give the Duke of Omnium advice in *The Prime Minister*. Contemporary critics sometimes caviled at Trollope's use of silly names, but "Drought" for the last name of a stiff, pompous old Tory seems inspired.

ORPHEUS *(Greek mythology name)* Orpheus was the great music maker and poet of Thrace. Ovid's *Metamorphoses* tells how

145

deeply he loved his wife Eurydice. She is bitten by a snake and dies. Orpheus descends to the underworld to find her, enchanting all its denizens with his music. Hades allows him to take Eurydice back to earth if he can lead her there without glancing back at her. Just as they reach earth, he looks at her, and she slips back into the underworld. Dante classes Orpheus with the Virtuous Pagans in Canto 4 of the *Inferno*.

ORSINO (*Italian, "little bear"*) Like many of the names in *Twelfth Night*, or indeed in any of Shakespeare's comedies, **Orsino** is a conventional rather than a naturalistic name: a true Italian duke is much more likely to bear a saint's name. It is a choice perfectly in keeping with the Illyrian fantasy, however. Orsino is madly in love—or so he thinks—with his subject Olivia. Ignoring her clear lack of interest in him, he languishes for her sake. The arrival of Viola, disguised as Cesario, and her twin brother Sebastian eventually provides a more willing mate for each.

> *In his father's eyes, Osborne was the representative of the ancient house of Hamley of Hamley, the future owner of the land which had been theirs for a thousand years. His mother clung to him because they two were cast in the same mould, both physically and mentally—because he bore her maiden name.* —ELIZABETH GASKELL, *WIVES AND DAUGHTERS*

OSBORNE (*Old English, "god bear"*) More commonly a last name. In Elizabeth Gaskell's *Wives and Daughters*, Osborne Hamley is the elder of two Hamley brothers. He bears his mother's maiden name as his first name. All the hopes of the family are pinned on him—he is handsome and clever, but perfectly undisciplined. His easy charm casts his reserved brother Roger in the shade. Osborne, however, ultimately disappoints his family.

OSWALD (*Old English, "god power"*) Also **Osvald.** Most of the characters in Chaucer's *Canterbury Tales* are known by their station in life, but the Reeve (an administrator on a lord's estate) is called Oswald. Another administrative type is Goneril's steward Oswald in Shakespeare's *King Lear*. He is, as Edgar calls him, "a serviceable villain," more than ready to collaborate with Goneril's wicked schemes.

A name that was current in Chaucer's time is truly old, and thus had extra appeal to antiquarian-minded Victorians. Better yet if it is an old family name, passed down without respite from the mists of time. Oswald Standish, Viscount Chiltern, in Trollope's *Phineas Finn*, is the scion of an old, aristocratic, and rich family. He is, furthermore, hotheaded, full of ire, wild, and proud. "He was a man with thick short red hair, and an abundance of very red beard. And his face was red,—and, as it seemed to Phineas, his very eyes."

English and Scandinavian names occasionally overlap (with some phonetic adjustment) as a result of their common linguistic roots. In Henrik Ibsen's *Ghosts*, Osvald Alving is the degenerate son of a degenerate father. He has come back to his mother's house after years on the Continent living as a free-spirited artist. He is syphilitic, and knows it, but still wishes to marry his mother's maid Regina. She, however, is his half sister, begotten by his father on an earlier housemaid. His mother's life has been an attempt to conceal this scandal.

> "Yes, my dear Osvald Alving, you have inherited the name of a man who undoubtedly was energetic and worthy."
> —HENRIK IBSEN, *GHOSTS*

OTTO *(Old German, "wealthy")* JohannWolfgang von Goethe's *Elective Affinities* is a study of a wealthy German couple, Eduard and Charlotte, whose marriage collapses when their ménage expands to include Charlotte's niece and Eduard's old friend the Captain. The latter is always known by his army rank rather than by his name, Otto. He and Eduard are school friends and they discuss the fact that Eduard's given name was also Otto, but he renounced it so that his friend could use it. He does virtually the same thing with his wife, all but handing her over formally to the Captain once he has fallen hard for the niece.

Olive Schreiner's *The Story of an African Farm* could not present a more different milieu. Set on a dusty, poor farm in South Africa, it illuminates the narrow possibilities for the characters marooned there. One of them is Otto, the kindly, simple-minded German overseer who is ejected from the farm after having been framed for a crime he did not commit. Without money to travel or skills to barter in that isolated place, he dies.

Othello is an Italian diminutive of Otto. A reasonable name for a Moorish soldier of fortune? Perhaps not, but Shakespeare's Moor owns it now. He is married to the fair Desdemona and is fatally susceptible to the jealousy that his "friend" Iago sows in his mind. At the end of the play, after he has killed Desdemona, he describes himself as "one that lov'd not wisely but too well."

> *Poor Owen went through life with a frank dread of people's minds.* —HENRY JAMES, THE SPOILS OF POYNTON

OWEN (*Welsh variant of* **Eugène:** *Greek, "well-born"*) In Thomas Hardy's *Desperate Remedies,* Owen Graye is the elder son of a prosperous architect who dies leaving considerable debts. Owen, despite his "good birth," goes out to work as a clerk in a different architect's office. He is of a markedly higher class than his fellow clerks. Henry James, in *The Spoils of Poynton,* does not play on the literal meaning of the name as Hardy does. Owen Gereth is the son of Adela Gereth, whose lifework is the house, Poynton, and its superb furnishings. Owen, alas, though officially the owner of the house, does not appreciate it. He is, in fact, not terribly bright: "robust and artless, eminently natural, yet perfectly correct, he looked pointlessly active and pleasantly dull." His engagement to the philistine Mona Brigstock threatens his mother's great achievement since Mona will want to put her own (vulgar) stamp on Poynton.

OZIAS *(Hebrew, "helper, supporter")* The tangled plot of Wilkie Collins's melodrama *Armadale* involves several generations of men named Allan Armadale. Ozias Midwinter is the son of one of them by a Creole woman. Abandoned by his mother, he was raised by a gypsy in horrendous circumstances, and has been taught by his hard life to be wary and suspicious. When young Allan Armadale takes care of him in an illness, he wins Ozias's unwavering loyalty.

> *"Whatever else we may doubt, I really think we may feel sure about the man's name! It is so remarkably ugly, that it must be genuine. No sane human being would assume such a name as Ozias Midwinter."*
>
> —WILKIE COLLINS, *ARMADALE*

PALAMON (*Greek, meaning unknown*) Also spelled **Palaimon** or **Palaemon**. In Greek myth, a sea god, but in Chaucer's *Canterbury Tales,* a Theban knight. In "The Knight's Tale" he is taken captive by Theseus and hauled off to Athens where he falls in love with Hippolyta's sister Emelye. Palamon's cousin Arcite also falls in love with Emelye, and the two fight over her. Arcite prays to Mars—wrong choice. Palamon prays to Venus, and wins. The tale is really about the relative merits of the two gods: Emelye is indifferent to both men.

PALMER (*English, "one who carries a palm"*) Palm branches indicated pilgrims in the Middle Ages. The symbolism may date from the celebration of Palm Sunday, the Sunday before Easter when Jesus was welcomed into Jerusalem by throngs casting palms on the ground before him. In Book Two of Edmund Spenser's *The Faerie Queen,* the hero Guyon (the embodiment of Temperance) is guided by Palmer.

PANGLOSS (*Greek, "all tongue"*) In Voltaire's *Candide,* Dr. Pangloss is the naive hero's pedantic old tutor. No matter what horror he witnesses or endures in the course of the tale—and by the end he is missing an eye and an ear—he maintains that "all is for the best in this best of all possible worlds."

PARFYON (*Russian from Greek, "virginal"*) In Fyodor Dostoyevsky's *The Idiot,* Parfyon Semyonovich Rogozhin is the antithesis of the cerebral, innocent Myshkin. Uneducated, crude, driven by his passions, he has a reputation for womanizing. Dostoyevsky, who chose his characters' names with great care, must have selected this one ironically, for Parfyon is sexually motivated.

PARIS *(Greek mythology name)* The son of Priam, king of Troy. He was exposed on a mountainside at birth and reared as a shepherd because of a dream his mother had before his birth. But he grew up to be the most beautiful man in Asia Minor, so he was chosen to decide which of three goddesses—Venus, Minerva, or Juno—should be awarded a golden apple inscribed "For the Fairest." As Dorothy Sayers writes in her introduction to Dante's *Inferno,* "Juno offered him riches and Minerva conquest, but Venus promised him the love of the most beautiful woman in the world." He fell for Venus's bait, and the result was the Trojan War, since Venus helped him kidnap Helen from Sparta. Dante places him with the Lustful in Hell, and Homer doesn't have many kind words for him either. Paris is pampered, shameless, and only a competent soldier. Worst, he never apologizes for causing the war that brought down his family and its kingdom. Shakespeare gave his name to Juliet's disregarded fiancé in *Romeo and Juliet.*

PATRICK *(Latin, "noble, well-born")* From the same root that gives us "patrician." The patron saint of Ireland was a missionary bishop of the fifth century who established an organized Christian presence in the face of Druid opposition. Less reliably, he is supposed to have driven the snakes out of the country as well. The name has always been very popular among the Irish. In Maria Edgeworth's *Castle Rackrent,* the narrator Thady Quirk's first employer is Sir Patrick Rackrent, a popular, hard-drinking gentleman who falls down dead at a party.

Stephen Crane's Pat Scully ("The Blue Hotel") comes from a very different kind of fiction. He is the Irish proprietor of the "Palace Hotel" in Fort Rompers, Nebraska. The hotel is blue because he thinks its added visibility will attract business. His relationship to his guests and their difficulties—one of them gets himself killed on the premises—is strictly businesslike.

PAUL *(Latin, "small")* A standard name in Europe, probably owing its prominence to one of the major saints of the Christian church, six popes, and various European royal figures. Dickens's novel *Dombey and Son*, despite its title, is really not about a father-son relationship. Mr. Dombey has his heart set on raising a son to inherit his business interests, so dreamy, frail, sensitive Paul is a disappointment—especially when he dies in childhood. Trollope names one of his amiable young men Paul Montague in *The Way We Live Now*. He is somewhat damaged goods as marriage material, having been far too close to the scandalous widow Mrs. Hurtle, but he has a good heart and wins his sweetheart Hetta Carbury in the end. In Henry James's *The Princess Casamassima*, Paul Muniment (the last name is a term for family papers) is a former Lancashire laborer who has become a leader of the anarchist movement that enmeshes Hyacinth Robinson. Calm, commanding, "for a revolutionary he was strangely unexasperated," says James.

Paul is one of the names that moves unchanged across the English Channel. In Charlotte Brontë's *Villette*, Paul Emanuel is a fellow teacher of Lucy Snowe's at boarding school in Brussels. Irascible, capable of arrogance, he is nevertheless loyal and kind. More important to Lucy (her last name is "Snowe" for a reason), he is perceptive, and tries to ignite her passions. His last name, "Emanuel," may indicate a savior, since it is another term for the Messiah. Some scholars suggest that he is based on a teacher in the Brussels boarding school where Charlotte Brontë herself taught. In Émile Zola's huge novel about coal mining, *Germinal*, Paul Negrel is the engineer, and thus on a social plane of his own, squarely between the workers and the owners. The workers are inclined to resent him, especially since he is the manager's nephew, but he wins their respect with his physical courage.

In Italian, Paul becomes **Paolo**, and the most famous literary character of that name is Paolo Malatesta of Dante's *Inferno*. He is the handsome younger brother of Francesca da Rimini's husband Giancotto Malatesta, whom she had married in a political alliance. They fell in love one day while reading about Lancelot, and were both killed by Francesca's husband. Dante places them in the second circle of Hell, where they are constantly tossed about by light winds symbolizing the lust that they made no attempt to resist.

The Russian version of the name is **Pavel,** and if Russian fiction is any indicator, it was widely used in the nineteenth century. The reign of Tsar Paul I may have influenced this usage, though his five-year rule was marked by cruel, reactionary policies and ended in his murder. Pavel Shubin in Turgenev's poignant *On the Eve* is a handsome young sculptor. "Everything about him seemed to breathe the joy, the gaiety of health, everything breathed youth— carefree, self-confident, charming, pampered youth." Discipline is not mentioned in this description, and there is an aimlessness to Shubin's behavior that suggests no happy future. Pavel Kirsanov, in *Fathers and Sons* by the same author, is a less important character; the brother of Nikolai Kirsanov, he lives on the estate with little to do but maintain his elegant wardrobe and remember the social successes of his St. Petersburg past. The enterprising ghoul of Gogol's *Dead Souls* is Pavel Ivanovich Chichikov, most often known by just his last name. A modest, unassuming man, he charms by his very ordinariness. His scheme to buy "dead souls" (serfs who have died within the year) from landowners is the third in a series of minor swindles that he hopes will bring him financial security. Dostoyevsky's *The Brothers Karamazov* deals with the sons of the reprobate Fyodor Karamazov. The three legitimate sons grow up with Pavel Smerdyakov, their illegitimate half brother. He is vain, dishonest, self-absorbed, and violent: it is he who kills their father, though he pins the crime on his half brother Dmitri.

PENTHEUS *(Greek, possibly "grief, sorrow")* In Euripides' *The Bacchae*, Pentheus is the young king of Thebes when the worship of Dionysos begins to sweep across Greece. Dionysian rites included libertine behavior that a ruler like Pentheus might consider threatening to civil order. Dionysos deals courteously but implacably with Pentheus's resistance of his worship, tricking the ruler into watching a group of women worshiping in a frenzy— after which they tear him limb from limb.

PERCIVAL *(French, "pierce the vale")* The German forms are **Parsifal** or **Perzival,** and it is sometimes spelled **Perceval** or **Percivale** in English. He appears in most of the Arthurian legends including *Le Morte D'Arthur* and *The Idylls of the King.* He is a hugely strong bumpkin who was raised alone by his mother in a forest, and when he comes to King Arthur's court, the polished manners of the knights confound him. But he learns courtly behavior without losing his essential purity of character, and he ultimately sees the Holy Grail.

In Wilkie Collins's *The Woman in White,* Sir Percival Glyde is a ghastly parody of the Round Table knight. He is crude, nasty, and contemptuous to his wife, Laura, whom he has only married for her money. He is, furthermore, illegitimate, and burns down a church to destroy the records of his base birth. Henry James makes lighter but still ironical use of the name in its shortened form, **Percy.** In his story "An International Episode," Percy Beaumont is an English businessman who visits the United States with a young friend, Lord Lambeth, in 1878. The story centers on the multiple opportunities for misunderstanding among Americans and Englishmen of similar classes in the two countries. Percy's function is to be a somewhat sophisticated but nevertheless archetypal Briton.

PETER *(Greek, "rock")* A standard name throughout Europe. Peter is one of the most prominent saints of the Christian church; in popular imagination it is he who guards the "pearly gates" of heaven. It is one of those names that is used frequently enough to be virtually neutral. In Henry Fielding's *Joseph Andrews,* for instance, Peter Pounce is the steward to the Boobys, the aristocratic family that employs the hero. Cheating the Boobys, he has gotten rich and brags often about it. Alliteration (and the suggestion that he may "pounce" on any spare pence) makes his name funny.

The name is neutral enough to be used for secondary characters without freighting them with too much significance. In George Eliot's *Middlemarch,* Peter Featherstone is the cranky and sickly old owner of Stone Court who is connected by marriage or kinship to many Middlemarch characters. He is thus the center of

RUSSIAN NAMES

It's difficult to keep the names straight in a sprawling novel like Tolstoy's *Anna Karenina*, even without the added unfamiliarity of Russian names. Compounding the problem is the Russian system of using a first name and a patronymic. Most confusing of all is the fact that Russians are constantly playing with names, creating a string of nicknames from a mere pair of syllables. Finally, a Russian character in high society is likely to bear a French name, owing to the aristocratic Russian affection for Western European habits.

The combination of first name and patronymic is used politely, by acquaintances, so upon meeting someone named Pyotr Ivanovich Lupachkin one might address him as **Pyotr Ivanovich**. (Not all translators render names thus, however.) In a ballroom, he might be known as **Pierre**. And his family might call him, variously, **Petya, Petrushka, Petr,** or **Petinka**.

the classic Victorian novel's "Who will inherit the money?" tension. In Mrs. Gaskell's *Cranford,* Peter Jenkyns is the long-lost brother of Matty and Deborah Jenkyns who is recalled from India to rescue his sister's finances, and who fits seamlessly into the social life of the female-dominated village. Henry James's *The Tragic Muse* is dominated by the actress Miriam Rooth, but her principal suitor is Peter Sherringham, a well-born and highly cultured diplomat who loses his heart to her. James's more memorable Peter, however, is the ghostly Peter Quint in *The Turn of the Screw.* Saint Peter was a fisherman when Jesus recruited him, saying, "I will make you a fisher of men." James may have been thinking of this ghastly notion of evangelism when he named Quint, for the narrator of the story believes she is fighting him for the souls of the children, Miles and Flora. He never appears in fleshly form, but his personality (brutal, drunken, pretentious) emerges from the other characters' discussion of him. In Benjamin

Britten's opera based on the novella, Quint is a dominating presence, but not visible to all the characters. His "fishing" for the children, however, is quite explicit.

Another sinister Peter appears in one of the earliest American novels, *The Coquette* by Hannah Webster Foster. Published in 1797 and written in epistolary form, it concerns eligible young Eliza Wharton, who must choose between a respectable cleric and the rakish aristocratic Major Peter Sanford. Sanford's attentions discourage the courtship of the minister but the major then drops Eliza and leaves town. He comes back, married to an heiress, and seduces Eliza when she's in a shaky mental state. She and her child die and he is punished by a lonely and penniless existence afterward.

Piers is an early form of Peter, closer to the French **Pierre**, but still used in England. William Langland's *Piers the Ploughman* dates back to the fourteenth century. As an allegory it concentrates on characters who are abstractions of certain qualities—Conscience, Reason, and so on. Piers the Ploughman offers himself to the narrator as a guide to the Truth, citing his innocence and common sense as his qualifications. The poetry is, like much Middle English verse, alliterative. His name may thus refer to Saint Peter, but may also have been chosen for its initial *P*.

Although **Pierre** is not the anglophone form of the name, it has been used by writers outside France. Herman Melville followed *Moby-Dick* with *Pierre, Or, The Ambiguities*. Its hero, Pierre Glendinning, is the pampered, wealthy youth whose life is changed when he meets a woman he believes to be his half sister. His desire for her, and the pressures of trying to support her by his writing, blend the Gothic with the autobiographical.

The aristocratic Russian fondness for French names is amply documented in Tolstoy's novels. Pierre Bezuhov is one of the pivotal figures of *War and Peace*. The illegitimate son of a count, he is a physically robust but aimless presence as the novel begins. An unexpected inheritance makes him lionized and he marries the corrupt Hélène Kuragin. An important facet of his character is his lack of focus, which is corrected by his experience as a French prisoner of war. He emerges from captivity a more humble, positive person, and embarks on a successful second marriage. Pierre

Gringoire is a secondary character in Victor Hugo's historical novel *Nôtre-Dame of Paris*. A poor and unsuccessful poet, he is the author of a morality play that is being performed at Nôtre Dame Cathedral when the action begins. He is captured by a gang of street thugs and only saved when the gypsy dancer Esmeralda offers to marry him. He falls madly in love with her but romance is not the point of this plot-driven novel. Gringoire is useful to Hugo in moving the action along, and he ends up alive—unlike Esmeralda's three other besotted suitors.

The Italian form of **Peter** is **Pietro,** but Molière's play *The Sicilian* doesn't bother much with realism. The Sicilian of the title is Don **Pedro**—actually a Spanish name. He is the jealous custodian of the beautiful Greek girl Isidore, a former slave. He has freed her and intends to marry her but loses her to a different, more attractive man. **Pyotr** and **Piotr** are the Russian forms of the name, and both Anton Chekhov and Ivan Turgenev make it clear that not every educated Russian affected French names. In fact, in Chekhov's short story "The Party," the host is Peter. In the course of the party it emerges that he is a spoiled, selfish flirt and an intolerant snob—but that his wife Olga is strongly attached to him nonetheless. Pyotr Vassilievich is the father of Vladimir, the narrator of Turgenev's *First Love*. A fine horseman, he unknowingly competes with his son for the attentions of the fair young Zinaida, who is apparently a courtesan. In Chekhov's drama *The Cherry Orchard,* Piotr Trofimov is a young intellectual, the former tutor to Madame Ranevskaya's son. Her daughter Anya is in love with him. In the discussion of how to save the estate, Trofimov takes an idealistic and forward-looking stance, hoping for a more egalitarian Russian. Pyotr Verkhovenski is one of the revolutionaries in Fyodor Dostoyevsky's *The Devils*. He spearheads the plot to murder Stahov, a defector from the group.

Petrushka (sometimes spelled **Petrouchka**) is a familiar variant of **Pyotr.** In Nicolai Gogol's *Dead Souls,* Pavel Chichikov's servant is Petrushka. The narrator mocks his hand-me-down clothes, his unwashed aroma, and his love of "reading": "the fact that a word of some kind always came out of the letters" is a thrill. **Petruchio** is probably a name invented by Shakespeare for the sham-Italian setting of *The Taming of the Shrew*. He is the high-handed suitor who manages to subdue the obstreperous Katherina to the extent that she later wins a contest, proving herself to be the most obedient wife. Petruchio is witty and determined, and fully as energetic as his willful bride.

PHILANDER *(Greek, "loving men")* Or loving women, for that matter—though it is not clear why an entire genus of marsupials, including woolly South American opossums, is called Philander. Perhaps they are highly sociable. In Aphra Behn's roman à clef *Love-Letters Between a Nobleman and His Sister*, Philander is the name for the historical character of Lord Grey, who seduced his virgin sister-in-law Lady Henrietta Berkeley. He is a rake and a libertine, and enjoys the seduction process as a form of domination, a fact that becomes clear when he moves on to his next mistress/victim.

PHILIP *(Greek, "lover of horses")* *Emma* is one of Jane Austen's more complicated fictions, with a large cast of characters, most of them managed capably by Emma herself. Philip Elton, the vicar, is one of these, a handsome and eligible clergyman whom Emma intends for her friend Harriet Smith. His own choice of a bride (after Emma declines the honor) is a vulgar snob, with whom he is very well pleased. Catharine Maria Sedgwick took great care in researching *Hope Leslie*, an 1827 historical novel about the early days of the Massachusetts Bay Colony. Characters' names clearly signal their roles: Puritan; Native American; unreconstructed, luxury-loving Anglican. Sir Philip Gardiner is one of these last (his title gives him away, too). He is in Boston posing as a Puritan, hoping to marry the wealthy Hope Leslie and recoup his political fortunes back in England. Further evidence of his bad character is evinced by the presence of a girl named Rosa masquerading as his male page after he has seduced her. In George Eliot's *The Mill on the Floss*, Philip Wakem is the clever, sensitive, crippled son of Edward Tulliver's great enemy. He is a schoolfellow of Tom Tulliver's and eventually Maggie Tulliver's suitor. Though the two are clearly compatible, their families' enmity keeps them apart.

One of the best-known characters in English literature, Philip

Pirrip, is known throughout *Great Expectations* simply as "Pip," his childhood nickname. In fact, he is the recipient of a generous legacy, on the condition that he keep his nickname. His unknown benefactor, the ex-convict Abel Magwitch, may have intended the condition as a link with their common past, but it has two further effects. First, as a would-be gentleman, Pip is somewhat hampered by his odd name. It sounds like something small, expressing potential more than achievement—not unlike Pip himself, whose full potential as a real gentleman is not reached until the end of the book.

The French version is **Philippe,** and the title character of Honoré de Balzac's *The Black Sheep* answers to the name of Philippe Bridau. He is a former captain in Napoleon's army who never integrated into civilian life, descending instead into a life of debauchery and crime. His victims include his doting mother and his unappreciated brother Joseph. Crafty and unprincipled, he victimizes his family until his mother finally grasps which of her sons truly is the black sheep.

> *The small bundle of shivers growing afraid of it all and beginning to cry was Pip.*
> —CHARLES DICKENS, *GREAT EXPECTATIONS*

PHINEAS (*Meaning unknown, possibly Hebrew, "oracle"*) Anthony Trollope sometimes indulged himself in silly names but his principal characters usually have naturalistic names with slightly exaggerated features, like "Glencora M'Cluskie" or "Plantagenet Palliser." The young Irish barrister Phineas Finn, protagonist in Trollope's series of Parliamentary novels, is an extremely handsome and charming striver who gets caught up in high society in the course of forging a political career in London. Trollope refers to him as "that child of fortune, Phineas Finn."

PHOEBUS (*fee' bus; Greek mythology name*) Phoebus is an epithet for Apollo, the god of light and poetry, so Victor Hugo's use of the name for the dashing, handsome Royal Archer in *Nôtre-Dame of Paris* is hardly subtle. In this book, where physical and moral beauty rarely coexist, Phoebus de Châteaupers is so attractive that Esmeralda falls madly in love with him, yet he is an unregenerate rake.

PITT *(Old English, "ditch")* An appropriate name for two generations of baronets in William Thackeray's *Vanity Fair.* Sir Pitt Crawley the elder could plausibly have been named for the great statesman William Pitt—in any case, the connotations of hardness (as in a fruit pit) suit this selfish, miserly aristocrat. His son, also Sir Pitt, is a conventionally staid politician who, although a cold fish, is more humane than his amoral father.

PLANTAGENET *(Old French, "sprig of broom")* The Plantagenet family ruled England in the thirteenth and fourteenth centuries. Theirs makes an unlikely first name, but by calling his blue-blooded statesman Plantagenet Palliser, Anthony Trollope conveys his pride in his lineage as well as the sacrifices high rank sometimes entails (imagine being called "Plantagenet" in tender moments). Palliser, later the Duke of Omnium, was one of Trollope's great creations and one he particularly cherished. He appears in *The Small House at Allington* and later in ever-larger roles in the political novels. Earnest, courageous, shy, and dull, he is a sympathetic character but not, perhaps, quite as interesting as Trollope found him.

PLATON (pla tohn´; *Russian from Greek, "broad-shouldered")* A name that works on two levels for the wise peasant Platon Karataev in Tolstoy's *War and Peace.* It is the name, of course, of the Greek philosopher, and Karataev exemplifies the philosophical outlook. He is also "broad-shouldered," especially in emotional terms, tranquilly bearing up under the hardships of French captivity.

PLUTO *(Greek, "wealth")* In Roman myth, Pluto is the god of the underworld, and the most remote planet in the solar system is named for him. (The radioactive metallic element plutonium is named for the planet.) His Greek name, **Hades,** means "unseen." Pluto refers to the precious minerals found underground. The most memorable story about Pluto is his kidnapping of Proserpine. Her mother, Ceres, goddess of the harvest, searched and searched for her daughter and neglected her fertility duties. Finally Proserpine was permitted to return to the upper world for six months of every year. Those six months represent the warm months, while the cold months occur when she goes back to the underworld with her husband Pluto, and Ceres goes into mourning.

POLONIUS *(Latin, "from Poland")* In Shakespeare's *Hamlet,* Polonius is a courtier, father of Laertes and Ophelia. He is a diplomatic, smooth-talking presence, and Hamlet mistakenly kills him early in the play, precipitating Ophelia's madness.

PORFIRY *(por fee′ ree; Russian from Greek, "purple")* The purple of the name may refer to royalty or to Saint Porphyry, a fourth-century bishop and custodian for a while of a piece of "the true cross." Dostoyevsky's names are always significant. As the investigator in *Crime and Punishment,* Porfiry Petrovich must play cat-and-mouse with Raskolnikov, whom he knows to be his criminal. He is Raskolnikov's intellectual equal, but he believes in the benefits of the social contract (is this the "true cross" for Dostoyevsky?) rather than in anarchy.

PORTHOS *(French, invented name)* Alexandre Dumas, in *The Three Musketeers,* pretends to have found his tale in a secluded library. He realizes that the names of the characters are pseudonyms for aristocrats of the French court. Porthos is the snob of the three: tall, arrogant, insistent on social distinctions, and originally suspicious of d'Artagnan.

POSEIDON *(Greek mythology name)* Poseidon is the god of the sea in Greek myth—**Neptune** is his Roman name. He creates earthquakes by striking the seabed with his trident. In *The Odyssey,* it is Poseidon who creates storms to delay Odysseus's return to Ithaka because Odysseus has killed his son the Cyclops.

He is a character in Euripides' *The Women of Troy*, which takes place just after the end of the Trojan War. At Athena's request, and because he is saddened by the destruction of the city he had built with Apollo, he pins the Athenians to the Trojan shore with adverse winds.

PRINCE *(Middle English from Latin, "first person, chief")* Horatio Alger, Jr., in *Struggling Upward*, names a character Prince Duncan. Alger's books are all about social opportunity for the modestly born, so this name is used ironically; Duncan is a bank president who has stolen bonds from his own bank. Charles Dickens's Prince Turveydrop in *Bleak House* is one of those unforgettable minor characters Dickens invented with such gusto. He is the son of the proprietor of a dancing and deportment academy, a small, slight, effeminate man with very formal manners, who becomes engaged to Caddy Jellyby. In spite of his slightly ridiculous exterior he has a very good heart.

> *"Young Mr. Turveydrop's name is Prince; I wish it wasn't, because it sounds like a dog, but of course he didn't christen himself. Old Mr. Turveydrop had him christened Prince, in remembrance of the Prince Regent."*
> —CHARLES DICKENS, *BLEAK HOUSE*

PROMETHEUS *(Greek mythology name)* In Greek mythology, Prometheus is a Titan, a cousin of Zeus, who steals fire from Mount Olympus and gives it to the human race, which Zeus had intended to exterminate. In revenge, Zeus has him chained to a rock in the Caucasus where vultures perpetually feast on his liver. Aeschylus's *Prometheus Bound* focuses on this phase of his existence. He is finally freed by Heracles.

PROSPERO *(Middle English, "to succeed, do well")* A Saint Prosper of Aquitaine was a fifth-century cleric in Rome, so a related name existed before Shakespeare named his magician in *The Tempest*. The dramatist explicitly links magic and theater in this, his last play. Prospero holds the reins of the entire project—shipwreck, love affair, revenge—masterfully in hand and then, once his purposes are accomplished, breaks his magical staff and drowns his book, relinquishing his unearthly powers. If Shakespeare identified with Prospero, then the latter's final speech, which begins, "Now my charms are all o'er thrown," is an extraordinarily moving valediction.

PROTEUS *(Greek mythology name)* Proteus, in Greek myth, is a sea god who can take on a wide variety of different forms. Shakespeare adopted this name for one of his *Two Gentlemen of Verona*. The character does not actually change form, but he casually transfers his passion from one woman to another in this comedy.

PUCK *(Middle English, "goblin, sprite")* In Shakespeare's *A Midsummer Night's Dream*, Puck is the attendant and lieutenant of Oberon, the fairy king. He is a shape-shifting jester, full of mischief and spells gone awry. It is Puck who charms Titania so that she loves Bottom, and Lysander so that he loves Helena rather than Hermia—thus shuffling the romantic deck in an unexpected way.

PYRAMUS *(Greek mythology name)* In a tale told by Ovid in *Metamorphoses*, Pyramus is a young Babylonian who loves Thisbe. Supposed to meet him at a nearby tomb, she is frightened away by a lion, leaving her scarf behind. When he arrives late and finds her scarf smeared with blood by the lion, Pyramus assumes her dead and kills himself. She, returning, finds his body, and follows suit. The mulberry tree beneath which the lovers killed themselves originally bore white berries, but after the carnage they were stained crimson. Geoffrey Chaucer includes the tale in "The Legend of Good Women," part of his longer *Love Visions*. Shakespeare's subversion of the story, as performed by two rustic buffoons in *A Midsummer Night's Dream*, is a classic piece of comedy.

QUINTUS *(Latin, "fifth")* In Anthony Trollope's Palliser novels, Quintus Slide is a semicomic character, a journalist who is not a gentleman. Trollope uses Slide to express his mistrust of the popular press. In *Phineas Finn*, Slide proposes to support the young Parliamentarian Finn by writing favorable articles in his paper, *The People's Banner*. Finn, as much a snob as his creator Trollope, rebuffs Slide, making an enemy who dogs him through *Phineas Redux*. Slide turns his ire on the powerful Palliser family in *The Prime Minister*.

QUIXOTE *(kee hoe' tay; Spanish, meaning unknown)* Also **Quijote**. The assumed name of Miguel de Cervantes' Alonso Quijano, a kindly gentleman whose mind has been addled by reading too many novels of chivalry. Assuming the title of "Don Quixote de la Mancha," he sets out on a series of quests whose humor often hinges on his misconceptions of the world. His earnest wrongheadedness has given us the adjective "quixotic."

RALPH *(Old English, "wolf counsel")* Ralph Touchett is a pivotal figure in Henry James's *The Portrait of a Lady*. He is Isabel Archer's cousin, an Anglicized American who persuades his wealthy but frail father to leave Isabel half of his fortune, which he sees as a way for Isabel to achieve her great potential. His name may allude to Transcendental thinker Ralph Waldo Emerson, a thorough optimist who believed in the "divine sufficiency of the individual." Charles Dickens had no such precedent in mind for Ralph Nickleby, the nasty uncle in *Nicholas Nickleby* who refuses his financial support to Nicholas's mother and sister, but tries to match beautiful Kate with his roué friend Sir Mulberry Hawk. Uncle Ralph turns out to be the father of Nicholas's pathetic protégé Smike. Undine Spragg, the protagonist of Edith Wharton's *The Custom of the Country*, accumulates several husbands in the course of the book. Number two, Ralph Marvell, is the mild-mannered scion of Old New York who is dazzled by Undine's beauty and ultimately a victim of her profound selfishness.

> *It had so long been clear to him that poor Ralph was a survival, and destined, as such, to go down in any conflict with the rising forces.*
> —EDITH WHARTON, *THE CUSTOM OF THE COUNTRY*

RANDOLPH *(Old English, "shield wolf")* A name used for spoiled brats by two very different writers. In Horatio Alger Jr.'s

Struggling Upward, Randolph Duncan is a bully, the son of the corrupt bank manager and constant nemesis of Our Hero Luke Larkin. In Henry James's *Daisy Miller,* Randolph Miller is Daisy's obstreperous nine-year-old brother. He runs utterly wild, says just what he thinks, and is oblivious to his European surroundings.

RAPHAËL *(Hebrew, "God has healed")* One of the principal angels of the Bible; in *Paradise Lost,* Milton refers to him as the "affable archangel." Honoré de Balzac, in *The Wild Ass's Skin,* plays explicitly on the name. When we meet the hero, the destitute young marquis Raphaël de Valentin, Balzac shows him on the verge of suicide: "The young man was standing there like an angel stripped of his halo, one who had strayed from his path." His discovery of the magical skin of the wild ass rescues and at the same time imprisons Raphaël, for each time it satisfies one of his desires, it docks time off his life span. He eventually dies in the arms of his fiancée, his life ended by his sexual desire for her.

RAWDON *(Old English, "rough hill")* When Becky Sharp in Thackeray's *Vanity Fair* is hired as governess by the decadent Sir Pitt Crawley, she meets his son Rawdon, a bluff, amiable, but slightly dim cavalry officer with financial expectations from his aunt. Becky marries him in secret, then neglects both him and their son, whom he adores. He doesn't comprehend her mercenary selfishness until it is much too late.

RAYMOND *(Old German, "counsel protection")* The handsome and polished French count Raymond de Chelles appeals immensely to Edith Wharton's Undine Spragg in *The Custom of the Country.* Yet her marriage to him is ruined by her absolute inability to comprehend the traditions and values of the French aristocracy—and her husband's inability to compromise them in any way.

REGINALD *(Old German, "counsel power")* Variations include **Reinhold, Renaud, Reynolds, Rinaldo, Ronald,** and many other names. In Sir Walter Scott's *Ivanhoe,* Sir Reginald Front-de-Boeuf is a Norman knight, owner of the castle of Torquilstone where Ivanhoe and his Saxon cohorts are imprisoned. Dickens uses the name for the shy clerk Reginald Wilfer in *Our Mutual Friend*. He is a cherubic-looking man always short of money, whose two daughters Bella and Lavinia greatly outshine him in the personality department.

In Ludovico Ariosto's *Orlando Furioso,* Rinaldo is Orlando's cousin and one of Charlemagne's heroic paladins. The famous brown horse Bayard is his traditional mount. Like Orlando, he is madly in love with the pagan princess Angelica. His exploits as a warrior occupy much of Ariosto's narrative.

REMUS *(Latin mythology name)* According to Roman myth, Remus is the twin brother of Romulus. The boys are descendants of Aeneas, the sons of vestal virgin Rhea Silvia and Mars. When she gave birth (as no vestal virgin should) the babies were thrown into the Tiber but washed ashore and were nursed by a she-wolf. Romulus later killed his brother in a fight over the location of Rome. It was not uncommon for American slave owners to give their servants names from classical myth. In Joel Chandler Harris's *Uncle Remus: His Songs and His Sayings,* Uncle Remus is a wise old slave. He is full of dignity and affection for the young boy to whom he tells his stories, yet the tales, in which Br'er Fox perpetually seeks to devour Br'er Rabbit, suggest an unreliable universe.

RENZO *(Diminutive of* Lorenzo: *Italian, "from Laurentium")* see **LAWRENCE**

REUBEN *(Hebrew, "behold, a son")* Plucky, resourceful Jeanie Deans is the heroine of Sir Walter Scott's *The Heart of Midlothian* who walks from Scotland to London to plead the case of her unfairly imprisoned sister. Reuben Butler is a sober, intelligent, but extremely poor teacher who loves Jeanie but cannot afford to support her as his wife. Scott, as he so often does, uses Old Testament names to distinguish his Dissenting (i.e., non-Anglican) peasants from aristocrats with their saints' names, like the villain George Robertson.

RICHARD *(Old German, "ruler hard")* A name common enough in the English-speaking world to be almost neutral in literature, despite the examples of the heroic King Richard I (the Lion-Hearted) of England and his complex descendant King Richard III. In fact **Richard** is that rare thing, a name with no class connotations. In Thomas Hardy's *The Mayor of Casterbridge,* Richard Newson is the sailor who buys Susan Henchard from her husband Michael, and brings up her daughter as his own. Later in Hardy's oeuvre comes Richard Phillotson, the schoolmaster in *Jude the Obscure.* It is he who inspires Jude Fawley with scholarly ambitions, yet fails to act on his own aspirations. He is a tragic figure of frustration, particularly in his marriage to Jude's cousin Sue Bridehead. James Fenimore Cooper's *The Pioneers,* written in 1823, is set in eighteenth-century New York State. Richard Jones, also known as Dickon, is cousin and steward to the great landowner Marmaduke Temple. Finally, Richard Enfield is a minor character in Robert Louis Stevenson's *Dr. Jekyll and Mr. Hyde.* A young relative of Dr. Jekyll's attorney, he is a witness to some of Mr. Hyde's excesses.

One common nickname for **Richard** is **Dick,** used by Horatio Alger, Jr., in his classic "rags to riches" story, *Ragged Dick.* A teenage boy who sleeps in a box on the street, he is honest, hard-working, and cheerful. Given opportunity, he makes the most of himself.

RINALDO see **REGINALD**

ROBERT *(Old English, "renown bright")* As a standard English name, Robert shows up frequently in the literary canon and, like **Richard,** seems to cut across classes. Some more modest characters, like Robert Loveday in Thomas Hardy's *The Trumpet-Major,* are known as **Bob.** He is a naval man who comes home to his village laden with treats from abroad, including a parrot, a marmoset, and a camp follower to whom he is engaged. Bob Cratchit, in Dickens's *A Christmas Carol,* is Scrooge's endlessly forgiving clerk, loyal to his employer even when he is treated most cruelly.

And *The Pickwick Papers* includes Bob Sawyer, a young medical student on a spree that includes some rather wild behavior.

A more dignified Robert is the "bad" Ferrars brother in Jane Austen's *Sense and Sensibility*. He is a tremendous dandy who disapproves of his brother Edward's clumsy manners, and ends up marrying the conniving Lucy Steele. He actually answers rather well to Samuel Richardson's description of Robert Lovelace at the beginning of *Clarissa:* "A man of birth and fortune, haughty, vindictive, humorously vain, equally intrepid and indefatigable in the pursuit of his pleasures." The difference is that Lovelace is hellbent on seducing Clarissa, and eventually drugs and rapes her. Such violent behavior would never occur in an Austen novel. Robert Moore in Charlotte's Brontë's *Shirley* is another dominating male, but his province is the Yorkshire mills he owns. By mechanizing his operations he is displacing workers, but refuses to acknowledge his responsibility for the miseries of unemployment. Only his sister and the woman who secretly loves him perceive his more sensitive side.

Robert the Bruce, King Robert I of Scotland, reigned in the fourteenth century and delivered that country from English control. The name has consequently been popular in Scotland, and Robert Kennedy of Anthony Trollope's *Phineas Finn* is in some ways a quintessential Scot. He is the stern, dour, joyless, but wealthy politician who marries Lady Laura Standish. His compulsion to control her behavior drives her to leave him—a drastic act in 1866.

In earlier times the common nickname for Robert was **Robin,** the real name of Puck in *A Midsummer Night's Dream*. Dr. Faustus's servant, in Christopher Marlowe's *Dr. Faustus,* was a Robin; he is turned into an ape as his master meddles in magic. Robin of Locksley or Robin Hood existed in legend before Sir Walter Scott wrote him into *Ivanhoe,* but he may have been based on a true outlaw who lived in Sherwood Forest. Daniel Defoe's heroine Moll Flanders marries a Robin, though he only lives for five years. A name as old and as common as Robert naturally spun off variations like Robson, Hopkins, or **Robinson,** as in Defoe's *Robinson Crusoe*. The novel was written in 1715 but set in the

1650s, and the narrator Crusoe states that Robinson had been his mother's maiden name. His tone throughout the book is one of rueful wonder at his folly, yet his resourcefulness, his courage, his patience, and his discipline bring him triumphantly through his ordeal.

RODERICK (*Old German, "renown rule"*) Tobias Smollett's *Roderick Random* is a picaresque novel that recounts with great charm the incredible adventures of the eponymous hero/narrator. He is cheerful and determined, but above all he is a figure to whom things happen. The name has not been very widely used in the United States and literary examples suggest it has acquired an effete aura. Roderick Usher, the central character in Edgar Allan Poe's "The Fall of the House of Usher," is neurasthenic and absurdly sensitive. He dies of shock—and his house collapses—when he realizes that he buried his ailing sister Madeline before she had actually breathed her last. Horatio Alger Jr.'s Roderick Crawford, in *Ragged Dick,* doesn't exhibit that level of over-refinement, but he is mean, lazy, and a snob. (In Alger's books foppish names always betray the villain.) Henry James's novel *Roderick Hudson* deals with a talented young American sculptor who, once taken to Europe, runs right off the rails. Handsome and charming, Roderick proves to have insufficient discipline to establish his claim to be an artist.

In Italian or Spanish the name is, interchangeably, **Roderigo** or **Rodrigo**. Shakespeare uses the first form for the Venetian soldier in *Othello* who loves Desdemona and plots, with Iago, to woo her. Tobias Smollett's Roderick Random discovers a rich South American father named Don Rodrigo. And in Alessandro Manzoni's historical novel *The Betrothed,* Don Rodrigo is the rake who brags that he will seduce the modest virgin, Lucia. He is later felled by the plague, and repents his wicked ways.

RODION (*Russian from Greek, "from Rhodes"*) The island of Rhodes was originally named by the Greeks for the roses that grew there. Fyodor Dostoyevsky's choice of this name for his superman Raskolnikov in *Crime and Punishment* is opaque. His last name incorporates the Russian word *raskol*, which means "split" or "schism." This is perfectly appropriate for the arrogant killer who is also deeply empathic and emotional. Anton Chekhov's use of the name Rodion for a blacksmith in his short story "The New Villa" suggests that it is a name for the common man. Raskolnikov is also known by multiple diminutives: Rodya, Rodenka, Rodka. Possibly the discrepancy between the meaning of his name and his violent act suggests his profound self-doubt and alienation.

RODOLPHE *(French form of* Rudolph: *Old German, "renown wolf")* Emma Bovary's first seducer in Flaubert's novel is Rodolphe Boulanger, a coldhearted but alluring young bachelor. Accurately sizing up her ennui and her romantic longings, he wins her over without a struggle. Boredom soon takes over, however, and Rodolphe abandons Emma when she is on the verge of leaving her husband for him.

RODOMONTE *(Italian invented name)* In Ariosto's *Orlando Furioso,* Rodomonte is a fierce, arrogant Moorish king. He is descended from Nimrod (the "mighty hunter") and kills many Christians, but is frustrated in his attempt to destroy Paris. The name has been absorbed into the English language as a term for a braggart, and a "rodomontade" is a boastful rant.

> *"I have never known a truer or warmer heart than Roger's; and I have known him boy and man."*
> —ELIZABETH GASKELL, *WIVES AND DAUGHTERS*

ROGER *(Old German, "renown spear")* One of literature's most odious characters is Roger Chillingworth, the mysterious white-haired physician of Nathaniel Hawthorne's *The Scarlet Letter.* He is Hester Prynne's husband and a cruel manipulator. When he suspects the ailing minister Arthur Dimmesdale of fathering Hester's illegitimate child, he assumes Dimmesdale's medical care in the hope that the cleric will betray himself. Anthony Trollope uses Roger as the name of a reliable English country squire in *The Way We Live Now*. Roger Carbury is a classic Tory landowner, the diametric opposite of the shady financier Augustus Melmotte, whom Trollope clearly sees as the unattractive avatar of the future. Elizabeth Gaskell also creates a squire named Roger in *Wives and Daughters*. Roger Hamley ("of Hamley," he says proudly more than once) is "awkward and ungainly in society, and so kept out of it as much as possible; and he was obstinate, violent-tempered, and dictatorial in his own immediate circle. On the other hand, he was generous, and true as steel." He adores his wife and two sons, but favors the weak-willed elder drastically, ignoring the scientific talents and quiet merits of the younger, another Roger. Young Roger is cast into the shade by his elder brother Osborne, but heroine Molly clearly perceives his worth and falls in love with him.

The Italian version of the name is **Ruggiero**, closer to the Germanic **Rutger**. Ruggiero is a crucial character in Ariosto's *Orlando Furioso*. The pagan king of Reggio, he is a descendant of the mighty warrior Hector. He suffers terrible trouble, however, with women. Enchanted by the sorceress Alcina, distracted by the pagan Angelica, scolded by the enchantress Melissa, he is finally reunited with the warrior maiden Bradamante who persuades him to convert to Christianity. He kills Rodomonte and is elected to assume the crown of Bulgaria. The princes of Este (Ariosto's patrons) were supposedly descended from him.

> "*Give me my Romeo, and when he shall die,*
> *Take him and cut him out in little stars,*
> *And he will make the face of heaven so fine*
> *That all the world will be in love with night*
> *And pay no worship to the garish sun.*"
> —WILLIAM SHAKESPEARE, *ROMEO AND JULIET*

ROLAND see **ORLANDO**

ROMEO *(Italian, "from Rome")* This is inescapably the name of the young Veronese lover from Shakespeare's *Romeo and Juliet*. The character himself is a youth in love with love before he even sets eyes on Juliet. But he and his beloved speak some of the most glorious love poetry ever written.

Romeo's name descends from that of **Romulus,** one of the twin sons of Mars and a vestal virgin. They were thrown in the Tiber at birth, and nursed by a she-wolf after being washed ashore. Romulus later killed his brother **Remus** when they disagreed over where to locate Rome. It was Romulus who invited the neighboring Sabine tribe for a festival and carried off their women. Ovid recounts this story in *Metamorphoses*.

RUFUS *(Latin, "red")* In George Eliot's *Felix Holt: The Radical,* Rufus Lyon is a preacher and politician, honest, thoughtful, and passionate about Scripture. He is the adoptive father of Esther Lyon, the beautiful young woman who marries the radical Felix.

SAGRAMOR *(Latin invented name, "holy love")* Also **Sagramore**. In *A Connecticut Yankee in King Arthur's Court,* Mark Twain mocks the conventions both of class and of the Arthurian legend. The Yankee Hank Morgan accidentally offends Sir Sagramor le Desirous (a character from Sir Thomas Malory's *Le Morte D'Arthur*). To satisfy the demands of honor, Morgan must meet the knight in a joust, but before he can do this, he must go on a quest.

ST. JOHN *(sin' jun; saint's name)* Readers tend to remember *Jane Eyre* as the tale of the governess and the compelling Mr. Rochester, but Jane has another suitor, her cousin St. John Rivers. A young and handsome clergyman, he courts her because he believes she would make a good wife for a missionary. Charlotte Brontë always describes him in terms of coldness, and it is no wonder that Jane prefers even her memories of the passionate Rochester to the priggish reality of Rivers.

SAMPSON *(Hebrew, "sun")* Also **Samson**. Despite appearances, not related to **Samuel** in the way a name like **Robinson** is related to **Robert**. In the second part of *Don Quixote,* which Cervantes published ten years after the first section, Sampson is a student who, having read Part I, wants to "cure" Don Quixote of his mania. It becomes apparent that, as "The Knight of the Mirrors" and "The Knight of the Full Moon," he enjoys "chivalry" as much as Don Quixote himself.

SAMUEL *(Hebrew, "told of God")* The second half of John Bunyan's *The Pilgrim's Progress* was published in 1684, after the great success of Part I. In it, Christian's wife Christiana follows him to the Celestial City with their children. Their third son is named Samuel, undoubtedly after the Old Testament judge and prophet. The name was still in robust circulation in the nineteenth century, especially in the professional classes. Samuel Pickwick, the founder of the Pickwick Club, is the guiding sensibility of *The Pickwick Papers*. Kindly, warmhearted, and naive, he is constantly stumbling into adventures. His valet, Sam Weller, provides him with some of the worldly wisdom he spectacularly lacks.

Anthony Trollope uses the name for two different characters. One, the Reverend Samuel Prong, is one of his semicomic clergymen. An "energetic, severe, hard-working, and I fear, intolerant young man," he appears in *Rachel Ray*. Samuel Camperdown is the Eustace family lawyer in *The Eustace Diamonds*. He is, in his way, as respectable and hardworking as Samuel Prong, but less obnoxious. Comedy results from the conflict between the charming, manipulative, and amoral Lizzie Eustace and the severe legal rectitude of Mr. Camperdown.

SANCHO *(Spanish from Latin, "holy")* In *Don Quixote*, Sancho Panza is Don Quixote's peasant sidekick. Though much more firmly rooted in reality than his master, he nevertheless gets caught up in every adventure and somehow collects even more physical punishment than the deluded Don. His name is a joke, since "panza" is Spanish slang for "belly."

SANDY see **ALEXANDER**

SASHA see **ALEXANDER**

SAVINIEN *(sah* vee nee yeh'; *French, meaning unknown)* In Honoré de Balzac's *Ursule Mirouet*, Savinien de Portenduère is the aristocratic young neighbor of the rich provincial maiden Ursule. Ursule's father is merely a country doctor, while Madame de Portenduère is a Breton aristocrat of ancient family. She regards the Mirouets as beneath her, but accepts their financial help when Savinien runs through her money and is jailed for debt.

SAVVA *(Russian from Arabic, "captive" or "slave")* Saint Sava was a twelfth-century bishop, and the patron saint of the Serbs, revered in both Eastern and Western Rite churches. In Chekhov's short story "Agafya," Savva Stukach is a tall, handsome ne'er-do-well who lives hand-to-mouth outside a village. He survives on the gifts and food that women bring to him. The story concerns his casual affair with the young wife of a signalman on the railroad.

SCAPIN *(ska pah'; French invented name)* Scapino is a traditional character in Italian comedy who reaches an apotheosis in Molière's *That Scoundrel Scapin*. A calculating rascal who serves Léandre as valet, Scapin stage-manages a complicated romantic imbroglio with entertaining chicanery. His sheer nerve (along with the success of his schemes) procures forgiveness from his master when his outrages are revealed.

SCYTHROP *(Greek, "gloomy countenance")* Thomas Love Peacock's *Nightmare Abbey* is a satiric novel that mocks the romantic passion for misery. Young Scythrop Glowry is modeled after the poet Shelley. The plot of the novel turns largely on finding the appropriately mournful wife for Scythrop.

> *This only son and heir Mr. Glowry had christened Scythrop, from the name of a maternal ancestor, who had hanged himself one rainy day in a fit of* toedium vitae . . . ; *on which account, Mr. Glowry held his memory in high honour, and made a punchbowl of his skull.*
> —THOMAS LOVE PEACOCK, *NIGHTMARE ABBEY*

SEBASTIAN *(Latin, "from Sebastia")* Saint Sebastian is one of the earliest of the Christian martyrs and a favorite subject of Renaissance painters, for his martyrdom consisted of being shot to death by arrows. This permitted artists an unimpeachable excuse to portray the human body. In Shakespeare's *Twelfth Night*, Sebastian is the handsome twin brother of the shipwrecked Viola. It could be said that he is pierced by love's arrows but in fact, he does the piercing. Olivia whisks him off to marry him virtually on sight.

SELAH *(Hebrew, meaning unknown)* "Selah" is an interjection that appears often in the Psalms. Scholars conjecture that it was an expression like "Amen" or "Hallelujah," or possibly a musical directive to temple musicians. It was adopted occasionally as a name in the Puritan quest for freedom from the taint of Rome, but it never became commonplace. When Henry James uses it in *The Bostonians* for the charlatan father of Verena Tarrant, it evokes the ardor of the true believer. Selah Tarrant, however, is no conventional churchman but a "mesmerist." James has only the harshest words for Tarrant: "He was false, cunning, vulgar, ignoble; the cheapest kind of human product."

SELIM *(Arabic, "to be safe")* Lord Byron's stock in trade was his experience in exotic corners of the world, which he combined with remarkable poetic skills and, occasionally, scandalous content. "The Bride of Abydos" is a narrative involving Zuleika, the fair young daughter of a pasha who has fallen in love with the wrong man, her "brother" Selim. He is in fact her cousin, and being proud, brave, and handsome, he is worthy of Zuleika's love, but he is nevertheless killed by her father's soldiers.

> *"Oh, Selim dear! Oh more than dearest!*
> *Say is it me thou hat'st or fearest?"*
> —LORD BYRON, "THE BRIDE OF ABYDOS"

SEPTIMUS *(Latin, "seventh")* A name used occasionally in the Victorian era of large families. There is something very fishy about the moneylender Septimus Luker in Wilkie Collins's *The Moonstone*. Fat, flamboyant, probably unscrupulous, he is a focus for the reader's suspicions in this novel of sensation. One dissonance that adds to the reader's unease is that Luker, like most

Victorian moneylenders, is probably Jewish, yet the Latinate name suggests a classically educated father. Is his first name assumed? If so, why? Is he otherwise trustworthy? In contrast, the clergyman Septimus Harding, who first appears in Anthony Trollope's *The Warden,* is clearly a man whose word is gold. Kindly, mild-mannered, unworldly, he resigns his tenure as warden of a charity home when he is criticized in the press for holding a sinecure. He appears throughout the Barchester novels, and though clearly saintly, is never sanctimonious. His son-in-law sums up his appeal just before his death by saying, "He couldn't go wrong. He lacked guile, and he feared God."

> *On the whole Sergey had great success with women. They loved his height, his powerful build, his strong features, his idleness and his tribulations.*
> —ANTON CHEKHOV, "WITH FRIENDS"

SERGEY (sair gay'; *Russian from Latin, "servant"*) A Roman martyr and an early pope were named **Sergius,** and Continental versions of the name include **Serge** and **Sergio,** but it is most common in Russia, where Saint Sergius of Radonezh, a fourteenth-century abbot, is popularly revered. It is sometimes spelled **Sergei.** In Chekhov's short story "With Friends," Sergey Losev is the husband of Tatyana, the narrator Podgorin's old friend. The action concerns a visit to Tatyana and Sergey's estate, in the course of which various "friends" badger Podgorin for financial advice and outright loans. Sergey, who has run his wife's estate into insolvency, is one of the worst offenders, though his greed is masked by attempted charm. Nikolai Leskov's "Lady Macbeth of Mtsensk" portrays a strong-willed woman who betrays her marriage vows for a passionate affair with her husband's clerk, Sergey. He is a classic rake, handsome, bold, a habitual seducer, who drops Katerina ("Lady Macbeth") when she begins to bore him.

SETH *(Hebrew, "appointed")* In the Old Testament, Seth is Adam and Eve's third son, after Cain and Abel. Charles Dickens uses the name for Mr. Pecksniff, a comically grasping hypocrite in *Martin Chuzzlewit*. He is kin to the dying Chuzzlewit, and hopes, by judicious display of emotion, to secure some of the Chuzzlewit fortune. When a Victorian mocks Victorian sentimentality, the oratory is truly outrageous.

SEXTUS *(Latin, "sixth")* The name of the seventh pope of the Christian church. Also **Sixtus**. Sixtus the Second was canonized as an early martyr. Anthony Trollope's Sextus Parker probably has less to do with these churchmen than with Trollope's earlier creation, Quintus Slide, the newspaperman in *Phineas Finn*. Sextus Parker is a man from the same modest walk of life as Slide, but he is portrayed in *The Prime Minister* as the unwitting dupe of the slimy foreign "financier" Ferdinand Lopez. In Honoré de Balzac's *Lost Illusions*, Sixte Chatelet begins as an elderly social climber with a government position. He is better equipped than the hero, though, for the cutthroat social competition of Paris. Lucien ends up discredited and Sixte de Chatelet ends up a count.

SGANARELLE *(French invented name)* A favorite name of Molière's, used for a variety of characters. In *Love's the Best Doctor*, Sganarelle is a tradesman, father of the desirable Lucinde. He is a bully and a boor, but roundly deceived by his daughter and servants. Molière's *Don Juan* is a purely comical piece, and Sganarelle plays that staple character, the valet who is smarter than his master. *A Doctor in Spite of Himself* features a woodcutter Sganarelle who, through simple common sense, manages to "cure" his patients, while spouting ersatz Latin and extorting money from every possible source.

SHAHRIYAR (shah ree' yahr; *Arabic, "famous, well-known"*) The sultan to whom the *Tales from the Thousand and One Nights* were told. Because he believed that no woman could be faithful, he insisted on marrying a virgin each evening, sleeping with her, and having her executed in the morning. Shahrazad put an end to this practice by telling him a story each night and breaking it off just before sunrise. He let her live to tell the end of the story—for a thousand and one nights. At that point he proclaimed her the liberator of her sex, and revoked his harsh decree.

SHYLOCK *(Origin unclear)* One of Shakespeare's most memorable characters, Shylock is the moneylender in *The Merchant of Venice*. He is a Jew in a Christian society, always on the outside, and Shakespeare makes much of this. The characterization is often seen as anti-Semitic, yet Shylock also delivers the heartrending speech that begins, "I am a Jew. Hath not a Jew eyes? Hath not a Jew hands, organs, dimensions, senses, affections, passions? . . . If you prick us, do we not bleed?"

SIDNEY *(French, "from St. Denis")* Tom Sawyer's odious half brother (in Mark Twain's *Tom Sawyer*) is called, simply, **Sid,** and he serves as dramatic foil for Tom. Clean, obedient, and self-righteous, he never misses an opportunity to undermine Tom in Aunt Polly's eyes. **Sid** is short for **Sidney** or **Sydney,** the spelling used for the antihero of Dickens's *A Tale of Two Cities*. He is a dissolute but brilliant lawyer who notices, during Charles Darnay's trial for spying, that he is Darnay's physical double. Like Darnay, he falls in love with Lucie Manette, but she finds his penchant for self-destruction alarming. The reader is likely to find Sydney Carton the more romantic of Lucie's two suitors, especially when he utters his final words: "It is a far, far better thing that I do, than I have ever done. . . ."

SIEGFRIED *(Old German, "victory peace")* Sometimes spelled **Sigfried.** Wagner's famous "Ring Cycle" of operas was based loosely on a set of German myths collected in *The Nibelungenlied,* written around 1200 A.D. Siegfried is a wild, impetuous warrior, a dragon slayer who has magical powers, including a cape that renders him invisible. Having bathed in dragon's blood, he is invincible except in one spot (like Achilles). He marries the beautiful Kriemhild of Burgundy, and helps her brother Gunther woo Brunhild of Iceland.

SILAS *(From Latin* Silvanus, *"woodsman")* In many of Dickens's novels readers meet memorable minor characters with biblical first names and marked peculiarities. Silas Wegg of *Our Mutual Friend* is a classic example of the type. A one-legged keeper of a fruit stand, he is hired by Noddy Boffin to read aloud *The Decline and Fall of the Roman Empire,* a task that is utterly beyond him. The far more famous Silas of English literature is George Eliot's Silas Marner. The novel was unusual for its time in focusing on a simple, modest character. Marner is a weaver who lives alone outside an English village. He is shunned by the villagers, having been accused of theft. Ugly, prone to fits, a victim of circumstance, he is ultimately redeemed by his love for an orphan girl. William Dean Howells's *The Rise of Silas Lapham* tells the story of a nouveau riche paint manufacturer from Vermont trying to establish himself in Boston society at the turn of the century. Brash and naive, he gets involved in shady business deals and offends the Boston Brahmins he wants so badly to impress. He finally retreats to Vermont, chastened by his experience.

Silas, as a biblical name, was revived by the Puritans and kept alive in "dissenting" or non-Anglican families. Though other forms of the name—like **Silvester, Sylvester, Silvanus,** or **Silvius**—were almost obsolete by the nineteenth century, they had occurred in earlier literature. In Molière's *That Scoundrel Scapin,* Silvester is Scapin's sidekick, the valet to one of the romantic young men, Octavio. Shakespeare, naturally enough, uses the name for a rustic swain in his pastoral comedy *As You Like It.* Silvius lives in the Forest of Arden and is preoccupied with courting Phebe (the name of a bird), thus permitting Shakespeare to mock the convention of "rustic" romances featuring shepherds and shepherdesses who speak in polished iambic pentameter.

SIMON *(Hebrew, "listening carefully")* Saint Peter, one of the twelve disciples, was originally called Simon until Jesus gave him his new Greek name to signify Peter's fundamental importance to Christianity. The evil plantation overseer in Harriet Beecher Stowe's *Uncle Tom's Cabin* is so memorable that a hard-driving taskmaster is still sometimes known as a "Simon Legree." His

slaves are desperately overworked and he effectively beats Uncle
Tom to death. Some scholars speculate that he may even represent
the Devil. Less one-dimensional yet still sinister is Simon Rosedale
in Edith Wharton's *The House of Mirth*. A nouveau riche aspirant
to the highest levels of New York society, Rosedale is crafty, controlled, and irresistible in his social climbing. Yet Lily Bart, in one
of her finer moments, finds the humanity in him.

SINDBAD *(Arabic, "city on the river")* Also **Sinbad.** In the *Tales
from the Thousand and One Nights,* Sindbad is a merchant who
has acquired wealth on his seven extremely eventful sea voyages.
On the first trip, for instance, he visits what he thinks is an island,
lights a fire, and is submerged when what is actually a whale dives
under the water. He also encounters the Cyclops, visits the Valley
of Diamonds, and sets foot on the mountain where Adam landed
once he was expelled from Eden.

SOLOMON *(Hebrew, "peaceful")* The biblical king of great wisdom. Dickens uses the name for a French spy in *A Tale of Two
Cities*. We know him for most of the novel as John Barsad; when
he suddenly turns out to be Solomon Pross, wayward brother of
the redoubtable Miss Pross, he is effectively diminished and do-
mesticated.

SPENCER *(Middle English, "provisioner, dispenser of food")*
The protagonist of Henry James's short story "The Jolly Corner"
is Spencer Brydon, an American bachelor of fifty-six who has
come home to his house on a "jolly corner" in New York after
thirty years in Europe. The neglected house, in an elusive way,
seems to be haunted, as does its owner, by neglect and lost opportunities.

STARBUCK *(Invented name)* In Herman Melville's *Moby-Dick*,
Starbuck is the hardworking, reliable first mate who provides
emotional ballast for crazy Captain Ahab. Melville describes him
as a "staid, steadfast man, whose life for the most part was a
telling pantomime of action, and not a tame chapter of sounds."

STEPHEN *(Greek, "crowned")* Also **Steven, Stefan.** Saint Stephen, in the lore of hagiography, was the first Christian martyr, stoned to death for his faith. Charles Dickens does not always concern himself with the connotations of his characters' names, but Stephen Blackpool in *Hard Times* clearly evokes the martyr. A weaver in a Coketown textile mill, he is married to an alcoholic. Refusing on principle to take sides in a union dispute, he is shunned by his coworkers and abused by the mill owner. George Eliot's Stephen Guest, in *The Mill on the Floss,* is a much less pathetic case. He is the handsome, rich son of the man who buys the Tulliver mill after Maggie's father's financial troubles. He woos Maggie, who is clearly attracted to him sexually, and carelessly allows her reputation to be compromised when the two are benighted on a long boat ride. Thomas Hardy's Stephen Smith, in *A Pair of Blue Eyes,* may be compared in some ways with the author himself. The architect son of a stonemason, he is an autodidact who moves uneasily in a higher level of society than the one he was born to.

In French, the name is **Étienne** *(ay tyen'),* as in Étienne Lousteau, the young journalist of Balzac's *Lost Illusions.* He serves as both guide and object lesson to Lucien Chardon when the latter first arrives in Paris. He introduces Lucien to the financial rewards of journalism and the pleasures provided by young actresses—yet at the same time, he despairs at his own moral compromises and warns Lucien against them. The Russian form of **Stephen** is **Stepan,** and Stepan Oblonsky in Tolstoy's *Anna Karenina* is another pleasure lover like Lousteau. Charming, sentimental, undisciplined, Oblonsky (often known by his nickname, Stiva) is an irresponsible spendthrift who cannot be faithful to his wife. His infidelities, which are condoned by society, highlight the double standard that condemns Anna for hers.

SVENGALI *(Invented name)* George du Maurier's 1894 novel *Trilby* was an immense commercial success. The character of Svengali teaches the young Trilby O'Ferrall to sing under hypnosis. Du Maurier's portrait of the musician is deeply anti-Semitic, but the plot is memorable, and since the book's publication

"Svengali" has become someone who remakes another person's image or character.

> *Svengali playing Chopin on the pianoforte . . . was as one of the heavenly host . . . Svengali walking up and down the earth seeking whom he might cheat, betray, exploit . . . was about as bad as they make 'em.*
>
> —GEORGE DU MAURIER, *TRILBY*

TALUS *(Latin, "man of iron")* Edmund Spenser's allegorical epic *The Faerie Queen* involves dozens of characters whose qualities are indicated by their names. Talus is, quite simply, a strongman, a groom of the queen Gloriana (standing in for Elizabeth I). In Book Five he is dispatched as sidekick to the knight Artegall, whom he aids in various acts of righteous violence.

TARTUFFE *(French invented name)* In Molière's play *Tartuffe,* the eponymous hero is a remarkable hypocrite. A religious conservative, he has attracted the attention and admiration of the credulous and wealthy Orgon. Espousing austerity for religious reasons, he is a glutton and a lecher when he thinks no one is looking. The term *tartufe* is still current in French, and means a "sanctimonious hypocrite."

TELEMACHUS *(Greek, meaning unknown)* Telemachus is the son of Odysseus and Penelope. *The Odyssey* finds him a young man, trying to establish his identity. The story of Telemachus's search for his wandering father and his attempts to get rid of his mother's unwanted suitors is parallel to the story of Odysseus's long voyage home from Troy.

TEREUS *(Greek, meaning unknown)* Ovid's *Metamorphoses* was well known in Europe, and authors from Boccaccio to Geoffrey Chaucer drew on it for their work. Chaucer included the tale of Procne and Philomela in "The Legend of Good Women," a portion of his *Love Visions.* Tereus is the king of Thrace, married to the Athenian princess Procne. He goes to Athens to escort her sister Philomela back to Thrace for a visit, but is so taken by Philomela that he rapes her, cuts out her tongue, and installs her in a castle as his sex slave. Philomela, unable to betray Tereus verbally, weaves a tapestry telling her sister of his deeds. In revenge, Procne kills their son, cooks him, and feeds him to Tereus. Procne, Philomena, and Tereus are all turned into birds at the end.

TERTIUS *(Latin, "third")* The Latin numbering names were not usually used until a fifth or sixth child was born; usually for a third, parents could still find friends or relatives to flatter. In George Eliot's *Middlemarch*, Tertius Lydgate is the idealistic doctor who hopes to reform medical care in Middlemarch. His disastrous marriage to the selfish, expensive Rosamond Vincy draws him into debt and disrepute. Like the heroine Dorothea, Lydgate has to face a pragmatic diminution of his youthful dreams.

THADY (tay' dee; *Irish variant of* Thaddeus: *Aramaic, meaning unknown)* The full name is usually spelled **Thaddeus** or **Thaddeaus**. It was sometimes used in Ireland as an anglicization of an old Gaelic name that meant "poet." Thaddeus was one of the Apostles. In Maria Edgeworth's *Castle Rackrent*, Thady Quick is the unreliable narrator of the Rackrent family saga. He is their steward and they are his prey in various schemes of extortion. One Rackrent baronet is more reprehensible than the next, and Quirk's nominal loyalty to them depends on how lavishly he expects to line his pockets.

THEMISTOCLIUS *(Invented name)* In Nikolai Gogol's *Dead Souls*, the protagonist Chichikov visits a series of estates hoping to buy the names of dead serfs from their owners. At the Manilov estate he is sizing up the lazy and intellectually pretentious owner when he meets the Manilov sons, one of whom is named Themistoclius. "Chichikov raised an eyebrow when he heard this Greek-sounding name, to which, for some mysterious reason, Manilov had given an *ius* [i.e., a Latinate] ending."

THEOBALD (*Old German, "people brave"*) An archaic name, unusual in anglophone countries. Samuel Butler's 1903 novel *The Way of All Flesh* features a portrait of a stern, violent, angry clergyman, Theobald Pontifex. He is the father of the protagonist, and some scholars believe his character is based on that of Butler's own father. In addition to sounding stiff and formal (and thus distancing the reader from the character), the name **Theobald** fits in with the Victorian enthusiasm for antique-sounding names. Variants like **Tybalt, Thibault,** and **Thibaut** occurred in Continental Europe as well. In Molière's *The Doctor in Spite of Himself,* Thibaut is a peasant who confidently approaches the "doctor" Sganarelle seeking a cure for his wife's dropsy. In Shakespeare's *Romeo and Juliet,* Tybalt is the hothead cousin of Juliet who is desperately eager to pick a fight with the Montagues, and with Romeo in particular. Romeo shows great restraint until Tybalt kills his friend Mercutio, at which point Romeo retaliates—lethally.

THEODORE (*Greek, "gift of God"*) Charles Brockden Brown was one of the earliest novelists in America. His gothic *Wieland* explores the boundary between sanity and madness as Theodore Wieland, a prosperous American landowner, comes under the influence of the mysterious Francis Carwin. Carwin, with his ventriloquist's ability, uses different voices to meddle with the Wielands' emotional lives. Ultimately Wieland kills his wife and four children. A much more engaging Theodore is the charming boyish Theodore Laurence, the "boy next door" to the March girls in Louisa May Alcott's *Little Women.* A wealthy orphan nicknamed both **"Teddy"** and "Laurie," he flirts with a life of idleness after being refused by Jo but returns to the straight and narrow path of hard work and virtue under Amy March's loving influence.

The calendar of saints includes several Theodores who were important in the Eastern Rite church, so **Fyodor** is a common Russian name. In Ivan Turgenev's *Home of the Gentry,* Fyodor Lavretsky is a well-meaning middle-aged man whose mercurial but alluring wife has left him. He visits a cousin's estate and falls in love with her young daughter. He is outmaneuvered by his wife, who returns to him demanding money, and dazzles the Kalitin family. If Fyodor Lavretsky is well-meaning and ineffectual, Fyodor Karamazov is his polar opposite. A drunkard, a womanizer, cynical and depraved, he thinks only of his own pleasures and treats those around him—including his four sons—with cruelty. Interestingly, this odious character bears the name of *The Brothers Karamazov*'s author, Fyodor Dostoyevsky.

THEOPHILUS *(Greek, "loving God")* Anthony Trollope indulged in a bit of irony when he named his archdeacon of Barchester Theophilus Grantly. In *The Warden,* the reader sees him as proud, efficient, always conscious of his dignity, a model administrator but somewhat lacking in human warmth. Trollope says, "He is always the archdeacon; unlike Homer, he never nods." By the writing of *The Last Chronicle of Barset,* Trollope has deepened this portrait so that Grantly's fundamental warmth, honesty, and faith emerge.

THERON *(Possibly Greek, meaning unknown)* Harold Frederic's *The Damnation of Theron Ware* is a late-nineteenth-century exposé of religion's role in small-town America. An ambitious Methodist minister, Theron Ware becomes virtually unhinged upon exposure to the aesthetic delights of the Catholic church, and to the broadminded sensual outlook of the cultured Celia Madden.

THESEUS *(Greek mythology name)* A towering figure in Greek myth who appears in later literary works as well, notably *The Canterbury Tales* and *A Midsummer Night's Dream.* Theseus is an Attic hero, the son of King Aegeus of Athens. One of his most famous deeds is the slaying of the Minotaur, which he accomplishes with the help of the Cretan princess Ariadne. But Theseus is interesting to writers not merely for his feats of strength and strategy. His emotional entanglements have fascinated dramatists as diverse as Euripides and Racine. He rescues Ariadne from Crete, but on his way home to Athens decides that he prefers her sister Phaedra, so he abandons Ariadne on the island of Naxos. (This is Chaucer's version in "The Legend of Good Women.") He also marries the Amazonian queen Hippolyta and has a son by her. The chronology of the various tales is confusing, but he does end up wed to Phaedra, whose infatuation with her stepson Hippolytus—and Theseus's reaction to it—forms the basis for Racine's *Phaedra*. In Shakespeare's *A Midsummer Night's Dream*, Theseus is simply the duke of Athens, about to marry the Amazonian Queen Hippolyta, and tragedy is in the distant future.

> *A gracious knight was Theseus to behold,*
> *And young, being only twenty-three years old,*
> *Yes, anyone who'd seen his face would weep*
> *In pity for the oath he'd sworn to keep.*
> —GEOFFREY CHAUCER, "THE LEGEND OF GOOD WOMEN"

THOMAS *(Aramaic, "twin")* Also **Tomas, Tom, Tommy.** A very common name throughout Europe, and one that changes form very little from country to country. Part of its significance comes from the story of Saint Thomas, who refuses to believe in Jesus' resurrection until he can see and touch Christ (hence the term "a doubting Thomas"). Jane Austen, whose male characters bear generally mundane names, used Thomas for the wealthy owner of Mansfield Park, Sir Thomas Bertram. Both he and his son Thomas are worldly and fashionable, and the modest Fanny Price is ill at ease in their company. Charles Dickens seems to be drawing on the example of Thomas the skeptic with another father and son, the Thomas Gradgrinds of *Hard Times*. Thomas the father believes in a strictly utilitarian universe and brings up his children with the most pragmatic education imaginable. Son Thomas, predictably enough, ends up on the wrong side of the law. Another, comical Dickens character is Thomas (usually known as Tommy) Traddles, David Copperfield's sidekick. David patronizes him, but Traddles is a dependable, hardworking friend. Anthony Trollope had a much-loved brother named Thomas, so it is no surprise that he should use the name in his novels. A comical example is Thomas Spooner, Esquire, the owner of Spoon Hall, who falls in love with Adelaide Palliser on the hunting field in *Phineas Redux*. Adelaide sees him as an elderly, vulgar man with a red nose, but he cannot comprehend why she should prefer the feckless, penniless Gerard Maule to him and his tidy acres. In *Doctor Thorne,* Trollope creates a rounded portrait of Thomas Thorne, the doctor of the title. Connected to the Barsetshire gentry, he is a modest but highly skilled rural medical man who deplores pretension wherever he finds it. He is clever, cultivated, and wise, especially in his dealings with the hypochondriac Lady Arabella Gresham. In *Framley Parsonage,* he marries the wealthy spinster Martha Dunstable.

Mark Twain used the name several times. In *The Prince and the Pauper,* Tom Canty is the young London boy who trades places with the youthful king Edward VI in sixteenth-century London. Another Thomas is involved in a swap in *Pudd'nhead Wilson*. The slave Roxana, one-sixteenth black, substitutes her son Valet de Chambre for her master's son Thomas à Becket Driscoll. The substitute Thomas is a nasty character, spoiled, selfish, and vicious. (After being freed, Roxana sells herself back into slavery to redeem his debts but he, ultimately, is sold down the river as punishment for a murder.) Mark Twain's famous Thomas, of course, is Tom Sawyer. *The Adventures of Tom Sawyer* presents a portrait of the quintessential American boy: plucky, curious, imaginative, and good-hearted. Tom is twelve or thirteen at the time of his adventures, an orphan being raised by his aunt. He is a charismatic leader who can manipulate his friends with almost uncanny adeptness.

Thomas is an unusual name in France, and especially unusual in the works of Molière, in which the characters usually have names that suit the baroque dramatic convention. The characters in *The Imaginary Invalid* include Argan, Béline, Angélique, Cléante . . . and Thomas Diafoirus. He is one of Molière's funniest creations, a pompous apothecary's nephew whom the hypochondriac Argan wishes his daughter Angélique to marry so that he can have lifelong free medical care. Thomas's idea of courtship is inviting Angélique to witness the dissection of a female corpse. In Ibsen's *A Public Enemy*, the title character is Thomas Stockmann. A genuinely skilled doctor (unlike Molière's Thomas), he has discovered that the public baths, the foundation of his town's prosperity, are making its citizens ill. He advocates closing down the baths and repairing the pipes at a great cost to the town—a position that makes him deeply unpopular with the community.

Sometimes characters are known by diminutives to signify affection, but often in works written before the nineteenth century, the diminutive indicates low social standing. When Edgar, in *King Lear*, is betrayed by his illegitimate brother, he goes out onto the "blasted heath" as simple Tom of Bedlam, impersonating a poor madman. Similarly Tom Jones, purportedly the son of a maid and given the same first name as Squire Allworthy, is always known merely as "Tom" in Henry Fielding's eponymous novel. "Even at his first appearance, it was the universal opinion of all Mr. Allworthy's family, that he was certainly born to be hanged," Fielding says of his hero. Certainly Tom Jones never behaves with the dignity that would make him "Thomas" to affectionate readers. American slaves, of course, took the names their masters gave them, and had no last names. Thus Uncle Tom, of Harriet Beecher Stowe's *Uncle Tom's Cabin*, is simply "Tom" to everyone. He is a Christlike figure in Stowe's book—dignified, warmhearted, capable, and even heroic. He saves Eva St. Clare's life and sacrifices his own when two slaves escape from Simon Legree's plantation.

By the time George Eliot wrote *The Mill on the Floss*, psychological intimacy was more of a feature of fiction. Tom Tulliver is virtually family to the reader. He is the older brother of the clever Maggie, not as intelligent as she but educated according to his father's ambitions for him. Maggie is always loyal to Tom, even when he disapproves of her, and she loses her life trying to save his. The narrator of Herman Melville's *Typee* is also a Tom, but the natives of the South Sea island where he is stranded cannot pronounce "Tom" so they call him **Tommo**. He lolls around for four months enjoying the indolence and sensuality of his native hosts. Though Tom, the narrator, is a romantic wanderer, his alter ego Tommo is a complete hedonist lost in the pleasure of the moment.

> *Tom swept his brush daintily back and forth—stepped back to note the effect—added a touch here and there—criticized the effect again—Ben watching every move and getting more and more interested, more and more absorbed. Presently he said:*
> *"Say, Tom, let me whitewash a little."*
> —MARK TWAIN, *THE ADVENTURES OF TOM SAWYER*

THURSTAN *(English, "Thor's stone")* Also occurs as **Thurston**. In Elizabeth Gaskell's *Ruth,* Thurstan Benson is the Unitarian minister who meets Ruth in Wales and takes her under his wing after she has been abandoned by her seducer. He is "long past middle life, and of the stature of a dwarf"—desexualizing characteristics that probably make him more trustworthy in Ruth's eyes. He is also quite saintly, and risks his reputation and livelihood in order to shelter this wronged girl and her child.

> *"Thurstan was called by his name because my father wished it; for, although he was what people called a radical and a democrat in his ways of talking and thinking, he was very proud in his heart of being descended from some old Sir Thurstan, who figured away in the French wars."*
> —ELIZABETH GASKELL, *RUTH*

TIMOTHY *(Greek, "fearing God")* A very early Timothy corresponded with Saint Paul, so two of the New Testament epistles are named for him. Trollope uses the name comically for one of his minor political characters in the Palliser novels. Sir Timothy Beeswax's name is redolent of stuffy offices, dust, and Victorian stationery. He is a conservative whose great moment comes when he serves in Plantagenet Palliser's coalition government. Far more famous is young Timothy Cratchit, the crippled son of Scrooge's clerk Bob Cratchit in *A Christmas Carol*. Uncomplaining despite his constant pain, he is known to his family as "Tiny Tim." Dickens cranks up the interest in Tim by having the Spirit of Christmas Present tell Scrooge that he sees in the future "a vacant seat in the poor chimney-corner, and a crutch without an owner, carefully preserved." It is the dawning of concern for others in Scrooge's hard heart.

> *"God bless us every one!" said Tiny Tim, the last of all.*
> —CHARLES DICKENS, *A CHRISTMAS CAROL*

TIRESIAS *(Greek mythology name)* A Theban prophet who appears in the Oedipus cycle of myths. Having seen Athena naked, he was blinded, but given second sight as a consolation prize. He delivers his predictions in a whisper. It is he who acquaints Oedipus with his own identity, as a result of which Jocasta commits suicide and Oedipus blinds himself. In Sophocles' *Antigone*, Tiresias warns Creon not to bury Antigone alive, but Antigone and Creon's son Haemon have already committed suicide.

TITO *(Italian from Greek, possibly meaning "honor")* Tito Melema is the handsome scholarly young Greek who enchants both Romola and her father in George Eliot's historical novel *Romola*. Unfortunately, though Tito is handsome and ambitious and well-educated, he is also lazy and unprincipled. His marriage with Romola does not prevent him from starting another family with an innocent peasant woman. The Latin form of the name is **Titus,** as in Shakespeare's *Titus Andronicus,* a shockingly violent tragedy. The title character is a Roman warrior who has successfully subdued the Goths, and returns home with their queen and her three sons as captives. In the sequence of revenge killings and brutality that follows, Titus is responsible for dispatching five characters, including two whose bodies he serves in a pie to their mother.

TOBY *(Hebrew, "the Lord is good")* Also **Tobias.** In *Twelfth Night*, Shakespeare crafts a priceless portrait of the drunken English roué. Sir Toby Belch is the uncle of the countess Olivia. Perpetually focused on his own interests, he meddles in his niece's love life in hopes of securing a comfortable future for himself. He is thwarted and discredited, of course. In Laurence Sterne's *The Life and Opinions of Tristram Shandy*, Tristram also has a comical Uncle Toby, but he is a different stamp of man. All but inarticulate, he expresses himself by whistling or emitting bursts of military jargon. His principal occupation is playing with toy soldiers.

In Dante's *Paradiso* we meet the linguistic ancestor of these two men in **Tobit.** The subject of an apocryphal book of the Bible, Tobit is a virtuous Jew living in the Babylonian city of Nineveh. Having gone blind, he sends his son Tobias to collect a debt. Tobias encounters the angel Raphael who helps him catch a fish in the Tigris River. The gall of the fish restores his father's sight.

TORRE *(Italian, "tower")* One of the most obscure of the Arthurian knights, Sir Torre was nevertheless the first to be invited to the Round Table. He is the son of King Pellinore by a milkmaid.

TORVALD *(Old Norse, "Thor's rule")* The egotistical, conservative banker husband of Nora Helmer in Ibsen's *A Doll's House.* In the Helmer household, his rule might as well be that of Thor, Norse god of thunder. Torvald expects his wife Nora to reflect him and his wishes in every way—to be, in effect, his doll.

TOUCHSTONE *(Invented name)* Originally a touchstone was a black stone that was used to test the purity of gold or silver; genuine metals, when rubbed against the touchstone, left streaks on it. The literal meaning was expanded to the metaphorical, so that a touchstone became any criterion that determined quality. In *As You Like It*, Shakespeare makes it the name of one of the denizens of the Forest of Arden. Touchstone sees through everyone's pretensions and reveals their true character.

TRACY (*Old French place-name*) Tracy Tupman, of Dickens's *The Pickwick Papers*, bears what was still, in the 1830s, a man's name. He is a middle-aged "beau," avid in pursuing women. But because they fail to respond, he ends up consoling himself with food instead.

TRISTRAM (*Meaning unknown, but the French word* triste *means "sad"*) **Tristan** is an alternate version. As the hero of a cycle of Celtic legends, Tristram is a tremendous hero: a dragon slayer, a musician, a seaman, a poet, and gloriously handsome. His story was grafted onto the Arthurian legends and included in Malory's *Le Morte D'Arthur*. In it, he is one of Arthur's knights, second in rank to Lancelot. His tragedy is that, because he drank a love potion, he is madly in love with his uncle's wife, Queen Iseult (or Isolde) of Cornwall. Dante takes a dim view of his lack of self-control and consigns him to the Circle of the Lustful in the *Inferno*. Spenser later borrows the name and makes Tristram a young Cornish squire in Book Six of the *Faerie Queen*. Tennyson took up the original tale in his reworking of the Arthur legends, *The Idylls of the King*, and Wagner's opera *Tristan und Isolde* set the story of the doomed lovers to music. One of the jokes of Laurence Sterne's long, chatty novel *The Life and Opinions of Tristram Shandy* is that young Tristram's father detested his son's name. Another joke is that in the more than seven hundred pages of the novel, the narrator, Tristram himself, only manages to recount the first few years of his life. His opinions, however, get a very thorough airing.

TROILUS (*Latin, "from Troy"*) Both Shakespeare and Chaucer adapted the story of Troilus and Cressida, a lovers' tragedy set

LAURENCE STERNE
ON NAMING

Early in Volume I of *The Life and Opinions of Tristram Shandy*, the narrator comments, in his discursive way, on his father's attitude to his own name. Walter Shandy is well established as a crank by Chapter 19, where the reader is exposed to his pronounced views on naming.

His opinion in the matter was, That there was a strange kind of magic bias, which good or bad names, as he called them, irresistibly impressed upon our characters and conduct. . . .

How many Caesars and Pompeys, he would say, by mere inspiration of the names, have been rendered worthy of them? And how many, he would add, are there, who might have done exceeding well in the world, had not their characters and spirits been Nicodemused into nothing? . . .

It was observable, that though my father, in consequence of this opinion, had, as I have told you, the strongest likings and dislikings towards certain names;—that there were still numbers of names which hung so equally in the balance before him, that they were absolutely indifferent to him. Jack, Dick, and Tom were of this class: These my father called neutral names;—affirming of them, without a satire, That there had been as many knaves and fools, at least, as wise and good men, since the world began, who had indifferently borne them;—so that, like equal forces acting against each other in contrary directions, he thought they mutually destroyed each other's effect; for which reason, he would often declare, He would not give a cherry-stone to choose amongst them. Bob, which was my brother's name, was another of these neutral kinds of Christian

> names, which operated very little either way . . . Andrew
> was something like a negative quality in Algebra with
> him;—'twas worse, he said, than nothing.—William
> stood pretty high:—Numps again was low with him;—
> and Nick, he said, was the Devil.
>
> But, of all the names in the universe, he had the most
> unconquerable aversion for Tristram.

during the Trojan War that has its roots in classical myth. Troilus
and Cressida are young lovers who have sworn eternal loyalty
during a truce in the Trojan War. As part of the negotiations Cressida is traded for Trojan prisoners-of-war. She betrays Troilus
with her Greek captor, Diomedes.

TURNUS *(Latin, meaning unknown)* Aeneas's great opponent in
The Aeneid. When Aeneas finally gets to Italy he finds that Turnus
is the chief warrior of the Latins. The Fury Alecto incites Turnus
to battle against Aeneas's Trojans, and the ultimate result is hand-
to-hand combat between the two heroes. Aeneas wins, winning
also the hand of the princess Lavinia and, ultimately, his stature
as founder of the glorious race of Romans.

ULYSSES see **ODYSSEUS**

UNCAS *(Mohegan, "the fox")* In James Fenimore Cooper's *The Last of the Mohicans,* Uncas is the son of Chingachgook and thus the ultimate Mohican. Cooper makes him a physically magnificent man, less prone to violence than his father. He falls in love with the English Cora, and she with him. They are both killed; in 1826, when Cooper published the novel, there was no future in mixed marriages.

UNFERTH *(Danish, "strife" or "un-peace")* The Anglo-Saxon poem *Beowulf* relates not only the great hero's struggle with the monster Grendel, but also his relations with fellow men. Unferth is a warrior at the Danish court who is cast into the shade by Beowulf's might and repelled by his boastful character. But he is finally won over by Beowulf's genuine might, and gives him a special sword that will kill the monster Grendel's mother.

URBAIN *(Latin, "from the city")* Although this is a perfectly plausible name for a nineteenth-century French aristocrat, Henry James is also playing with its meaning. Urbain de Bellegarde in *The American* is quintessentially urbane—smooth, civilized, and, to the American hero Christopher Newman, perfectly impenetrable. (The last name "Bellegarde" means "beautiful to see.") Newman wants to marry Bellegarde's widowed sister Claire de Cintré and Urbain, as head of the family, forbids the marriage in a courteous and baffling fashion.

URIAH *(Hebrew, "my light is the Lord")* Despite the Old Testament pedigree, a name claimed for eternity by Charles Dickens's Uriah Heep. In *David Copperfield*, Heep is the hypocritically meek, hand-wringing villain whose fate intersects with David's. David describes him as "looking as like a malevolent baboon, I thought, as anything human could look." As clerk to Mr. Wickfield, Heep slyly and gradually takes over the business and attempts to court Agnes, the daughter of the house.

> " 'Be umble, Uriah,' says father to me, 'and you'll get on.' "
> —CHARLES DICKENS, *DAVID COPPERFIELD*

UTHER *(Meaning unknown)* In Arthurian legend, beginning with Geoffrey of Monmouth's twelfth-century *The History of the Kings of Britain*, Uther Pendragon is the father of King Arthur. Versions of the tale differ. In several, Igraine is the innocent wife of Gorlois, Duke of Tintagel. Merlin's magic turns Uther into Gorlois's likeness, and he visits her bedroom in this guise. Other variants have Uther and Gorlois fighting and Uther, victorious, bedding Igraine. Arthur, of course, grows up ignorant of his glorious parentage.

VALENTIN *(French from Latin, "strong man")* Also **Valentine**. February 14 is the feast day of the saint about whom very little is known, except that a church was built in his honor in Rome in the fourth century. His feast day may have coincided with a pagan lovers' festival, thus acquiring the romantic overlay that has long since obscured the saint himself. One of Shakespeare's *Two Gentlemen of Verona* is a Valentine, an adventure-loving soul who eagerly leaves Verona to see the world, starting with Milan. Once there, however, his wanderlust turns into physical lust for the duke of Milan's daughter, Silvia. In *The American,* Henry James names Claire de Cintré's younger brother Valentin de Bellegarde. More approachable than his brother Urbain, he approves of Newman's courting his sister. He becomes entangled with a young lady of dubious background and ends up dying in a duel over her—an anachronism even in 1876. James may have wanted his name to indicate that he is a martyr for love. So, in a way, is Valentine in Goethe's *Faust.* He is Gretchen's brother, who attempts to protect his sister from the seduction of Faust, but is killed by Mephistopheles.

The Latin root from which **Valentin** comes is *valere,* which means "to be strong." In French, a close modern word is *valeur,* which means "value." *Valeureux,* however, means "gallant" or "full of valor." These qualities are both hinted at in the name **Valère,** which Molière uses several times in his plays. One of his Valères, to be sure, is nothing more than a steward. In *Tartuffe,* he is the youthful love interest, a suitor for Mariane, whom her father wishes to marry off to the hypocrite Tartuffe. In *The Miser,* Valère is a more compelling figure. Having rescued Élise, the daughter of Harpagon (the miser of the title) from a shipwreck, he is in love with her. To be near her, he acts as a servant to her father, whom he flatters outrageously. "There are some people you can't deal with except by humouring them," he explains. Naturally with such a pragmatic view of human nature, he wins Élise in the end.

VASILY see **BASIL**

VERNON *(French, "alder tree")* George Meredith's *The Egoist* is a portrait of Sir Willoughby Patterne, a handsome, intelligent, perfectly humorless, and self-absorbed young man. His cousin Vernon Whitford is part of his household, and appears to Willoughby to be meek, grateful, and insignificant. Yet Vernon manages to pursue his literary ambitions and his romantic intentions despite Willoughby's objections.

> *Vernon seemed a sheepish fellow, without stature abroad, glad of a compliment, grateful for a dinner, endeavouring sadly to digest all he saw and heard.*
> —GEORGE MEREDITH, *THE EGOIST*

VESEY *(Origin unknown)* This is a last name transferred to a first name, an affectation of the upper classes of England and America especially in the nineteenth century. As such it provides the reader with a clue to the pretentions of Dr. Vesey Stanhope, a clergyman in *Barchester Towers*. Trollope has great fun at Stanhope's expense, depicting him as a lazy snob who has lived in Italy for years on the income from his clerical appointments in Barchester. "The great family characteristic of the Stanhopes might probably be said to be heartlessness," says Trollope.

VICTOR *(Latin, "conqueror")* The Gothic story of a monster created out of parts of dead men's bodies is familiar, but the monster is often confused with his creator. In Mary Shelley's 1818 novel *Frankenstein*, Victor Frankenstein is the brilliant Swiss scholar who discovers an elixir of life and brings the monster to life. He is identified with Prometheus, who brought fire to mortals and was horribly punished. Frankenstein's punishment is to see his brother, his best friend, and his best friend's wife all killed by the monster. In Charlotte's Brontë's *The Professor*, Victor Crimsworth is the young son of the narrator. William Crimsworth is a model of the self-made man who, with no help from his family, scrambles his way to a firm position in the upper middle class. He is chilly and disciplined, and his son's name may refer to victory over any number of human weaknesses that Crimsworth had to overcome to reach his goals. Leopoldo Alas's *La Regenta*, a Spanish novel akin to Flaubert's *Madame Bovary*, features Don Victor Quintana as the cuckolded husband of the flighty Ana Ozores. Elderly, impotent, but kindhearted, he makes a dangerously ill-suited spouse for the young and passionate Ana. When he discovers her affair with the rake Alvaro, he feels honor bound to challenge the latter to a duel, with disastrous results.

Victorin is a French variant of the name, used by Balzac for Victorin Hulot in *Cousin Bette*. He is a distinguished lawyer who works hard to repair the damage—financial and emotional—that his vain and foolish father brings to his family.

> *"Victor learns fast. He must soon go to Eton, where, I suspect, his first year or two will be utter wretchedness; to leave me, his mother, and his home, will give his heart an agonized wrench."* —CHARLOTTE BRONTË, *THE PROFESSOR*

VINCENT (*Latin, "to conquer"*) In *Nicholas Nickleby*, Charles Dickens created a memorable depiction of a small-time acting troupe. Vincent Crummles is its manager, an affected, pompous man and a perfectly dreadful actor. The Italian form of the name, **Vincentio**, is used by Shakespeare for the duke in *Measure for Measure*. He is aware that the public morals in Vienna have declined under his lenient rule, so he delegates his power to Angelo and leaves town. But he sneaks back in, disguised as a friar, to see what happens with a sterner man in charge. He is obligated to intervene when Angelo's passion for rectitude goes too far.

VLADIMIR *(Slavic, "famous prince")* A name used by Turgenev for two important characters in his novels. The narrator of *First Love,* a dreamy, romantic sixteen-year-old, is Vladimir Petrovich. He is restless, melancholy, full of poetry he's learned by heart, and completely defenseless against the wiles of the courtesan Zinaida. In *Home of the Gentry,* Vladimir Panshin is an elegant threat to the romantic dreams of Fyodor Lavretsky. Tall, handsome, rich, with an official job in St. Petersburg, he is superficially everything a young woman would want in a husband. Lizaveta Kalitin, however, prefers Lavretsky, and when she makes this clear, Panshin turns his attentions all too easily to a married woman—Lavretsky's wife. He is known affectionately as **Volodya** and also as **Woldemar.** Alexander Pushkin's *Eugene Onegin* relates the destructive career of a gifted but deeply selfish man. Vladimir Lensky is an eighteen-year-old student, a neighbor of Onegin's in the country, who worships Onegin. Yet when they come into conflict over a woman, Onegin kills Lensky in a duel.

> *From fifteen years of age Vladimir Nikolaich knew how to enter any drawing-room without embarrassment, engage in pleasant chit-chat and withdraw at the right moment.*
> —IVAN TURGENEV, *HOME OF THE GENTRY*

VULCAN *(Latin mythology name)* The Roman name for Hephaestus, the god of fire and metalworking. His mother Hera, one of his few partisans on Mount Olympus, valued his remarkable skill and promoted his ill-fated marriage to Venus. The word "volcano" comes from his name, for his forge was supposedly located inside Mount Aetna. The process of "vulcanization" involves treating various materials at very high heat to change their texture.

WALDO *(Old German, "rule" or "power")* In *The Story of an African Farm,* Olive Schreiner describes the bleak existence on a Boer farm in South Africa. The hardest lot falls to Waldo, the young son of the German overseer. The harsh religious outlook, the desolate landscape, his loneliness, and his father's death render his life a misery.

WALTER *(Old German, "rule people")* The story of "patient Griselda" was adapted by Chaucer from Boccaccio to be the clerk's offering in *The Canterbury Tales.* The virtuous and beautiful peasant girl Griselda marries a king who spends years testing her virtue and good nature, first by taking away her children, next by sending her back to her parents in disgrace, finally by recalling her to the castle to wait on his "new bride"—who is actually her daughter. The fellow who thought up all these clever tests is named Walter. Even more quixotic is Walter Shandy, the father of the narrator in Laurence Sterne's *The Life and Opinions of Tristram Shandy.* With his numerous outlandish and firmly held opinions, he is what we today would call a crank. Jane Austen's Sir Walter Elliot in *Persuasion* tests the heroine of that story as does the Walter in Chaucer's "Clerk's Tale." But as her silly, vain, snobbish, and improvident father, Sir Walter can only neglect and undervalue his daughter Anne. He cannot actually keep her apart from the man she loves. Walter Hartright is the not very subtly named hero of Wilkie Collins's *The Woman in White.* He is an artist and the drawing teacher of the beautiful and victimized Laura Fairlie. The events of the novel—numerous and startling as they are—prove him tenacious, loyal, and energetic, so he finally gets the girl. A subplot of Elizabeth Gaskell's novel *Ruth* concerns the wealthy merchant Bradshaw and his partner Walter Farquhar, who loves Bradshaw's daughter Jemima. Farquhar is kind and reliable but slightly stiff, so his courtship with the proud Jemima does not go smoothly.

An old-fashioned nickname for **Walter** is **Wat** or **Watt**. Charles Dickens does not often bother with literary or historic connotation for his names, but Watt Rouncewell in *Bleak House* must be intended to recall Wat Tyler and the Peasant's Rebellion of 1381, in which a group of peasants sacked Canterbury and portions of London, demanding an end to serfdom. Watt Rouncewell is the grandson of the housekeeper at Chesney Wold, the bleak, barren, aristocratic stronghold of Sir Leicester Dedlock. He has gone up north and become a successful ironmaster, a fact that introduces the double threat of insubordination and industrialization into the bleak Dedlock landscape.

"Kind, Jemima!" he repeated, in a tone which made her go very red and hot; "must I tell you how you can reward me?—Will you call me Walter—say, thank you, Walter—just for once."

Jemima felt herself yielding to the voice and the tone in which this was spoken, but her very consciousness of the depth of her love made her afraid of giving way, and anxious to be wooed, that she might be reinstated in her self-esteem. "No!" said she, "I don't think I can call you so. You are too old. It would not be respectful." She meant it half in joke, and had no idea he would take the allusion to his age as seriously as he did. He rose up, and coldly, as a matter of form, in a changed voice, wished her "Good-by." Her heart sank; yet the old pride was there. But, as he was at the very door, some sudden impulse made her speak:

"I have not vexed you, have I, Walter?"

He turned round, glowing with a thrill of delight.

—ELIZABETH GASKELL, *RUTH*

WELLINGBOROUGH *(Old English, "town with the well")* Herman Melville's early reputation as a writer was made by semiautobiographical seafaring tales like *Typee, Omoo,* and *Redburn.* The protagonist of the last, Wellingborough Redburn, is a gently reared young man from the Hudson Valley who goes to sea equipped with nothing more than his brother's hunting gun and fancy shooting jacket. (His pretentious name gives a clue to his background.) In the course of his voyage to England as a foremast hand he becomes a sailor and a man.

WENCESLAS *(Old Slavic, "garland of glory")* The King Wenceslas of the famous Christmas carol is based on a tenth-century Czech saint. Count Wenceslas Steinbock of Balzac's *Cousin Bette* is not Czech but Polish, and a formidably talented sculptor who falls into the toils of the manipulative old spinster Bette Fischer. She foils his suicide attempt, bullies him into working, and holds documents that could put him into prison for bankruptcy. He is the great love of her life, compellingly handsome and naive, but he loves the daughter of a French baron and never suspects the depth of Bette's passion for him.

WERTHER *(vair' tair; Old German, includes an element that means "army")* Goethe's *The Sorrows of Young Werther* had a tremendous impact on the intellectual life of his era. Written in 1774 when the Age of Reason was apparently in full flourish, it is the tale of a highly emotional young man who falls madly, inappropriately in love with someone else's fiancée. The depth of his emotion is perhaps more interesting to him than the object of it— he certainly gives no thought to her discomfort at his hounding her. In the end he commits suicide with her fiancé's pistol. Literary legend has it that Werther's suicide inspired a wave of copycat suicides.

WILFRED *(Old English, "will peace")* Sir Walter Scott's antiquarian research gave the flavor of authenticity to his historical novels. When he named his Anglo-Saxon hero Wilfred of Ivanhoe, readers could believe that Wilfred was a genuine Anglo-

Saxon name. As a character, he is no more nuanced than any of Scott's heroes: mighty, handsome, modest, courageous, hot-tempered, kind to women and his social subordinates. He is certainly a sturdy central figure for Scott's most popular novel, *Ivanhoe.* Anthony Trollope echoes the antiquarian theme with his Wilfred Thorne of *Barchester Towers:* Thorne is the rich, conservative squire of Ullathorne, exceedingly proud of his family's ancient lineage. His name suggests that an unbroken chain of Wilfred Thornes have lived at Ullathorne since the Norman Conquest. Trollope manages to expose the man's vanity without making him odious.

WILLIAM *(Old German, "will helmet")* A useful name for novelists since it is common enough to be neutral and classless, yet it can also be used to hint at strength of will. Oliver Goldsmith has no such thing in mind in *The Vicar of Wakefield.* Sir William Thornhill is the great landowner in the neighborhood where the hapless Primrose family ends up, and his influence pervades the book. Though they hear tales of his wealth and power, they do not meet him until the end, when he reveals himself in the amiable "Mr. Burchell" who has been a great friend to the family. Jane Austen uses the name three times, once for the pleasant William Price in *Mansfield Park.* He is nothing more important than the naval brother of the heroine Fanny. In *Persuasion,* William Elliot is that familiar Austen figure, the handsome, charming schemer, "a man without heart or conscience; a designing, wary, cold-blooded being." Most memorable of all is William Collins, the complacent clerical buffoon of *Pride and Prejudice.* As Mr. Bennet's heir he attempts to court Elizabeth Bennet, but when she will have none of him, he woos her best friend. His fawning fondness for the arch-snob Lady Catherine De Bourgh provides some of the sharpest comedy of the book. Like Austen, William Thackeray makes nothing special of the name William—it is his own, after all, and perhaps that is significant, for he gives it to his mundane hero William Dobbin in *Vanity Fair.* Dobbin's central characteristic, signaled by his last name, is his ordinariness. Steady, unexciting, kind, he treads carefully through life, loving Amelia Sedley and witnessing Becky Sharp's antics with shock. It is his tragedy to realize, toward the end of the novel, that Amelia does not merit his lifelong devotion.

Charlotte Brontë's William Crimsworth, of *The Professor,* lives up to his name—both first and last. Willpower is his defining trait, and the hard, "grim" connotations of his last name suit him as well. He is the self-made man of his era, abandoned by his family with nothing but a good education. He manages to scrabble his way into the upper middle class by determination and discipline. Similarly motivated, though in a different direction, is William Boldwood of Thomas Hardy's *Far from the Madding Crowd.* As a farmer in Weatherbury, he is Bathsheba Everdene's social peer. Hardy says of him that "he had no light and careless touches in his constitution, either for good or for evil." Earnest, hardworking, he loves Bathsheba obsessively but courts her in a way that offends rather than charms her: "It was a fatal omission of Boldwood's that he had never once told her she was beautiful," Hardy says. When he dies, his closets are found to be full of clothes for Bathsheba, who had promised to marry him in six years. George Eliot's Will Ladislaw, of *Middlemarch,* could be considered a victim of his will rather than the master of it. Idealistic, talented, full of energy—what he lacks is focus. Will he direct his talents to writing? Politics? Does he have the discipline to be successful? These are pressing questions, especially to the widowed Dorothea Casaubon as she contemplates marrying him.

> *Willoughby looked older than his years, not for want of freshness, but because he felt that he had to stand eminently and correctly poised.* —GEORGE MEREDITH, *THE EGOIST*

WILLOUGHBY *(English, "farm near the willows")* The protagonist of George Meredith's *The Egoist* is Sir Willoughby Patterne, "rich, handsome, courteous, generous, lord of the Hall, the feast and the dance," as Meredith says. Unfortunately, he is also completely humorless and incapable of seeing any point of view besides his own. This shortcoming is a pronounced drawback when it comes to wooing the appropriate wife and getting her to the altar.

XAVIER *(Basque, "new house")* Boys are usually called **Xavier** to honor Saint Francis Xavier, the great sixteenth-century Jesuit missionary. In Émile Zola's *Nana*, however, Xavier de Vandeuvres is merely an aristocratic playboy of a particularly emphatic type: "Last scion of a great family, of feminine manners and witty tongue, he was at that time running through a fortune with a rage of life and appetite which nothing could appease." Among his more expensive pleasures are his racehorses, his betting, and his mistresses.

YEGOR *(Russian from Scandinavian, "soldier of Ing")* Also **Igor** and **Ygor.** Ivan Turgenev's *On the Eve* concerns the shifting relationships among a group of prosperous Russians on a country estate. Elena Stahov is the twenty-year-old daughter who attracts the interest of several young men. Yegor Kurnatovski is the eligible, dull young man whom her parents have chosen for her. Principled, steady, with a government job, he appears to Elena to be "perpetually on *duty*." In the end he is outshone by the revolutionary Insarov.

YERMOLAI *(Russian, possibly a variant of* **Jeremiah***)* Also **Yermolay.** Chekhov's drama *The Cherry Orchard* sets up a conflict between the old world of aristocratic estate owners and the new world in which money and ambition matter more than sentiment and lineage. Yermolai Lopahin represents the New Man, a descendant of serfs who is now rich enough to buy the estate where his father and grandfather worked. His ruthless ambition and energy blind him to the family's emotional attachment to the land he owns.

YONEC *(Breton derivative of* **John:** *Hebrew, "the Lord is gracious")* *The Lais of Marie de France* is a twelfth-century collection of Breton love stories. Yonec is the miraculous offspring of a woman who has been imprisoned in a tower by her elderly jealous husband, and of a hawk that flew in her window and turned into a knight. The husband kills the hawk/knight, but Yonec is born. When he comes of age, he travels to claim the kingdom of his mysterious father.

ZACHARIE *(French variant of* **Zachary:** *Hebrew, "the Lord remembers")* Émile Zola's *Germinal* is a sprawling novel about coal mining in nineteenth-century France. Zacharie Maheu is emblematic of the miners; expert in his field, the son and grandson of miners, he is tough and hardworking but limited by his circumstances. He has two children by a local mistress but lives with his parents because he cannot afford a house of his own.

The Russian form of the name is **Zakhar** *(zak har´)* or **Zahar.** In Ivan Goncharov's *Oblomov,* Zakhar is the hero's privileged manservant, loyal and bossy, who treats Oblomov more like a child than a master. He remembers the grandeur of the great estate that Oblomov's lassitude has lost for both of them. When Oblomov dies, Zakhar becomes a beggar because his indolent, irresponsible master has made no financial provision for him.

ZERBINO *(Italian, meaning unknown)* Many of the characters' names in Ariosto's *Orlando Furioso* are literary conventions. Neither meaning nor verisimilitude should be expected of them. Zerbino is the duke of Ross, son of the king of Scotland—though Ariosto's version of Scotland would no doubt come as a surprise to most Scots. He is one of the Christian heroes who perform heroically at the siege of Paris.

ZEUS *(Greek mythology name)* Zeus, known in Roman mythology as **Jupiter** or **Jove,** is the chief god of the Olympians. The son of the Titan Cronus and Rhea Silvia, he is a testy, proud, and mighty figure. When angered, he throws lightning bolts. He is also perpetually casting lecherous eyes on nymphs and mortal

THE OLYMPIAN PANTHEON

Greek and, later, Roman theology posited twelve beings who lived on Mount Olympus and were responsible not only for natural events but also for human behavior. Certain Greek heroes were favored by certain gods. The deities meddled during the Trojan War; they made the sun rise and set. Unlike later gods, the Greek versions were not perfect—far from it. In fact their weaknesses, like concupiscence and hasty tempers, were human weaknesses writ very, very large.

Zeus was the thunder god, and ruled the sky. The Romans knew him as *Jove* or *Jupiter*. Like the other gods, he could transform himself at will, but he most commonly did so to satisfy his lust.

Hera or *Juno* was his sister and wife. Because Zeus had a roving eye, Hera was always jealous.

Poseidon, called *Neptune* by the Romans, was Zeus and Hera's brother. His realm was the sea and he controlled earthquakes.

Hades, another sibling, also known as *Pluto,* was the god of the underworld, where the shades of the dead wandered forever.

Pallas Athena was Zeus's daughter, a powerful virgin and goddess of battle. Athens was her city.

Apollo, a son of Zeus, was the sun god. His twin *Artemis* (*Diana* to the Romans) was the moon goddess and a virgin like Athena.

Aphrodite or *Venus,* goddess of love, was born of the foam on the ocean, though some legends have her also a daughter of Zeus. She was none too careful with her favors and had numerous offspring by numerous fathers.

> *Hephaestus* or *Vulcan* was always distressed by his wife Aphrodite's wanderings, but as the lame, ugly blacksmith to the gods, he was at a considerable disadvantage.
>
> *Ares,* the war god (also called *Mars*) was far more attractive to Aphrodite, and she bore three of his children though he was a fearful bully.
>
> *Hermes*, the messenger god, was also Zeus's son. A quicksilver trickster, he was called *Mercury* by the Romans.
>
> *Hestia,* the remaining full sibling of Zeus, Hera, et al., was the virgin goddess of the hearth, identified with the Roman *Vesta.* Yet in post-Homeric Greece Hestia was booted out of Olympus by *Dionysos* or *Bacchus,* the god of wine and religious ecstasy.

women, whom he seduces in astonishing guises such as a shower of gold (Danae), a bull (Europa), or a swan (Leda). His children by some of these couplings include Heracles and Perseus.

ZINOVY *(Russian version of* Zenobius: *Greek, "life of Zeus")* Nikolai Leskov's "Lady Macbeth of Mtsensk" features a number of unpleasant characters, but Zinovy Izmaylov, the husband of Katerina, is one of the nastiest. A dishonest merchant who is much older than his wife, he suspects her of having an affair and threatens to torture her to extract a confession. His malice prompts the reader to muster a measure of sympathy for Katerina before she embarks on her killing spree.

GIRLS' NAMES

ACRASIA *(Greek, "bad mixture")* Possibly invented by Edmund Spenser for a terrifying enchantress in Book Two of *The Faerie Queen*. She represents "Intemperance," and it is her habit to lure men to her "Bower of Bliss" where she turns them into animals, like Circe in Homer's *Odyssey*. In the modern era, the name is used for a genus of fungi related to the slime molds.

ADELAIDE *(Old German, "nobility")* A German name imported to England in 1818 when the Duke of Clarence married Princess Adelaide of Saxe-Meinigen, twenty-seven years his junior. She was rumored to be the seventh woman he proposed to—despite his rank, his long-standing liaison with an actress had tarnished his appeal in the marriage market. He ascended the throne as William IV in 1830, and the city of Adelaide, Australia, was named for Queen Adelaide in 1836. Aristocratic Adelaides turn up in novels that Hardy, Collins, and Trollope published around 1870. Though secondary characters, their presence suggests that the name was commonplace in English drawing rooms of the era. Dostoyevsky used the Russian variant, **Adelaida,** for lesser characters in both *The Brothers Karamazov* and *The Idiot*. For him, the European name indicated educated, upper-class affiliation.

Ada, a simpler variant, appears in Charles Dickens's *Bleak House,* where Ada Clare is the sweet, golden-curled, blue-eyed, passive heroine and one of the heirs to the famously tangled legal case of *Jarndyce* v. *Jarndyce*. A variant form, **Adah,** can also be traced to a Hebrew word for "decoration, adornment."

Adele and its variants were also widely used by nineteenth-century writers. Jane Eyre's charge at Thornfield Hall was called

Adele, probably to remind Charlotte Brontë's readers of her "flighty" French background. In Kate Chopin's *The Awakening*, set in turn-of-the-century Louisiana, Adèle Ratignolle is a reliable character; her warmth, conventionality, and boundless maternal energy contrast with the high-strung sensuality of Edna Pontellier. Henry James rang a change on the French form to name Mrs. Gereth in *The Spoils of Poynton*. **Adela,** a slightly more elaborate version, suits the English widow who has furnished the house called Poynton in impeccable taste. **Adeline** *(a de leen')* includes the French diminutive ending *ine*. In Balzac's *Cousin Bette* the beautiful baroness Hulot is named Adeline. Unfortunately her family includes her jealous cousin Bette as well as a womanizing husband and a beautiful daughter who falls in love with a penniless Polish sculptor. Throughout the novel she behaves with generosity and dignity toward all of them.

> *Adeline . . . was comparable in her loveliness to the famous Madame du Barry. . . . She belonged to the company of perfect, dazzling beauties.*—HONORÉ DE BALZAC, *COUSIN BETTE*

ADRIANA *(Latin, "from Adria")* Shakespeare's *The Comedy of Errors* is a comedy bordering on farce, involving as it does two sets of identical twins who were separated in early childhood. Adriana is the wife of Antipholus of Ephesus, energetic and jealous. Her possessiveness toward her husband—and toward his twin, whom she mistakes for her husband—contributes to the general hilarity.

AETHRA *(Greek, meaning uncertain)* Possibly related to a Greek word meaning "kindle, set afire," or to a different word meaning "clear," as in "ether" and "ethereal." In Euripides' *The Suppliant Women*, Aethra is the mother of Theseus, the statesman and king of Athens. The play concerns the right of various suppliants to bury their dead warrior kin—all fallout from the Oedipus tragedy.

AFFERY *(Hebrew, "dust")* This is probably an informal spelling for **Aphra** or **Afra**, a name used by the Puritans in seventeenth-century England. Affery Flintwich is a minor character in Dickens's *Little Dorrit,* the housekeeper to Mrs. Clennam, the hero Arthur's mother. Yet she is the repository of some of the novel's crucial secrets, which ultimately her conscience demands she reveal.

> *Agathe embodied the ideal of the housewife brought up in the provinces without ever leaving her mother's side.*
> —HONORÉ DE BALZAC, THE BLACK SHEEP

AGATHA *(Greek, "good")* Never an especially popular name in anglophone countries, though the martyrdom of Saint Agatha (a virgin whose breasts were cut off as a part of her torture) ensured her veneration in Catholic countries. She is often depicted carrying her breasts on a plate, and in some churches, bread is blessed on her feast day. To Catholics the name carries a connotation of sacrifice that Balzac takes advantage of in *The Black Sheep,* using the French **Agathe** *(a gaht'),* naturally. Agathe Bridau is the doting, self-sacrificing mother of two sons in post-Napoleonic Paris. The elder, Philippe, is selfish, lazy, and dishonest, stealing even from his mother, who continues to love him even when she apprehends his amorality.

In Russian, the name is **Agafya** *(ah gahf' yah).* In nineteenth-century Russia, where the upper class looked to European culture as a model, it was a lower-class name. Ivan Turgenev names a gentle, aristocratic estate-owner's wife **Agafokleya** in *Fathers and Sons,* but she is usually called Agatha. Anton Chekhov wrote a story entitled "Agafya" about a young, married peasant girl who recklessly has an affair with a village womanizer, while in Ivan Goncharov's *Oblomov,* Agafya Matveyevna is the lazy, slatternly landlady who ultimately marries the passive Oblomov.

AGAVE *(Greek, "noble, brilliant, illustrious")* In the United States, the agave is a kind of cactus common to the Southwest, often known as a century plant. In Euripides' *The Bacchae,* Agave joins the Maenads, women who worship Dionysos. Her son Pentheus, king of Thebes, finding this new religion threatening in the social chaos it unleashes, tries to ban the wild rites. But Dionysos casts a spell on the king that sends him to the hills, disguised as a woman, to spy on the Maenads. They discover him, and in a divine frenzy that does not permit her to recognize him, his mother joins the other women in tearing Pentheus to pieces. When the unfortunate Agave awakens from the god's spell, she finds her son's (severed) head in her hands.

AGLAYA *(Greek, "brilliance")* Also occurs as **Aglaia.** In Greek myth, Aglaia was one of the three Graces, to whom Fyodor Dostoyevsky may be referring when he names one of the three lovely Yepanchin sisters Aglaya in *The Idiot.* She falls in love with Prince Leo Myshkin, the "idiot" of the title, so called for his naiveté and humility, which make him somehow otherworldly. But Aglaya, impulsive and passionate, becomes disenchanted with Myshkin and jilts him.

> *He even called me "Agnes": the name had been timidly spoken at first, but, finding it gave no offence in any quarter, he seemed greatly to prefer that appellation to "Miss Grey"; and so did I.* —ANNE BRONTË, *AGNES GREY*

AGNES *(Greek, "chaste, pure")* In Latin, *agnus* means "lamb," and in Christian art Saint Agnes is often pictured with a lamb. The name was popular in England in the Middle Ages, then revived by cultured Victorians with a penchant for the medieval. In 1847, Anne Brontë named the eponymous heroine of her first novel Agnes Grey. She is the narrator, a resourceful, sensible clergyman's daughter who works as a governess after her father's death. Endearingly, she finds the challenge of earning a living "exhilarating," and her pointed observations about some of her employers' child-rearing methods are refreshing. Charles Dickens creates a much more conventional Agnes in *David Copperfield,* published just a few years later. She is, like Agnes Grey, sensible, but she is a motherly, bustling little soul who hides her love for David for much of the novel until he finally realizes her true worth.

In Italian, the name is **Agnese** *(ah nyai' zeh).* Alessandro Manzoni's *The Betrothed,* published in 1827, is set in seventeenth-century rural Italy. The heroine's mother, Agnese Mondella, is a strong, pious, cheerful peasant woman who faces with practicality each of the numerous blows that Manzoni's plot deals her. A diminutive is **Agnesina** *(ah nyai see' nah),* which Henry James uses in *The Awkward Age,* his tale of young women and the corruptions of London society. Agnesina is the Italian niece of a duchess, who has raised her to be perfectly sheltered and innocent, to the extent that she is supervised as closely as a small child. After her marriage, "Little Aggie" (as she is generally known) rapidly embraces the aura of sexual impropriety that she has been so carefully shielded from.

ALCESTIS *(al ses' tis; Greek, meaning unknown)* Also **Alceste.** In Euripides' comedy *Alcestis,* the title character is the wife of Admetus, king of Thessaly. Because Admetus had done him several favors, Apollo vowed that he would not have to die if he could find someone to die in his stead. Alas, he can't, until his loving wife Alcestis volunteers, and goes down to Hades in his place. She is rescued by Heracles. This is just the kind of story that impressed Chaucer, who includes Alcestis in his poem "The Legend of Good Women." Alceste is the queen who suggests to the author in a dream that he record the tales of women who suffered greatly for love.

ALCINA *(Invented name)* Alcina is one of several evil sorceresses in Ludovico Ariosto's *Orlando Furioso.* She captures and seduces two of the mighty warriors of the epic, Astolfo and Ruggiero.

They become enslaved to her sexually, losing sight of their properly bellicose pursuits.

ALCYONE *(al kee oh' nee or al see ohn'; Greek, "kingfisher")* In Ovid's *Metamorphoses,* Alcyone is the daughter of Aeolus, god of the winds. Her husband, King Ceyx, goes on a sea journey in spite of her premonitions of disaster. When his ship is wrecked, Alcyone prays so earnestly to Juno that the goddess sends her a vision of the dead Ceyx, whose body washes up on shore shortly thereafter. Then both Ceyx and Alcyone are turned into birds. Our word "halcyon," meaning "a calm time," comes from this myth.

> *Their love endured, even after they had shared this fate. . . . They still mate and become parents, and for seven days of calm in the winter Alcyone broods on the sea, wings outstretched over her nest: then the waves lie still and Aeolus, keeping guard over the winds, prevents their going out.*
> —OVID, METAMORPHOSES

ALDONZA *(Invented name)* The robust, good-natured peasant girl upon whom Cervantes's Don Quixote hangs his fantasy of the ideal woman. In his mind, she is the fair, noble, and unapproachable Dulcinea.

ALECTO *(Greek, "never-resting")* Also **Allecto.** One of the Furies, three appalling sisters who sprang from the blood of Uranus after his son Cronos castrated him. They live in the underworld and venture on earth to persecute humans who have committed crimes like patricide, usually by driving them to madness. After the events of the Oresteia, in which they hound Orestes, they are tamed by Athena and called "the Eumenides," or "the Kindly Ones." They appear in Aeschylus's *The Eumenides* and also in Virgil's *Aeneid.*

ALETHEA *(Greek, "truth")* Samuel Butler's *The Way of All Flesh* is a scathing portrait of an upper-middle-class Victorian family. Ernest Pontifex, the protagonist, is raised by a bully of a father to be a clergyman, despite his lack of enthusiasm for the career. His aunt Alethea (pointedly named) is the only family member who encourages his true talents. By leaving him her fortune, she enables him to embark on a new career as a writer.

ALEXANDRA *(Greek, "defender of man")* A name that was popular in Russia and on the Continent before it became widely used in England. In Dostoyevsky's *The Idiot*, Alexandra Yepanchin is one of three beautiful sisters, cultured, graceful, and delightful. Chekhov uses the diminutive, **Sasha**, for a character in his drama *Ivanov*. The title character, Nikolai Ivanov, is a married man of thirty-five, worn out by his intellectual work and efforts at reform, and facing his wife's imminent death of tuberculosis. Sasha Lebedev is the daughter of a neighboring landowner to whom Ivanov owes money. Sasha is bright and energetic, and she finds Ivanov's passivity somehow alluring.

Alexandra was more widely used in England once the Hanoverian dynasty of kings ended. Queen Victoria's first name was **Alexandrina**, and Alexandra of Denmark became Princess of Wales in 1863. Anthony Trollope surely had the former in mind when he created Lady Alexandrina De Courcy in *The Small House at Allington*. The thirtyish daughter of Earl De Courcy, she is not particularly attractive, either physically or morally, but Adolphus Crosbie allows himself to be maneuvered into marriage with her, jilting Lily Dale in the process. Trollope has fun with the pretentiousness of the De Courcy daughters, giving them all multisyllabic names: Alexandrina's sisters are Rosina, Margaretta, and Amelia.

Alice was immoveable. As a matter of course she was immoveable. —ANTHONY TROLLOPE, *CAN YOU FORGIVE HER?*

ALICE *(Old German, "nobility")* From the same root as **Adelaide.** It was used in this form in England as early as the late fourteenth century, for the Wife of Bath in Chaucer's *Canterbury Tales* is named Alice. She is one of the most memorable of Chaucer's creations, a bawdy, practical, humorous woman who maintains that woman's only happiness in marriage lies in domination of her husband. Having had five victims, she should know.

After several centuries of disuse, the name was revived in the nineteenth century. In James Fenimore Cooper's *The Last of the Mohicans* (1826), Alice Munro is one of the pair of English girls trying to reach their father at a remote fort in the American wilderness during the French and Indian War. They are escorted by English soldiers and friendly (Mohican) Native Americans, but are attacked by Hurons allied to the French. Alice is a conventional English girl, intimidated by her surroundings, and she falls in love, predictably, with the English officer escorting the party. Elizabeth Stoddard's *The Morgesons,* dating from the mid-nineteenth century, is an American tale of a different kind, recounting the emotional adventures of a girl from small-town New England. Tempestuous Cassandra Morgeson goes to visit her rich cousin Charles and falls, reluctantly, in love with him. Alice is his wife whose good nature and kindness cannot win over the difficult Cassandra. After Charles's death in a carriage accident, however, Alice's dignity and acceptance of Cassandra's grief earns the younger woman's respect.

In Trollope's *Can You Forgive Her?* it is the character named Alice whose temperament is difficult. Alice Vavasor, an independent-minded woman of twenty-four, is courted both by her reprehensible cousin George and by the impeccable if dull John Grey. Her error, referred to in the title, is that she becomes engaged to George though she truly loves John Grey. With his usual psychological acuity, Trollope depicts a proud woman who feels compelled to punish herself for what was considered, in those days, a virtually unforgivable mistake. George Gissing, in *The Odd Women,* creates a portrait of a very different kind of Alice, a meek, downtrodden spinster. Alice Madden and her sisters were cast onto the world unprovided for when their father died suddenly. Raised as "gentlewomen," they have no skills. Alice earns a paltry living as a governess, and her health has suffered from years of poor food and miserable accommodations. The most famous Alice in English literature, of course, is the Alice whom Lewis Carroll sent down the rabbit hole in *Alice's Adventures in Wonderland* and *Through the Looking-Glass*. The story goes that mathematician Charles Dodgson (Carroll's real name) wrote the tales to entertain Alice Liddell, the daughter of a friend. The fictional Alice, aged seven, undergoes remarkable adventures in the topsy-turvy world at the bottom of a rabbit hole. For the most part, she accepts with a calm curiosity the wonders she encounters, though her frustration occasionally provokes outbursts of temperament.

Alison or **Alisoun** was also a form of the name Geoffrey Chaucer used. In "The Miller's Tale," a comic turn involving adultery and horseplay, Alison is the young wife who readily deceives her husband with their lodger, Nicholas. Chaucer vividly sketches her allure by comparing her slender body to that of a weasel. Sir Walter Scott, in *Old Mortality*, creates a stingy, tyrannical, but utterly loyal housekeeper named Alison. His grandparents had a maid by that name, so a portrait is possible. Another Scottish Alison is Robert Louis Stevenson's Alison Durie, of *The Master of Ballantrae*. An heiress and kinswoman to James and Henry Durie, she is brought up with them and intended as bride for James, the magnetic elder son. After he is exiled from home for offenses ranging from debt to rape, she obediently marries the younger son, Henry, out of pity. When James returns he maliciously manipulates her love for him, setting the entire household at emotional loggerheads and provoking the two brothers to fight a duel over her.

A more Continental-sounding variant of Alice is **Alicia**, used by Mary Elizabeth Braddon for a secondary character in *Lady Audley's Secret*. Alicia Audley is the adult daughter of Sir Michael Audley, an English widower of mature years who falls for the wiles of governess Lucy Graham. Alicia not only loathes her calculating stepmother, she pines for her cousin Robert, who loves another woman. Alicia is a pretty, intelligent young woman, trapped in circumstances that hold no satisfaction for her. Mark

Twain elaborates Alice further to **Alisande,** the name of the female love interest in *A Connecticut Yankee at King Arthur's Court.* At the direction of King Arthur, protagonist Hank Morgan is assigned a quest: he must rescue forty-four virgins from three monstrous giants. Alisande is one of the virgins, a capable, practical young woman whose competence outstrips Morgan's. He calls her "Sandy," and eventually marries her.

> *"I can't explain* myself, *I'm afraid, sir,"* said Alice, *"because I'm not myself, you see."*
> *"I don't see,"* said the Caterpillar.
> —LEWIS CARROLL, *ALICE'S ADVENTURES IN WONDERLAND*

ALMA *(Latin, "nurturing," or Italian, "soul")* In Edmund Spenser's allegorical poem, *The Faerie Queen,* most of the characters represent attributes or traits rather than human beings. Book Two recounts the legend of Sir Guyon, and the theme throughout is Temperance. Alma, the chatelaine of a castle, is besieged by the enemies of temperance. Sir Guyon and Prince Arthur rout the troops (which embody the seven deadly sins and the lusts of the five senses).

ALMIRY *(Variant of Almira: Arabic, "high born, princess")* In Sarah Orne Jewett's *The Country of the Pointed Firs,* Almiry could be either a genuine given name or the rustic pronunciation of **Almira.** The character, Almiry Todd, is the landlady with whom the narrator lives for a summer in a small Maine village. An expert in herbs and the village's de facto apothecary, she is also the repository for much of the history of the place. She tells these stories to the narrator as a way of keeping them, and the village, alive.

AMANDA *(Latin, "lovable")* The characters in Henry James novels often bear names that sound naturalistic but, on examination, comment on the characters themselves. Thus, Amanda Pynsent in *The Princess Casamassima* is a dressmaker ("pin sent") who brings up the young Hyacinth Robinson after his mother is imprisoned for prostitution. Though James makes clear her innate silliness, he also insists on her genuine, selfless love for Hyacinth.

AMELIA *(Old German, "industrious")* Edmund Spenser's *The Faerie Queen* includes a character with a variant spelling, **Aemylia**. She is a noblewoman who falls in love with a mere squire and elopes with him. Naturally this disruption of the natural order cannot be sanctioned in the sixteenth-century worldview, so she and her lover undergo several nasty adventures before being rescued by Prince Arthur. Shakespeare uses a similar form of the name, **Aemilia**, for the virtuous wife of Aegeon in *The Comedy of Errors*. After a shipwreck in which she thinks her twin sons are drowned, she becomes an abbess—unnecessarily, as it turns out.

Henry Fielding's novel *Amelia*, written in 1751, concerns the long-suffering Amelia Booth. Beautiful (though her beauty is marred by a carriage accident), she is sensible, sweet, and plain-spoken. Captain Booth, alas, though loving and kindly, is also an immoderate hothead and leads her on a merry dance as he is imprisoned, has an affair with an adventuress, then is released only to fall into debt. An inheritance sets them aright again, to Amelia's everlasting contentment.

The name was most widely used by the Victorians. Anthony Trollope created three Amelias, for instance. Two of them (Amelia Fawn and Lady Amelia Gazebee) are secondary characters, aristocratic young ladies from large families with pretentious names. Amelia Roper, in *The Small House at Allington*, is a very different story. The daughter of the house where young John Eames lodges in London, she is a vulgar, brassy creature who almost entraps Eames into marriage. Trollope hints that, as a woman of thirty who has worked in a shop in Manchester, she is probably "no better than she should be," i.e., not a virgin. On the other hand William Thackeray's Amelia Sedley of *Vanity Fair* is the perfect specimen of the young Victorian lady. In fact, Thackeray paints her with such a broad brush that by the end of the novel the reader sees her pliancy, dependence, and lack of initiative as irritants rather than the Victorian virtues they seemed at first.

The consort of French king Louis Philippe, who reigned from 1830 to 1848, was Marie-Amélie. No wonder, then, that Balzac created two prominent characters named **Amélie** *(ah ma´y lee)*. *Cousin Pons* includes a scathing portrait of Amélie de Marville, wife of the president of the Court of Appeals, a snobbish and malicious woman caught up in the competitive melee of Paris society: "A temper naturally shrewish was soured till she grew positively terrible. She was not old, but she had aged; she deliberately set herself to extort by fear all that the world was inclined to refuse her, and was harsh and rasping as a file." Amélie Camusot, in *A Harlot High and Low,* is a similarly dominating wife, but less offensive. Her husband, an attorney, has been useful to a number of important people, and Amélie's is the strategy that helps him remain successful as a judge without offending any of his powerful patrons.

AMORET *(Invented name, based on* amour, *the French word for* love) In modern times an *amourette* is a love affair, but in Edmund Spenser's *The Faerie Queen* a fleeting reference to love is probably all that's intended. Amoret is twin sister to the virgin huntress Belphoebe; both girls were reared by Venus. She is in love with the knight Scudamore ("shield of love") but is captured by the wicked enchanter Busirane. Britomart, the female knight representing chastity, liberates Amoret and helps her to find Scudamore.

AMY *(French, "beloved")* The French word, and the French spelling of the name, is **Aimée.** In Elizabeth Gaskell's last novel, *Wives and Daughters,* Marie-Aimée Hamley is the French wife of Osborne Hamley. He has kept her existence a secret from his family, knowing that they would disapprove of her, but after his death, when she comes to the family home, they find her to be a patient, modest, loyal woman, a wonderful mother to the youngest Hamley, and well-deserving of the name **Aimée.**

Daniel Defoe's *Roxana,* written in 1724, is the narrative of a fallen woman whose success as a mistress to the powerful never blinds her to the error of her ways. Though few of the characters in the book have names, one who does is Roxana's maid Amy. Amy is worldly wise, and more practical than her mistress; it is she who urges Roxana to sleep with her first protector after her husband's disappearance. But the very confidential relations between the two sour after Roxana insists that Amy also share her common-law husband's bed. Thereafter, Amy turns against her mistress, with tragic results.

One of English literature's best-loved characters named Amy is rarely known by her name: she is called, instead, "Little Dorrit." Charles Dickens's novel of the same name focuses on the debtor's prison known as the Marshalsea, where Little Dorrit was born and raised, taking care of her impractical father and helping to raise her siblings by working as a seamstress. Her strange nickname (Dorrit is her last name) works to desexualize her and remove her from the ranks of Victorian womanhood, to the extent that it takes the hero, Arthur Clennam, over seven hundred pages to figure out that she is a woman. (She possesses, needless to say, all the virtues of a Dickensian heroine: patience, selflessness, loyalty, and wonderful nursing skills.)

Amy March of Louisa May Alcott's *Little Women,* on the other hand, claims none of those virtues. But she is an American heroine created by an American woman, and thus can flourish outside the strict English mold. She is the youngest of the four March sisters and the one among them who hankers after a more luxurious life. Pretty, vain, and artistic, she comes very close to turning into a worldly little snob, but recovers her bearings in the end. There is also a character named Amy in *The Inheritance,* which Alcott wrote when she was seventeen. Amy Hamilton is a secondary character, a pretty, charming, and rich young aristocrat with a warm heart.

> *Amy, a gay and lovely girl whose life was all a summer day.*
> —LOUISA MAY ALCOTT, *THE INHERITANCE*

ANAÏS see **ANNE**

ANASTASIE *(ah nah stah' zee; French from Greek, "resurrection")* When Honoré de Balzac's characters give their children grandiose names, it's a sure sign that some strenuous social climbing is going on. Anastasie de Restaud, married to a Parisian aristocrat, is the beautiful, haughty daughter of the former vermicelli manufacturer Goriot, in *Old Goriot*. She is much too proud to acknowledge her poor and adoring father, though he continues to support her and, indirectly, her lover. When he dies, she is at the Vicomtesse de Beauséant's ball, a social triumph for her.

ANDROMACHE *(an drah' ma kee; Greek, meaning unknown)* One of the casualties of the Trojan War, Andromache is the wife of Hector, the Trojans' greatest hero. In *The Iliad*, Homer calls her "white-armed Andromache" and shows her with Hector and their son Astyanax, pleading with her husband not to fight the Argives. Her plight and her emotions demonstrate the price of war. Indeed, in Euripides' play *The Trojan Women*, she is presented to Neoptolemus, the son of Achilles, as a slave. Astyanax has been killed, on Odysseus's orders, lest he grow up to seek revenge, and Andromache envies those women who have been sacrificed or killed. In Racine's *Andromache*, written in 1667, Pyrrhus, the son of Achilles, is in love with her. She agrees to marry Pyrrhus in order to save Astyanax, planning to commit suicide afterward.

> *Andromache pressed the child to her scented breasts,*
> *smiling through her tears. Her husband noticed,*
> *and filled with pity now, Hector stroked her gently.*
> —HOMER, *THE ILIAD*

ANDROMEDA *(an drah' meh da; Greek, "thinking man, meditator")* An Ethiopian princess whose story is told in Ovid's *Metamorphoses*. Her mother Cassiopeia bragged that she was more beautiful than the Nereids, or sea nymphs. Since such hubris could not go unpunished, the Nereids persuaded Poseidon to humble Andromeda. A sea monster attacked Ethiopia and an oracle stated that Andromeda must be sacrificed to it, so she was chained to a rock. She was rescued, however, by Perseus, who married her. According to Ovid, both she and her mother were placed among the stars when they died, and have constellations named after them. Andromeda is also the name of a flowering ground cover native to cool climates.

ANGELICA *(Latin, "like an angel")* The most alluring feminine character in Ariosto's *Orlando Furioso,* Angelica is a pagan, the daughter of the king of Cathay (China). Both Orlando and Rinaldo are in love with her and she is proud enough to spurn them. But she is humbled by the love of the handsome, modest Moorish soldier Medoro, and marries him. The French version of the name is **Angélique** *(aw zhay leek'),* and Molière uses it for the daughter of Argan, the protagonist of *The Imaginary Invalid.*

> *Anne was fair, very fair, in a poetic sense; but in complexion she was of that particular tint between blonde and brunette which is inconveniently left without a name.*
> —THOMAS HARDY, *THE TRUMPET-MAJOR*

ANNE *(Hebrew, "grace")* Also **Ann.** Saint Anne is the mother of Mary, and thus a significant saint, while Queen Anne ruled England for a dozen years at the beginning of the eighteenth century. Yet the name is not used with terrific frequency in anglophone literature, possibly because by the nineteenth century (arguably the great era of the novel), it was unfashionable in the educated classes. One exception to this generalization is Anne Elliot, the unappreciated heroine of Jane Austen's *Persuasion.* Austen makes it clear that all the women in this family of snobs are named for English queens, and that Anne, "with an elegance of mind and sweetness of character," is the only one worth knowing. In Thomas Hardy's *The Trumpet-Major,* Anne Garland is an unsophisticated country girl. The novel is one of Hardy's less complicated pastoral pieces, focused on the sensible Anne's choice between Bob Loveday and his brother John, the trumpet major of the title. One of the staple features of Wilkie Collins's sensational fiction is confusion of identity, and Anne Catherick, of *The Woman in White,* is one of a pair of women whose identities are purposely blurred by the villain. Anne, half sister of the heroine Laura Glyde, is the woman of the title who, dressed in white, makes occasional portentous appearances. Edith Wharton uses a European form of the name, **Anna,** for one of the central characters in her novel *The Reef.* Anna Leath is a reserved widow who sees George Darrow's reentry into her life as an opportunity to redeem her lost opportunities for emotional fulfillment. Having been alarmed by Darrow's intensity when he courted her as a girl, she finds the courage to accept him as a future husband—until a romantic indiscretion on his part betrays them both.

French writers consistently spell Anne with the final *e.* In Dumas's *The Three Musketeers,* the queen of France, formerly Anne of Austria, inspires fierce loyalty in her musketeers. However, the villainess Milady de Winter is also named Anne, a kind of eerie doubling that intensifies when Athos discovers she is the woman he had married when they were both young. In Spanish, **Ana** is the usual spelling. The heroine of *La Regenta* by Leopoldo Alas is Ana Ozores, a dreamy and intelligent young beauty in a small town, who is married off by her grasping aunts to an elderly, impotent gentleman. Her boredom and her yearning for passion result in the same kind of trouble Emma Bovary experienced. **Anaïs** is a Provençal form of the name, used by Balzac in *Lost Illusions.* Anaïs de Bargeton, known to her friends as Naïs, is the crème de la crème of Angoulême society. The handsome and ambitious poet Lucien Chardon succeeds in her salon because he flatters her intellectually as well as attracting her physically. But when the pair go to Paris, he sees her for the aging provincial that she is and drops her—with disastrous results.

In Russian, the name is **Anna,** and it appears often in the greatest Russian novels. Most notable, of course, is Anna Karenina, the tempestuous heroine of Tolstoy's eponymous novel. Beautiful and spirited but fatally selfish, she leaves her child and her husband to live with Count Vronsky, but he cannot satisfy all of her emotional needs and she becomes increasingly jealous and cruel. Turgenev used the name for significant characters in two of his novels. Anna Sergeyevna Odintsov in *Fathers and Sons* is a fascinating widow who entrances both aristocratic Arkady Kirsanov and his friend, the proto-Bolshevik Barsanov. She extracts from Barsanov the admission that he loves her, but decides not to become emotionally involved with him, reasoning, "God alone knows what it might have led to; this was not something to trifle with. After all, a quiet life is better than anything else in the world." Anna Stahov, in *On the Eve,* is the rich, well-educated wife of Nikolai Stahov who passively tolerates his infidelities and her empty life: "She was an affectionate, tender-hearted woman, and life had quickly crushed her." Chekhov, too, uses the name often. The title character of "Lady with Lapdog"—a naive newlywed who embarks on an affair with a rake—is called Anna. So is the young factory owner in "A Woman's Kingdom," which watches Anna Glagolev try to balance her loneliness and her responsibilities in a life of luxury.

The most common elaboration is **Annabel,** made famous by Edgar Allan Poe's hypnotic poem "Annabel Lee." We know nothing about her but that she was "a child" like the narrator, and her

> For the moon never beams, without bringing me dreams
>   Of the beautiful Annabel Lee;
> And the stars never rise, but I feel the bright eyes
>   Of the beautiful Annabel Lee;
> And so, all the night-tide, I lie down by the side
> Of my darling—my darling—my life and my bride.
>   —EDGAR ALLAN POE, "ANNABEL LEE"

aristocratic relatives disapproved of their romance, and she died. It all sounds much better in verse. Another elaboration is **Annabella,** used by Anne Brontë in her novel *The Tenant of Wildfell Hall.* Annabella Lowborough is a minor character, a shallow socialite who marries purely for ambition and has an affair with the husband of the heroine, Helen Graham. It is striking that, in choosing a name for this deeply unsympathetic character, Anne Brontë selects one that sounds aristocratic yet is a variant of her own name.

ANTIGONE *(an tih' goh nee; Greek, meaning unknown)* In Sophocles' *Antigone,* the title character is a model of loyalty. She is the daughter of Oedipus and Jocasta who stands up for her father and her brother Polyneices to the last. After the latter's death she defies the decree of King Creon and buries her brother. Though she is betrothed to his son Haemon, Creon sentences Antigone to be buried alive. The pair commit suicide and so does Creon's wife Eurydice when she hears the news.

ANTONIA *(Feminine version of* **Anthony:** *Latin clan name, possibly meaning "of great value")* In Byron's *Don Juan,* Antonia is the maid of Donna Julia, the young rake's first sexual conquest. The name is nominally Spanish in that context. A French variant is **Antoinette,** used by Balzac for the title character in his tale "The Duchess of Langeais." She is the daughter of a ducal family, married at eighteen to the scion of a family as high-ranked as her own. She and her husband go their separate ways in the Paris of the Bourbon Restoration, and she is haughty, beautiful, and coldhearted. "Her life was a sort of fever of vanity and perpetual enjoyment, which turned her head," says Balzac. She has allowed several men to fall in love with her, but is emotionally untouched until the advent of military hero Armand de Montriveau, who will not submit to her heartless flirtation. She ends, unhappily, in a convent as Sister Theresa. **Toinette,** a diminutive version of the name, appears in *The Imaginary Invalid* for one of Molière's sensible, plain-spoken soubrettes. She is the maid of the invalid Argan, who disguises herself as a doctor to free her master from his reliance on quacks.

APHRODITE *(Greek, "foam born")* In Greek myth, Aphrodite (her Roman equivalent is **Venus**) was born from the foam on the sea and rode a shell to the shores of Cythera, a Greek island. Botticelli's famous painting *The Birth of Venus* depicts this unusual genesis. She is the goddess of love and lust, married very unhappily to Hephaestus (Vulcan to the Romans). A born troublemaker, she has at least ten children by various gods and mortals, and her meddling in human affairs launches many a tragedy. Euripides' *Hippolytus* recounts her involvement in the sad tale of Phaedra, Hippolytus, and Theseus. It was also Aphrodite who persuaded Paris to choose her as "the fairest" by promising him the love of the most beautiful woman in the world—Helen of Troy.

AQUILINA *(Latin, "eagle")* The name assumed by a prostitute in Balzac's *The Wild Ass's Skin.* Having lost a lover when he was executed for a republican conspiracy, she has sworn revenge on men, and achieves it by mastering them sexually. Her pride and her intimidating, distinguished looks make her irresistible to Paris's jaded young dandies. "Just as Popes give themselves new names when elected to sovereignty over men, I took another name when I achieved sovereignty over all women," she claims.

ARABELLA *(Latin, "yielding to prayer")* Elaborate three-syllable feminine names were fashionable among eighteenth-century English aristocrats. Thus, Clarissa Harlow's elder sister—characterized by Samuel Richardson as "ill-natured, overbearing, and petulant"—is called Arabella. In Oliver Goldsmith's *The Vicar of Wakefield,* written in 1766, Miss Arabella Wilmot is the wealthy clergyman's daughter whom George Primrose is supposed to marry. When the Primrose family loses its money, the betrothal is called off, but in this cheerful tale, everyone ends up happily paired, including Arabella and George. In George Eliot's *Felix Holt: The Radical,* Arabella is the rarely used first name of the somewhat pathetic Mrs. Transome. Chatelaine of Transome Court, she is the wealthy but deeply unhappy gentlewoman whom fate has used very badly. Arabella Donn of Thomas Hardy's *Jude the Obscure* doesn't wait for fate to trip her up.

Rather, she sets her cap at ambitious Jude Fawley and traps him into marriage by pretending to be pregnant. Marriage to what Hardy calls "a complete and substantial female animal" spells the end of Jude's aspirations to higher education. Anthony Trollope makes the name comical in *Can You Forgive Her?* by assigning it to a blowsy, common flirt. The subplot balancing Alice Vavasor's tortured choice between two suitors consists of Arabella Greenow's practical and hardheaded version of the same dilemma.

ARACHNE *(a rak' nee; Greek, possibly related to the word for "net")* Ovid's *Metamorphoses* tells the story of the young woman who was such a good weaver that she challenged Athena to a contest. To demonstrate her craft, she made a tapestry depicting the amorous misadventures of the gods. Athena was so incensed at this hubris that she began to beat Arachne with the weaving shuttle and Arachne, incensed, took her thread and attempted to hang herself. Athena then said, "You may go on living, you wicked girl, but you must be suspended in the air like this, all the time"—and turned Arachne into a spider. An entire class of wingless arthropods, including spiders, scorpions, and mites, is called arachnids after her.

ARETHUSA *(Greek mythology name)* A nymph in classical myth. She was pursued by the river god Alpheus, and Diana turned her into a fountain or a stream to evade capture. In Ovid's *Metamorphoses,* it is Arethusa who informs Ceres that Proserpine has been taken off to the underworld. A genus of bog orchids with purple-fringed blossoms is named after the nymph.

ARIADNE *(Greek mythology name)* The daughter of the Cretan king Minos, she provided Theseus with a thread so that he could retrace his steps through the labyrinth after having slain the monstrous Minotaur. She fell in love with the great hero and left Crete with him as his wife. On the voyage home, however, the perfidious Theseus decided he preferred his sister-in-law Phaedra, and abandoned Ariadne on the island of Naxos. She later married

WOMEN WHO LOVE TOO MUCH

Western literature abounds in tales of passion that make average love stories look insipid. Anna Karenina's dramatic end—suicide under an oncoming train—follows the precedent of Dido, queen of Carthage, who threw herself on a funeral pyre after Aeneas's departure. Never mind the intervening two thousand years: there's no telling what a woman may do when she's unhinged by love. Around 1386, Chaucer wrote a poem called "The Legend of Good Women" that celebrated women who had suffered for love—or at the hands of men. Among the ladies he termed "Cupid's saints" were Dido and the following:

Cleopatra, who killed herself with an asp when told that her lover Mark Antony was dead.

Thisbe, a suicide upon discovering the body of her lover Pyramus.

Medea, the sorceress who used her powers to boost Jason's career, only to be divorced by him. She killed his two sons and remarried.

Lucrece, a Roman matron who stabbed herself in front of her husband and his friends, out of the shame of having been raped.

Ariadne, who left Crete with the hero Theseus only to discover that he really preferred her sister. She was abandoned on the island of Naxos.

Philomela, raped by her brother-in-law, who also cut out her tongue so she couldn't betray him. She wove a tapestry telling her sister the story, and in the end was turned into a nightingale.

Dionysos. Chaucer tells her story in "The Legend of Good Women."

Chekhov wrote a short story entitled "Ariadne" about a beautiful and alluring but utterly venal young girl. The tale is told from the point of view of a young man whom she captivates and ruins financially. Even in retrospect, he says, "I still cannot help thinking that nature had some sweepingly grand and wonderful design when she created that girl." But he also says, "The chief and as it were fundamental quality of that woman was her amazing cunning."

> *What struck me most of all was her unusual and beautiful name—Ariadne. It suited her so marvellously! She was a brunette, very thin, very slender, supple, shapely, extraordinarily graceful.* —ANTON CHEKHOV, "ARIADNE"

ARICIA *(Greek mythology name)* In his tragedy *Phaedra,* the French playwright Racine builds on the story told by Euripides in *Hippolytus:* Phaedra, Theseus's wife, falls in love with her stepson Hippolytus. She commits suicide, leaving a note for Theseus that accuses his son of trying to rape her. Theseus then curses Hippolytus, who is killed when a bull rises from the sea, frightening his carriage horses into crashing. In Racine's version, Aricia is a princess, daughter of the ruling house of Athens which Theseus has supplanted, and Hippolytus is in love with her. Her existence changes the effect of the tale, for in Euripides' version, Aphrodite casts the love spell on Phaedra out of pique that Hippolytus is more interested in hunting than in women. By introducing Aricia, Racine replaces the Olympian meddling with mere human passion.

ARINA see **IRINA**

ARKADINA *(Russian from Greek, "from Arcadia")* Arcadia was an area in southwestern Greece, and a fourth-century bishop named Arkadios is honored in Eastern Rite churches. In Chekhov's play *The Seagull,* Irena Arkadina Trepliov is known as "Madame Arkadina." A middle-aged actress, she competes with and constantly undermines her sensitive playwright son Konstantin. She is equally domineering with her younger lover, Trigorin. In our era she can be characterized as a monster of egotism.

ARTEMIS *(Greek mythology name)* One of the twelve Olympians, the virginal goddess of the moon who is Apollo's twin. Artemis is known in Roman myth as **Diana,** but she is also referred to as **Delia** (for Delos, the island where she was born) and as **Cynthia** (for Mount Cynthus or Kynthos, the mountain on Delos that was her birthplace). She is the patroness of hunting, and in Euripides' *Hippolytus,* she defends the young Hippolytus's lack of interest in women. A low, flowering shrub common in temperate areas is known as artemisia, possibly invoking the goddess's affinity for greenery.

ASPASIA *(Greek, "welcome")* An erudite joke in Anthony Trollope's *Phineas Finn.* The great Athenian statesman Pericles had a beautiful and intelligent mistress named Aspasia, a courtesan of the very highest level. Trollope's version is the Honourable Aspasia Fitzgibbon, the acid-tongued spinster sister of Laurence Fitzgibbon, Phineas Finn's Irish mentor in Parliament. She arrives on Phineas's doorstep to repay the money her brother owes him, thus averting a financial crisis and scandal—but there is nothing of tenderness or sexual commerce in her act. Of course Phineas Finn doesn't much resemble Pericles either.

ASTARTE *(Mythology name)* Astarte was the Babylonian goddess of love and war, known also as **Ishtar, Ashtoreth,** and **Athtar.** Widely worshipped in the Middle East, she was a fearsome deity with a chancy temper, whose worship included ritual prostitution. In some versions of her myth, she chooses an incestuous lover. When Byron wrote his verse drama "Manfred" in 1816–17, he was passionately in love with his half sister, a connection that had already caused scandal in England. Thus, when the hero Manfred (seeking the limits of sensual knowledge) summons the spirit of Astarte as his lover, the poet is consciously building on his own myth.

ATALANTA *(Greek mythology name)* In Ovid's *Metamorphoses,* Atalanta is a young Greek girl who can run like the wind. When she asks Apollo whether or not she should marry, he is not encouraging. Yet, determined to marry only a man who is her equal, she sets up a footrace. The man who beats her will be her suitor—any losers will be put to death. Hippomenes, with the help of Venus, wins the race by dropping golden apples in front of Atalanta. When she stoops to pick them up, he passes her.

> *Now she consulted the god Apollo on the subject of a husband, and he gave her this reply: "You have no need of a husband, Atalanta. You should avoid any experience of one. But assuredly, you will not escape marriage and then, though still alive, yet you will lose your own self."*
>
> —OVID, *METAMORPHOSES*

ATHENA *(Greek mythology name)* The fierce virginal goddess of wisdom in the Greek pantheon. Also known as **Pallas** and—to the Romans—as **Minerva,** she was born of Zeus and Metis. When an oracle told Zeus that Metis would bear him a child who would rule the gods, he swallowed the woman whole. Athena duly manifested herself as a crashing pain in Zeus's head. When Hephaestus split his father's head with an axe to relieve the headache, Athena sprang out, fully armed. She was the special protector of her city, Athens, and appears frequently in *The Odyssey* of Homer as "sparkling-eyed Athena," Odysseus's guardian. She also intervenes in the Trojan War. Like her father Zeus, Athena is quick to take offense when she feels she has been slighted.

AUDREY *(Old English, "noble strength")* An earlier form is Etheldreda, the name of a seventh-century English saint who founded a Northumberland convent. In Shakespeare's *As You Like It,* Audrey is one of the rustic inhabitants of the Forest of Arden. Touchstone the fool attempts to court her, vowing to abandon her afterward, but she outwits him by insisting that he tend her goats before she'll even listen to him.

An uncommon French form of the name is **Aude,** found in *The Song of Roland.* Aude is the betrothed of Roland and the sister of Olivier. Upon learning of Roland's betrayal and defeat at Roncesvalles, she dies.

> *Augusta Gresham had perceived early in life that she could not obtain success either as an heiress or as a beauty, nor could she shine as a wit; she therefore fell back on such qualities as she had, and determined to win the world as a strong-minded, useful woman.*
>
> —ANTHONY TROLLOPE, *DOCTOR THORNE*

AUGUSTA *(Latin, "venerable")* The name was brought to England by Augusta of Saxe-Gotha-Altenburg, wife of Frederick, Prince of Wales, and mother of George III. It was used with some enthusiasm in the upper classes—the half sister of whom Lord Byron was so scandalously fond was named Augusta. By the mid-Victorian era, the name had stuffy or pretentious connotations, and was used humorously by both Dickens and Trollope. In Dickens's *Bleak House,* the skinny, downtrodden maid of the Snagsby family is Augusta, called "Guster." Her unlucky lot in life is emphasized by her tendency to have "fits." Trollope uses the name as comic relief in *The Eustace Diamonds,* where Augusta Fawn is a virginal young woman of thirty, one of seven Fawn maidens still living at Fawn Court. *Doctor Thorne* is the Barsetshire novel that introduces a number of Trollope's best-loved characters, but Augusta Gresham is not one of these. A terrible snob, she aims to secure a husband for worldly advantage rather than for love—and ends up destined for spinsterhood. In *Phineas Finn,* we meet Lady

THE FAWN SISTERS

Anthony Trollope often amused himself with names, especially with what he saw as the pretentious names of the upper classes. In *The Eustace Diamonds*, the timid peer Lord Fawn has eight sisters. With a couple of exceptions, they are not even characters, just names: **Clara, Augusta, Amelia, Georgina, Diana, Lydia, Cecilia,** and **Nina.**

Augusta Boreham, the tedious daughter of Lady Blockhead, who is headstrong Violet Effingham's aunt and chaperone. She is no more than a dull foil to her tempestuous cousin, but Trollope has a joke at her expense when she is reappears in *Phineas Finn* as Sister Veronica John—a Catholic nun.

> *"Your name, like mine, represents a flower,"* said the little woman in the bed. *"Mine is Rose Muniment and her ladyship's is Aurora Langrish. That means the morning or the dawn; it's the most beautiful of all, don't you think?"*
> —HENRY JAMES, *THE PRINCESS CASAMASSIMA*

AURORA *(Latin mythology name)* Aurora was the Roman goddess of the dawn; certain phenomena of light, like the aurora borealis, or northern lights, refer to her. Lord Byron created an austere young heiress in *Don Juan* whom he called Aurora with some irony. Though she is only sixteen and an orphan, Don Juan wins her over, perhaps for the challenge of the thing. A warmer-blooded character refers to her as "that prim, silent, cold Aurora Raby." Lady Aurora Langrish in Henry James's *The Princess Casamassima* is a different kind of aristocrat. A warm and unconventional spinster, she finds pleasure in visiting the poor invalid Rose Muniment. "She was plain and diffident and she might have been poor," from the way she is dressed, says the narrator. Instead, she is one of a noble family of thirteen, and Byron's epithet of "prim, silent, cold" could refer to the Langrish home life in Belgrave Square.

AVICE *(Latin, "bird")* The name of a series of women in Thomas Hardy's novel *The Well-Beloved*. Jocelyn Pierston, the protagonist, has a mental image of the "well-beloved" woman. He falls in love as he mentally invests women with her characteristics, but on repeated occasions, reality overwhelms his ideal. His first romantic object is Avice Caro, a beautiful, refined girl on the isolated Isle of Slingers. Pierston proposes to her after a month's acquaintance, but impulsively leaves the island with another woman. The jilted Avice later marries a cousin and has a daughter, also called Avice, whom Pierston falls in love with when he returns to the island twenty years later. This Avice is as pretty as her mother, but neither as clever nor as well educated; Pierston hires her as his housekeeper but eventually sends her back to her husband. Another twenty years later, he meets and tries to marry *her* daughter, a third Avice—but finally realizes that she loves another man. In the course of the novel Pierston also falls in love with two women who are not named Avice.

> *Of all the girls he had known he had never met one with more charming and solid qualities than Avice Caro's.*
> —THOMAS HARDY, THE WELL-BELOVED

AZELMA *(French invented name)* Victor Hugo makes clear, in *Les Misérables*, that he holds strong and conservative opinions about the choice of names. The vile Thénardier family, for instance, has two daughters with names chosen out of the "cheap novels" that Madame Thénardier enjoys. Azelma is the younger of these, called Zelma by Cosette. Inasmuch as the name has legitimate roots, they would be found in the name **Anselm** or its feminization **Anselma**.

BARBARA *(Greek, "foreign")* Saint Barbara, a virgin martyr, was walled up in a tower to discourage her suitors, and her father attempted to kill her when she became a Christian. She is often portrayed in medieval art holding a small-scale tower. Margaret Oliphant may have been playing with the notion of imprisonment when she named Barbara Lake, in her 1866 *Miss Marjoribanks*. Barbara was not a common choice in the Victorian era, and Oliphant's choice of her heroine's name, **Lucilla** (see **Lucy**) suggests she considered connotations. Barbara Lake is the daughter of the drawing master in the small town of Carlingford. She both resents the patronage of Lucilla Marjoribanks, and is drawn to her elevated social circle. Her farouche manners, however, prevent her assimilation into Lucilla's group: "She was a young woman without any of those instincts of politeness, which make some people pleasant in spite of themselves."

The Russian form of the name is **Varvara,** sometimes shortened to **Varya** or **Varia.** Turgenev's *Home of the Gentry* describes what happens when middle-aged Fyodor Lavretsky visits his aunt Marfa at the estate where she lives. Though Lavretsky falls in love with the young Liza Kalitin, he is interrupted in his courting by the arrival of his estranged wife Varvara. Beautiful, clever, and artistic, she is also immoral. Her indiscriminate love affairs have broken Lavretsky's heart, and she has tracked him down to get him to pay her debts. Turgenev says, "She had much practical sense, much taste, a great fondness for comfort and much ability in obtaining such comfort for herself." In Chekhov's *The Cherry Orchard,* one of the characters with the greatest stake in the outcome of the plot is Varia, the adopted daughter of the owner

Liubov. Varia manages the estate, and is in love with Lopahin, the merchant who wants to buy the land and cut down the cherry orchard. Since he barely notices her presence, it's just as well that her fallback ambition is to enter a convent.

> *And then Barbara possessed a kind of beauty, the beauty of a passionate and somewhat sullen brunette, dark and glowing, with straight black eyebrows, very dark and very straight.* —MARGARET OLIPHANT, *MISS MARJORIBANKS*

BATHSHEBA *(Hebrew, "daughter of oath")* Thomas Hardy lavished imagination on the process of choosing names for his characters, and Bathsheba Everdene in *Far from the Madding Crowd* is one of his liveliest creations. The biblical Bathsheba was the beautiful wife of Uriah the Hittite whom King David seduced. The king had Uriah placed in the front line of battle where he was promptly killed, allowing David to marry his widow. Hardy's Bathsheba has no less sex appeal. The beautiful and headstrong heiress to a large farm, she turns all heads when she arrives in the village of Weatherbury. She is courted by three men, marries the wrong one (Sergeant Troy), and wreaks havoc on another (Farmer Boldwood) before ending happily with the modest farmer Gabriel Oak.

> *Bathsheba loved Troy in the way that only self-reliant women love when they abandon their self-reliance.* —THOMAS HARDY, *FAR FROM THE MADDING CROWD*

BEATRICE *(Latin, "she who brings gladness")* Scholars speculate that Dante's muse Beatrice (the Italian pronunciation is *bay a tree' chay*) is based on Beatrice Portinari, daughter of the powerful

Portinari family. Yet the Beatrice readers know through *La Vita Nuova* is only nominally a real person. Dante idealizes the young woman (whom, in fact, he saw only twice) to the extent that she becomes a symbol of the divine. It is in this guise that she reappears in *The Divine Comedy*. Shakespeare's Beatrice, in *Much Ado About Nothing*, is a more definite kind of heroine. Proud, pretty, and possessed of a very tart tongue, she scorns men. "She speaks poniards, and every word stabs: if her breath were as terrible as her terminations, there were no living near her; she would infect to the north star," says one character about her. Through a ruse, however, she is brought to see the appeal of the eternal bachelor Benedick.

> *"Beatrice is so strong and healthy, she never takes any medicine; but if I had had twenty girls, and they had been delicate, I should have given them all camomile tea."*
> —GEORGE ELIOT, "MR. GILFIL'S LOVE STORY"

The literary Beatrices since then tend to be ironic responses to Dante's creation. The name—and its variant **Beatrix**—was little used until the nineteenth century, when Queen Victoria named her youngest daughter (born in 1857) Beatrice Maud. William Thackeray's *The History of Henry Esmond* is set in the late seventeenth and early eighteenth centuries. The narrator, Henry Esmond, is the legitimate heir to the viscountcy of Castlewood, but believes himself to be illegitimate. Beatrix Castlewood is his beautiful and tempestuous niece, with whom he falls in love. She ultimately chooses as her consort James Stuart, the Catholic pretender to the throne of England. Beatrix Castlewood is not a "bringer of gladness" to Henry Esmond. Beatrice Assher, in George Eliot's tale "Mr. Gilfil's Love Story," brings happiness of a backhanded sort. Mr. Gilfil is a minister, the dependent of a noble family, who has fallen in love with the tempestuous Caterina, their Italian ward. She loves the heir, Captain Wybrow, but Beatrice Assher is chosen as his socially proper consort, throwing

Caterina into Gilfil's arms. Eliot describes Beatrice as "tall, and gracefully though substantially formed, carrying herself with an air of mingled graciousness and self-confidence."

BELA (*Hungarian variant of German* Adalbert, *"noble bright"*) In Mikhail Lermontov's *A Hero of Our Time,* Bela is a Cossack girl whom the protagonist, Grigory Pechorin, seduces. Pechorin is a restless, heartless, underoccupied aristocrat, and Bela, for him, represents little more than a wild episode. She falls in love with him and he becomes bored with her adoration, though he does stay by her bedside when she dies of a stab wound incurred in a quarrel. Even her death elicits no emotion from him.

BÉLINE (*French invented name*) Béline is one of the formal names Molière created for his characters. It may have roots in the French word for "to bleat" (like a sheep) or possibly *belle,* which means beautiful. The former, however, is more likely, because Béline is the second wife of the hypochondriac Argan in *The Imaginary Invalid.* She has married him for his money, and encourages his delusions of ill health, while at the same time urging him to put his beautiful daughter into a convent.

BELLA (*Italian, "beautiful"*) Usually a diminutive for a longer name like **Arabella.** In Dickens's *Our Mutual Friend,* Bella Wilfer is the spoiled, giddy daughter of Reginald Wilfer, a clerk in the Veneerings' drug concern. The novel's hero, John Harmon, is left a large sum of money on the condition that he marry Bella Wilfer—which he finds himself able to do, for though she lacks any moral weight, she does live up to her name.

BELPHOEBE (bel fee′ bee; *Greek, "sharp light"*) The name may have been coined by Edmund Spenser for a character in *The Faerie Queen.* The Greek word *belos* means "dart" while *phoibos* (root of the familiar **Phoebe**) means "light." Spenser's Belphoebe is a well-armed virgin huntress, a version of both the goddess Diana and Queen Elizabeth I, and a militant personification of chastity. Her fighting skills are repeatedly tested and proven.

BÉRÉNICE *(bay ray nees´; Greek, "bringer of victory")* In Jean Racine's *Bérénice,* the title character is the queen of Palestine, in love with the Roman emperor Titus. The latter, when he finds out that his people resent his choice of a foreign bride, sacrifices his love for the loyalty of his constituency. In Honoré de Balzac's *Lost Illusions,* Bérénice is the loving, loyal maid of Coralie, Lucien de Rubempré's mistress. Fat, ugly, but endlessly loyal, Bérénice stands by her mistress when Coralie's acting career disintegrates, nurses her through an illness, and in the end even prostitutes herself to come up with the money to send Lucien home to his sister in Angoulême.

BERTHA *(Old German, "bright")* Catharine Maria Sedgwick wrote her historical novel of early America, *Hope Leslie,* in 1827. In this tale set in Puritan Massachusetts, names are significant. The Puritans use virtue names, but those characters still attached to the frivolity of England and the established church are identified by their equally lightweight names. Bertha Grafton, the incorrigible aunt of Hope Leslie, has her fondest thoughts pinned not on her salvation but on her personal adornment. (The fashion term "bertha," for a deep collar of lace, didn't become current for another thirty-five years after the writing of the book.) In Charlotte Brontë's *Jane Eyre,* Bertha Mason is the beautiful but unstable woman to whom Edward Rochester is married—and whom he keeps in the attic at Thornfield Hall since she has lost her sanity.

BLANCHE *(French, "white")* In *Jane Eyre,* Blanche Ingram is Jane's competition for the heart of Mr. Rochester. Quiet, observant Jane sees through Blanche's charms: "She was very showy, but she was not genuine. . . . She was not good; she was not original; she used to repeat sounding phrases from books; she never offered, nor had, an opinion of her own. . . . Tenderness and truth were not in her." Yet Rochester pretends to Jane that he is going to marry Blanche, hoping to provoke a show of emotion from the governess. Having elicited it, he then proposes to Jane.

The Italian form of the name is **Bianca,** and in Shakespeare's

The Taming of the Shrew, Bianca, like Blanche Ingram, serves as a contrast to the heroine. Her father has decreed that she cannot marry until her spitfire sister Katherina finds a mate. Constantly referred to as "fair Bianca" and "sweet Bianca," she is much in demand among the swains of Padua.

> *One can't have too much of such a very excellent thing as my beautiful Blanche.* —CHARLOTTE BRONTË, *JANE EYRE*

BRADAMANTE *(Italian invented name)* One of the principal female characters in Ludovico Ariosto's *Orlando Furioso.* She is Rinaldo's sister, a virginal female warrior as fierce as any man. She is often referred to as "the Maid," an epithet that emphasizes her chastity. Her love interest throughout the epic is Ruggiero, the pagan king of Reggio and descendant of the great warrior Hector. After thousands of pages of adventures, in which she saves Ruggiero from enchantment or captivity, he finally agrees to be baptized and to marry her. The happy pair found the noble Este family, rulers of Ferrara—and Ariosto's patrons.

BRIANA *(English invented name)* A name that sounds like a twentieth-century development but actually has roots in the sixteenth—alas, not especially positive ones. The books of Edmund Spenser's *The Faerie Queen* focus on specific "moral virtues." Book Six, in which Briana appears, concerns itself with courtesy and rudeness. Briana is the mistress of a castle and the lover of Sir Crudor: the pair are emblems of discourtesy.

BRIDGET *(Irish Gaelic, "strength" or "the high one")* An ancient goddess of Ireland as well as that country's female patron saint. Saint Bridget was the foundress of an order of nuns in Kildare in the late fifth century. In Henry Fielding's *Tom Jones,* Bridget Allworthy is the unmarried sister of Squire Allworthy, who comes home one day to find a baby in his bed. Though the infant Tom is passed off as the son of a maid, Bridget is really his mother. Shortly afterward she marries Captain Blifil and has another son, who becomes Tom's nemesis.

Bridget (or **Brigid**) is usually used in Catholic countries, with specific reference to the Irish saint and to a Swedish saint of the eleventh century (**Birgitta**). The veneration of these holy ladies throughout Europe resulted in forms like **Brigitte, Birgit**, and **Brigida** and nicknames like **Bride** and **Bridey**. George Eliot's *Romola* is set in fifteenth-century Florence, under the sway of Savonarola. Mona Brigida is the kindly, vain aunt of the scholarly Romola. Eliot gently mocks her frivolity and her close attention to fashion.

The most commonly used nickname for Bridget is **Biddy**. Fanny Burney, in her epistolary novel of manners *Evelina* (1778), uses it to signal class. The gently reared Evelina is appalled to meet her vulgar cousins the Branghtons, whose father is a silversmith. The two Branghton daughters are pushy and ill-mannered. In the formal eighteenth century, their insistent use of nicknames ("Biddy" and "Poll") marks them especially as ill-bred. Biddy is just as crude as her sister Poll, and malicious to boot. Charles Dickens uses the name in *Great Expectations* in a similar way. Biddy is the loyal, affectionate village girl who is a friend to Pip. At the end of the book, after his "great expectations" and their consequences have been revealed, Pip asks Biddy to marry him, but she has already married the widowed blacksmith Joe Gargery.

BRITOMART (*Greek mythology name*) **Britomartis** was an ancient Cretan goddess who caught the fancy of King Minos and fled into the sea to escape him. The Britomart in Edmund Spenser's *The Faerie Queen* borrows her name and her chastity. She is one representation of Elizabeth I (the Virgin Queen). Book Three of the epic deals with chastity and features Britomart as a maiden knight. Merlin predicts that she will marry the knight Artegall ("equal to Arthur") whose face she has seen once in a mirror and adored. In Book Four, Britomart fights Artegall in a tournament and unhorses him, but when he knocks off her helmet to reveal the woman inside the armor, he falls in love with her and the two become betrothed. The kings of Britain, in Merlin's augury, will be their descendants.

BRUNHILD *(Old German, "armed for battle")* Also **Brunhilde, Brunnhilde, Brunhilda.** *The Nibelungenlied* is a German epic poem written around 1200 and based on existing German and Scandinavian legends. It owes much of its current fame to Richard Wagner's operatic adaptations. Brunhild, in the original version, is a physically mighty queen of Iceland who is wooed by the Burgundian king Gunther. He is not strong enough to subdue and bed her, however. Instead, Siegfried dons his cloak of invisibility and wrestles Brunhild into submission, stealing her ring and girdle at the same time. He gives them to his wife, Kriemhild, who in a malicious moment shows them to Brunhild. Tragedy and multiple deaths ensue.

CALIXTA *(Greek, "most beautiful")* Also **Callixta, Callista, Calista.** Kate Chopin's fiction takes readers to the exotic setting of the Creole South at the turn of the century. "At the 'Cadian Ball" describes a love triangle between the bourgeois Alcée, his cool, elegant girlfriend Clarisse, and the alluring Calixta. Chopin makes clear that Calixta's appeal is highly sexual; she is voluptuous, blue-eyed, with very curly hair and a thrilling low voice. Though Alcée flirts heavily with Calixta at the ball, Clarisse manages to reassert her claim on him.

CALLIOPE *(cah ligh' oh pee; Greek, "lovely voice")* In Greek myth, as related in Hesiod's poem the *Theogony*, Calliope is one of the nine Muses, daughters of Zeus and Mnemosyne. The mother was a Titan, the goddess of memory—our word "mnemonic" comes from her name. Each one of the Muses inspired the artists and intellectuals who practiced her particular craft; Calliope was the muse of epic poetry and the leader of the group. (The musical instrument was named after the literal sense of her name rather than her area of interest.) The tragic Orpheus was her son.

> *And Calypso stowed two skins aboard—dark wine in one,*
> *the larger one held water—added a sack of rations,*
> *filled with her choicest meats to build his strength,*
> *and summoned a wind to bear him onward, fair and warm.*
> *—HOMER, THE ODYSSEY*

CALYPSO *(Greek, "one who hides")* One of the most appealing characters in *The Odyssey,* Calypso is the goddess who has enchanted Odysseus and kept him on her island for eight years rather than releasing him to return to Ithaka. Homer refers to her as "the bewitching nymph" and "the lustrous goddess." When Hermes intervenes and instructs Calypso to release Odysseus, she does so, outfitting him with generosity, and genuinely mourning his departure.

CAMILLA *(Latin, meaning unknown)* In *The Aeneid* of Virgil, Camilla is the virgin warrior queen of the Volscians who assists Turnus in his battle against Aeneas. Dante, in the *Inferno*, places

---

AMUSEMENT

Zeus sired an extraordinary number of children, most of whom had extraordinary powers. Among the most constructive were the Muses, his nine daughters by the Titaness Mnemosyne. She was the goddess of memory, and recounted to her children the entire history of the world. Each daughter was patroness or inspirer of a specific art:

Calliope: epic poetry
Clio: history
Erato: love poetry
Euterpe: lyric poetry
Melpomene: tragedy
Polyhymnia: sacred poetry
Terpsichore: choral song and dance
Thalia: comedy
Urania: astronomy

Each Muse also had a specific attribute by which she could be identified. The tragic mask of Melpomene and the comic mask of Thalia are probably the most familiar of these attributes today.

her among the Virtuous Pagans. Balzac may allude to her when he uses the French form of the name, **Camille,** for a young novelist whom Lucien Chardon encounters in *Lost Illusions.* Camille Maupin, whose pen name is Mademoiselle des Touches, is wealthy, proud, beautiful—and utterly immune to Lucien's potent sexual charm. (She is also, scholars suggest, based on the novelist George Sand.)

CAROLINE *(Old English, "man")* Also **Carolina, Carolyn.** George II of England married the German princess Caroline of Brandenburgh-Anspach in 1705, and George IV married another German princess, Caroline of Brunswick-Wolfenbuttel, in 1795. He had already been married, to the scandalous divorcée Mrs. Fitzherbert, and submitted to the new marriage only because the government agreed to pay his debts. It was a wretched match, involving desertion and separation and even unsuccessful adultery proceedings (against the queen), and it did the Crown a great deal of damage. When Oliver Goldsmith wrote *The Vicar of Wakefield* he created a minor character named Carolina Wilhelmina Amelia Skeggs—her string of multisyllabic names (followed by the deflating monosyllable) is a comic device. Curiously, Wilhelmina was the middle name of the first Queen Caroline and Amelia the middle name of the second, who wasn't born until two years after *The Vicar of Wakefield* was written.

One of Jane Austen's deliciously hateful characters is Caroline Bingley in *Pride and Prejudice,* a cold, ill-mannered snob who has set her cap for Mr. Darcy. Wilkie Collins makes a joke on the queenly associations of the name by calling a minor character in *The Moonstone* Caroline and naming her sister Adelaide—the name of the wife of William IV, George's IV's equally discreditable brother, who reigned after him. The most common nickname is probably **Carrie,** but Dickens uses **Caddy** for the eldest daughter of the unfortunate Jellyby family in *Bleak House.* Mrs. Jellyby is so focused on the well-being of poor children in Africa that she utterly neglects her own offspring. Caddy serves as unpaid secretary ("I suppose nobody ever was in such a state of ink," says Dickens) as well as nanny. She ultimately marries the gloriously named Prince Turveydrop.

> "Miss C. Morgeson, *we will call you,*" she said, *in our first interview;* "*the name of Cassandra is too peculiar.*"
> —ELIZABETH STODDARD, *THE MORGESONS*

CASSANDRA *(Greek, meaning unknown)* Cassandra, the daughter of King Priam of Troy, was given the gift of prophecy by Apollo, who lusted after her. But when she refused to become his mistress, he amended his gift so that no one would believe her predictions. After the debacle of the Trojan War she was Agamemnon's prisoner and concubine. In Aeschylus's *Agamemnon* she foretells not only Agamemnon's death but also her own. The chorus, however, cannot understand her prophecy. Euripides, in *The Trojan Women,* gives her long speeches (her listeners believe her to be raving) that also foresee the fall of the house of Atreus.

Curiously enough, given this discouraging example, the name has been used with some consistency in anglophone countries. Jane Austen's much-loved sister, for instance, was named Cassandra. Yet in the provincial nineteenth-century Massachusetts of Elizabeth Stoddard's *The Morgesons,* it is seen as a strange name for a very strange girl. Cassandra Morgeson, who narrates, is a willful, intelligent young woman with a rebellious attitude toward the restrictions of her narrow world.

It was not uncommon for slave owners to give their servants grandiose names from classical literature; hence **Cassy,** in *Uncle Tom's Cabin,* short no doubt for Cassandra. She is the half-white former mistress of a slave owner, brought up in a convent and highly strung, who turns out to be Eliza's mother. She is forced to be the mistress of the odious Simon Legree, but escapes to Montreal and is reunited with Eliza.

CATHERINE *(Greek, "pure")* Also **Katherine, Katharine, Kathryn, Catharine,** as well as **Kathleen, Caitlin, Katrina,** and many more variations. A saint's name and a royal name in many European countries. Saint Catherine of Alexandria was an early martyr whose colorful history (a beautiful virgin, she was tortured on a wheel after refusing to marry the emperor Maxentius) seems to have no basis in fact. Three of Henry VIII's six wives were named Catherine, as was Russia's great empress. It is no surprise that the name occurs frequently in literature, in many different forms.

> *"Cathy, do come. Oh, do—once more! Oh! My heart's darling! Hear me this time, Catherine, at last!"*
> —EMILY BRONTË, *WUTHERING HEIGHTS*

The *C* spelling was the most common in nineteenth-century England, and Jane Austen used it twice. The arch-snob Lady Catherine De Bourgh in *Pride and Prejudice* is one of Austen's most delicious creations, while the credulous Catherine Morland of *Northanger Abbey,* wishing to find gothic horror in everyday life, is less broadly comic. In contrast, Emily Brontë takes Catherine Earnshaw in *Wuthering Heights* utterly seriously. She is the pretty but headstrong and ultimately selfish young girl who captivates Heathcliff as a boy. The housekeeper, Nelly, remembers: "A wild, wicked slip she was—but she had the bonniest eye, and sweetest smile, and lightest foot in the parish." Yet, though she loves Heathcliff, she marries her neighbor, Edgar Linton, who is rich and refined. She dies while giving birth to her daughter, Cathy Linton, who in turn marries Heathcliff's son. George Eliot, in *Daniel Deronda,* creates a portrait of an intelligent, highly musical, but homely young woman who is the heiress to a large new fortune. Catherine Arrowpoint bears with dignity the necessity to submit to the wooing that was the sole function of a rich young girl in the Victorian era. Eliot, who was herself quite plain, not only makes Miss Arrowpoint likable but gives her as a lover the irascible musical genius Julius Klesmer (based, some scholars think, on Liszt). Another rich and homely Catherine is Miss Sloper in Henry James's *Washington Square*. The shy daughter of the exacting Dr. Sloper, she is a perpetual disappointment to her father, who thus cannot believe that the handsome Morris Townsend is courting his daughter for any reason beyond her fortune. Finding no charm in her, he cannot imagine that Townsend would. When Townsend abandons her, Catherine retreats from the world, and repulses him coldly when he contacts her again twenty-five years later.

In French, the spelling is the same but the name is pronounced *cah treen´*, while the Italian form is **Caterina**. Zola's coal-mining novel, *Germinal,* includes a portrait of Catherine Maheu, a young woman who is born into the harsh poverty of a mining town. She longs for a life of more refinement, but ends up as the mistress of one of the crudest miners. George Eliot's "Mr. Gilfil's Love Story" tells the poignant story of a clerical romance. Maynard Gilfil is a mild young minister who falls madly in love with Caterina, the Italian ward of his aristocratic patrons. She marries Gilfil when her true love is persuaded into a match with a fellow aristocrat.

The name is also popular in Russia, and novelists have used several forms and spellings, including **Yekaterina**, **Katerina**, and **Katya** (a diminutive). In Dostoevsky's *The Brothers Karamazov,* Katerina Ivanovna (also called Katya) is the fiancée of Dmitri Karamazov. Fond of self-dramatization, she pledges eternal loyalty to Dmitri even though it is his brother Ivan whom she loves. What's more, Dmitri, the "earthy" brother, really loves the working-class Grushenka, who goes into exile with him. In Russia it was an upper-class affectation to prefer Western European names or nicknames to Russian options. Hence **Kitty** as a nickname for Yekaterina Turkin in Chekhov's tale "Ionych." In the Turkin household the father Ivan is known as "Jean" and Kitty, the daughter, spends hours of every day pounding away at the piano. At first district medical officer Dmitri Ionych Startsev finds the family's level of culture thrilling, but he eventually sees it as pure pretension. In *Anna Karenina,* Kitty is one of the three beautiful Shcherbatsky daughters, courted briefly by the dashing Count Vronsky but won by the staid Konstantin Levin. Tolstoy makes her a flighty young flirt who matures into a strong, practical helpmeet to her husband.

Kitty, of course, occurs in English novels as well, as a nickname for Katherine. One of the bouncing young Bennet daughters in *Pride and Prejudice* is named Kitty. More common, though, is **Kate** (other variations are **Katie** and **Katy**). The most famous Kate is of course the sharp-tongued heroine of *The Taming of the Shrew*. Having set his play in Italy, Shakespeare gives her the Italian name **Katherina,** but she is widely known as "plain Kate." In fact, she blazed such a trail as an outspoken woman that later Kates may intentionally echo her frankness. Kate Nickleby, sister of Dickens's Nicholas, is a classic Dickensian heroine: sweet, beautiful, pure, hardworking, and innocent—the polar opposite, in fact, of Kate the shrew. But Kate Vavasor in Trollope's *Can You Forgive Her?* shares some of the earlier Kate's abrasive nature. She is one of Trollope's conflicted characters, obstinately loyal to her selfish brother George, difficult and prickly in society, and unexpectedly kind to her silly aunt and crotchety, sickly grandfather. Kate Croy in Henry James's *The Wings of the Dove* is another complex woman who, in her pride and her awareness of a woman's limited role, conjures the shrew. Poor, intelligent, but a lady, she is launched in society by her ambitious aunt. While her aunt drives her toward a monied marriage, she carries on her relationship with journalist Merton Densher until the rich and ailing American heiress Milly Theale enters—and transforms—their lives.

> *You lie, in faith; for you are called plain Kate,*
> *And bonny Kate and sometimes Kate the curst;*
> *But Kate, the prettiest Kate in Christendom*
> *Kate of Kate Hall, my super-dainty Kate,*
> *For dainties are all Kates.*
> —WILLIAM SHAKESPEARE, *THE TAMING OF THE SHREW*

CECILIA (*Latin, clan name possibly meaning "blind"*) In Chaucer's *Canterbury Tales* "The Second Nun's Tale" recounts the history of Saint Cecilia, a martyr who persuaded her pagan fiancé Valerian to be baptized before their marriage. He is killed, and so is she, but only after strenuous efforts by her murderers. She is also referred to as **Cecile** or **Cecilie** in the story. Although modern scholars scoff at the origin of her cult, Saint Cecilia is the patroness of music. Her name was not very widely used in England. Trollope includes a Cecilia in the long list of elaborately named Fawn daughters (*The Eustace Diamonds*)—Cecilia is the sixth, between Lydia and Nina. Dickens, too, draws attention to the pretentious air of the name in *Hard Times*. Sissy Jupe, the daughter of a clown and an acrobatic rider, joins the utilitarian Gradgrind household and is renamed Cecilia because "Sissy is not a name." Her essential warmth and humanity, however, also unusual in the Gradgrind family, are not so easily displaced.

Scholars draw a distinction between **Celia** and Cecilia, pointing out that the former name descends from a different Latin clan name, but for centuries Celia has been understood as a variation of Cecilia. In Shakespeare's *As You Like It*, Celia is Rosalind's cousin and sidekick, and a witty woman in her own right. She ends up, after the magical effects of the Forest of Arden, as the beloved of Oliver. In George Eliot's *Middlemarch*, Celia Brooke is the gentler, more conforming sister of the serious Dorothea. Celia's ease with the world points up Dorothea's intensity and earnestness. Harold Frederic's *The Damnation of Theron Ware* is a turn-of-the-century fable about the lost innocence of a naive Methodist preacher. Celia Madden is the beautiful, hedonistic Catholic woman who exposes him to the mystical, sensual appeal of religion as well as culture.

The French form of the name is **Cécile** and it is fairly common, perhaps because of the popularity of Saint Cecilia. In Choderlos de Laclos's *Les Liaisons Dangereuses*, Cécile de Volanges is the young virgin deflowered by the rakish Vicomte de Valmont. Fifteen years old, convent raised, and perfectly innocent, she does not even understand, after her seduction, what Valmont has done. Balzac's Cécile Camusot de Marville, in *Cousin Pons*, is also a young woman of marriageable age, but a different character altogether. The daughter of a bureaucrat and his grasping, ambitious wife, she is principally concerned with making an advantageous match, regardless of the personal qualities of her projected spouse. In Émile Zola's *Germinal*, Cécile Gregoire is the pampered daughter of the family that owns the Montsou mines. "She was not pretty, being too heavy and full-blooded and quite mature at eighteen, but her perfect flesh was white as milk," says Zola. She is thus a complete contrast to the scrawny, dirty, ill-nourished Maheu family that works in the mines.

> *Cécile, a red-haired young woman, with a touch of pedantic affectation, combined her father's ponderous manner with a trace of her mother's hardness.*
> —HONORÉ DE BALZAC, *COUSIN PONS*

CÉLIMÈNE *(French invented name)* A name, possibly based on Cécile, created by Molière for a character in *Le Misanthrope*. Célimène is a heartless, flirtatious young widow whom the misanthrope of the title loves. She has a small pack of suitors, and gossips cruelly about each to the others. When her malice is unmasked at the end of the play, they all abandon her.

CERES *(Latin mythology name, possibly from* crescere, *meaning "to grow")* Ceres is the Latin name for Demeter, goddess of the harvest: our word "cereal" comes from her name, since it was under her auspices that grain flourished. She is the mother of Proserpine, and in *Metamorphoses* Ovid tells how she searched all over the world for traces of her daughter when the latter was kidnapped by Pluto. She found Proserpine's girdle in Sicily, and in her anger broke up the earth and made it barren and inhospitable to crops.

CÉSARINE *(say zah reen´; French, from Latin* caesar *which, though it originally meant "hairy child," has taken on the mean-*

ing of "emperor") In Balzac's *César Birotteau,* Césarine is the daughter of the wealthy but modestly born perfumer. Often in Balzac's novels—particularly those that take place in Paris, which Balzac saw as a corrupting influence—children are vicious and ungrateful to their hardworking parents. Césarine Birotteau, loving, pretty, kindly, and modest, breaks this pattern. She appreciates her parents and hopes to make a good marriage that will please them.

CHARITY *(English virtue name)* The principal of the three "Theological Virtues" in the Christian faith, the other two being Faith and Hope. More recent translations of Scripture render it as "love," since "charity" has taken on the meaning of philanthropy. In Edmund Spenser's allegorical *The Faerie Queen,* the characters tend to be ideas rather than human beings, hence **Charissa,** an embodiment of Christian love. She lives with her sisters Fidelia (Faith) and Speranza (Hope) in the House of Holiness, and teaches Saint George about the meaning of love. Charles Dickens uses the name in *Martin Chuzzlewit* for the sour spinster daughter of Mr. Pecksniff. She is called **Cherry,** but her given name is Charity. As she cares for her ailing, elderly father, it becomes clear that she does, in fact, deserve her name. Charity Royall, in Edith Wharton's *Summer,* is named to memorialize the impulse that prompted an attorney in rural Massachusetts to adopt her. Born in poverty to a feckless teenager, Charity is raised by lawyer Royall in the tiny town of North Dormer. Her life is brightened—briefly—by the appearance of Lucius Harney, a clever architect.

CHARLOTTE *(French from Old German, "man")* The Old English word is *ceorl,* and it meant "man" in terms of "the fellow who tills the fields"—a man as a unit of labor. The obsolete word "churl" is a remnant of the concept. **Charlotte,** of course, is a feminization of Charles. The name has been current for centuries, showing up in Molière's version of *Don Juan* in which Charlotte is a humble peasant girl, an easy victim of Don Juan's charms. In Samuel Richardson's *Clarissa,* Lady Charlotte Harlowe is

Clarissa's mother: "mistress of fine qualities, but greatly under the influence not only of her arbitrary husband but of her son." Susanna Rowson, considered to be America's first professional female novelist, wrote *Charlotte Temple* in 1791, basing her story on the saga of a clergyman's daughter, Charlotte Stanley, who was seduced by Rowson's own cousin. The fictional Charlotte, beautiful, innocent, and only fifteen, is lured to the Colonies by a dashing lieutenant in the army, who impregnates and then abandons her. The book was America's best-selling novel at one time.

Though Charlotte is a French name heavily used in England, the German writer Goethe was apparently fond of it, for he used it in two of his novels. *The Sorrows of Young Werther* (1774) concerns a young man who, rusticating to recover from an unhappy love affair, falls madly in love with the modest country girl Charlotte, called **Lotte.** He is especially drawn to her simple, maternal air, and is not discouraged by her marriage to a steady bourgeois. Ultimately his hopeless love drives him to suicide. Goethe's *Elective Affinities,* written in 1809, concerns a marriage that derails under the stress of strong sexual attraction. Charlotte is happily married to Eduard, a wealthy baron, but when her lovely young niece Ottilie comes to stay with the couple, Eduard is overwhelmed by longing. Meanwhile practical, mature Charlotte is attracted to an army captain who is their houseguest. The forces of attraction ultimately destroy the marriage, and two of the characters die.

Many of the great novelists of the nineteenth century used the name Charlotte for major or minor characters. Charlotte Lucas, in Austen's *Pride and Prejudice,* is the Bennet sisters' friend who marries the fatuous Mr. Collins to achieve a home of her own. In Dickens's *Bleak House,* Charley Necket (christened Charlotte) is the humble orphan whom the saintly Esther Summerson takes under her wing as a maid, vastly improving her lot in life. Trollope created Charlotte Stanhope of *Barchester Towers,* the cold and efficient spinster daughter of the Reverend Vesey Stanhope, who facilitates her father's idle and selfish approach to life. Henry James's Charlotte Stant, in *The Golden Bowl,* is one of his most memorable heroines. Young, beautiful, educated, but penniless, she is a friend of Maggie Verver's and arrives in London for Maggie's wedding to Italian prince Amerigo. She has no family and no real means of support, so she accepts an invitation to stay with her friend in London. She ends up marrying Maggie's immensely rich father—and it is not until then that Maggie discovers Charlotte's previous love affair with the prince. The marriage to Adam Verver has only made it easier for Charlotte and the prince to resume their relationship. Proud and sensitive, Charlotte is often referred to by the other characters as "magnificent."

CHLOE *(klow' ee; Greek, "young green shoot")* A traditional name in pastoral poetry. The source is Longus's fourth-century poem "Daphnis and Chloe" which concerns the romance between the offspring of a goatherd and a shepherd. In Harriet Beecher Stowe's *Uncle Tom's Cabin,* Aunt Chloe is the wife of Uncle Tom, a wonderful cook, warm and loving, who is saving money to buy his freedom. When he dies, she is heartbroken.

> *"Your name?"*
> *"Christie Devon."*
> *"Too long; I should prefer to call you Jane as I am accustomed to the name."*
> *"As you please, ma'am."*
> —LOUISA MAY ALCOTT, WORK: A STORY OF EXPERIENCE

CHRISTINA *(Greek, "anointed")* This name has taken several different forms over the ages and in different countries. **Christian** was used for women, then **Christiana** became more popular. **Christina** and the French **Christine** can be considered contractions, and **Christie** is a common nickname often rendered in Scotland as **Kirstie. Kristin** and **Kirsten** appear in Scandinavian countries. John Bunyan's *The Pilgrim's Progress* tracks the voyage of Christian (Everyman) to the Celestial City. Part Two, written six years later, tells the story of his wife Christiana who misses him so much that she sets out in his wake. She is no more a naturalistic character than he is. Christie Devon, in Louisa May Alcott's *Work: A Story of Experience,* is also a bit schematic. In fact, *The Pilgrim's Progress* was one of Louisa's father Bronson Alcott's favorite books, and Christie's story is also a kind of pilgrimage or voyage. She is an intelligent, idealistic, educated young woman, but not a wealthy one, and *Work* follows her as, not unlike the author, she pursues various careers en route to a way of life that will bring her independence and satisfaction. Christina Allaby Pontifex, in Samuel Butler's *The Way of All Flesh,* is not a seeker like her literary antecedent Christian. Rather, she is a clergyman's wife who flees her own miserable existence in daydreams and sometimes fails to protect her children from their violent father. Her name seems inspired by savage irony.

In Henry James's many novels, only one character recurs. Christina Light appears in *Roderick Hudson* (1875) as a European-raised American girl of astounding beauty who is being trolled around Europe in search of a magnificent match. "We are looking for a husband and none but tremendous swells need apply," she says sardonically. She is attracted to a brilliant but penniless American sculptor who falls far short of the matrimonial standard, and she is effectively blackmailed by her mother into wedding an Italian prince. She returns as the title character in *The Princess Casamassima.* She is still beautiful, separated from her dull husband, and she dangerously impulsive. Her dabbling on the fringes of English anarchist circles has bitter consequences for the novel's hero Hyacinth Robinson.

In Ibsen's *A Doll's House,* Christina Linde functions as a foil to Nora's high-strung charm. She is the ant to Nora's grasshopper, a serious, practical woman who has worked hard and made sacrifices for her family. She disapproves of Nora's rashness. It is Christina's quest for rectitude that forces the climax of the play. Robert Louis Stevenson died before he could finish *Weir of Hermiston,* but a character named Kirstie seems, in the remaining fragment, to be on the verge of playing a similarly pivotal part. Kirstie Elliott is the maternal housekeeper of the Weir family who adores the hero, Archie, but scorns his gruff father. Her niece, also

Kirstie Elliott, is a pretty, superficially sophisticated maiden with whom Archie falls in love. His rakish friend Frank is on the verge of seducing Kirstie when the novel breaks off, with this potential conflict looming. August Strindberg's *Miss Julie* deals with the headstrong young aristocrat Julie and her ill-judged fling with her father's valet Jean. Kristin is the family cook, engaged to Jean, who frustrates the unsuitable couple's attempt to elope.

> *"Christina I suspect is very clever. When I saw her I was amazed at her beauty, and certainly if there is any truth in faces she ought to have the soul of an angel."*
> —HENRY JAMES, *RODERICK HUDSON*

CIRCE (sir' see; *Greek mythology name*) In *The Odyssey,* Homer refers to Circe as "the nymph with lovely braids." She lives on the island of Aeaea and when Odysseus and his men land, she enchants them, delaying their departure for over a year. Her particular mischief is to turn men into swine. Hermes finally arrives to help Odysseus overcome her wiles.

CLARA (*Latin, "bright, shining"*) The Latin word *clarus* has spawned numerous feminine names, many of which (**Clarice, Clarissa, Claribell, Clarine**) are elaborations. This form, however, was very popular in Victorian England, and thus appears in several Victorian novels. Clara Wieland of Charles Brockden Brown's novel *Wieland* cannot be called Victorian; the novel was published in 1798. But Clara's personality is as passive as that of many a heroine in a nineteenth-century novel. She is a young woman of wealth and education who lives contentedly with her brother in rural Pennsylvania until the mysterious Francis Carwin appears on the scene. Carwin's talent of ventriloquism and Clara's brother's murderous intentions make for a lurid tale. Clara Copperfield, mother of David in Dickens's eponymous novel, is a classic Dickensian heroine: beautiful, dreamy, and somewhat elusive. David's nursemaid and longtime defender, Peggoty, is also named Clara. She has all the attributes of practicality and warmth that Clara Copperfield lacks; between them, the two Claras add up to one effective mother.

The name was also used for more romantic heroines. In George Meredith's *The Egoist* (1879), Clara Middleton is the pretty young clergyman's daughter who catches the eye of the monstrously self-centered Sir Willoughby Patterne, the egoist of the title. Sir Willoughby's witty aunt characterizes Clara as "a rogue in porcelain," and she is indeed clever and somewhat irreverent. He refuses to see this side of her character, though: "There was nothing of rogue in himself, so there could be nothing of it in his bride." She is eventually extricated from his attentions and marries his cousin. In Mary Elizabeth Braddon's *Lady Audley's Secret*, Clara Talboys is a woman of great self-possession and resourcefulness, who defies her tyrannical father to trace the fate of her much-loved brother. In so doing, she captures the affections of Robert Audley, the nephew by marriage of the dangerous and beautiful Lady Audley.

> *His cousin was pretty, his uncle's wife was lovely, but Clara Talboys was beautiful.*
> —MARY ELIZABETH BRADDON, *LADY AUDLEY'S SECRET*

Henry James pays attention to the names of his characters, and it is entertaining to witness him doing so in French as well as English. In *The American,* Christopher Newman (an American exploring Europe) falls in love with the beautiful aristocratic widow Claire de Cintré. **Claire,** the French form of Clara, of course means "light." Her last name means "tightly fitted" or even "squeezed," which she certainly is. Her poor but immensely proud family will not, in the end, permit her to marry this alien from the New World. In Edmund Spenser's *The Faerie Queen,* names often indicate qualities that characters represent. In the case of Claribell, who appears in Book Two, the name is simply an elaborate fantasy. The character is a virtuous young woman whose suspicious fiancé kills her because he thought her unfaithful. The theme of this section of the book is Temperance, which the fiancé clearly lacks. Another similarly elaborate name, **Clarinda,** is used ironically in Thomas Love Peacock's *Crotchet Castle.* Lady Clarinda Foolincourt is the practical daughter of Lord Foolincourt. Her visit to Crotchet Castle is supposed to display her merits as a potential wife. She is perfectly happy to marry into the nouveau riche Crotchet family: "I dare say, love in a cottage is very pleasant; but then it positively must be a cottage ornée." Charles Brockden Brown, author of *Wieland* mentioned above, wrote a frankly gothic tale called *Edgar Huntly: Or, Memoirs of a Sleep-Walker.* In this 1799 novel Clarice Wiatt is the illegitimate daughter of the villain, raised by his sister. She unfortunately attracts the amorous attentions of Clithero Edny, an Irish immigrant to America who turns out to be savagely violent. A French spelling of the same name is **Clarisse,** found in Kate Chopin's story "At the 'Cadian Ball." This tale of a love triangle features the earthy Calixta, cool, elegant Clarisse, and the suitor Alcée who is torn between them. Clarisse, with class on her side, prevails.

When Samuel Richardson wrote *Clarissa* in 1747–48, it was the longest novel in the English language, at over a million words. In letters from a wide array of characters, it tells of the travails of Clarissa Harlowe, "a young lady of great delicacy . . . having the greatest notions of filial duty." Her duty, as seen by her parents, is to marry the odious but wealthy Roger Solmes, "a man of sordid manners." She is driven instead into the arms of the seducer Richard Lovelace. Indeed, a great portion of the novel concerns Clarissa's ultimately futile attempts to maintain her virginity.

CLELIA *(Latin, "glorious")* Variants are **Cloelia** and, in French, **Clélie.** In the legends about the founding of Rome, Cloelia is a Roman maiden who is taken hostage by the Etruscans but escapes their camp by swimming across the Tiber. French novelist Mlle. de Scudéry took up the tale in 1654 and spun it into a ten-volume romance—for Cloelia made her swim in order to be with her lover. Stendhal, in *The Charterhouse of Parma,* created a Clelia who is quite as willing to risk everything for love. The handsome hero Fabrizio is jailed in Parma, and Clelia is the gentle, intellectual daughter of his jailer. Less glamorous than his previous conquests, she is nevertheless utterly smitten by him. Though she marries another man and swears to the Virgin never to see Fabrizio again, she cannot keep her vow. The two make love in his jail cell—in the dark, so that she does not, strictly speaking, *see* the man. She dies of remorse.

CLÉMENCE *(French from Latin, "merciful")* From the root that gives us "clement" and "inclement" as well as names like **Clementine** and **Clementina**. In Balzac's short story "Ferragus," Clémence Desmarets is the innocent bourgeoise banker's wife with whom the aristocrat Auguste de Maulincour falls in love. Trailing her around Paris, he notices her visits to a house of ill repute. She is actually visiting her father, a former shipbuilder who has become leader of a powerful group of secret criminals. Angered by Auguste's unwelcome advances toward his daughter, the father has him maimed and poisoned.

CLEOPATRA *(Meaning unknown)* The famous Macedonian queen of Egypt, who was consort to Ptolemy XIII, Julius Caesar, Ptolemy XIV, and finally Mark Antony, her great love. In "The Legend of Good Women" Chaucer sees her as one of Cupid's saints, who gave all for love, but he overlooks her ruthlessness. Shakespeare, in *Antony and Cleopatra,* creates a more complex character, a capricious but sincere lover and a woman of immense allure. Chekhov uses the name in the short story "My Life," a bleak narrative of a well-born Russian who chooses, out of idealism, a life of manual labor. He is called Misail (rather than the more common "Mikhail") and his sister's name is Cleopatra. Both of these odd names were chosen out of vanity by their father, who intended to show thereby that he was an interesting and cultivated man.

CLIO (kligh′ oe; *Greek, "one who praises"*) One of the nine Muses, the daughters of Zeus and Mnemosyne, who inspired artists and intellectuals and performed on Mount Olympus to entertain the gods. Hesiod's poetry outlines their careers and talents. Clio's special province was history and she is usually pictured with a scroll.

> *Clotilde was more than five feet four in height; if we may be allowed to use a familiar phrase, which has the merit at any rate of being perfectly intelligible—she was all legs.*
> —HONORÉ DE BALZAC, *A HARLOT HIGH AND LOW*

CLOTILDE (*Old German, "loud battle"*) Also spelled **Clothilde**, and a primarily French name. Saint Clothilde was the wife of Frankish king Clovis I in the sixth century. Honoré de Balzac has some fun at the expense of the aristocratic Clotilde de Grandlieu in *A Harlot High and Low*. She is the homely twenty-seven-year-old daughter of the Duc de Grandlieu ("famous place" in English) and Lucien Chardon de Rubempré aspires to marry her. Yet her family insists on stringent financial guarantees before Lucien will be allowed to marry this mature maiden. Lucien, in the meantime, is in love with his actress mistress.

George Washington Cable's *The Grandissimes* is a novel about Creole society in early nineteenth-century New Orleans. It traces the entwined fates of Honoré Grandissime and his half brother Honoré Grandissime f.m.c., or "free man of color." Clotilde Nancanou is the beautiful and well-born Creole woman who falls in love with a Yankee entrepreneur of German descent. She ultimately marries Frowenfeld, whose business success discomfits the landowning Creoles.

CLYTEMNESTRA (*Greek, meaning unknown*) Sister of Helen, wife of Agamemnon, Clytemnestra is a pivotal figure in the tragedy of the house of Atreus, and thus figures in dramas by

Aeschylus and Euripides. While Agamemnon is off at the Trojan War (a voyage that included the sacrifice of his and Clytemnestra's daughter Iphigenia), his wife takes Aegisthus as a lover. Shortly after Agamemnon comes home, the two guilty parties slay him in his bath. Years later her son Orestes, as a grown man, kills his mother. Euripides, in *Electra,* portrays Clytemnestra as a proud woman who dresses magnificently and lives in utter splendor.

CLYTIE *(Greek mythology name)* In Ovid's *Metamorphoses,* Clytie is a nymph who falls abjectly in love with Apollo. She turns into a flower that follows Apollo in his sun chariot wherever he goes—a sunflower.

COELIA *(Latin, "sky")* Another symbolic character from Edmund Spenser's allegorical epic *The Faerie Queen.* Coelia is the Heavenly Spirit in Book One, and the mother of Fidelia (faith), Speranza (hope), and Clarissa (charity).

CONCHA *(Spanish diminutive of* Concepción, *"conception," referring to the Immaculate Conception of Mary)* Balzac's "The Girl with the Golden Eyes" is the kind of fiction that gave French writers such a scandalous reputation in straitlaced England. It concerns the dandy Henri de Marsay's seduction of a mysterious young woman named Paquita, who seems to be the carefully guarded mistress of a Spanish marquis. Concha Marialva, a strikingly beautiful woman in her own right, is Paquita's duenna.

Constance frankly abdicated the more brilliant destiny to which, like all shop-girls, she may at times have aspired. She wished to be an honest woman, a good mother of a family, and looked at life according to the religious programme of the middle classes.—HONORÉ DE BALZAC, *CÉSAR BIROTTEAU*

CONSTANCE *(Latin, "firmness, steadfastness")* A notion related inextricably to the Christian faith in its earliest use. For instance, "The Man of Law's Tale" in Chaucer's *Canterbury Tales* concerns a young Christian woman named Constance who is married off to a Muslim and undergoes many trials, but remains true to her faith. In Dumas's *The Three Musketeers* the notion of loyalty is still implied, but the object is different. Constance is the beleaguered Queen Anne's linen maid, and an envoy between her mistress and the Duke of Buckingham. D'Artagnan rescues her from nasty Cardinal Richelieu's bullies, and falls in love with her. Even Balzac, that incomparable cynic, employs the name to signal character in *César Birotteau*. The wealthy perfumer of the title has been made deputy mayor of Paris and has been bitten by the ambition to fly high in society. His practical, loyal wife, Constance, mistrusts his fantasies and would prefer to invest the perfume profits in a small country estate.

George Meredith elaborates the name to **Constantia** in *The Egoist*, with subtly comic effect. Constantia Durham is beautiful, grand, and rich, and somehow the ornateness of her name makes her just less than human as a character. The egoist of the title, Sir Willoughby Patterne, condescends to solicit her hand in marriage. When she grasps the true nature of his character, she jilts him.

> Still Constantia's beauty was of a kind to send away beholders aching. She had the glory of a racing cutter in full sail on a whining breeze; and she did not court to win him, she flew.
> —GEORGE MEREDITH, *THE EGOIST*

CORA *(Greek, "maiden")* Probably coined by James Fenimore Cooper in *The Last of the Mohicans*. Cora Munro is the half sister of Alice Munro; both girls are caught in the forest in the French and Indian War, en route to their father at Fort William Henry. Cora's mother was Creole, so Cora is a half-breed by English standards. She is also the more spirited, resourceful, courageous, and open-minded of the sisters. She falls in love with the Mohawk Uncas, who is the last of his tribe. The two lovers are killed: there was no future for mixed marriages in 1826.

Coralie is a French elaboration of Cora, though it looks to anglophones as if it were related to Coral. In Balzac's *Lost Illusions,* Coralie is the actress/mistress of Lucien Chardon. Coralie, of course, is a stage name, and she is known by no other. She is completely uneducated, and sacrifices her career to Lucien. Ultimately, she can no longer act and falls ill when all of his ambitious schemes come to naught. He has to prostitute his poetic talents by writing popular ballads in order to raise the money for her funeral.

> *But like many actresses Coralie was without intelligence.*
> —HONORÉ DE BALZAC, *LOST ILLUSIONS*

CORDELIA *(Possibly related to the Latin word for "heart," cor)* Literature's famous Cordelia is the youngest daughter of King Lear in Shakespeare's tragedy of that title. Early in the play Lear demands that his three daughters prove their love for him: Cordelia alone refuses to play along, which angers him immensely. She marries the king of France and he is left to the tender mercies of her two scheming sisters. After her father has lost his senses she returns to England and helps him regain his sanity—but she is killed by the schemer Edmund and Lear carries her body onto the stage at the end, in an immensely powerful moment of tragic drama.

COSETTE *(French diminutive)* The familiar name by which the young heroine of Victor Hugo's *Les Misérables* is known. She is the daughter of Fantine by a careless journalist. Raised by the Thénardiers, she is later adopted by the heroic Jean Valjean. Cosette is a beautiful blonde like her mother, and a classic nineteenth-century heroine: virginal, biddable, and ladylike.

> For Cosette, read Euphrasie. The name of the little one was Euphrasie. But the mother had made Cosette out of it, by that sweet and charming instinct of mothers and of the people, who change Josefa into Pepita, and Françoise into Sillette. It is a kind of derivation that confuses and disconcerts the entire science of etymology. We knew a grandmother who succeeded in changing Theodore to Gnon.
>
> —VICTOR HUGO, LES MISÉRABLES

CRESSIDA *(Origin unknown)* The name occurs in Chaucer's 1385 narrative poem *Troilus and Criseyde,* which was the source for Shakespeare's *Troilus and Cressida.* The young lady in question is a Trojan who succumbs to the charms of the prince Troilus, yet manages to transfer her affections to the Greek Diomedes, leaving Troilus heartbroken.

CUNÉGONDE *(German, "brave in battle")* In Voltaire's novel *Candide* one cannot look for naturalistic characters or events. Cunégonde is the fair daughter of the baron with whom Candide is staying at the opening of the novel. Candide is kicked out of the castle for making a pass at her, and embarks on a wild series of adventures. Cunégonde undergoes a similarly harrowing set of trials, and at the end of the novel the lovers are reunited and Candide reluctantly marries his much-battered inamorata.

CYANE *(sy' an; Greek, "bright blue enamel")* "The most famous of Sicilian nymphs" according to Ovid's *Metamorphoses,* Cyane lived in a pool that shared her name. She tried to stop Pluto from kidnapping Proserpine and, out of grief, turned into the water itself. The term *cyan* means "deep blue" and occurs in the names of a number of chemical compounds, including cyanide. Presumably a small pond lit by the Sicilian sun would be deep blue.

CYNTHIA *(Greek, "from Mount Kynthos")* Cynthia is an epithet for Diana, who was also known as **Delia,** since she was born on the island of Delos. Mount Kynthos is a peak on that island. Diana is the twin of Apollo, a virgin huntress and goddess of the moon. She is very modest: In *Metamorphoses,* Ovid tells how Actaeon accidentally glimpsed her naked as she bathed in a stream; to punish him, she turned him into a stag and he was torn to pieces by his own dogs. The Cynthia in Elizabeth Gaskell's *Wives and Daughters* is nowhere near as vengeful, nor as skittish around men. She is the neglected but beautiful daughter of Hyacinth Kirkpatrick, a former governess who marries Dr. Gibson of Hollingford. Gaskell's portrait of a rebellious daughter is psychologically penetrating: Cynthia is hostile and resentful toward her vain, calculating mother, but cannot resist manipulating men just as her mother always has.

> *"But, Mr. Gibson, you must not call her Miss Kirkpatrick. Cynthia remembers you with so much—affection, I may say. . . . Pray call her Cynthia; she would be quite hurt at such a formal name as Miss Kirkpatrick from you."*
>
> *"Cynthia seems to me such an out-of-the-way name, only for poetry, not for daily use."*
>
> *"It is mine," said Mrs. Kirkpatrick, in a plaintive tone of reproach. "I was christened Hyacinth, and her poor father would have her called after me. I'm sorry you don't like it. . . . Hyacinth Clare! Once upon a time I was quite proud of my pretty name; and other people thought it pretty too. . . . Perhaps I did wrong in yielding to his wish, to have her called by such a romantic name."*
>
> —ELIZABETH GASKELL, WIVES AND DAUGHTERS

CYTHEREA (sih ther' ee eh; *Greek place-name*) The name of the Greek island where Aphrodite (Venus to the Romans) washed ashore on her seashell. Thomas Hardy makes use of this allusion, none too subtly, in an early novel, *Desperate Remedies.* Two women in the book bear this remarkable name. The elder,

HARDY'S HEROINES

Thomas Hardy's novels feature some of the most compelling heroines in English literature. They also, however, feature some of the most extraordinary names. Readers are hardly likely to forget the rolling cadences of "Bathsheba Everdene" or "Eustacia Vye," but even the author's lesser-known works offer wonderful examples of Hardy's naming powers.

Desperate Remedies: Cytherea Graye
Far from the Madding Crowd: Bathsheba Everdene
The Hand of Ethelberta: Ethelberta Petherwin, Picotee Chickerel
Jude the Obscure: Arabella Donn, Sue Bridehead
A Laodicean: Paula Power
The Mayor of Casterbridge: Lucetta LeSueur, Susan Henchard
A Pair of Blue Eyes: Elfride Swancourt
The Return of the Native: Eustacia Vye, Thomasin Yeobright
Tess of the D'Urbervilles: Tess Durbeyfield
The Trumpet-Major: Anne Garland
Under the Greenwood Tree: Fancy Day
The Well-Beloved: Avice Caro

Cytherea Aldclyffe, is a handsome widow of forty-some years. The other, Cytherea Graye, is the daughter of an architect who dies at the beginning of the book. He had named his daughter for a woman he once loved; only in a sensation novel of the 1870s could readers have accepted the interlocking fates of these two women. To further stretch credulity, Cytherea Graye (beautiful and spirited, of course) falls in love with the mysterious Aeneas Manston. Classically educated readers would know that the mythical Aeneas was the son of Venus—as this Aeneas is the son of Cytherea Aldclyffe. Further plot details descend to the lurid and include bigamy, attempted murder, and fornication, but Cytherea Graye does finally end in the arms of the sober, sensitive farmer who has loved her all along.

"Do you remember what poor papa once let drop—that Cytherea was the name of his first sweetheart in Bloomsbury, who so mysteriously renounced him? A sort of intuition tells me that this was the same woman."

"O no—not likely," said her brother skeptically.

"How not likely, Owen? There's not another woman of the name in England."

—THOMAS HARDY, *DESPERATE REMEDIES*

DAISY *(Old English, "day's eye")* The late nineteenth century saw a vogue for flower names: Rose, Pansy, Violet, Lily, and so on. Daisy was one of the most popular of them, and was often used as a nickname for Margaret (the French name for the flower and the French version of Margaret are both *marguerite*). *Daisy Miller,* Henry James's short novel about the clash between European and American manners, follows the adventures of a brash yet innocent beauty from Schenectady, New York. "I'm a fearful flirt," she says: "Did you ever hear of a nice girl that was not?" She gallivants around Rome with little sense of what is proper for a young girl on her own. Despite all warnings, she goes into the Colosseum at night with her Italian suitor, Giovanelli, and contracts a fever, which kills her. Yet throughout her adventures, she maintains a faith in the benevolence of the world—a classically American characteristic.

DANAE *(dah' nay ee; Greek, meaning unknown)* In Greek myth, the daughter of King Acrisius of Argos. The king had been told by the Delphic oracle that he would be killed by his daughter's son, so he shut Danae up in a tower built of brass. But, as Ovid tells us, Jupiter visited her in the form of a shower of gold pouring into her lap. The offspring of this unconventional union was the hero Perseus. Still hoping to avoid his fate, Acrisius set mother and child adrift on the ocean in a trunk, but they were rescued by Jupiter.

DAPHNE *(Greek, "laurel")* Ovid tells the tale of Daphne in some detail. The daughter of a river god, she was Apollo's first love.

Although she wanted nothing more than to rove the slopes of Mount Parnassus as a virgin, like the goddess Diana, Apollo pursued her relentlessly. Finally exhausted, Daphne prayed to her father to transform her, to rid her of the beauty that entranced Apollo. On the spot, she was turned into a laurel tree. Apollo still loved her in this form, saying, "Since you cannot be my bride, surely you will at least be my tree. My hair, my lyre, my quivers will always display the laurel." He also made her an evergreen. The name *Daphne* was given to a genus of shrubs, and heroes still wear laurel wreaths.

DEBORAH *(Hebrew, "a bee")* Oliver Goldsmith's comic novel *The Vicar of Wakefield* mocks the weaknesses and pretensions of its characters in a gentle manner, but there is no overlooking the folly of Deborah Primrose, the vicar's wife. She is kindly and silly, and cherishes social ambitions for her daughters that are utterly undone when misfortune overtakes the family. Deborah is one of the few female names to figure in the Old Testament—she was a prophetess and a judge in Israel. Elizabeth Gaskell plays on the former role for a character in her very popular *Cranford*. Deborah Jenkyns is the dominant elder of the two Jenkyns sisters, who has spent a lifetime benevolently bullying the younger Matty. Gaskell points out that she is "not unlike the stern prophetess in some ways." A small example of Miss Jenkyns's authority is that she insists her name be pronounced "De bor' ah."

> *Poor Deborah, instead of reasoning stronger, talked louder, and at last was obliged to take shelter from a defeat in clamour.*
>
> —OLIVER GOLDSMITH, THE VICAR OF WAKEFIELD

DEIANIRA *(day ah nee' rah; Greek mythology name)* Also sometimes spelled **Deyanira**. The second wife of Hercules (the Roman name for Heracles). In *Metamorphoses,* Ovid characterizes her as "a most lovely girl who, in days gone by, roused jealous hopes in the hearts of many suitors." Her beauty was ultimately her downfall, and that of Hercules as well. She was kidnapped by a centaur, Nessus. When Hercules shot Nessus, in revenge the centaur gave Deianira the tunic he had been wearing. It was soaked with his blood and with the Hydra's poison Hercules had smeared on the tip of the arrow that killed Nessus. The centaur told Deianira that the tunic was a love charm. When she later heard rumors that Hercules' attentions were straying, she sent the tunic to him. It clung to his flesh and burned him so badly that he set himself on fire to end the torture. Deianira hanged herself in remorse.

DELIA *(Greek, "from Delos")* Delos is the island where the twins Apollo and Diana were born, so **Delia** is another name for the virgin goddess. See **Diana** and **Cynthia**.

DELPHINE *(French from Greek, "dolphin")* Refers also to the Greek oracle at Delphi, which the Greeks believed to be the womb of the earth. Most French names are drawn from the calendar of saints, but during the years immediately following the French Revolution, Catholicism was in disfavor. Thus the slightly fantastic choices of Delphine and Anastasie make sense for the daughters of wealthy vermicelli manufacturer Goriot in Balzac's *Old Goriot*. In the novel, Goriot has fallen on hard times and is ignored by the daughters who were launched into society with his money. Delphine, married to the immensely rich German banker Nucingen, is socially ambitious and somewhat ashamed of her crude husband. She falls in love with handsome Eugène de Rastignac, who urges her to show some kindness to her husband. Later, in *A Harlot High and Low*, she coolly tolerates her husband's mad infatuation with the beautiful Esther Gobseck.

DESDEMONA *(Greek, "misery")* All too suitable a name for the misunderstood wife in Shakespeare's *Othello*. The beautiful young daughter of a Venetian senator, she marries the Moor Othello in secret. Although Desdemona loves her husband desperately, he is nevertheless persuaded by Iago that she is unfaithful to him. In a rage, he strangles her.

DESIRÉE *(French, "longed for")* Kate Chopin's tale "Desirée's Baby" illuminates the issue of race in turn-of-the century Louisiana. Desirée Valmonde is the gentle, pretty, loving, adopted daughter of the owners of Valmonde plantation. She was left at their gates as a baby. Proud Armand Aubigny marries her despite her obscure origin. Three months after they have a baby, however, he begins to obsess about the baby's racial purity, and comes to believe that the child bears traces of African origin. Thus, he reasons, Desirée must be of mixed race—and he bans her and the child from his house. Ironically, he later discovers that it is his own ancestry that is not purely white.

DIANA *(Latin, "divine")* The Roman name for the virgin goddess Artemis (see also **Delia** and **Cynthia**). She is the moon goddess, partial to hunting and extremely modest. In Ovid's *Metamorphoses* she turns a human hunter into a stag in punishment for having seen her bathing in a stream. Shakespeare may be alluding to the chaste goddess in *All's Well That Ends Well* when he has the despicable Bertram attempting to seduce the virgin Diana. Bertram's long-suffering wife Helena takes advantage of her husband's lust to strengthen her own claim on the man. Anthony Trollope uses her name as a quick joke in *The Eustace Diamonds;* Diana is the fourth of eight sisters of Lord Fawn, all of whose names end with *a*. In *A Harlot High and Low,* Balzac uses the French version of the name, **Diane** *(dee yahn´)*, which conjures the memory of Diane de Poitiers, the mistress of King Henri IV. Diane de Maufrigneuse is one of a group of powerful aristocratic beauties who concern themselves in the fate of Lucien Chardon de Rubempré. Mme de Maufrigneuse was Lucien's mistress and when he gets in trouble with the law, she makes an unconventional foray to the courts to ensure that her love letters to him do not reach the public.

DIDO *(digh´ doh; Greek, meaning unknown)* In Virgil's *Aeneid*, Dido is the queen of Carthage, Venus's favorite city. Venus prompts Dido to fall in love with Aeneas, even though the queen, when widowed, had sworn never to marry again. Under Venus's influence, Dido neglects her reputation, the rule of her country—

everything that had previously mattered to her. When Aeneas obeys the summons of the gods and leaves her for Italy, she commits suicide after directing that her body be burned on a vast funeral pyre visible to her departed lover out at sea.

DINAH *(Hebrew, "justified, judged")* The name **Dinah** was widely used among Puritans in seventeenth-century England, and many of the Old Testament names revived by the Puritans lingered in rural areas well into the nineteenth century. George Eliot's *Adam Bede* portrays rural English life in 1799. Dinah Morris is a serious young preacher in the Methodist church, and a millworker in the town of Snowfield. She is beautiful in an ethereal way, and full of practical charity rather than abstract theology. Several of the male characters are drawn to Dinah, but she resists courtship until the end of the book, feeling that her call to preach rules out marriage. She finally renounces her ministry to marry Adam Bede.

DOLLY *(see also* **DOROTHEA***)* In Tolstoy's *Anna Karenina*, Dolly is a nickname for **Darya** (Russian from Old Persian, "king"). It was part of the affectation of the aristocratic characters in nineteenth-century Russia to use Westernized names. Dolly is married to Prince Stepan Oblonsky, who holds a high rank in the government and is a cheerful, charming, spendthrift rake. Dolly, plain and very sincere, is tortured by his faithlessness; in fact the book opens with a scene between the two in which Dolly, having discovered a new adultery, threatens divorce. But she truly loves her husband and refuses to jeopardize the emotional well-being of their five children, so she remains with him.

DORA see **DOROTHY**

DORALICE *(Invented name)* Ludovico Ariosto's *Orlando Furioso* is a sixteenth-century epic set in the ninth century, around the era of Charlemagne. Naturalism in naming is unimportant, even undesirable, since a different historic period is being evoked. This name is a combination of **Dora** and **Alice** which, though they come from different linguistic roots (Dora is Greek, Alice Old German), could be considered to mean "noble gift." The character is the daughter of the king of Granada, which was Muslim-dominated in the ninth century. Doralice is affianced to the African king Rodomonte, but swashbuckling Mandricardo captures and seduces her. She is completely won over by her captor despite Rodomonte's love.

DORIGEN *(Meaning unknown)* In Geoffrey Chaucer's *Canterbury Tales,* "The Franklin's Tale" is a story of ancient Brittany, which had a culture and language of its own before assimilation into the rest of France. Dorigen is the faithful wife of a Breton knight, Aurelius, who is strenuously wooed by a neighboring knight. Putting him off politely, she tells him that she will leave her husband for him when the cliffs of the coast disappear. Her suitor Arveragus finds a magician who performs the feat, and her husband tells her that she is honor bound to keep her word. But Arveragus, impressed by her nobility, sends her back to Aurelius unmolested. The tale is thus really about two men's demonstrations of honor—Dorigen is more or less a desirable chattel.

DORINE *(French, meaning unclear)* Possibly a diminutive of **Dora.** Dorine, in Molière's *Tartuffe,* is one of his tart, saucy maids who see the foibles of their masters and never hesitate to speak the truth. About a neighbor lady, Dorine says, "We all know that she's virtuous only because she has no alternative." She retains an exasperated affection for her stupid master, and discreetly stage-manages the love affair of her mistress Mariane.

DOROTHEA *(Greek, "gift of God")* Although in real life **Dorothy** is the more common form of this name, authors beginning with Miguel de Cervantes seem to have preferred **Dorothea.** In *Don Quixote,* Dorothea is one of the most appealing characters, a clever, beautiful, and strikingly quick-witted young woman of substance who encounters Don Quixote and Sancho Panza in their wanderings. She poses as the Princess of Micomicona to dissuade Don Quixote from one of his more dangerous follies.

George Eliot, who used the name in *Middlemarch,* could easily have known this Dorothea from her reading. Her "Prelude" to her novel, however, draws the reader's attention to a different Spanish woman, Saint Teresa of Avila. Eliot compares Saint Teresa with other women of high spirit and limited opportunity. Readers may further draw the implied parallel between heroine Dorothea Brooke and the Spanish saint, since on the second page of her story, Eliot characterizes Dorothea as "enamoured of intensity and greatness, and rash in embracing whatever seemed to her to have those aspects." It is this rashness that sends her into the arms of the desiccated scholar Edward Casaubon. She is faithful to Casaubon, though lonely and disillusioned; when she is widowed, Dorothea must choose a new life, and new potential for love, with great care. Clever women since 1871 have found a soul mate in Dorothea Brooke.

A shorter version of the name is **Dora,** which was popular in the Victorian era. David Copperfield, hero of Dickens's eponymous novel, marries Dora Spenlow and lives to rue his choice. She is his "child-wife" and the girlish charm that captured his heart is eclipsed by her abysmal inability to be a housekeeper or, indeed, take on any adult responsibility. She wastes away and dies, considerately freeing David for a more satisfying union. **Dora** and **Dorothy** were also frequently turned into **Dolly.** As early as 1747, Dolly Hervey appears in Samuel Richardson's *Clarissa.* She is the daughter of Clarissa's aunt Hervey, "good-natured, gentle, sincere, and a great admirer of her cousin Clarissa," according to Richardson. All that gentleness, however, means that she is unable to object to the Harlowe family's cruel treatment of Clarissa.

George Eliot's *Silas Marner* is set in a small village; part of Eliot's intention was to focus on the emotional lives of simple, unsophisticated people. Dolly Winthrop is a neighbor of the weaver Silas. She is an efficient, warmhearted woman who unintentionally draws Silas out of his isolation because she sees that he needs help raising the foundling Eppie. Probably the most famous Dolly in English literature is Dolly Varden, the heroine of Dickens's early novel *Barnaby Rudge.* This is one of Dickens's historical novels, set in 1780 during a series of anti-Catholic riots in England. Dolly is a cheerful, charming flirt, always colorfully dressed and fond of flowered hats. The eminent painter W. P. Frith created an enduring image of her, and her name was given to a dance, a style of dress, and ultimately, a species of immense olive-colored trout with large red or orange spots.

DRUSILLA *(Latin, meaning unknown)* Drusilla is one of the few female names to appear in the New Testament, so it was current in Roman times. It is used comically by Wilkie Collins in *The Moonstone;* Drusilla Clack is the old-maid cousin of Lady Verinder, who has a terrible crush on her young kinsman Godfrey Ablewhite. A sanctimonious, self-righteous busybody, she participates in all of his good causes and puts on a great show of Christian charity. She and Collins's forceful heroine Rachel loathe each other—more comedy.

> *"If I have not already mentioned that my Christian name is Drusilla, permit me to mention it now."*
> —WILKIE COLLINS, *THE MOONSTONE*

DUESSA *(Latin, "two")* An especially transparent name from Edmund Spenser's allegorical epic *The Faerie Queen.* Una, the heroine, is single-minded, personifying at once Truth, Protestantism, and Queen Elizabeth I of England (under whose aegis, of course, the work was written). Duessa, in complete contrast, represents falsehood, Catholicism, Queen Mary Tudor, and Mary, Queen of Scots. As an evil enchantress she takes a number of forms, attempting to seduce the Red Cross Knight away from his true mission. She appears to him in the guise of Fidessa, or faith—but she represents Catholicism, the *wrong* faith. Queen Elizabeth was bent on establishing the Protestant church in England after her half sister Mary's Catholic reign.

DULCINEA *(Spanish, "sweet")* The aristocratic beauty beloved by Don Quixote. He sees her as a ravishing beauty: "Her flowing hair is of gold, her forehead the Elysian fields, her eyebrows two

celestial arches . . . her bosom whiter than the new-fallen snow."
In fact, the real woman whom Quixote has transmuted into this
vision (see **Aldonza**) is a crude, stout peasant.

DUNYA *(Diminutive of* Avdotya: *Russian, "well-regarded")* Another form is **Eudoxia** or **Eudoxie**. Dostoyevsky names his characters allusively. Thus, while the last name Raskolnikov means
"split" or "schism"—drawing attention to the fissure in the character of Rodion Raskolnikov of *Crime and Punishment*—his
beloved sister Dunya is always "well-regarded." Dunya responds
courageously to terrible pressure, resisting the evil Svidrigailov
when he tries to blackmail her into sleeping with him. Her ability
to live as part of a community and to resist her own urges to violence provide stark contrast to her brother's weaknesses.
Chekhov uses the diminutive form, **Dunyasha**, for the ladies'
maid in *The Cherry Orchard*.

> *Her name is Echo, and she always answers back.*
> —OVID, *METAMORPHOSES*

ECHO *(Greek, "sound")* In *Metamorphoses,* Ovid tells the story of the nymph Echo. She was a chatterbox who protected the other nymphs by distracting Juno while Jupiter dallied with her friends. As a punishment, Juno took away her power of saying anything original; she could only repeat the last words spoken to her. Then unfortunate Echo made the mistake of falling in love with Narcissus, who was incapable of loving anyone. She wasted away until only her voice was left.

> *Although borne down by the misfortunes and imminent danger of the man she loved, Edith was touched by the hopeless and reverential passion of the gallant youth.*
> —SIR WALTER SCOTT, *OLD MORTALITY*

EDITH *(Old English, "rich war")* A name that was adopted with great enthusiasm in the Victorian English wave of revivalism. The sheer variety of characters named Edith in nineteenth-century fiction reflects the popularity of the name but also suggests that it was used as a generic female name, with no important connotations. Sir Walter Scott, for instance, generally aimed for accuracy in his historical novels (hence **Rowena** and **Cedric** in *Ivanhoe*, for instance). *Old Mortality* is set in seventeenth-century Scotland during the religious struggles that racked the country. Yet its heroine is named Edith Bellenden. It's an unlikely choice for a Scots family of the era, but to Scott's readers a beautiful, sensitive heroine named Edith made perfect sense. Similarly, Edith Millbank in Benjamin Disraeli's *Coningsby* hints at conventional Victorian womanhood. To be sure, her last name signals her manufacturing origins (as in fabric mill, perhaps) but she is little more than a demure, pretty pawn in this political fable. Edward Bellamy, too, in his time-traveling *Looking Backward: 2000–1887*, names his heroines Edith. The novel concerns a wealthy young Bostonian dilettante of 1887 who has himself hypnotized and transported into the future. In both 1887 and 2000, his love interest is a lovely young lady named Edith. The future version is conveniently already in love with him, having read his love letters to his fiancée of 1887. But in spite of new, utopian social conditions in 2000, she is still a Victorian maiden: deferential, patient, attuned to his pleasure.

Edith was such a standard-issue name that Louisa May Alcott used it for the heroine of her first novel, *The Inheritance,* a gothic tale of love in the English aristocracy that Alcott produced at the age of seventeen. Edith Adelon is an Italian orphan who has been raised with the noble Hamilton family. Lady Hamilton is chilly to her but the handsome Lord Percy is swift to see her real charms. It transpires that Edith is the true inheritor of the Hamilton estates and riches, but of course she is noble enough to share them with the family that has treated her with bare civility.

> *With an angel's calm and almost holy beauty, Edith bore within as holy and as pure a heart—gentle, true, and tender.* —LOUISA MAY ALCOTT, *THE INHERITANCE*

EDNA *(Hebrew, "enjoyment, pleasure")* A fashionable name in late-nineteenth-century America, and thus a perfect choice for Edna Pontellier, the protagonist of Kate Chopin's novella *The Awakening.* Edna is a twenty-eight-year-old matron who realizes in the course of the story that her life is insupportable. Her awakening includes realization of her unsatisfied sexual needs and her profound incompatibility with her insensitive husband, who regards her as "a valuable piece of property that has suffered some damage."

EFFIE *(Greek, "pleasant speech")* A short version of **Euphemia** that was widely used as an independent name in the nineteenth century. One of Sir Walter Scott's best-loved novels, *The Heart of Midlothian,* set in the 1730s, concerns the tribulations of Effie Deans, the modest daughter of a strict Presbyterian dairy farmer who is seduced by a dissolute rake. Her baby vanishes (kidnapped by the midwife) after the birth, and Effie is imprisoned for killing it. She refuses to name her seducer, and her sister Jeanie (the heroine of the piece) walks to London to plead Effie's case in a higher court.

The German form is **Effi,** the name of the heroine of one of Germany's great nineteenth-century novels by Theodor Fontane. Scholars suggest that Fontane may even have named Effi in part for Effie Deans, since the name is unusual in Germany. *Effi Briest* is the story of an energetic, joyous young girl who is shackled at the age of sixteen to a formal, conventional civil servant. The marriage, planned by her parents for purely worldly reasons, proves to be Effi's downfall. Her husband takes her to a small town with a rigid social structure and, largely out of boredom and ignorance, Effi embarks on an affair with a man she does not love. Years later her indiscretion (long finished) is discovered and her husband challenges her lover to a duel. Effi's adultery is exposed and she goes back to live with her parents. She accepts this punishment with equanimity and dies equally passively.

EGERIA *(Latin, meaning unknown)* In legend, Egeria is the female advisor of Numa Pompilius, the second king of Rome who taught the race of Latins how to live peacefully together. The name is sometimes used as a term for a wise woman counselor. In Ovid's *Metamorphoses* Egeria is a nymph, and when her husband dies, she cries so long and hard that she disturbs Diana. The goddess finally turns her into a spring.

EGLENTYNE *(Middle English, "sharp-edged")* Also **Eglantine,** another name for the shrub known as sweetbriar or dog rose. This is the first name of the Prioress in Chaucer's *Canterbury Tales,* though it seems unusual for a woman of the church to have a secular name. Chaucer describes her as a great beauty, very genteel and ladylike; he uses terms like those in the French romances of the day. Her Tale, when she comes to tell it, concerns a young boy who is murdered while singing a hymn of praise to the Virgin Mary.

> *"Esteem him! Like him! Cold-hearted Elinor! Oh! Worse than cold-hearted! Ashamed of being otherwise!"*
> —JANE AUSTEN, *SENSE AND SENSIBILITY*

ELAINE, ELLEN see **HELEN**

ELEANOR *(Origin unclear: possibly related to Greek, "light")* Alternate English spellings include **Elinor** and **Ellinor,** and there does not seem to have been a preferred spelling: both Jane Austen and Anthony Trollope employed two versions of the name. In *Northanger Abbey* Eleanor Tilney is the sensible, clever friend of heroine Catherine Morland. Her brother Henry is the love interest in the novel. Austen seems to have associated the name with a certain coolness of temperament because the "sense" sister in *Sense and Sensibility* is Elinor Dashwood. Austen notes approvingly that she "possessed a strength of understanding and coolness of judgment," but "sensibility" sister Marianne disapproves.

Trollope also apparently liked the name: he had kind words about Ellinor Greystock in *The Eustace Diamonds* (a "good-humored, kindly being") who is the elder sister of feckless hero

SISTER ACTS

The idea of sisters is very powerful in Western literature. We occasionally hear of brothers, like the Brothers Karamazov, but sisters seem to be more fascinating. In addition to those divine creatures the Muses, the Furies, the Graces, and the Fates, Greek literature tells the stories of Procne and Philomela, Helen and Clytemnestra, Ariadne and Phaedra. The trope retained its mystique right through the nineteenth century, as authors wrote about sets of sisters like:

Goneril, Regan, and Cordelia in *King Lear*

Jane, Elizabeth, Mary, Lydia, and Kitty Bennet in *Pride and Prejudice*

Elinor, Marianne, and Margaret Dashwood in *Sense and Sensibility*

Ethelberta, Picotee, Emmeline, Faith, Georgina, Gwendoline, Cornelia, and Myrtle Chickerel in *The Hand of Ethelberta*

Jane, Susan, Sophy, and Elizabeth Dodson in *The Mill on the Floss*

Dorothea and Celia Brooke in *Middlemarch*

Alexandra, Adelaida, and Aglaya Yepanchin in *The Idiot*

Cora and Alice Munro in *The Last of the Mohicans*

Alice, Virginia, and Monica Madden in *The Odd Women*

Meg, Jo, Beth, and Amy March in *Little Women*

Anastasie and Delphine Goriot in *Old Goriot*

Frank Greystock. And in Eleanor Harding, Trollope created a character who was obviously dear to him. She is the younger daughter of Barchester Warden Septimus Harding. In *The Warden*, Trollope describes her as pretty in an unassuming way. She is twenty-four, with mild manners but a fundamental independence and stubbornness. In *Barchester Towers* she is a wealthy widow, and much of the comedy of the novel arises from her ineligible but determined suitors.

> *You might pass Eleanor Harding in the street without notice, but you could hardly pass an evening with her and not lose your heart.* —ANTHONY TROLLOPE, THE WARDEN

Wilkie Collins's novels are often less psychologically subtle than those of Trollope, and in terms of plot, *Armadale* is infinitely more lurid than the tame goings-on in Barsetshire. Yet Collins's female characters are often quite complex and rarely conform to Victorian standards of womanhood. In *Armadale* one of the protagonists falls swiftly and carelessly in love with Eleanor Milroy, the daughter of his tenants. Spoiled, lonely, and bumptious, Neelie is just what you would expect as the offspring of a domineering, invalid mother and a loving but passive and remote father.

A more exotic form of the name is **Eleanora,** which Edgar Allan Poe uses in a parable of perfect love. "Eleanora" is a short

> "*I think Eleanor is a beautiful name; and yet, I don't know why, I think the major made an improvement when he changed it to Neelie.*"
>
> "*I can tell you why, Mr. Armadale,*" *said the major's daughter, with great gravity. "There are some unfortunate people in the world, whose names are—how can I express it?—whose names are, Misfits. Mine is a Misfit. I don't blame my parents, for of course it was impossible to know when I was a baby how I should grow up. But as things are, I and my name don't fit each other. When you hear a young lady called Eleanor, you think of a tall, beautiful, interesting creature directly—the very opposite of me! With my personal appearance Eleanor sounds ridiculous—and Neelie, as you yourself remarked, is just the thing.*"
>
> —WILKIE COLLINS, ARMADALE

piece detailing the bond between the narrator and his flawlessly beautiful cousin who is marked for an early death—themes familiar to Poe's readers. Benjamin Constant's *Adolphe,* written in 1815, is one of the forerunners of the modern psychological novel. Its eponymous protagonist, a young man of means, travels to the court of a German prince where he encounters a Polish woman called **Ellénore**. Older than he, the long-term mistress of an aristocrat by whom she has two children, Ellénore chafes somewhat at her ambiguous social position. Adolphe seduces her, she falls madly in love with him, and he soon finds her boring. As he pulls away, she becomes more possessive, fractious, and needy. The novel is thought to be based on Constant's affair with Madame de Staël.

ELECTRA *(Greek, "beaming sun")* Long before the tragic events of the Oresteia, Greek myth told of an Electra who was the daughter of Atlas. Her son founded the city of Troy. Electra and her six sisters were raised to heaven in the form of the stars and became the Pleiades, but Electra lost her gleam just before the Trojan War. She is thus known as "the lost Pleiad." Her name comes from the same root as the word "electricity."

By far the more famous Electra, however, is the tragic daughter of Agamemnon and Clytemnestra. Aeschylus, Euripides, and Sophocles all lingered over her history and that of her brother Orestes. When the mighty warrior Agamemnon went off to the Trojan War, Clytemnestra transferred her affections to Aegisthus. The pair woefully mistreated Electra, turning her into a virtual slave (Aeschylus's *The Libation Bearers*). When Orestes returned from exile to avenge his father's death at Clytemnestra's hands, Electra was overjoyed. In telling of the subsequent bloodshed the three tragedians focus on different aspects of the drama, but Electra can be said to supply the moral force for Orestes' actual physical act of murder.

ELFRIDE *(Old English, "elf power")* *A Pair of Blue Eyes* was the first novel Thomas Hardy published under his own name, and it was successful enough to launch him into his career as a novelist.

Hardy created a series of fascinating women who strain to transcend the narrow roles provided for them by Victorian society. Elfride Swancourt, the naive, impulsive daughter of a snobbish Anglican vicar, sees marriage as her road to fulfillment, though she has written a novel called *The Court of King Arthur's Castle*. She is assiduously courted by a series of men: a self-made architect (very reminiscent of Hardy himself), a widowed local aristocrat, and a clever but effete scholar named Henry Knight.

> *Elfride Swancourt was a girl whose emotions lay very near the surface.* —THOMAS HARDY, *A PAIR OF BLUE EYES*

ELISE see **ELIZABETH**

ELISSA *(Meaning unknown)* Now construed as a variant of Elizabeth, Elissa actually has ancient roots. Dido the queen of Carthage was also known as Elissa. What's more, there is an Elissa in Spenser's *The Faerie Queen*. She appears in Book Two, an allegory about the virtue of temperance; the protagonist visits the castle where she lives with her half sisters Medina (or the Golden Mean) and Perissa (Excess). Elissa herself represents Deficiency.

ELIZABETH *(Hebrew, "promised to God")* One of the standard female names in Western Europe for hundreds of years. Made famous among the populace by rulers and saints before culture provided other naming inspirations, Elizabeth has spawned nicknames and variations galore including **Eliza, Lisa, Betty, Bette, Betsy,** and **Lizzie.** The standard version without tricky spelling (**Elisabeth,** for instance) dominates early in the nineteenth century. Jane Austen, whose limited experience shows nowhere more clearly than in her names, created the sublime Elizabeth Bennet in *Pride and Prejudice*. The most discerning of the numerous Bennet daughters, she "had a lively, playful disposition, which delighted in anything ridiculous" including the snobbery of some of her acquaintances. A later creation is Elizabeth Elliot of *Persuasion,* a proud, vain, and silly spinster who sees no value at all in her warmhearted and sensitive sister Anne. Nathaniel Hawthorne's 1836 tale "The Minister's Black Veil" is a mysterious evocation of the presence of sin in seventeenth-century New England. The Reverend Mr. Hooper suddenly takes to wearing a black veil over his face, to the shock of his parishioners and the consternation of his fiancée Elizabeth. She is more a structural element than an actual person, however: though she urges him to reveal his reasons for veiling himself, he declines. She never marries, and attends his (veiled) deathbed.

Four syllables is a fairly unwieldy length for everyday use of a name; in literature as in life, characters choose to shorten Elizabeth in a variety of ways. Elizabeth Tulliver, mother of the spirited Maggie in George Eliot's *The Mill on the Floss,* is known to her three sisters as **Bessy.** Eliot gently mocks the sisters' pretensions, but Elizabeth Tulliver's petty discontents and relentless focus on household goods feed the uneasy atmosphere in the Tulliver household. Dickens's Elizabeth Hexam of *Our Mutual Friend* is known as both **Lizzie** and Elizabeth. The use of a nickname by nonfamily members can serve as a class marker; Lizzie is the daughter of a waterman, who makes a living by searching for bodies in the Thames. She eventually marries the gentleman Eugene Wrayburn, whom she had rescued from drowning. Her full name, Elizabeth, has more dignity than mere Lizzie and can help bridge the huge gap in status between her and her husband. Anthony Trollope uses Lizzie somewhat derisively as a nickname for his brilliant creation Lizzie Eustace in *The Eustace Diamonds.* Trollope compared her, with complete justice, to Thackeray's Becky Sharp: she is a beautiful, amoral, and fascinating adventuress. "As she was utterly devoid of true tenderness," says Trollope, "so also was she devoid of conscience." She becomes somewhat infamous in London owing to her insistence on keeping a diamond necklace that belongs to her dead husband's family. Trollope indicates general disrespect by having men in clubs refer to her as "Lizzie Eustace" rather than the more seemly "Lady Eustace." And sometimes a nickname is merely an affectionate shortening, as in *Little Women*'s **Beth.** The sweet, musical, shy, and physically fragile March sister is based on a sister of Louisa May Alcott's who was also named Elizabeth, though called Betty. She died when Louisa was twenty-six—her last words, worthy of Beth March, were "Now I'm comfortable and so happy."

Some characters, like Beth, are known primarily by their nicknames, indicating a confidential or warm relationship or character. Aunt Betsey Trotwood, in *David Copperfield,* rescues the pathetic child hero from the terrifying Murdstone family. David soon realizes that her seeming fierceness is a comically inadequate disguise for her soft heart. Henry James uses nicknames for Elizabeth—**Bessie** and Lizzie—in two fictions that explore the European reaction to American informality. "An International Episode" deals with a pair of young Englishmen who travel to Newport, Rhode Island, and meet the delightful Bessie Alden. (Echoes of John Alden of the Plymouth settlement were probably intended.) Lord Lambeth, heir to a dukedom, falls in love with frank, openhearted Bessie, who is intrigued by her first English suitor. In *The Europeans,* set in 1830, a faintly disreputable European-raised brother and sister visit wealthy cousins in rural Massachusetts. Lizzie Acton is the vivacious, pert family friend who provides another example of the fresh charm of American womanhood.

One of the offshoots of Elizabeth that is used as a name in its own right is **Eliza** or **Liza.** Hannah Webster Foster's *The Coquette,* written in 1797, is an epistolary tale about a young woman torn between a respectable marriage and a passionate if illicit attachment. Eliza Wharton, a lively, charming damsel, is sorely tempted by the dashing Major Sanford, an aristocratic rake. The minister who offers her his name repudiates Eliza when he catches her flirting with Sanford, and she ultimately succumbs to passion with tragic results. Anne Brontë, in *The Tenant of Wildfell Hall,* uses Eliza for a secondary character. Narrator Gilbert Markham, a jejune young farmer, flirts with the vicar's daughter Eliza Millward, "a very engaging little creature, for whom I felt no small degree of partiality." Harriet Beecher Stowe's Eliza, of *Uncle Tom's Cabin,* is probably the most famous of the nineteenth-century Elizas. She is the brave, intelligent slave who runs away from the Shelby plantation when her son Harry is supposed to be sold. In a dramatic scene she crosses the Ohio River to freedom by leaping across its crumbling ice floes.

Other fragments of the name Elizabeth are also names in themselves. Molière, for instance, uses **Élise** (an ingenue in *The Miser*) and **Lizette** (a saucy maid in *Love's the Best Doctor*). A minor character in George Eliot's *Adam Bede* is **Lisbeth,** while Chekhov uses **Lisa** in "A Boring Story" for the spoiled daughter of the narrator. In *War and Peace,* Tolstoy gives Prince Andrei Bolkonsky a pretty, immature wife named **Lise.** Though physically engaging, she is not his intellectual equal and when she dies in childbirth he is freed for a more fulfilling match.

While Lise is a Frenchified version of Elizabeth, **Lizaveta** is the more purely Russian form. Lizaveta Mikaylovna Kalitin, known as Liza, is the young woman who enchants Nikolai Lavretsky in Ivan Turgenev's *Home of the Gentry.* Stern, cultured, pious, she refuses the eligible Vladimir Panshin because she does not love him. When Lavretsky's amoral wife Varvara appears on the scene, Liza insists the two try to reconcile, and enters a convent. In Fyodor Dostoyevsky's *The Idiot,* Madame Lizaveta Yepanchin is a relative of Prince Leo Myshkin, the idiot of the title. Dostoyevsky's naming system is explicitly symbolic, and since Myshkin is his Christlike man, it makes sense that his kinswoman be named Elizabeth, like the kinswoman of Jesus.

Honoré de Balzac's novels are short on Christlike figures and Bette Fischer, the title character of *Cousin Bette,* is a personage of purely secular menace. Born Lisbeth Fischer in eastern France, she is brought up with the beautiful Adeline, five years her elder. A homely face, a sour disposition, and a childhood's worth of inequities make her the unwitting Adeline's bitter enemy. She spends the novel engineering the downfall of the Hulot family with a kind of sly inevitability.

ELLEN, ELAINE see HELEN

ÉLODIE *(French from Greek, "marsh flower")* Émile Zola's novels took a panoramic look at every level of nineteenth-century French society. *The Earth* is his examination of the brutal life of the rural poor. One branch of the Fouan family struggles at bare subsistence level, but a sister, married into the family that keeps the town brothel, flourishes. Élodie is their daughter, whose existence—supported by prostitution—is infinitely more comfortable than that of her cousins. Zola calls her "a pallid, plain little girl with a flabby, puffy face and pale wispy hair, a bloodless little creature who was moreover repressed by the virginal innocence of her upbringing to the point of idiocy."

ELVIRA *(Spanish, meaning unknown)* A stock "Spanish" name, perhaps, to the dramatists of seventeenth-century France, who also used **Elvire**. Pierre Corneille employed it in *Le Cid* for the governess of Ximena, the fierce heroine. With more lasting literary effect, Molière gave this name to the wife of Don Juan in his version of that story. Molière's Elvira is a stern, pious creature who takes her marriage vows seriously. When Don Juan abandons her, she seeks vengeance, uttering the famous line, "If Heaven itself has no terrors for you, then beware, at least, the fury of a woman scorned!" She later warns him that God has prepared retribution for him, which it took Lorenzo da Ponte, in his libretto for Mozart's *Don Giovanni,* to clothe in a terrifying form.

> *Emelye, that fairer was to sene*
> *Than is the lylie upon his stalke grene.*
> —GEOFFREY CHAUCER, *THE CANTERBURY TALES*

EMILY *(Latin clan name)* In use as a first name from very early times. In "The Knight's Tale" of *The Canterbury Tales,* the sister of Hippolyta the Amazon is named, improbably, **Emelye**. She goes to Athens with her sister, and two knights of Thebes fall madly in love and fight for the right to woo her. Emelye barely knows they're alive and would prefer to remain a virgin, but when Palamon (having prayed to Venus) kills his cousin Arcite (who prayed to Mars for help), she is more or less obliged to marry the victor. David Copperfield's childhood friend Emily Peggoty is the niece of his much-loved nursemaid. She is socially a cut above her family, having learned to speak in a refined way and having pretensions to a finer life. Emily falls victim to David's heedless friend James Steerforth. After her seduction (and Steerforth's death in a shipwreck—Dickens is swift to deal out retribution), she emigrates, a "fallen woman."

Anthony Trollope used the name Emily for principal female characters in two novels. Emily Rowley in *He Knew He Was Right* is the unwitting victim of Louis Trevelyan's unbalanced moral scruples. Trevelyan is offended by an old family friend of Emily's who continues to call her by her first name after their marriage, when etiquette would normally have her become "Mrs. Trevelyan." His mind becomes nearly unraveled by this obsession, with terrible effects on his marriage. Emily Trevelyan is one of those Trollopian heroines who cannot be pushed around, which certainly sharpens the conflict in *He Knew He Was Right*. Emily Wharton of *The Prime Minister*, written only six years later, is similarly stubborn. The daughter of an eminent barrister, she falls in love with a tremendous bounder, the con man Ferdinand Lopez. She proudly endures all of his mistreatment, and then—this is the touch of Trollope's psychological genius—refuses to forgive herself for her mistake. Though the gentlemanly, lovable Arthur Fletcher is only too willing to pick up the pieces, Emily wallows in her guilt and misery in an irritating but utterly human way.

Continental versions of the name include **Emilie** and **Emilia**. The latter is used by Shakespeare in *Othello* for the wife of Iago. She is a close companion of Desdemona's and ultimately understands how evil her husband is. Shortened, Emily becomes **Em,** the name of one of the characters in Olive Schreiner's *The Story of an African Farm*. We never know Em's last name, nor indeed what Em is short for, which adds to the sense of claustrophobia and limitation in the novel. In contrast with her friend and playmate Lyndall, Em is slow, chubby, and plain. Schreiner says "her only idea of love was service." She does attract the love of Gregory, the farm's English tenant, but he soon shifts his attentions to Lyndall and Em is left stoically alone.

EMMA *(Old German, "all-embracing")* Jane Austen's portrait of Emma Woodhouse in *Emma* combines acute discernment and immense affection. Charming, generous, headstrong, and arrogant, Emma fancies herself as the social queen of her neighborhood. Unfortunately, she is young and foolish enough so that her social engineering amounts to little more than meddling, some of which is unintentionally cruel. Her heedlessness is forgiven by the observant Mr. Knightley, whose friendship, to her surprise, turns out to be more passionate than avuncular. The other great Emma of European literature is the protagonist of Gustave Flaubert's *Madame Bovary*. But while Emma Woodhouse is one of the "happily ever after" heroines, whose happy fate as a wife and helpmeet seems assured, Emma Bovary belongs to the camp of the passionate malcontents along with Anna Karenina and Hedda Gabler. Emma is the wife of a provincial French doctor, whose life fails to provide her with the excitement she expects. Disillusioned by her marriage, she embarks on affairs with first a cynical young rake, and then a lawyer. Financial folly compounds her infidelity, and she ultimately commits suicide.

> *"Emma has been meaning to read more ever since she was twelve years old."*
> —JANE AUSTEN, *EMMA*

EMMELINE *(Old German, meaning unclear)* One of the minor slave characters in *Uncle Tom's Cabin*, Emmeline is a pretty young woman whom the terrifying overseer Simon Legree intends to make his mistress. She manages to escape to Canada.

> *"Enid, the pilot star of my lone life,*
> *Enid, my early and my only love,*
> *Enid, the loss of whom hath turned me wild."*
> —ALFRED, LORD TENNYSON, *IDYLLS OF THE KING*

ENID *(Welsh, "spirit, soul")* Brought to prominence by Alfred, Lord Tennyson in *Idylls of the King.* One long narrative section of the epic called "Geraint and Enid" recounts the marital trials suffered by this pair. Geraint, one of the Round Table knights, is seriously rattled by Guinevere's adultery with Lancelot. He begins to doubt his own wife, Enid, and clings close to her rather than embarking on knightly adventures. Then he becomes unhinged and drags Enid off on a voyage that will test her obedience and virtue. He not only humiliates his wife, he actually puts her in danger, but she rises to every challenge with a saintly acceptance that sets modern female teeth on edge.

ÉPONINE *(French, meaning unknown)* Victor Hugo took a conservative stance when it came to names. The upstart, morally dubious Thénardier family of *Les Misérables* (innkeepers, grave robbers, ultimately new aristocrats) name their daughter Éponine because Madame gets pretentious ideas from all the cheap novels she reads. Hugo does permit Éponine to redeem herself personally, though, by falling in love with the young hero Marius and sacrificing herself for him during the battle on the barricades in Paris.

EPPIE see **HEPZIBAH**

ERATO *(Greek, "passionate")* One of the nine Muses, a daughter of Zeus and Mnemosyne, the Titaness whose responsibility was memory. Each Muse inspires artists and intellectuals in a different field: Erato's realm is erotic poetry (note the link in her name to Eros, the god of love). She is often depicted with a lyre.

ESMERALDA *(Spanish, "emerald")* In Victor Hugo's *Nôtre-Dame of Paris,* the gypsy girl Esmeralda fulfills several functions. Most obviously, she is the classic nineteenth-century heroine, beautiful, sweet, and innocent, intent on maintaining her virtue. As a secondary issue she evokes passion in a number of the male characters, and she is ill-equipped to rebuff them. Finally, as a Gypsy, Esmeralda is in a minority: uneducated, isolated, with no social structure to protect her. This makes her the glamorous fem-

VICTOR HUGO ON NAMES

One of the unexpected charms of *Les Misérables* is its author's habit of interrupting the narrative to lecture the reader. He is particularly sharp about the pretensions of the despicable Thénardier family, with whom Cosette passes the most miserable years of her childhood. Madame Thénardier is much given to reading trashy romantic novels, of which Hugo disapproves. She has chosen the names for her children from the pages of these fictions, with—according to the author—deplorable results.

People do not read stupidities with impunity. The result was that her [Mme Thénardier's] eldest child was named Éponine, and the youngest, who had just escaped being called Gulnare, owed to some chance pleasure wrought by a novel by Ducray Duminil, the less problematic name of Azelma.

However, let us say in passing that all things are not ridiculous and superficial in this singular era to which we are alluding, which might be termed the anarchy of baptismal names. Besides this romantic element we have just noted, there is the social symptom. Today it is not infrequently that we see shepherds named Arthur, Alfred, and Alphonse, and viscounts—if viscounts still exist—named Thomas, Peter, or James. This change, which places the "elegant" name on the plebeian and the country appellation on the aristocrat, is only an eddy in the tide of equality. The irresistible penetration of new inspiration is there as in everything else: Beneath this apparent discord there is a great and profound reality—the French Revolution.

inine equivalent to the novel's hunchback, Quasimodo, and like Quasimodo, she ends up dead.

> *"One night he brought her here asleep, and I called her Estella."* —CHARLES DICKENS, *GREAT EXPECTATIONS*

ESTELLA *(Latin, "star")* See also **Stella**. Charles Dickens does not often engage in the allusive naming that authors like Hardy and James were so fond of, but Estella, in *Great Expectations,* is as beautiful and distant as any star. She has been raised by Miss Havisham as an instrument of vengeance; she will punish men for Miss Havisham's own aborted wedding day. In the course of the novel her cruelty is mitigated by her miserable marriage, and she and Pip—who has worshipped her from afar for hundreds of pages—finally meet as equals.

> *Esther Downing was of a reserved, tender, and timid cast of character.* —CATHARINE MARIA SEDGWICK, *HOPE LESLIE*

ESTHER *(Persian, "star")* See also **Hester**. One of only two women in the Bible with a whole book devoted to her. A beautiful Jewish girl known as Hadassah, she was chosen as a wife by the Persian king Ahasuerus. She concealed her religion until she learned of a plot to destroy all Jews, at which point she courageously put in a plea to save them. With the Puritan swing away from saints' names in the seventeenth century, Esther came to prominence. Catharine Maria Sedgwick's *Hope Leslie* is an early (1827) historical novel set in colonial Massachusetts. Esther Downing is the niece of Governor Winthrop and everything a Puritan maiden should be: honest, scrupulous, principled, and sub-

missive to her elders. She is even capable of the sacrifice of her fiancé Everell to title character Hope, when she realizes where his
affections truly lie. Esther Summerson of Charles Dickens's *Bleak
House* is saintly in much the same mold. Dickens uses her as narrator for portions of the novel, so she is required to protest a great
deal about her modesty ("I know I am not clever. I always knew
that") and her unworthiness of the other characters' affections.
She tends to define herself by the way she ministers to the other
characters like Ada Clare, to whom she is a companion. George
Eliot uses the name for the heroine of *Felix Holt: The Radical.* Esther is the refined young daughter of independent minister Rufus
Lyon. Again, the name denotes fairly homespun origins. A Dissenting minister in a northern English town did not lead a grand
life. Esther's intelligence and education set her apart, as does her
fondness for refinement: wax candles instead of tallow, silk stock-
ings instead of woolen. Her potential for frivolity is alarming in
the eyes of the radical hero, Felix, who has no patience with such
things.

> *Esther had that excellent thing in a woman, a soft voice with
> a clear fluent utterance.*
> —GEORGE ELIOT, *FELIX HOLT: THE RADICAL*

Esther Gobseck is the young lady of the title in Balzac's *A Harlot High and Low.* That thorough cynic practically invented the
whore with a heart of gold, and Esther is the prototype. As a
"rat," or young chorus girl in the Paris Opéra, she was introduced to vice by young men-about-town, and then graduated to
being a proper courtesan, or kept woman. She becomes the contented mistress of Lucien Chardon (in this novel, Lucien de Rubempré). Alas, Lucien is under the control of the arch-villain
Vautrin, who has only worldly advantage in mind for his protégé.
Vautrin whisks Esther off to a convent and threatens disasters to
befall Lucien unless she cooperates. Selflessly, Esther allows her-

self to be used, and goes back to her ostensibly gold-digging ways as the mistress of the banker Nucingen. Lucien is thus free to court his aristocratic Clotilde. But Esther holds out, refusing to sleep with Nucingen for as long as possible, thus remaining faithful to Lucien.

> *"You are flippant, Ethelberta. You are too much given to that sort of thing."*
> —THOMAS HARDY, *THE HAND OF ETHELBERTA*

ETHELBERTA *(Old English, "noble bright")* Thomas Hardy's *The Hand of Ethelberta,* one of his earlier novels, focuses on the struggles of a young woman who moves in London society with neither money nor a family background. Her father, in fact, is a butler. Ethelberta (named, Hardy makes plain, after the daughter of an aristocratic house where her father was a servant) is clever, resourceful, and charming. She wishes to make an advantageous marriage in order to help her numerous siblings, but circumstances and her own high spirits tend to interfere with this somewhat soulless objective. **Ethel,** which was eventually more widely used than Ethelberta, seems to be an offshoot of this name or of Ethelinda (see below). Scholars suggest that Thackeray's use of the name in *The Newcomes* may have encouraged its use. Certainly Ethel Newcome is an appealing character. The cousin of hero Clive Newcome, she is the daughter of a banker and granddaughter of an earl. As a wealthy, highborn beauty, Ethel is destined for the highest ranks of the marriage mart. But as an intelligent and analytical young woman, she is fiercely aware of her stature as near chattel, and refuses to submit completely to the marketing process. Thackeray makes her a complex creature, a flirt with a vein of self-hatred.

> *A girl of great beauty, high temper, and strong natural intel-*
> *lect, who submits to be dragged hither and thither in an old*
> *grandmother's leash, and in pursuit of a husband, who will*
> *run away from the couple, such a person, I say, is in a very*
> *awkward position as a heroine; and I declare if I had an-*
> *other ready to my hand . . . Ethel should be deposed at this*
> *very sentence.*
>
> —WILLIAM THACKERAY, THE NEWCOMES

ETHELINDA *(Old German, "noble serpent")* Eighteenth-century poet Christopher Smart took command of his craft (and, it appears, the perquisites of manhood) early. At age thirteen he was in love with Anne Vane, the daughter of the owners of Raby Castle where he was a guest. He wrote a very competent little poem to her, but called her Ethelinda instead of Anne. Perhaps the meter of his verse demanded it—the name was certainly far from common, then or since.

> *Happy verses! That were prest*
> *In fair Ethelinda's breast!*
> *Happy muse, that didst embrace*
> *The sweet, the heav'nly-fragrant place!*
> *Tell me, is the omen true?*
> *Shall the bard arrive there too?*
>
> —CHRISTOPHER SMART, "TO ETHELINDA"

EUDOXIE (euh dawk see'; *French from Greek, "well-reputed")* The vast majority of Russian names derive from the Orthodox Calendar of Saints. They are thus Greek in origin, though cultured Russians of the nineteenth century often Frenchified their names. In Ivan Turgenev's *Fathers and Sons,* Eudoxie Kukshin is known also as **Yevdoxia** or **Avdotya,** depending on who is addressing her. The two male protagonists, Kirsanov and Bazarov, meet her while visiting a provincial town, and both are attracted to the clever, unconventional blonde.

> *Charlotte and Gertrude acquired considerable facility in addressing her, directly, as "Eugenia"; but in speaking of her to each other they rarely called her anything but "she."*
> —HENRY JAMES, *THE EUROPEANS*

EUGENIA *(Greek, "well-born")* Henry James may have been playing with the literal meaning of the name when he chose it for the fascinating Baroness Eugenia Munster of *The Europeans.* He may also have wanted to evoke the French empress Eugénie, her era's version of a celebrity. In either case, Eugenia brings a whiff of exoticism to the small Massachusetts town where her American cousins live. (Her full name, overwhelmingly, is Eugenia-Camilla-Dolores, and she is morganatically married to a minor German princeling, from whom she is separated.) James wrote the novel in 1878, but set it thirty years earlier when contact between Europe and the United States was extremely limited. Eugenia and her feckless brother Felix discover with some discomfiture the relative freedoms and restrictions that control European and American lives.

The French form of the name is **Eugénie** *(euh zhay nee'),* as in the title character of Balzac's *Eugénie Grandet.* She is a kindly, handsome, straightforward young woman of twenty-three, the only daughter and heiress of the town miser. Though her father lives in shabby squalor, Eugénie possesses a dowry of six thousand francs. There are two suitors for her hand in the town of Saumur, but she falls in love with her handsome, unsteady cousin Charles. He takes her dowry, meaning to return to Saumur for her, but goes off to join the slave trade and forgets Eugénie. She lives on in Saumur, and finally makes a loveless marriage.

> *In short, Eugénie, so vigorous and built on such a generous scale, had nothing of the prettiness that pleases the crowd; but she was beautiful with the unmistakable beauty that only artists delight in.*
>
> —HONORÉ DE BALZAC, *EUGÉNIE GRANDET*

EULALIE *(Greek, "speaking sweetly")* Another one of the lost young ladies in Edgar Allan Poe's poetry. "Eulalie" is one of Poe's shorter works and we learn only that Eulalie has blond curls and violet eyes. She is also still alive when the poem ends—something of a departure from Poe's usual form.

> *I dwelt alone*
> *In a world of moan*
> *And my soul was a stagnant tide,*
> *Till the fair and gentle Eulalie became my blushing bride—*
> *Till the yellow-haired young Eulalie became my smiling bride.*
>
> —EDGAR ALLAN POE, "EULALIE"

EUNICE *(Greek, "victorious")* *Desperate Remedies* was Thomas Hardy's first published novel, and it shares more with the tradition of sensation fiction than it does with Hardy's later, more contemplative works. The male protagonist, Aeneas Manston, is an all-around bad'un. He courts Cytherea Graye, believing himself to be a widower. Doubt arises as to the means by which his previous wife died. Eunice Manston was at a certain inn when it burned down. Did Aeneas set the fire? Did he know she was there? Knowledgeable Hardy fans may remember that the author adored classical allusion, and that the meaning of Eunice's name should be taken literally.

EUPHEMIA *(Greek, "well spoken of")* From the same roots that give us "euphemistic." Saint Euphemia was an early Christian martyr, and her feast day on the Christian calendar gave her name continual exposure in Catholic countries. Charles Brockden Brown's *Edgar Huntly* is one of a handful of very early American gothic novels that take advantage of their American setting in striking ways. In *Edgar Huntly,* for instance, the Atlantic Ocean functions almost as a permeable membrane for the characters. They are raised here, born there, work on this continent, emigrate to that one. The surpassingly strange Clithero Edny once worked as the steward to Euphemia Wiatte Lorimer in Ireland. Though benevolent and well-meaning, Euphemia is secretly married to a mysterious doctor, and even has an evil twin brother, whose illegitimate daughter she has raised to adulthood.

EUPHRASIE *(euh frah zee'; Greek, "good cheer")* A name adopted by a prostitute in Honoré de Balzac's *The Wild Ass's Skin.* Pretty, gentle, barely adult, she is described by one man as "an ingenuous naiad" and by another as "soulless vice." Presumably she chose her name for its grandiose ring rather than for its evocations of a fourth-century Egyptian saint. In Victor Hugo's *Les Misérables,* the character known as **Cosette** is actually named Euphrasie.

EUROPA *(Greek, meaning unknown)* Europa is a Phoenician princess who bewitches Jupiter with her beauty. Ovid (one of the chief chroniclers of Jupiter's sexual peccadilloes in his *Metamorphoses*) tells how he turns himself into a snowy white bull in a herd near where Europa is frolicking on the seashore with her maidens. She is enchanted by the tameness of the powerful beast, and he carries her off to sea. The pair end up in Crete, and Minos is one of their offspring. The continent of Europe is named for her.

EURYDICE *(you rih' dih see; Greek, meaning unclear: the Greek particle eury means "broad" or "wide")* In *Metamorphoses,* Ovid tells the tragic story of musician Orpheus and his dryad wife Eurydice, who died of a snakebite shortly after they were wed. Or-

NYMPHS AND DRYADS

Though the Olympians are the deities most familiar to us today, there were also many lesser divinities in the Greco-Roman pantheon. The immortals included minor gods, nymphs, dryads, naiads, and nereids, all of whom appear frequently in myths. Orpheus's wife Eurydice, for instance, was a dryad, or tree spirit. Naiads lived in rivers or lakes or fountains while nereids were daughters of Poseidon and often rode seahorses while attending him. The most common category were nymphs, beautiful maidens who lived in the wild. They gave life and permanence to the beauty of nature. They also frequently had complicated love lives. Echo, for instance, faded away for the love of Narcissus, while Pomona refused to marry anyone. Clytie pined for Apollo and Io caught the lustful eye of Zeus/Jupiter—a fate she shared with many women both human and divine.

pheus went down to the underworld to seek her out, and with his music so charmed Pluto that he was permitted to take Eurydice back to the world of the living. But there was one condition: while leading her to the sunny lands, Orpheus was not permitted to look at her. He glanced back just once, and she returned to the land of the dead. Musicians have found this story very appealing, and operas by Monteverdi, Haydn, and Gluck treat the subject. This is also the name of Creon's wife in Sophocles' tragedy *Antigone*.

EUSTACIA *(Greek, "fruitful")* Another one of Thomas Hardy's passionate, headstrong heroines. *The Return of the Native* takes place in the small village of Egdon Heath. Eustacia Vye finds her life stultifying and hopes for escape when Clym Yeobright ("the native") comes back. She ends up marrying him but he does not whisk her off to a more exciting life, so she succumbs to the attentions of the village rake, Damon Wildeve.

> *Eustacia Vye was the raw material of a divinity. On Olympus she would have done well with little preparation. She had the passions and instincts which make a model goddess, that is, those which make not quite a model woman.*
> —THOMAS HARDY, *THE RETURN OF THE NATIVE*

EUTERPE *(yoo ter' pee; Greek, "the one who gladdens")* The Muse of lyric poetry and of certain kinds of music. She is often pictured with a double flute, which she invented. The word "euterpean" means "related to music."

EVANGELINE *(Greek, "good news")* Henry Wadsworth Longfellow was a hugely popular poet in his day. "Evangeline," a narrative poem dating from 1847, tells the story of the gentle, beautiful French-Canadian Evangeline Bellefontaine. She is a kind of latter-day Patient Griselda, ever faithful to her fiancé Gabriel, though they are separated for decades. In the mid-nineteenth century the somewhat heavy-handed Christian symbolism of the lovers' names (the "good news" referred to is the gospel of Christ) was not a weakness. Longfellow is usually given credit for bringing the name **Evangeline** to the attention of English-speakers, and Harriet Beecher Stowe followed hard on his heels by using the name in *Uncle Tom's Cabin*. Her Evangeline, generally known as "little **Eva**," is also pointedly named. She is a pious child of the sort so beloved by the Victorians. On a riverboat traveling to New Orleans the slave Uncle Tom meets little Eva and saves her from drowning. Her father Augustine buys Uncle Tom, and when Eva falls ill and is about to die (events that often befall pious children in literature of the day), she makes him promise to free the slave.

EVE *(Hebrew, "life")* In the Bible, the name of the first woman created. When Honoré de Balzac portrays a good woman, she usually fits the mold of the ideal Victorian helpmeet, and Eve

Chardon, in *Lost Illusions,* is one of these. Her brother Lucien (protagonist of this novel and *A Harlot High and Low*) is a handsome, ambitious poet with a dubious moral character, but Eve is blind to his weaknesses. She is the first woman to believe in him. She is also practical, courageous, and resourceful, especially when her beloved husband David's printing business encounters hard times.

EVELINA *(Origin unclear)* Scholars dispute whether Evelina is French or German in origin: it does not, surprisingly, seem to be an elaboration of **Eve.** Fanny Burney's *Evelina,* published in 1778, is the epistolary account of a young lady's introduction to polite society. Her mother's maiden name, "Evelyn," is probably the source of the heroine's first name. She is a kind, careful, well-educated young lady who happens to have a number of louche relatives. She is vigorously pursued by a rake, and methodically wooed by a lord.

FAITH *(English virtue name, "belief")* The first of the "Theological Virtues," Faith, Hope, and Charity. Writers have not been able to use this name without freighting it with meaning. It was popular, of course, in the seventeenth century among Puritan families, so Catharine Maria Sedgwick's *Hope Leslie,* set in early Massachusetts, naturally enough features a character named Faith. The sister of Hope Leslie, Faith was originally christened Mary but was renamed when the family arrived in America. Unlike Hope, she is timid and clinging.

As a young child, she is captured by the Pequot Indians, later married to one of their braves, and converted to Catholicism. When captured back and returned to her family, she pines for her earlier life with the Pequots. Nathaniel Hawthorne uses the name almost allegorically in his historical tale of Puritan Salem, "Young Goodman Brown." Faith is the honest, warmhearted wife of the protagonist whose life is disturbed by a vision of evil in the heart of his community. Thomas Hardy names a secondary character Faith in *The Hand of Ethelberta;* she is the ever-loyal and supportive sister of Christopher Julian, a young musician who is torn between his attraction to the expensive Ethelberta Petherwin and

> *"It seems a pity that the name of Faith was given to her, since her shrinking timid nature doth not promise, in any manner, to resemble that most potent of the christian graces."* —CATHARINE MARIA SEDGWICK, *HOPE LESLIE*

his musical career. Faith Julian believes in his music, but not in Ethelberta. Elizabeth Gaskell wrote a faithful sister into *Ruth* as well: Faith Benson is the loyal sister of minister Thurstan Benson. When her quixotic brother chooses to rescue Ruth the unwed mother, Faith objects at first. But she grows to love Ruth and soon her energy and pragmatism are harnessed to Ruth's benefit.

> *"Your incomprehensible summons has just reached me, and I obey, thereby proving my right name of Faith."*
> —ELIZABETH GASKELL, *RUTH*

FANCY *(English, "elaborate")* Thomas Hardy's *Under the Greenwood Tree* is one of his earliest novels, published anonymously in 1872. It is a kind of rural fantasia, looking back to innocent days in an English village. Young schoolmistress Fancy Day is the object of yearning among all the rustic menfolk. Having been "away," she brings a new level of sophistication to the village. Her name can be read as a pun: the men "fancy" her, and she is more "fancy" than the other village women.

FANNY *(Latin, "French")* Fanny originates as a nickname for **Frances**, but by the middle of the eighteenth century it was used very widely on its own along with **Fannie**. It was a favorite name among the Victorians, and appears often enough in literature to suggest that it was a neutral, nondescript name for a well-educated woman. Henry Fielding wrote significant characters named Fanny into both *Joseph Andrews* and *Amelia*. In the former, satiric novel, Fanny Goodwill is the simple, beautiful country girl who loves the hero. She travels to London to find him and her virtue is under constant threat. Fanny Matthews of *Amelia* is exactly the opposite. Our hero Captain Booth encounters her while he is serving a prison sentence, and she entices him into an affair despite the many virtues of his wife Amelia. Jane Austen also uses the name twice. The grasping wife of John Dashwood in *Sense* *and Sensibility* is Fanny, a proud and mercenary woman who dissuades her husband from helping his half sisters and stepmother financially. Fanny Price is the heroine of *Mansfield Park,* a modest girl thrown into exalted circumstances who keeps her head and wins the appropriate suitor.

Many of the English Victorian novelists used Fanny for characters of various importance. In Charles Dickens's *Nicholas Nickleby,* Fanny Squeers is a lonely female denizen of Dotheboys Hall, shrill, bitter and trapped. Anne Brontë writes a childish Fanny into *Agnes Grey:* Fanny Bloomfield is one of the diabolical children to whom Agnes is a governess, "a mischievous, intractable little creature." More conventional is the ladylike Fanny Robarts of Anthony Trollope's *Framley Parsonage.* She is the wife of the vicar at Framley, and the very model of a Victorian wife, except that she can be quite fierce where her husband's interests are concerned. Fanny Davilow in George Eliot's *Daniel Deronda* is incapable of any fierceness at all: she is merely a silly, shallow, well-meaning woman who somehow managed to produce the magnificent Gwendolen Harleth as a daughter. And in Thomas Hardy's *Far from the Madding Crowd,* Fanny Robin is a victim. Bathsheba Everdene's servant, she falls in love with the dashing Sergeant York and comes close to marrying him. She bears his child and dies, along with the infant, prompting much remorse from York.

Henry James is modern enough to be suspected of irony, especially in the creation of secondary characters. In *The Awkward Age,* Fanny Cashmore is a magnificent but stupid member of Nanda Brookenham's social circle. She is always on the verge of leaving the comforts of Mr. Cashmore's home for the thrills of life with her lover. Fanny Assingham in *The Golden Bowl* is not a fool like Mrs. Cashmore. Having promoted the marriage between Maggie Verver and Prince Amerigo, she watches with horror as the prince and Maggie's friend Charlotte Stant seem to resume a love affair.

Fanny is also the rare name that transferred to France without etymological roots there (ironic, considering its meaning). In Émile Zola's *The Earth,* Fanny Delhomme is the one member of the unfortunate Fouan family to have avoided the miseries of agricultural life. Her husband is both rich and kind to her, so she escapes hunger and domestic violence, unlike most of the female characters in the book.

FANTINE *(French, meaning unknown)* Victor Hugo's *Les Misérables* is very explicit about social conditions in early nineteenth-century France. Fantine, the mother of Cosette, was born during the Revolution, when the use of last names was suspended and the French practice of naming children after saints was also in abeyance. Fantine is beautiful and naive, and she falls madly in love with an intellectual who drops her when she gets pregnant. She has no recourse but to work as a prostitute to support her daughter Cosette, eventually selling her hair and her teeth to ensure Cosette's well-being.

> She was called Fantine—Why? Because she had never been known by any other name. At her birth, the Revolutionary Directory was still in power. She could have no family name, because she had no family; she could have no baptismal name, because at the time there was no church. She was named at the whim of the first passerby who found her, an infant wandering barefoot in the streets. Her name came to her like water from the clouds on her forehead when it rained. She was called little Fantine. Nobody knew anything more about her. —VICTOR HUGO, *LES MISÉRABLES*

FATIMA *(Arabic, "she who weans" or "she who abstains from the forbidden")* Traditionally Fatima (also **Fatma** or **Fatimah**) is the name of Muhammad's favorite daughter, one of four perfect women in the world. It is also the name of Bluebeard's last wife. In *Tales from the Thousand and One Nights,* Fatima is a female hermit murdered by a magician, a casualty of a larger plot against Aladdin.

FAUSTA *(Latin, "lucky, fortunate")* Also occurs as **Faustina.** Fabrizio del Dongo, the womanizing hero of Stendhal's *The Charterhouse of Parma,* falls in love with an opera singer named Fausta. She serves primarily as a glamorous conquest; Fabrizio's real interest in her is that she already has a lover, whom he displaces. Matthew Arnold also uses the name in a poem called "Resignation." He is actually addressing it to his sister Jane, but Fausta seems to fit better into his metrical scheme.

> *This world in which we draw our breath,*
> *In some sense, Fausta, outlasts death.*
> —MATTHEW ARNOLD, "RESIGNATION"

FAYAWAY *(Origin unknown) Typee* was Herman Melville's first book, a kind of travel memoir about his experiences sailing the South Seas. The narrator is, practically speaking, the captive of a Polynesian tribe called the Typees, and Fayaway is the beautiful young island woman who treats his leg wound, shares his bed, and nearly undermines his American moral vigor. Fayaway is gentle, generous, and graceful, a sort of natural ideal woman of her era.

FÉLICITÉ *(French, "happiness")* The English form is **Felicity.** In Gustave Flaubert's "A Simple Life," Félicité is a deeply pious servant. Having been jilted as a young girl, she has spent the remainder of her life working as a maid to one woman. She is capable of (even prone to) deep devotion. Her nephew, the son and daughter of her employer, even her parrot, named Loulou, are objects of this devotion. Critics have suggested that Félicité is Flaubert's version of a saint.

FERNANDA *(Old German, possibly "peace" or "bold voyager")* Could Henry James have been aware of the ancient meaning of this name? It seems unlikely, yet in *The Awkward Age* he creates a heroine who steers a very courageous course out of the world of her childhood. Fernanda Brookenham, known as **Nanda,** is the daughter of a selfish, pretty London socialite (also named Fernanda). The mother has never taken the trouble to shelter her daughter from the vulgarities and scandals of London society, with the unfortunate consequence that Nanda is considered damaged goods by the strictest standards of the marriage market. Yet she somehow retains her innocence on a profound level and, deploring the cynicism of society, opts simply to drop out and live in the country.

> "Do you *call her Fernanda?*"
> Vanderbank *felt positively more guilty than he would have expected.* "You think it too *much in the manner we just mentioned?* . . . In point of fact, I don't *call Mrs. Brookenham by her Christian name.*"
> —HENRY JAMES, THE AWKWARD AGE

FIAMMETTA *(Italian, "little flame")* Though the name is Italian, in Ludovico Ariosto's *Orlando Furioso* Fiammetta is a Spanish girl purchased by a pair of young bucks, Astolfo and Giocondo, for their sexual pleasure. She is clever enough, however, to cheat both of them with a young man from her hometown—summarily proving to Astolfo and Giocondo that women are utterly faithless.

FIDELIA *(Latin, "faith")* In Edmund Spenser's allegory *The Faerie Queen,* Fidelia is one of three daughters of Coelia in the House of Holiness. (The others are Speranza, or hope, and Charissa, or charity.) She bears a chalice containing wine and water, and represents the most important of the three "Theological Virtues" of the Christian faith.

FIONA *(Gaelic, "fair, pale")* A highly improbable name for a Russian convict, yet Fiona is a character in Nikolai Leskov's "Lady

Macbeth of Mtsensk." The protagonist, Katerina, is being transported to Siberia with her lover Sergey, who tires of her. Fiona is the first object of his attentions, and she happily sleeps with Sergey, but she is not malicious. In fact, when Sergey turns against Katerina, Fiona is kind to her.

FIORDILIGI *(fyoer dee lee' jee; Italian, "lily blossom")* The French equivalent is the more familiar *fleur de lis*. In Ariosto's *Orlando Furioso*, Fiordiligi (also known as **Fiordelisa**) is a princess who was stolen from her parents and raised by the family of the knight Brandimarte. She grows to love him, follows him on all his adventures, and eventually the pair marry. Fiordiligi even frees him from the sorceress Atalante when he is captured. He is killed soon after, though, and she builds him a beautiful tomb, where she takes up residence, waiting to die herself.

FLAVIA *(flah' vee yah or flay' vee yah; Italian, clan name meaning "yellow")* A minor character in William Dean Howells's *A Modern Instance*. An example of what was called "social realism," the novel traced the development of a bad marriage between the impulsive and rich Marcia Gaylord and brilliant, lazy Bartley Hubbard. They name their daughter Flavia, in honor of Marcia's father Flavius, who is more generally known as "Squire."

> *Fleda Vetch, whom from the first hour no illusion had brushed with its wing.*
>
> —HENRY JAMES, *THE SPOILS OF POYNTON*

FLEDA *(Origin unknown)* Henry James does not usually invent names, but Fleda is unprecedented outside of *The Spoils of Poynton*. Even her last name, Vetch, is unusual, being the name of a very modest legume. The two names together may suggest "fledgling" or "fletcher," both terms having to do with feathers and arrows. Fleda herself is a clever, quiet young woman who is taken up by a widow, Mrs. Gereth. Mrs. Gereth's lifework is the house called Poynton, which is full of artistic masterpieces, all acquired with little money but great connoisseurship. Fleda's "only treasure," says James, is "her subtle mind." Mrs. Gareth thinks of Fleda as a potential daughter-in-law but her son Owen prefers the vulgar Mona Brigstock.

FLORA *(Latin, "flower")* The root of a number of names that have been steadily used, especially in the eighteenth and nineteenth centuries. Edmund Spenser, in *The Faerie Queen*, creates a character called **Florimell**, which may be a combination of "flower" and the Latin word particle for honey, *mel*. Florimell is a personification of Chastity and she spends Book Three of *The Faerie Queen* desperately eluding rape and seduction. A wizard even creates a False Florimell (also known as "the Snowy Florimell") who deceives some of her pursuers. **Florinda** is another elaboration, used casually by Anthony Trollope in *The Warden* for a young daughter of Archdeacon Grantly. She originally appeared with her sister Griselda, and she was the elder. By *Barchester Towers*, she is the younger, and this is her last appearance in Trollope's works. In Honoré de Balzac's *Lost Illusions* we meet **Florine**, a young actress of dubious morals. Her name, another variant on the Flora theme, is invented, like those of many of Balzac's prostitutes (**Coralie** in the same book being an example). Florine is only sixteen, slender, delicate-looking, but extremely hardheaded and practical about earning her keep.

Flora has been one of the two most commonly used forms of the name. It has a certain Scots flavor, probably owing to the fame of Flora McDonald, the Scottish woman who helped Bonnie Prince Charlie escape British troops. She was a great celebrity in her day, and when Sir Walter Scott names a character Flora MacIvor in *Waverley* he clearly invokes the heroics of Flora McDonald. Scott's Flora is the sister of an ambitious clan chieftain who aids Charles Stuart in the hope of material advantage. She doesn't approve of her brother's scheming, and serves the Jacobite cause out of pure passion. Though the hero, Edward Waverley, proposes to her, she ultimately retires to a convent. Scott wrote

Waverley in 1814 and there may have been something nostalgic about the name by Dickens's time, for he gives it to Flora Finching, Arthur Clennam's old flame in *Bleak House.* Clennam has remained a bachelor and cherished the memory of Flora for twenty years. But when he finally meets her again, she turns out to be a kindly, garrulous, raddled, and irritating woman. Critics suggest that this episode is based on Dickens's own experience with his childhood love, Maria Beadnell. In Henry James's *The Turn of the Screw,* Flora is the daughter of the household. James manages to suggest that although Flora is pretty, well-mannered, and charming, there is something eerie about her. Her only actual peculiarity is a tendency to wander at night.

Flora is a short step from the French **Flore,** which historians suggest might be its source for anglophone use. In Balzac's *The Black Sheep,* Flore Brazier is a staggeringly beautiful peasant girl purchased by a country doctor from her venal uncle when she was a child. Dr. Rouget educates Flore, houses and feeds her, and trains her to be his housekeeper, but he is not able to make her his mistress, because he is impotent. After Rouget's death she gets her revenge, however, by seducing his foolish son, Jean-Jacques. Flore turns out to be merciless and manipulative, bending Jean-Jacques to her will and bringing her own lover Max into the household as well.

Florence means, literally, "blossoming" or "in flower." Its use as a girl's name was increased by the fame of nurse Florence Nightingale (who was actually named for the Italian city). Florence Dombey, of Dickens's *Dombey and Son,* became famous a bit earlier, however. She is in some ways the true hero of the book. When young Paul Dombey dies, his father despairs, but strong, sensible, affectionate Florence could console the father, were she only permitted to do so. Dickens effects redemption by having Dombey senior live with Florence after his business fails. He becomes a loving grandfather to her children. In Horatio Alger, Jr.'s *Struggling Upward* we see the casual nineteenth-century use of the name: Florence Grant is "the prettiest girl in Groveton," and Alger calls her "a general favorite, not only for her good looks, but on account of her pleasant manner and sweet disposition." That was back when a sweet disposition was an asset.

> *How can one explain the fascination of a name?* Foedora
> *haunted me like an evil thought that one tries to compro-*
> *mise with.* —HONORÉ DE BALZAC, THE WILD ASS'S SKIN

FOEDORA *(feh doe' rah; Russian from Greek, "gift of God")*
Many of Honoré de Balzac's Parisian novels are about self-
invented characters, and many of those have names that they have
assumed or changed. When Raphaël de Valentin falls for Countess Foedora in *The Wild Ass's Skin,* it seems likely that her real
name is something else entirely. She is beautiful, rich, half Russian, and lives without ties to any man. "She was more than a
woman, she was a romantic novel," says Balzac. But Raphaël, in
his desperation to get close to her, hides in her bedroom and finds
that her hauteur covers emotional emptiness: "In order to satisfy
the natural human need, however undeveloped it might be in her,
to open her heart to a fellow-creature [she] was reduced to chat-
ting with her chambermaid."

> *"If only you could've seen her! Fortunata's eyes were like*
> *stars, almost like the ones on the Virgin in Carmen*
> *Church.... Let's see... Fortunata's hands were rough*
> *from working so hard. Her heart was pure innocence. For-*
> *tunata hadn't had any education. Such a pretty mouth, and*
> *it left out letters right and left and mixed up others. She used*
> *to say 'indilgences,' 'goin,' 'sorta.' She spent her childhood*
> *taking care of the 'cattle.' You know what the 'cattle' were?*
> *Hens."* —BENITO PÉREZ GALDÓS, FORTUNATA AND JACINTA

FORTUNATA *(Spanish, "born of chance")* Benito Pérez Galdós
has been termed the Spanish Balzac, a nineteenth-century novelist
working in the realistic tradition. *Fortunata and Jacinta* follows

the lives of two very different women who are linked by their love for handsome, feckless Juanito Santa Cruz. Fortunata is a girl of the streets, a ravishing beauty whom Santa Cruz seduces and abandons. Pérez Galdós treats with sympathy her attempt to achieve respectability and her loosening hold on sanity.

FRANCES *(Latin, "French")* Though **Frances** has not been a favorite with writers, two of the three Brontë sisters used it in their novels. The heroine of Charlotte Brontë's *The Professor* is Frances Evans Henri, a plucky, resourceful teacher at a Brussels boarding school. It seems likely that she is in some way an alter ego of Charlotte herself, who worked in Brussels as a schoolteacher. Frances is a strong-minded woman who, even after she marries fellow teacher William Crimsworth, insists on continuing to teach, and never allows her marriage or her motherhood to interfere with her career. Emily Brontë writes a much smaller part for Frances Earnshaw in *Wuthering Heights*. She is merely Hindley Earnshaw's wife, Cathy's sister-in-law, who bears Hindley a son and dies before she can lose her optimistic high spirits.

The French form of Frances is **Françoise** *(fraw swahz´)*, the Italian form **Francesca** *(fran ches´ kah)* or **Francisca**, which Shakespeare uses for a nun in *Measure for Measure*. In Émile Zola's *The Earth,* many of the characters, like Françoise, do not even have last names. They are not far removed from the animals, preoccupied with subsistence alone. Françoise is an earthy but innocent fourteen-year-old peasant at the beginning of the book. She has an affair with one of the most brutal of her neighbors, despite her attraction to the better-educated, more refined visitor, Jean Macquart. Her teenage aspirations are soon mired in the daily grind for survival. Francesca da Rimini in Dante's *Inferno* is not a fictional character but one of the most famous inhabitants of Dante's Hell. She falls in love with the handsome younger brother of her husband, while reading with him one day. (The inauspicious subject was Lancelot, who cuckolded his best friend King Arthur.) Francesca's husband kills his wife and his brother, and they spend eternity in the second circle of Hell, blown hither and thither by light winds that symbolize the lust they succumbed to.

GEORGIANA *(Latin, "farmer")* Use among grand English families (in honor of the Hanoverian kings of England) gives **Georgiana** (or **Georgina, Georgianna,** and even **Georgia**) a certain aristocratic aura that authors have taken advantage of. In Jane Austen's *Pride and Prejudice*, for instance, Georgiana Darcy's name contrasts with plain Elizabeth and Jane Bennet. Like her brother Fitzwilliam Darcy, Georgiana initially seems haughty but improves on acquaintance. Dickens's use of Georgiana for Mrs. Joe Gargery, Pip's sister in *Great Expectations*, is purely comical. Mrs. Joe, the wife of a blacksmith, is a severe and practical housewife with no pretensions at all. Georgiana Longstaff, in Trollope's *The Way We Live Now*, is almost the exact opposite of Mrs. Joe. Trollope had great scorn for mercenary society marriages, and as a noble spinster of thirty, desperate to marry a rich man, Georgiana is an object of derision. Her Germanic name, like that of her brother Adolphus, signals that the Longstaff family's days of glory had occurred in the previous century. Trollope's other Georgina, the third Fawn sister in *The Eustace Diamonds*, is nothing more than Trollope's little joke about the timid Lord Fawn's family. There are eight sisters, all of whose names end in *a*.

GERTRUDE *(Old German, "spear strong")* The name of two influential saints, one a medieval mystic and the other a seventh-century abbess who was revered in Belgium and the Netherlands. Shakespeare, who named Hamlet's mother Gertrude, may have known the name from the church. Gertrude's great sin, in Hamlet's eyes, was to remarry after his father's death, but even Hamlet's wildest imaginings do not connect his mother with his father's murder. Modern productions of *Hamlet,* however, often suggest that Hamlet and Gertrude have a more sexual relationship than is usual between mother and son. In Alessandro Manzoni's *The Betrothed,* Sister Gertrude is also known as "The Nun of Monza." She is the daughter of a powerful family who was sent unwillingly to a convent. Her lack of vocation and her bitterness about her fate have led her into evil ways, including murder and a sexual relationship. When the chaste heroine Lucia falls into Sister Gertrude's hands, she thinks she is safe from her pursuer, but Sister Gertrude readily betrays her. Henry James takes up the name for an unconventional American girl in *The Europeans.*

GERVAISE *(French, feminization of a saint's name of unknown origin)* Émile Zola's linked Rougon-Macquart novels attempted to describe a cross-section of contemporary French society. *L'Assommoir* dissects life in the slums of Paris from the point of view of good-natured, feckless Gervaise. Abandoned, early in the book, by the father of her two children, she takes up with a roofer who is seriously injured and can no longer work. She ends up as a prostitute. Her daughter Anna reappears in the Zola oeuvre as the courtesan Nana.

GINA *(Source unclear)* To English ears **Gina** sounds like a variant of **Jean,** which would relate it to **John,** but scholars suggest that it is a diminutive of longer names like **Georgina** or **Virginia.** An Italian source seems most likely for Gina Sanseverina, Fabrizio's young aunt in *The Charterhouse of Parma.* Stendhal had an Italian mistress named Gina, who probably served as a source for the character. Gina is a spirited, passionate promoter of Fabrizio's interests, and though she constantly reassures herself that her feelings for him are purely familial, her behavior indicates otherwise. Throughout the book her actions and choices serve to either promote his worldly career or keep him from the clutches of other women. Gina in Henrik Ibsen's *The Wild Duck* presents a stark contrast to Stendhal's worldly aristocrat. Gina Ekdal was the housemaid and mistress of the unsavory Old Werle. She married Hjalmar Ekdal without informing him that she was pregnant. She runs Hjalmar's house and photography business with efficiency, and genuinely loves Hjalmar, though he mocks her lower-class mannerisms.

GINEVRA *(Source unclear)* Some scholars propose that **Ginevra** is related to **Jennifer** and thence to **Guinevere,** while others suggest a link to the Dutch word for a juniper tree, *genever*. Improbably, Ginevra is the daughter of the King of Scotland in Ariosto's *Orlando Furioso*. She is in love with the Italian knight Ariodante and when the two are married, becomes the Duchess of Albany. Almost as unlikely is Ginevra Fanshawe, a young English girl in Charlotte Brontë's *Villette*. Ginevra is everything that the heroine Lucy Snowe is not: pretty, rich, fascinating to men, and profoundly selfish. Lucy loses a suitor to Ginevra, who ultimately prefers a rakish aristocrat to the worthy Dr. John Bretton. Yet Brontë takes almost a savage satisfaction in contrasting the observant, reserved Lucy's ambiguous fate to Ginevra's more conventional success, suggesting that if Lucy is an alter ego for Charlotte, Ginevra is the alter ego of all the showy women who eclipsed Charlotte's feminine attractions.

> *"I won't be called Lady Glencora. Call me Cora."*
> —ANTHONY TROLLOPE, *CAN YOU FORGIVE HER?*

GLENCORA *(Invented name)* For this headstrong Scottish heiress (his favorite female character), Anthony Trollope created a name that sounded simultaneously Scottish and grand. Lady Glencora M'Cluskie appears first in *The Small House at Allington* as a beautiful, vivacious, and stubborn young woman who must be married off to the respectable Plantagenet Palliser instead of to her beloved but improvident Burgo Fitzgerald. In *Can You Forgive Her?* Lady Glencora is bored with her marriage and strongly tempted to run away with Burgo. Her husband makes an immense sacrifice at the end of the book and whisks her off to Europe rather than taking the prized political role of Chancellor of the Exchequer. The Pallisers' complex marriage forms part of the narrative thread of the rest of the political novels, and its basic conflict never changes. Plantagenet Palliser loves Glencora deeply but is appalled by her frivolity, her lively instinct for mischief, and her propensity to meddle.

GLORIANA *(Latin, "glory")* An elaborated form of **Gloria**; the earliest name with this root was **Gloriosa**. **Gloriana** is the form used by poets to refer to Elizabeth I. In Edmund Spenser's *The Faerie Queen*, Gloriana is the Faerie Queen herself, seen by Prince Arthur in a vision of Faery Land and eagerly sought thereafter.

GLORVINA *(Invented name)* First appeared in a minor English novel in 1806, apparently coined by the author, Lady Morgan. William Thackeray took it up in *Vanity Fair* for an incidental character. William Dobbin's regimental commander has an Irish wife, Peggy O'Dowd. Her sister Glorvina Maloney comes into the story as an unattached female who makes a play for the impervious Dobbin. Pretty and vivacious, Glorvina Maloney is a contrast to the ladylike Amelia Osborne, whom Dobbin loves in vain.

GONERIL *(Possibly Old Norse, "battle maiden")* The eldest sister in *King Lear*. Shakespeare manages to develop her character even within the parameters of outlandish cruelty. She begins as a mean-spirited follower of her sadistic sister Regan, but in the course of the play her capacity for evil develops. She always retains, however, a semblance of reason, which is possibly even more frightening than her sister's violence.

> *No girl ever lived with any beauty belonging to her who had a smaller knowledge of her own possession than Grace Crawley.*
> —ANTHONY TROLLOPE, *THE LAST CHRONICLE OF BARSET*

GRACE *(Latin, "grace")* In Christian theological terms, grace is the undeserved generosity that God shows to mankind. Anthony Trollope, steeped in the culture of the English church, certainly knew this when he named the eldest daughter of the Reverend Josiah Crawley. The Crawley family appears first in *Framley Parsonage* as the poor dependents of the excessively proud Crawley who, despite his immense talents, holds an unremunerative position in the church. Grace is being taught Greek and Latin because, as her father says, "It is all that I can give [her]." In *The Last Chronicle of Barset,* Grace has matured into a modest, intelligent and, yes, graceful young lady who supports her father through terrible troubles. She attracts the love of Henry Grantly, son of the archdeacon, whose family objects to what they see as a mismatch, until they come to know Grace better.

GRETCHEN see **MARGARET**

GRISELDA *(Old German, "gray battle maiden")* Chaucer, in *The Canterbury Tales,* spells the name **Grisild** or **Grisilde,** depending on the edition, while in Boccaccio's *Decameron* she is **Griselda.** Her story is essentially the same in both versions. Griselda is a beautiful peasant girl who is chosen to marry the king. After a few years he gets it in his head to test her by taking away their children, telling Griselda that he has killed them. Then he sends Griselda back to her poor parents, pretending she was an unsatisfactory wife. Then he brings her back to the palace to wait on his new "wife," who is actually her daughter. Throughout, Griselda is patient and meek and submissive, thus passing her husband's test. He finally reinstates her as his queen. Trollope clearly draws on this story when he names Griselda Grantly in *The Warden.* One of two daughters of Archdeacon Grantly, Griselda promises to be a beauty. One of the great pleasures of reading Trollope is participating in his development of characters over the course of a series of books, and his treatment of Griselda Grantly is deeply entertaining. By *Framley Parsonage,* she is "decidedly a beauty, but somewhat statuesque in her loveliness." Comparisons to

Chaucer's Griselda are made, but humorously; Griselda Grantly is barely human and has nary a thought in her head that does not pertain to her appearance. She marries very grandly, becoming Lady Dumbello, vaulting into the stratosphere of English society. In *The Small House at Allington* Trollope indulges himself by describing an excruciatingly dull flirtation between Lady Dumbello and Plantagenet Palliser, neither one of them an exemplar of charm. She makes walk-on appearances in several other novels as a cold and empty-headed aristocrat.

GUDRUN *(Old Norse, meaning unclear)* The *Laxdaela Saga* was written around A.D. 1000 in Iceland. Its heroine is Gudrun, an imperious and animated woman who marries four times without ever managing to wed her true love Kjartan Olafsson. Her fierce pride and misunderstandings with Kjartan precipitate many a bloody feud and power play among the brutal clans of Iceland and Norway. In a startling reversal, Gudrun ends her days as Iceland's first nun.

GUDULE *(Probably Old Norse in origin)* The church of Sainte-Gudule in Brussels is dedicated to a seventh-century laywoman who lived an especially holy life. Little else is known about her. Victor Hugo adopted her name for the mother of the Gypsy Esmeralda in *Nôtre-Dame of Paris*. Gudule is a former prostitute who was imprisoned in a cell in the Cathedral of Nôtre Dame for fifteen years after Esmeralda was stolen away by Gypsies. She has long since gone mad. When she realizes that her daughter is in the cell next door she tears down the cell bars to reach her.

GUILLERMINA *(Spanish from German, "will helmet")* The English cognate would be **Wilhelmina,** since the name is a feminization of **Guillermo** (**William** or **Wilhelm**). Benito Pérez Galdós is evenhanded with his characters in *Fortunata and Jacinta*. They are human, worthy of understanding and compassion even when they cause each other great pain. Guillermina Pacheco is no exception: she is a wealthy woman who works tirelessly to support fallen women and their children. Guillermina shamelessly bullies her acquaintances into donating money and goods to her projects. Yet Pérez Galdós, though he refers to her as "the saint," does not shrink from depicting her fits of impatience and temper.

GUINEVERE *(Welsh, "fair and smooth")* In various versions of the Arthurian legends Guinevere (also known as **Ganor, Gaynor,** and **Guenever**) plays different roles in Arthur's reign and his demise. She is always a woman of staggering beauty, whose looks cause men to lose their senses. She is also unfaithful to Arthur, usually with Lancelot, though Geoffrey of Monmouth's *The History of the Kings of Britain* has her seduced by Arthur's son and nemesis Mordred. In Malory's *Le Morte D'Arthur,* Guinevere renounces her love for Lancelot after Arthur is killed in battle with Mordred, and she becomes a nun.

GWENDOLEN *(Welsh, "fair bow")* Also **Gwendolyn, Gwendoline.** Henry James's tale "The Figure in the Carpet" concerns a critic's obsession with the meaning of another writer's work. Gwendolen Corvick is the wife of an editor who feels he has found the secret. The narrator hounds Gwendolen but she refuses to reveal this key ("the figure in the carpet" of the title), even after her husband's death. George Eliot uses the name for one of the principal characters of *Daniel Deronda.* Gwendolen Harleth is the beautiful, talented, and spoiled young lady whose life becomes entangled with Daniel's. She marries the cold Henleigh Grandcourt because her family has lost all its money and as a petted Victorian beauty she has no other resources. Eliot manages to make Gwendolen an object of compassion without ever making her likable.

> *In Gwendolen's habits of mind it had been taken for granted that she knew what was admirable and that she herself was admired.*
> —GEORGE ELIOT, *DANIEL DERONDA*

HAIDÉE *(Arabic, possibly "serene, calm")* Part of the appeal of Lord Byron's poetry in its era was the exoticism of setting and character, which extended to the names of characters. An epic poem about Don Juan, of course, cannot be expected to feature just one heroine, so Haidée is not the only female to catch the hero's lustful attention. She is the beautiful seventeen-year-old daughter of a Greek smuggler who (shades of *The Odyssey*) finds Don Juan washed up on the shore of the island where she lives. She falls madly in love with him and succumbs to his charms. When her fierce father discovers her in Don Juan's arms, she dies of shock. Dumas takes up the name, spelling it **Haydée**, in *The Count of Monte Cristo*. Again, exoticism is the keynote: Haydée, the daughter of a dethroned Turkish ruler, has been sold into slavery as a result of the evil doings of the book's villain. Dumas is more culturally cautious than Byron, though, and does not throw his Haydée into his Christian hero's arms.

HARRIET *(Old German, "home ruler")* Also appears as **Hariett** and **Harriot**; it is considered the "spoken" form of **Henrietta**.

> *And Haidée, being devout as well as fair,*
> *Had doubtless heard about the Stygian river*
> *And hell and purgatory, but forgot*
> *Just in the very crisis she should not.*
> —LORD BYRON, *DON JUAN*

Used by authors almost exclusively for secondary characters in the eighteenth and nineteenth centuries. The exception is William Hill Brown, whose *The Power of Sympathy,* published in 1789, was one of America's first novels. It is the epistolary tale of the pretty, respectable orphan Harriot. She catches the eye of young Harrington, her social superior and, it transpires, her half brother. (Both names are derivatives of **Henry**.) She is made ill by the shame of being illegitimate, and Harrington's love for her is not diminished by knowledge of their common blood. Poet Christopher Smart fell in love with a real Harriot, Miss Harriot Pratt of Norfolk, when he was very young, and naturally enough wrote a poem to her—infinitely more sophisticated than most juvenile poetry. In Fielding's *Tom Jones* the heroine Sophia has a cousin named Harriet, a selfish, rather raffish married woman, and in Austen's *Emma* the illegitimate Harriet Smith is one of Emma's matchmaking projects.

Charles Dickens's sympathy for the downtrodden colors his portrait of Harriet Beadle in *Little Dorrit*. She is known as "Tattycoram," the young girl adopted by a middle-class family, the Meagles. She refuses to show adequate gratitude and meekness, but instead is subject to fits of rage. Regretfully Mr. Meagles says, when she has left the family, "Who were we that we should have a right to name her like a dog or a cat?" Trollope seems to associate the name Harriet with something less than sterling morals. Harriet Roby in *The Prime Minister* is the vulgar, silly aunt at whose house Emily Wharton is courted by the louche Ferdinand Lopez. In *Framley Parsonage,* Harriett Smith is the ambitious sister of the disreputable Sowerby, a woman "with a keen sense of the value of all worldly things." Elizabeth Gaskell has no such axe to grind. In her last novel, *Wives and Daughters,* Lady Harriet Cumnor is the least stuck-up and the prettiest daughter of the grand Cumnor family. She becomes a very good friend to the modest heroine Molly.

Jane Austen uses the more formal name, **Henrietta,** for a minor character in her last novel, *Persuasion*. Henrietta Musgrove is "perhaps the prettiest" of the two Musgrove sisters, sisters-in-law to the heroine Anne Elliot. If Harriet had racy connotations for

Trollope, Henrietta did not. The conventional heroine of *The Way We Live Now* (his most satiric novel) is ladylike Henrietta Carbury, known as **Hetta.** She is the self-effacing sister of rogue Felix Carbury, beloved by her conservative cousin Roger. Henry James uses the name for comic effect in *The Portrait of a Lady.* Henrietta Stackpole is Isabel Archer's sardonic journalist friend. The contrast between her highly feminine first name and the prosaic "Stackpole" is faintly ludicrous. James, however, makes her a trenchant observer of English ways, and a staunch friend to Isabel.

> *Incomparable Harriot, loveliest fair,*
> *That e'er breath'd sweetness on the vital air,*
> *Whose matchless form to us below is giv'n,*
> *As a bright pattern of the rest of heav'n,*
> *Blest with a face, a temper and a mind*
> *To please, to soothe, and to instruct mankind!*
> —CHRISTOPHER SMART,
> "TO MISS H——— WITH SOME MUSIC"

HECUBA *(Greek, meaning unknown)* In *The Iliad* and later works, Hecuba is the wife of Priam and mother of Hector, Paris, and Cassandra. Euripides takes up her fate after the Trojan War in *The Trojan Women* and *Hecuba.* She is a central figure of suffering in both plays, overcome with grief at all of her losses. In *Hecuba* her last two children are killed and in revenge she blinds Thracian king Polymestor and kills all of his sons.

HEDDA *(Old German, "warfare, strife")* **Hedda** is a variant of **Hedvig** or **Hedwig.** The title character of Ibsen's *Hedda Gabler* is the clever, beautiful, and spoiled wife of dull academic George Tesman. Bored and anxious, she begins to meddle with a former admirer, Ejlert Lovberg, who is a rival of her husband's. By the end of the play she has driven him back to alcohol and ultimately to his death, which she follows with her own. Ibsen uses Hedvig in another tragedy, *The Wild Duck*. Hedvig Ekdal is the fourteen-year-old daughter of Gina Ekdal, and passes for the daughter of Gina's husband Hjalmar. She lavishes affection on her pet wild duck, which she identifies with.

HELEN (*Greek, "light"*) One of the great beauties of Western literature, Helen is the daughter of Leda and Zeus, who came to her mother in the form of a swan. She is virtuously married to Spartan king Menelaus when Paris carries her off to Troy, thus sparking the Trojan War. She is portrayed as a pawn of the gods by authors like Euripides (in *The Trojan Women*). In *Helen* he even weaves a narrative around the "false Helen" who went to Troy and the "real Helen" who fled to Egypt and remained loyal to Menelaus. In *The Iliad,* Homer has her pining for Sparta and regretting her relationship with Paris, for whom she has little respect, and in *The Odyssey* she appears at Menelaus's side as the restored queen of Sparta.

> *And catching sight of Helen moving along the ramparts,*
> *they murmured one to another, gentle, winged words:*
> *"Who on earth could blame them? Ah, no wonder*
> *the men of Troy and Argives under arms have suffered*
> *years of agony all for her, for such a woman.*
> *Beauty, terrible beauty!*
> *A deathless goddess—so she strikes our eyes!"*
> —HOMER, *THE ILIAD*

Helen appears in later works as the epitome of feminine allure, and both Marlowe's and Goethe's versions of the Faust story include encounters with her. Goethe's Faust even has a child by her. In Anne Brontë's *The Tenant of Wildfell Hall,* Helen Graham is irresistibly attractive like Helen of Troy. The narrator, farmer Gilbert Markham, falls under her spell despite her occasional attempts to limit his ardor. She is the mysterious, slender, dark-haired widow who rents Wildfell Hall and refuses to reveal her history to Gilbert. It transpires that she has left her husband, a cruel alcoholic. Shakespeare uses an elaborated form of the name, **Helena,** in *A Midsummer Night's Dream,* his play that is nominally set in Greece. Helena is a young Athenian woman who loves Demetrius and wins him with Puck's help. In *All's Well That Ends Well,* the playwright uses the name for the resourceful and determined young woman who manages to cling to the snobbish and unfaithful Bertram, eventually holding him to his marriage vows.

> *Was this the face that launched a thousand ships,*
> *And burnt the topless towers of Ilium?*
> *Sweet Helen, make me immortal with a kiss.*
> *Her lips suck forth my soul; see, where it flies!*
> —CHRISTOPHER MARLOWE, *THE TRAGICAL HISTORY OF*
> *DOCTOR FAUSTUS*

Anne Brontë's sister Charlotte uses the name without invoking beauty in *Jane Eyre.* Helen Burns is Jane's young friend at the dreadful Lowood School. She dies of tuberculosis in a saintly fashion, stating that "by dying young, I shall escape great sufferings." American novelist Elizabeth Stoddard plays on names in her novel *The Morgesons.* Prickly, quixotic heroine Cassandra has one school friend, Helen Perkins. Helen is prettier than she, and more skilled at managing the social strictures of early nineteenth-century Massachusetts. The parallel with the two women of Troy is hardly exact, but Cassandra is certainly the character with an eye to a malignant future while Helen is feted by their mutual community. Helen Alving, in Ibsen's *Ghosts,* is forced to reap the tragic harvest of decades of hypocrisy. Her late husband, Captain Alving, was a syphilitic rake who passed along his disease to his son Osvald and impregnated his housekeeper. Helen is nevertheless about to dedicate an orphanage to his memory.

Constantine the Great was the Roman emperor who converted to Christianity in A.D. 313, and made Constantinople, formerly Byzantium, the seat of the Roman Empire. His mother Helen worked tirelessly to promote Christianity and is an important saint in the Orthodox Church. In Russian her name is **Yelena** or **Elena,** though in Tolstoy's *War and Peace* Princess Kuragin is known as **Hélène,** the French form of the name. She is a sinister creature, possibly a nymphomaniac, who marries Pierre Bezuhov for his money. The marriage also provides cover for her sexual adventuring. Hélène even refuses to have Pierre's children but engages in sex purely for pleasure, a startling notion for a nineteenth-century woman.

> *Mrs. Graham and I were now established friends—or brother and sister, as we rather chose to consider ourselves. She called me Gilbert, by my express desire, and I called her Helen, for I had seen the name written in her books.*
> —ANNE BRONTË, *THE TENANT OF WILDFELL HALL*

Chekhov's short story "The New Villa" features a more conventional woman, Yelena Kucherov, the young wife of an engineer who is isolated in a small village because of her husband's work. She is unable to accommodate herself to her only neighbors, the local peasants. In *On the Eve,* Turgenev depicts the passionate, idealistic, even severe Elena Stahov. She is compelling enough to attract the notice of several young men but falls in love with the romantic Bulgarian revolutionary Insarov. They secretly marry, but he dies in Venice en route to his homeland.

A modern version of the name, **Ellen,** has been infrequently used in literature, but Edith Wharton's Ellen Olenska is one of that writer's most memorable characters. Connotations of Helen of Troy are probably intentional, for the Countess Olenska certainly wreaks havoc with protagonist Newland Archer's heart. She is the unconventional daughter of Old New York whose misery with her noble Polish husband sends her back to her American relatives for succor in *The Age of Innocence.* Her outsider's view of the provinciality of his city changes Archer's perspective on it permanently—but only after he has married one of its most conventional maidens.

> *"It's odd," Janey remarked, "that she should have kept such an ugly name as Ellen. I should have changed it to Elaine."* She glanced about the table to see the effect of this.
>
> *Her brother laughed. "Why Elaine?"*
>
> *"I don't know; it sounds more—more Polish," said Janey, blushing.*
>
> *"It sounds more conspicuous; and that can hardly be what she wishes," said Mrs. Archer distantly.*
> —EDITH WHARTON, *THE AGE OF INNOCENCE*

Elaine is an early English form of the name influenced by the French **Hélène**. It appears in Sir Thomas Malory's *Le Morte D'Arthur* and its Victorian descendant, Tennyson's *Idylls of the King*. In the earlier version Elaine, the daughter of King Pelles, secretly loves Lancelot and uses a spell to disguise herself as Guinevere for one night. The resultant offspring is Galahad. Tennyson's handling of the story was a huge hit in his day—he had Elaine simply pine away when Lancelot, however kindly, rejects her. Then, according to her wishes, her body was sent on a barge to Arthur's castle, with a lily in one hand and a letter to Lancelot in the other. Victorian painter John William Waterhouse's romantic image of Elaine in her barge was widely admired. Tennyson took up her story again in *The Lady of Shalott*.

> *Elaine the fair, Elaine the loveable,*
> *Elaine, the lily maid of Astolat,*
> *High in her chamber up a tower to the east*
> *Guarded the sacred shield of Lancelot.*
> —ALFRED, LORD TENNYSON, *IDYLLS OF THE KING*

HENRIETTA see **HARRIET**

> *Her scowl had done Miss Hepzibah a very ill office, in establishing her character as an ill-tempered old maid.*
> —NATHANIEL HAWTHORNE, *THE HOUSE OF THE SEVEN GABLES*

HEPZIBAH *(Hebrew, "my delight is in her")* Also **Hepsibah** or **Hephzibah.** One of the Old Testament names adopted by the Puritans in the sixteenth century when saints' names were looked at askance. By the nineteenth century these names were by and large the province of the lower classes or those who cherished their Puritan antecedents, like Hepzibah Pyncheon in Nathaniel Hawthorne's *The House of the Seven Gables.* She is the last of her family to live in the famous house, an elderly spinster who rents rooms to a lodger. Miss Hepzibah has to stoop even lower to support herself by opening a small shop in the house. This is a terrible blow to her pride, and she survives it only with the help of her cheerful little cousin Phoebe. A common nickname for Hepzibah was **Hepsey,** but its use seems to have been linked with particularly low social standing. In Louisa May Alcott's *Work,* the heroine Christie Devon learns a few lessons about practicality and humility from the freed slave Hepsey who cooks at the first house where Christie works as a maid. Christie fusses about the servility of her work until she contemplates Hepsey's calm acceptance of her situation. *The Morgesons* by Elizabeth Stoddard is set before the Civil War, but also features a cook named Hepsey, who exhibits the independence—even cussedness—of a New England servant who considers herself quite on a social par with her employers. **Eppie,** which is used as an independent name, can be considered a version of Hepzibah or of **Euphemia.** In *Silas Marner,* George Eliot's tale about life in rural England, the half-crazed weaver Silas adopts a golden-haired foundling. She turns out to be the illegitimate daughter of the squire's son Godfrey Cass, by a local barmaid who died in a snowstorm. Eppie is the redemptive fact in Silas's life, reweaving his connections to his fellow villagers, and her sweet, simple character amply rewards him for bringing her up.

> *"My mother's name was Hephzibah," said Silas, "and my little sister was named after her."*
>
> *"Eh, that's a hard name," said Dolly. "I partly think it isn't a christened name."*
>
> *"It's a Bible name," said Silas, old ideas recurring.*
>
> *"Then I've no call to speak again' it," said Dolly, rather startled by Silas's knowledge on this head; "but you see I'm no scholard, and I'm slow at catching the words. My husband says I'm allays like as if I was putting the haft for the handle—that's what he says—for he's very sharp, God help him. But it was awk'ard calling your little sister by such a hard name, when you'd got nothing big to say, like—wasn't it, Master Marner?"*
>
> *"We called her Eppie," said Silas.*
>
> *"Well, if it was noways wrong to shorten the name, it 'ud be a deal handier."* —GEORGE ELIOT, *SILAS MARNER*

HERA *(Greek, meaning unknown)* The sister and wife of Zeus, known to the Romans as **Juno.** Hera is the mother of three of Zeus's children—Ares, Hebe, and Hephaestus—and the perpetual thorn in his side. A suspicious, jealous scold, she generally appears in Greek myth to punish someone for an offense. She was Heracles' mortal enemy, and in *The Iliad* of Homer she is the foe of the Trojans because Paris, a Trojan, had named Aphrodite as the fairest woman.

HERMIONE *(Greek, meaning unknown)* A feminization of **Hermes.** In Greek myth, Hermione is the daughter of Spartan king Menelaus and his wife Helen, whom Paris carries off to Troy. Euripides' play *The Trojan Women* has Hermione married to

Achilles' son Neoptolemus, who had previously loved Andromache. Jean Racine's *Andromache* (1667) rearranges the pairings somewhat: Hermione loves Pyrrhus, but Pyrrhus marries Andromache. Hermione orders her staunch admirer Orestes to kill Pyrrhus, then throws herself on Pyrrhus's burial pyre. Orestes goes mad. Shakespeare may have coined **Hermia** as a more manageable form of Hermes without the tragic baggage. Hermia in *A Midsummer Night's Dream* is loved by both Demetrius and Lysander. Her father—and the law—say she must marry Demetrius, but she elopes with Lysander, ending up in the forest where magic takes over. On the other hand, the playwright uses Hermione in *The Winter's Tale* for the uncomplaining and long-suffering wife of Leontes. Though the source of the story is a 1588 romance by one Robert Greene, Hermione's trials are reminiscent of Patient Griselda's in *The Canterbury Tales*.

HERO *(Origin murky, possibly adapted from* **Hera***)* In Greek legend, the young Leander swam across the Hellespont every night to court his beloved Hero—no mean feat considering that the swift-flowing body of water that divides the Aegean and the Sea of Marmara is a mile wide at its narrowest point. In Shakespeare's *Much Ado About Nothing,* Hero is the ill-used love interest of Claudio. Her reserved personality sets off her cousin Beatrice's wit.

HERSILIE *(Greek, "delicate")* Also appears as **Hersilia** or **Ersilia**. Ovid's *Metamorphoses* tells how Hersilie, the wife of Rome's founder Romulus, mourned him terribly after his death. A star fell to the earth, setting her hair alight, and she ascended to heaven, becoming the goddess Hora and consort of the deity Quirinus, formerly Romulus.

HESTER *(Greek, "star")* A variation of **Esther**, which, as an Old Testament name, was acceptable to Puritan reformers. Nathaniel Hawthorne, in choosing it for the heroine of *The Scarlet Letter,* may have wanted to invoke the ravishing Jewish woman who was plucked from the harem of Persian king Ahasuerus to become his queen. Hester Prynne is beautiful, of course: tall, with dark eyes and luxuriant dark hair and a majestic carriage. The citizens of seventeenth-century Boston are outraged when she becomes pregnant, since her husband has been missing for years. Outrage only deepens when she refuses to name her lover. She is constrained to wear a brilliant red letter *A* on her clothes. Her lover is a minister, the Reverend Arthur Dimmesdale, and his courage compares unfavorably to hers: while Hester faces society's odium for her sin, her partner Dimmesdale goes unsuspected and makes no effort to share her burden.

HETTY (*Diminutive of* **Hester** *or* **Henrietta,** *used independently*) Akin to **Eppie** or **Hepsey** in its connotations of social insignificance. The garrulous spinster Miss Bates in Jane Austen's *Emma* is a Hetty; Emma feels free to mock the woman in part because of her low social standing. James Fenimore Cooper's *The Deerslayer* is set in upstate New York when control for that area was still being fiercely disputed by Native Americans and English settlers. Hetty Hutter is the daughter of Tom Hutter who patrols Glimmerglass (modeled on Lake Otsego in Cooperstown) from a "castle" and an arklike boat. Hetty, a devout Christian, believes that converting the Native Americans to Christianity will end all the conflict. Ultimately, she is killed. In George Eliot's *Adam Bede* Hetty Sorrel is the vain, silly, but ravishingly pretty love object in the village of Hayslope. Upstanding Adam Bede can't compete with dashing Captain Arthur Donnithorne in the glamour stakes, even though he wants to marry Hetty. Alas, the aristocratic Donnithorne wants only one thing, and gets it, leaving Hetty pregnant when his regiment is transferred to Ireland.

HILDA (*Old German, "battle"*) An element in many German names like Hildegarde or **Brunhilde,** used independently at least since the seventh century when Saint Hilda founded a convent in Yorkshire. In Hawthorne's *The Marble Faun* Hilda is a young New Englander, a descendant of Puritans, on her own in Rome where she is engaged in copying Old Master paintings. Her strict moral code is her primary characteristic, and when she inadvertently witnesses her friend Donatello push a mysterious friar off a cliff, her conscience is tortured. Some scholars suggest that Hilda's purity represents the fine, clean morals of the New World as opposed to the decadence of Europe.

HIPPOLYTA *(Greek, meaning related to "horses")* In Greek myth, Hippolyta is the queen of the Amazons whom Theseus married. Shakespeare, in *A Midsummer Night's Dream,* follows up on the myth and portrays Hippolyta as the proud woman on the verge of marrying Theseus, the duke of Athens.

HONORIA *(Latin, "woman of honor")* Charles Dickens doesn't often bother with ironic names, tending more toward the fantastic (Tattycoram, Uriah Heep). But Lady Dedlock in *Bleak House* is, we find, called **Honoria** by her family, and she is emphatically not a woman of honor. Theoretically childless, she is in fact the mother of virtuous Esther Summerson. Her youthful error and her lifetime of denying it have ostensibly turned her to stone emotionally. Honoria is an eighteenth-century form of the name, which also appears as **Honor** or **Honour** or even, in France, **Honorine**. Henry James, in *The Tragic Muse,* names a retired actress Honorine. She is better known as Madame Carré, the renowned tragedienne who coaches Miriam Rooth in the fundamentals of the acting craft.

> *Before the children were separated, they were baptised by the Reverend Mr. Cotton, and in commemoration of the christian graces of their mother, their names were changed to the puritanical appellations of Hope and Faith.*
> —CATHARINE MARIA SEDGWICK, HOPE LESLIE

HOPE *(English virtue name)* The second of the three Christian "Theological Virtues" (the others being **Faith** and **Charity**). Catharine Maria Sedgwick's *Hope Leslie* was one of America's earliest historical novels. Written in 1827, it is set in seventeenth-century Massachusetts. Hope Leslie, born in England, was originally called Alice, but was renamed when she arrived in the strict Puritan colony. Hope's free-spirited character comes into conflict with the authoritarian culture of Boston, and is contrasted with several more conventional, biddable Massachusetts maidens. Scholars suggest that Hope, in her individualism and courage, represents what Sedgwick saw as crucial characterititics of America itself.

> *All heads turned to watch Hortense.*
> —HONORÉ DE BALZAC, *COUSIN BETTE*

HORTENSE (*Latin clan name*) A related word means "garden" and *hortensia* is the French word for hydrangea. In Balzac's *Cousin Bette,* Hortense Hulot is the ravishing daughter of Baron and Baroness Hulot. They are deeply in debt because of the Baron's endless womanizing, but Hortense has reached marriageable age and needs a dowry. She is madly in love with brilliant Polish sculptor Wenceslas Steinbock who has no money of his own. In *Bleak House,* Dickens gives a French maid named Hortense to the unhappy Lady Dedlock. Hortense serves her mistress well but is jealous and suspicious, "like a very neat She-Wolf imperfectly tamed."

> *"Hyacinth!" said Molly, entirely bewildered.*
> *"Yes! Hyacinth! It's the silliest name I ever heard of; but it's hers, and I must call her by it. . . . And the worst is, she's gone and perpetuated her own affected name by having her daughter called after her. Cynthia! One thinks of the man in the moon . . . I'm thankful you're plain Molly, child."*
> —ELIZABETH GASKELL, *WIVES AND DAUGHTERS*

HYACINTH *(Greek plant name)* In Elizabeth Gaskell's last novel, *Wives and Daughters,* Hyacinth Kirkpatrick is one of the former. She enters the novel as a former governess to the grand Cumnor family, then manages to enthrall kind Dr. Gibson of Hollingford, who marries her. She is utterly self-absorbed, vain, and silly, and Dr. Gibson eventually rues his choice as she makes his daughter Molly unhappy as well. Even more unhappy is Mrs. Gibson's daughter Cynthia, the child of a previous marriage and largely neglected throughout her upbringing.

The Spanish version of the name is **Jacinta** *(hah seen' tah)*, used by Benito Pérez Galdós for one of the two female protagonists of *Fortunata and Jacinta.* Jacinta is the gently reared bourgeoise chosen to be the wife of young Juanito Santa Cruz. In the course of the novel she goes from a naive young girl madly in love with her husband to a worried matron who cannot conceive and whose fantasy life offers more comfort than reality. Pérez Galdós stresses her purity and refers to her in angelic terms, but life spares her no punches.

> *Jacinta was a girl with excellent qualities: modest, delicate, affectionate, and very pretty too. Her lovely eyes were already announcing the readiness of her soul to fall in love and be loved.*
> —BENITO PÉREZ GALDÓS, *FORTUNATA AND JACINTA*

IDA *(Old German, meaning unknown)* A fashionable name in the mid-nineteenth century, as evidenced by Louisa May Alcott's use of it in *The Inheritance*, written when she was seventeen. Lady Ida Clare is the poor but proud and disagreeable cousin of the Hamilton family with whom the heroine, Edith Adelon, lives. Lady Ida is especially cruel to poor Edith, who wants only to be loved as part of the family. In *What Maisie Knew,* Henry James portrays an Ida who is unpleasant in a different and possibly more damaging way. She is the good-looking, stylish, and morally vapid mother of Maisie Farange, who quarrels with her husband Beale. In the course of the novel both of Maisie's parents take different partners and attempt to avoid taking responsibility for their daughter. Ida is not a common name in France, but the young women of the demimonde in Balzac's novels often christen themselves more or less fantastically, and this may have been the case with Ida Gruget, a *grisette* in "Ferragus." (A *grisette* is a young dressmaker or milliner who is prepared to supplement her income with a little casual prostitution.) Ida Gruget is a corset-maker, kept by a man whom she calls Henri. He is actually Ferragus, the ruthless leader of a powerful secret society of criminals, and he betrays Ida.

Ida bristled with monograms.
> —HENRY JAMES, *WHAT MAISIE KNEW*

IGRAINE *(Origin unknown)* The name also appears as **Igerne** or **Ygraine** or **Ygerne**. In the Arthurian legends, Igraine is the mother of King Arthur. She is the wife of King Gorlois of Cornwall and lives at Tintagel Castle. Most versions of the myth suggest that English king Uther Pendragon, with the magical help of Merlin, turned himself into a facsimile of Gorlois and visited Igraine in this guise.

IMOGEN *(Origin disputed: some sources suggest Latin "last born" while others prefer Latin "innocent.")* "Innocent" is the more appropriate connotation for Shakespeare's Imogen, the wronged wife of *Cymbeline,* and indeed in the source of the tale, Holinshed's *Chronicles,* the name appears as **Innogen.** In Shakespeare's adaptation, Imogen is married to Posthumus Leonatus, who makes a bet with the cynical Iachimo that she is faithful to him in his absence. Iachimo attempts to woo Imogen, who will have none of him, so he fabricates evidence of her "infidelity." As part of the exceedingly complex plot, Imogen at one point disguises herself as a page and calls herself "Fidele," or "faithful."

INEZ *(Spanish from Greek, "chaste, pure")* The English cognate is **Agnes.** Lord Byron's 1819 retelling of the Don Juan story follows the traditional version in only the bare outlines. He gives his hero a rakish father and a strict, prudish mother, Donna Inez. When Don Juan is seduced by his mother's best friend, it seems natural, even nearly excusable, that he should proceed into a life of lechery.

IO *(Greek, meaning unknown)* Yet another of Zeus/Jupiter's quarries. She is, according to the source, variously a nymph and a mortal woman, even a priestess of Hera, who catches Zeus's eye. To protect Io from Hera's wrath, Zeus changes her into a heifer, but Hera sends a gadfly after her. The fly pursues poor Io all over Greece and Asia. In Ovid's *Metamorphoses,* suspicious Hera/Juno sets Argus with the hundred eyes to watch over Io. Hermes, under orders from Zeus, kills Argus and Hera changes him into a peacock, which has a hundred eyes in its tail.

SILLY NAMES

One of the easiest ways to tell the difference between comedy and drama in, say, eighteenth-century fiction, is to look at the names. In Samuel Richardson's *Clarissa* we read about Clarissa Harlowe, Roger Solmes, and Robert Lovelace; in Henry Fielding's *Joseph Andrews* the action takes place at Booby Hall. Fielding, in giving his characters ridiculous names (like *Tom Jones*'s Rev. Mr. Thwackum), drew on a tradition dating back to Shakespeare. Funny characters get silly names in plays by Molière (Géronte) and Sheridan (Mrs. Malaprop) as well as in novels by Thackeray, Dickens, and even Trollope. The latter was one of the last authors to betray the authorial presence by concocting names like Sir Timothy Beeswax or Mr. Chaffanbrass.

IPHIGENIA *(Greek, "sacrifice")* In Greek myth, Iphigenia is Agamemnon and Clytemnestra's eldest daughter. When the Greek fleet is becalmed at the harbor of Aulis, Agamemnon sacrifices Iphigenia to obtain favorable winds. Euripides' two plays *Iphigenia in Tauris* and *Iphigenia in Aulis* focus on different facets of the tale. In the *Tauris* version Artemis has rescued Iphigenia from death and spirited her off to Tauris, where her brother Orestes finds her after his murder of their mother. In the earlier play, *Iphigenia in Aulis*, Euripides focuses on Agamemnon's difficulties in holding together the Greek command. Achilles offers to defend Iphigenia but she willingly goes to the sacrifice. Racine and Goethe later wrote versions of the tale, both of which allowed Iphigenia to escape death.

Trollope takes up the name as a joke in *Can You Forgive Her?*, poking fun at pretentious aristocratic names. An elderly Palliser cousin, related to the Duke of Omnium, is named Iphigenia, called "Iphy" by her family.

> *Miss Palliser whose Christian names, unfortunately for her, were Iphigenia Theodata.*
> —ANTHONY TROLLOPE, *CAN YOU FORGIVE HER?*

IRENE *(Greek, "peace")* Wiliam Dean Howells's *The Rise of Silas Lapham* tells the story of a Vermont paint manufacturer who moves his family to Boston in a quest for wider business and social horizons. Lapham has two daughters, Penelope and Irene. Irene, the younger, is a real beauty, so the Laphams believe she is the magnet for young Tom Corey, a Boston blueblood. It turns out, however, that Corey is really interested in Penelope, the elder daughter. She dismisses him, afraid to hurt Irene's feelings. Although Irene is the most common version of this name in English, **Irena** also occurs, as in Edmund Spenser's *The Faerie Queen*, where Irena is a queen besieged by the tyrant Grantorto. Artegall vanquishes Grantorto, freeing Irena—who represents Ireland in the allegory.

> *Arina Vlassyevna was a true Russian gentlewoman of the old school; she ought to have lived a couple of centuries ago, in the early days of Muscovy.*
> —IVAN TURGENEV, *FATHERS AND SONS*

Irina or **Irena,** the Russian form of the name, is popular in that country and Anton Chekhov used it for important characters in two of his plays. Madame Irena Arkadina Trepliov of *The Seagull* is usually known simply as "Arkadina." She is the egotistical middle-aged actress whose narcissism has crippled her son Konstantin. She also dictates the terms of her lover Boris Trigorin's life. In *The Three Sisters,* Irena Prozorov is the youngest and prettiest of the sisters. She has hopes, both of finding work that she likes and of marrying well. Ultimately she finds she must settle for an engagement with the dull Baron Toozenbach. Even this option is closed to her when he is killed in a duel. Ivan Turgenev uses a variation of the spelling, **Arina**, for a character in *Father and Sons*. Arina Bazarova is the kindly, superstitious, barely literate mother of the ferocious reformer Yevgeny Bazarov. She and her husband adore their son who returns to live with them after his stay with the Kirsanov family.

IRIS *(Greek, "rainbow")* One of the messengers of the gods, along with Hermes, and a minor deity in her own right. She was especially favored by Juno. She appears in Ovid's *Metamorphoses,* and Dante mentions her several times in *Paradiso*.

> *At [Juno's] behest Iris put on her trailing robe of a thousand colours and, tracing a curved arc across the heavens, sought the cloud-wrapped palace of the king she had been told to visit.* —OVID, METAMORPHOSES

ISABEL *(Spanish variant of* **Elizabeth:** *Hebrew, "promised to God")* Also appears as **Isabelle, Isobel,** even **Ysabel.** The most elaborate and legitimately Spanish form is **Isabella,** used by Shakespeare in *Measure for Measure*—which is set in Vienna. Isabella, about to take her vows as a nun, is the sister of Claudio, who is sentenced to death for fornication. Willy-nilly she gets drawn into a scheme that saves him and substantially alters her own fate. In Maria Edgeworth's *Castle Rackrent* (1800), Isabella is one of a string of greedy aristocrats who run the Irish Rackrent estate into the ground. Isabella Thorpe in Jane Austen's *Northanger Abbey* is another grasping individual, a coldhearted young woman who befriends heroine Catherine Morland in Bath. The naive but warmhearted Catherine at first admires Isabella's sophistication. In Emily Brontë's *Wuthering Heights* the exoticism of Isabella Linton's name contrasts with the simplicity of **Cathy**

AMERICAN HEIRESSES IN VICTORIAN ENGLAND

Anthony Trollope was always interested in America. He closely observed the subtle differences between his own country and the large anglophone cousin across the water, which he visited frequently. When he wrote *The Way We Live Now,* in 1876, he made a wealthy American father and daughter, visiting London, important characters. Lord Silverbridge falls in love with Isabel Boncassen and wants to marry her.

Silverbridge would not have been the first—or the last—English aristocrat to marry a rich American girl. In 1874, Lord Randolph Churchill wed Jennie Jerome, whose father was a New York stockbroker. Two years later, in New York, Viscount Mandeville married Consuelo Yznaga, from a Southern family. By 1895, the trickle had become a flood, culminating with the union of Consuelo Vanderbilt and the Duke of Marlborough.

Trollope dwells on the Duke of Omnium's attitude to Isabel Boncassen as a potential daughter-in-law. In real life, many of these transatlantic matches were made cynically, an outright swap of dollars for titles. The Duke of Omnium has no need of the Boncassen money. Furthermore, he is very fond of Isabel in her own right, as a charming and intelligent young woman. He simply has difficulty accepting her as a future duchess. In point of fact, by 1901, when Edward VII was crowned, many American women wore peeresses' coronets at the ceremony. Isabel Silverbridge, had she been a real person, would have been among them.

and **Heathcliff**—it brings a whiff of an outside world to the hermetic universe of the moors. By the time Trollope wrote *The Small House at Allington* the foreignness seems to have bled away from Isabella, for nothing could be more soundly English than pretty Isabella Dale. She is a conventional blond heroine who sets off the sardonic nature of her younger sister Lily. Isabella Dale is always known as "Bell," which erases any hint of the name's Spanish origin.

In Herman Melville's *Pierre,* the dark-eyed, half-French Isabel Banford contrasts with blond All-American Lucy Tartan, and the protagonist Pierre Glendinning is torn between the two. Isabel turns out to be his half sister, his father's daughter by a French emigré, and her life has been difficult. She longs for only one thing—the security of a family, which Pierre gives her by pretending to marry her. The ménage becomes troublesome when his feelings for her overstep the bounds of the fraternal. Anthony Trollope creates an American Isabel in *The Duke's Children.* She is Isabel Boncassen, the intelligent, well-bred daughter of the American millionaire Ezekiel Boncassen. She is flattered but disconcerted when the Duke of Omnium's son Lord Silverbridge wants to marry her. Isabel Archer, the heroine of Henry James's 1881 *The Portrait of a Lady,* is another pretty young American abroad. The clever, refined orphan from Albany, New York, travels to visit English cousins and inherits an unexpected fortune. Her sudden wealth opens unlimited possibilities to Isabel, freeing her from the necessity to marry either of her persistent suitors—yet the choice she innocently makes, to wed the corrupt Gilbert Osmond, makes her deeply unhappy.

> *"And remember this, that if you've been hated, you've also been loved. Ah but, Isabel—adored!"*
> —HENRY JAMES, *PORTRAIT OF A LADY*

ISEULT *(Origin unclear)* Possibly an Old German name meaning "ice ruler," or perhaps derived from the Welsh, "fair." Variations include **Isolde, Isolt, Isoud,** and **Yseult.** The story of Tristram and Iseult is told in a series of medieval poems and sometimes intersects the Arthurian legends: Malory incorporates it into *Le Morte D'Arthur,* and Tennyson into *The Idylls of the King.* Iseult is a beautiful Irish princess betrothed to marry King Mark of Cornwall. He sends his nephew Tristram to bring her to Cornwall and the pair drink a love potion that binds them together eternally. Iseult marries her king, and Tristram goes to Brittany where he marries Iseult of the White Hands, but their love for each other never fades.

ISIDORE *(Greek, "gift of Isis")* In English, the name occurs more commonly as the obviously feminine **Isadora,** but when Molière used it in *The Sicilian,* it was as a genuinely Greek name to give color to a comedy that was full of exoticism. Isidore herself is a beautiful, sensible, and good-natured slave to Don Pedro. He frees her and intends to marry her but she objects to his high-handed methods of wooing, saying, "Affection is very insecure when you seek to retain it by force." When the young Frenchman Adrastes courts her, she is skeptical about his fulsome flattery but tolerates it and eventually agrees to marry him.

ISMENE *(Greek mythology name)* In Sophocles' *Antigone,* Ismene is the heroine's sister. Though she lacks the courage to bury her brother Polyneices along with Antigone, she petitions to share Antigone's harsh punishment—burial alive.

JACQUELINE *(zhah kleen′; French, diminutive of* **Jacob:** *Hebrew, "he supplants")* In Molière's comedy *The Doctor in Spite of Himself,* Jacqueline is a minor character, one of the rural folk full of bawdy country wisdom who have sport at the expense of the overcivilized and credulous. In Balzac's novel *A Harlot High and Low,* Jacqueline is the real name of a deeply sinister confederate of the arch-criminal Vautrin. Jacqueline Collin is the fat Malayan cook whom Vautrin puts in place as part of Esther Gobseck's household. She is a marvelous cook but an even better spy, with an endless repertoire of disguises and a relentless loyalty to Vautrin. She is known as "Asie," or Asia. Shakespeare uses an unusual version of the name, **Jacquenetta,** in *Love's Labours Lost,* for "a country wench."

> *"Jane, you look blooming, and smiling, and pretty."*
> —Charlotte Brontë, *Jane Eyre*

JANE *(Feminine version of* **John:** *Hebrew, "Jehovah is gracious")* Early in the nineteenth century, **Jane** seems to have had some glamour. Jane Austen, whose powers of invention were somewhat limited concerning names, used her own name for several characters. Jane Bennet of *Pride and Prejudice* is the prettier, kinder, less defensive older sister of Elizabeth. Her winning characteristics are readily perceived by Mr. Bingley. In *Emma,* Jane Fairfax is the equal in accomplishment and looks to Emma Woodhouse, but she is destined to become a governess. Emma never quite warms to Miss Fairfax, finding her "too reserved." A generation after Jane Austen, the Brontë sisters also created significant characters named Jane. Anne Brontë's *The Tenant of Wildfell Hall* features a farmer's daughter named Jane Wilson with whom the narrator Gilbert Markham has flirted often—until the appearance at the Hall of the fascinating Helen Graham. He characterizes Jane Wilson as "a young lady of some talents, and more ambitions." The enduring Brontë Jane is, of course, the narrator of Charlotte Brontë's *Jane Eyre*. Jane breaks ground because she is "a little, small thing," physically and socially insignificant but passionate and determined. Mr. Rochester's discernment of the governess's charms has given hope to unspectacular women ever since the book was written.

The other great Victorian English novelists all used the name Jane as well, in ways that demonstrate its general utilitarian nature. Dicken's Miss Murdstone, for instance, the terrifying sister of David Copperfield's stepfather, is called Jane (though given her harsh character, only her brother uses her first name). Maggie Tulliver's aunt Glegg, in George Eliot's *The Mill on the Floss,* is a Jane. Her family is a bit more substantial than the mill-owning Tullivers, but nothing like as grand as that of Lady Jane Crawley in *Vanity Fair*. One of the few amiable characters among Thackeray's throng of corrupt or grasping creations, Lady Jane shows genuine affection and loyalty to her husband and her brothers-in-law, Pitt and Rawdon Crawley. In *Phineas Finn* Trollope uses the Bunce family, Phineas's landlords, to exemplify the rising English middle class. They are hardworking, respectable, and suspicious of the aristocracy. Jane Bunce tempers her husband Jacob's revolutionary tendencies and has a soft spot in her heart—as do all women—for the handsome, plausible Phineas. *The Eustace Diamonds*, Trollope's answer to *Vanity Fair,* includes almost as many raffish characters as Thackeray's tale, one of the more reprehensible being the mysterious widow Jane Carbuncle, whose "friendship" with Lizzie Eustace is based on mutual need for respectability. She is chaperoning the American beauty Lucinda Roanoke and attempting to chivvy the girl into a heartless marriage with violent Sir Griffin Tewett. Finally, Henry James uses

Jane to gently comic effect in *The Awkward Age*. An English-woman married to an Italian nobleman, she is known as "the Duchess" and insists on an exalted level of grandeur and formality in all her social contacts. It is thus somewhat deflating to hear an intimate call her "Jane."

Charlotte Brontë's Mr. Rochester sometimes calls Jane Eyre **Janet** in his fond moments, but this diminutive is also used as an independent name. George Eliot's first published fiction, *Scenes of Clerical Life,* featured three stories. "Janet's Repentance" tells the tale of Janet Dempster, the intelligent strong-willed woman whose great mistake was to marry an alcoholic. The controversial evangelical preacher Mr. Tryan manages to rescue Janet from drink and degradation on her own behalf. This form of the name is familiar in Scotland and Robert Louis Stevenson uses it in "Thrawn Janet," a story of retribution in an isolated Scots village. "Thrawn" is an old Scots word meaning "misshapen" or "sullen," and Janet fits the bill. Odd, perhaps crazy, she has had a child out of wedlock and the villagers believe her to be a witch. Stevenson even suggests she may be a ghost.

> *Robert Dempster was the cleverest man in Milby; and there weren't many young men fit to talk to Janet.*
> —GEORGE ELIOT, SCENES OF CLERICAL LIFE

Another Scottish name from the same source is **Jean** or **Jeanie**. Sir Walter Scott's fiction is out of fashion now, but in the nineteenth century Jeanie Deans, the heroine of *The Heart of Midlothian,* loomed large in the popular culture. Her achievements were based loosely on those of a historical figure who walked, as Jeanie does, from Scotland to London to plead for her sister's life. The novel is set in the early eighteenth century and Jeanie's sister Effie has borne a child out of wedlock. Effie won't reveal the name of the father, and since the baby has disappeared, she is in prison for murder. Jeanie's heroism saves the day.

Continental feminizations of John include **Juana, Joana,** and

Johanna or **Joanna**, while **Joan** is another anglophone version of the name. In Thomas Hardy's *Tess of the D'Urbervilles*, Tess's mother is the downtrodden, hardworking Joan Durbeyfield, for whom an evening drinking at the pub is the sole respite from a harsh life. Sarah Orne Jewett's *The Country of the Pointed Firs* can be characterized as "local color writing," focused tightly as it is on a small seafaring village in Maine. Joanna Todd is not even a living character, but a personage in the village nevertheless. Having been jilted by her lover, Joanna left the village to live alone on Shell Heap Island, eight miles offshore. She spent the rest of her life there, visited occasionally by fishermen and villagers, a proud exile. Though she has been dead for twenty-two years by the time the narrator visits Dunnet Landing, her story is still current in the village.

The French use **Jeanne** *(zhawn)*, the name of the protagonist in Guy de Maupassant's *A Woman's Life*. Critics have suggested the novel may be based on his mother's experience. Jeanne de Vauds is the innocent daughter of a provincial baron; she is married out of the convent to a local vicomte. He is systematically unfaithful to her and later her spendthrift son puts her in debt. Throughout, Jeanne is sweet, passive, and helpless.

> "Do you remember the discussion there was about Miss Bradshaw's name, Thurstan? Her father wanting her to be called Hepzibah, but insisting that she was to have a Scripture name at any rate; and Mrs. Bradshaw wanting her to be Juliana, after some novel she had read not long before; and at last Jemima was fixed upon, because it would do either for a Scripture name or a name for a heroine out of a book."
>
> "I did not know Jemima was a Scripture name," said Ruth.
>
> "Oh yes, it is. One of Job's daughters; Jemima, Kezia, and Keren-Happuch. There are a good many Jemimas in the world, and some Kezias, but I never heard of a Keren-Happuch; and yet we know just as much of one as of another. People really like a pretty name, whether in Scripture or out of it."
>
> —ELIZABETH GASKELL, *RUTH*

JEMIMA *(Hebrew, "dove")* In Elizabeth Gaskell's *Ruth,* Jemima Bradshaw is the daughter of the most prominent citizens in the town of Eccleston, where Ruth eventually settles. Kindly and warmhearted, she is very fond of Ruth, but the friendship is threatened by a romantic misunderstanding between Jemima and her suitor, Walter Farquhar.

JENNY *(Diminutive of* **Jane** *or* **Jennifer:** *Welsh, "smooth, fair")* Scholars maintain that **Jenny,** as an independent name, derives from **Jane,** since **Jennifer** was scarcely used until the twentieth century. Literary employment of Jenny suggests that it was a name with modest connotations. In Henry Fielding's *Tom Jones,* Jenny Jones is the maid who is paid to confess that Tom is her child. Sir Walter Scott's *Old Mortality* also features a maid named Jenny, while in Dickens's *Bleak House,* a bricklayer's wife named Jenny, a victim of the most dire poverty, keeps turning up in increasing stages of desperation. In nineteenth-century France, by contrast, the name had a slightly jaunty air. One of Baron Hulot's mistresses in Balzac's *Cousine Bette* is named Jenny Cadine.

JESSICA *(Hebrew, "he sees")* An Old Testament name. The Jewish moneylender Shylock in Shakespeare's *The Merchant of Venice* has a daughter named Jessica who shocks him by running away with a Christian—as well as with some of his money. In Maria Edgeworth's satiric *Castle Rackrent,* Jessica is the rich Jewish wife cynically chosen by ne'er-do-well Sir Kit Rackrent. Stubborn and practical, she refuses to relinquish her jewels to her husband and as a result is confined to her room for seven years. When Sir Kit is killed in a duel over another woman, she hightails it back to London, abandoning the castle to her husband's feckless heir.

JOCASTA *(Greek, meaning unknown)* In Greek myth, Jocasta is the sister of Creon of Thebes. When plague comes to the city, Creon offers Jocasta in marriage to whoever can answer the riddle of the Sphinx. Alas, the man who does so is Oedipus, whom Jocasta does not recognize as her son. They marry and raise four children, and when Jocasta realizes what she has done, she hangs herself, while Oedipus blinds himself with her brooch and becomes an outcast. The story is told in Sophocles' *Oedipus the King,* while Euripides' *The Phoenician Women* focuses on a later point in the story when two of Jocasta's sons fight over control of Thebes.

JOSEPHINE *(Feminization of* **Joseph:** *Hebrew, "Jehovah adds")* The given name of **Jo** March in Louisa May Alcott's *Little Women.* The tomboyish, hot-tempered writer is clearly the March daughter with whom the author identifies most, and her portrait of Jo gives the reader a sense of how difficult it could be for a woman of spirit to fit herself into the meek mold of Victorian womanhood. Though **Josephine** is a French name, it is **Josépha** that Honoré de Balzac used for one of his demimondaines in *Cousin Bette.* It is, of course, an assumed named, based on her real name, Mirah Josephs. The character is a singer who has become the mistress of Baron Hulot and then left him for the richer Duc d'Hérouville, who keeps her lavishly. Josépha, though hardheaded and devoted to her own well-being, always treats Madame Hulot with the utmost respect and even kindness.

JOYCE *(Possibly Latin, "joyous")* A name that was uncommon as a last or first name when Wilkie Collins wrote *No Name.* He used it for the mentally subnormal wife of the scheming Captain Wragge. Magdalen Vanstone allows Wragge to manage her acting career for a while, but when she has made enough money to become independent of him, she leaves, taking Joyce with her. Magdalen is much kinder to poor Joyce than Wragge has ever been.

Judy never owned a doll, never heard of Cinderella, never played at any game. —CHARLES DICKENS, *BLEAK HOUSE*

JUDITH *(Hebrew, "Jewish")* The apocryphal Book of Judith tells the story of the Hebrew heroine who secretly sneaked into the tent of the Assyrian general Holofernes and decapitated him. When she showed his head to the Hebrew army, the forces were inspired to defeat the invading Assyrians. In his *Divine Comedy* Dante places Judith in Paradise, with other Hebrew women enthroned in the Empyrean (the dwelling place of God himself). James Fenimore Cooper takes up the name in *The Deerslayer*, using it for Judith Hutter. One of the nominal daughters of Tom Hutter, who lives on Lake Glimmerglass and patrols it in his "ark," Judith is no sheltered Victorian heroine. Pretty, courageous, spirited, she is the product of her life in the wild, prone to flirtation and fond of the small luxuries that come her way. One of the characters refers to her as a "light-minded jilting jade." She loves Natty Bumppo and tries to persuade him to marry her, but in vain. The common nickname for **Judith** is **Judy**. Though the name is a perfectly likely one for a young working-class woman of the nineteenth century, it also provides echoes of the famous Punch and Judy puppet shows that entertained Londoners for years. The essence of the comedy was Punch's uncontrollable temper and his adeptness with a bat—Judy often got the worst of it. In Dickens's *Bleak House* poor Judy Smallweed gets the worst of life. She is the housekeeper for the noxious Smallweed grandparents, carrying out the responsibilities of an adult. Dickens makes the Smallweed ménage comical, but Judy's plight jerks at the reader's heartstrings.

JULIA *(Latin, "youthful")* Shakespeare's use of this name in *The Two Gentlemen of Verona* suggests that it may have been quite exotic in England at the end of the sixteenth century. Julia is a well-bred girl who undertakes the adventurous voyage from Verona to Milan to be with her beloved Proteus. She passes herself off as his page, "Sebastian," and thus has a front-row seat for his rough and ready courtship of the Milanese Silvia.

By the nineteenth century, the name was unremarkable enough to be used by many authors for secondary characters. In Jane Austen's *Mansfield Park*, Julia is the sister of the calculating Maria Bertram. Trollope uses the name for two "ladies of a certain age." Miss Julia Macnulty, in *The Eustace Diamonds*, has the unenviable job of serving as the irrepressible Lizzie Eustace's chaperone. Trollope describes her as being "as utterly destitute of possessions or means of existence as any unfortunate, well-born, and moderately-educated, middle-aged woman in London. . . . She could do nothing—except dress like a lady with the smallest possible cost." He is slightly kinder to Lady Julia DeGuest in *The Small House at Allington,* calling her "a tedious, dull, virtuous old woman." Wilkie Collins names the heroine's mother Julia in *The Moonstone.* Lady Verinder is a practical, strong-minded, and fair widow, a good mistress to her servants and a good mother to her equally stubborn daughter.

Henry James's Julia Dallow is another such strong-minded widow. In *The Tragic Muse,* she is a cousin of the Dormer family who has an abiding interest in politics. She would like to see dilettante Nicholas Dormer run for Parliament, and offers to finance his campaign, but he is irresolute and offers her marriage instead—not exactly what she'd bargained for. In James's *The Awkward Age,* Lady Julia is not a living character, but rather the grandmother of young Nanda Brookenham, constantly held up as an example by her elderly admirer Mr. Longdon. Unlike Nanda, she was always a perfectly pure young debutante. An older, elaborated version of the name is **Juliana,** and perhaps James wishes to invoke the sense of antiquity for Juliana Bordereau in *The Aspern Papers.* She is the elderly and crafty woman who was once poet Jeffrey Aspern's lover and who has custody of his papers. The narrator is confounded, first by her age and greed, and secondly by her evident intention that he marry her niece Tita as part of the price for the papers.

On the Continent, the name is used in the same form. The early portion of Byron's *Don Juan* is set in Spain. Donna Julia is Don Juan's first conquest, the unhappily married twenty-three-year-old wife of a neighbor, who succumbs to the precocious sixteen-year-old rake's charms. In Russia the name is sometimes spelled **Yulia.** Chekhov's tale "Three Years" recounts the first few disillusioning years of marriage between Alexei Laptev and Julia Belavin, the daughter of his sister's doctor. Julia has married the undistinguished Laptev to escape from the tiny, stultifying village where she lives, while Laptev truly loves her. The relationship brings neither partner what they had imagined, but improves as the two mature. The most common nickname for **Julia** is the

French form **Julie,** which Swedish playwright August Strindberg uses for the protagonist of his play *Miss Julie.* She is the daughter of a count, raised as an independent, even hoydenish young woman. Her mother has taught her to hate men, and in the course of the play she permanently alienates her fiancé and seduces her father's footman.

Juliet is the name of two Shakespeare characters, though the girlfriend of Claudio in *Measure for Measure* is cast in the shade by the young daughter of the Capulet family in *Romeo and Juliet.* The poetic speeches that Shakespeare wrote for the young and passionate pair, no less than their ineluctably tragic end, has made them perhaps the most famous lovers in Western literature.

> *But, soft! What light through yonder window breaks?*
> *It is the east, and Juliet is the sun!*
> *Arise, fair sun, and kill the envious moon,*
> *Who is already sick and pale with grief,*
> *That thou her maid art far more fair than she.*
> —WILLIAM SHAKESPEARE, *ROMEO AND JULIET*

JUNE *(French form of the Latin* Junia, *a clan name)* Jean Racine's *Britannicus* followed the outlines of the intrigue involving Nero's usurpation of the Roman leadership as told by Tacitus. June was the fiancée of Britannicus, Nero's half brother and the legitimate ruler. After Britannicus's death by poison, which he orders, Nero attempts to woo June. She escapes the palace and becomes a vestal virgin.

JUNO *(Latin mythology name)* **Juno** is the Latin name for the Greek goddess Hera. The sister and wife of Jupiter, she is the mother of three of his children—Mars, Vulcan, and Hebe. She is also the perpetual thorn in her husband's side, constantly monitoring his amours and punishing mortals for offenses against her pride.

JUSTINIA *(Latin, "just, fair")* An elaborate form of a name that more commonly occurs as **Justine** or even **Justina.** In *Framley Parsonage* Trollope uses the name to once again make gentle fun of aristocratic pretentious names. Lady Meredith is the daughter of the proud Lady Lufton, whose sins include saddling her daughter with this mouthful of a name. Known to her husband as "Justy," Lady Meredith is actually a warm and kind woman.

KATE, KATHERINE see **CATHERINE**

KIRSTIE, KRISTIN see **CHRISTINA**

LAETITIA *(Latin, "gladness")* A name that also appears as **Letitia.** Anthony Trollope uses the second spelling for the ironically named Letitia Quiverful. She is the staunch wife of the Reverend Quiverful in *Barchester Towers;* the surname refers to the family's "quiver full" of children, for they have fourteen. Mrs. Quiverful's life cannot be said to be full of the gladness that her name indicates, for feeding and clothing her huge family on a minor cleric's salary is a constant challenge. Henry Fielding's *Jonathan Wild* is the satiric pseudobiography of a genuine criminal who was hanged in London in 1725. Miss Laetitia Snap is a worldly-wise harridan who manages to disguise her true nature long enough to secure Wild in marriage. Fielding refers to her sardonically as "the chaste," making plain that "Miss Tishy" has been around the block once or twice. George Meredith's *The Egoist* features a Laetitia in a different mold altogether. The daughter of a retired army surgeon, a writer of poetry and a modest soul, Laetitia Dale is a neighbor of Sir Willoughby Patterne, the egoist of the title. He confides all of his romantic trials to Laetitia, never noticing that "she was pretty; her eyelashes were long and dark, her eyes dark-blue, and her soul was ready to shoot like a rocket out of them at

> *The lovely Laetitia, either out of prudence, or perhaps religion, of which she was a liberal professor, was deaf to all his promises, and luckily invincible by his force.*
> —HENRY FIELDING, *JONATHAN WILD*

a look from Willoughby." Henry James uses the nickname, **Tishy,** in *The Awkward Age* to make a point about the informality of London society at the turn of the century. In a certain fast set the women are all known casually not only by their first names but by their nicknames: Carrie, Tishy, Nanda. Tishy Grendon in particular is considered a terrible influence on the debutante Nanda, who, as an unmarried girl, should be sheltered from any hint of the racy and immoral.

> *"You've known ever since we came to England what I feel about the proper persons—and the most improper—for her to meet. The Tishy Grendons are far from the proper."*
> —HENRY JAMES, *THE AWKWARD AGE*

LAURA *(Latin, "laurel")* The reference to the laurel can point to the literal shrub or, more likely in literature, to the laurel as a metaphor for worldly acclaim. The Italian Renaissance poet Petrarch wrote a set of verses to "Laura" and scholars are still debating about whether she was an actual person or an abstraction. Byron, in his comic poem "Beppo," plays with the notion of the woman as poetic inspiration; *his* Laura is a well-preserved Venetian whose husband Beppo is absent for many years, perhaps taken captive by Turks. She comforts herself with a count, but when Beppo returns it takes her no time (and no effort) to turn her allegiance back to him. One of Trollope's more poignant characters is Lady Laura Standish of *Phineas Finn*. Phineas, the Irish newcomer to London, is very taken by courageous, majestic, red-haired Laura, and considers asking her to marry him. She loves Phineas, but when the dour, wealthy Scot Robert Kennedy proposes to her first, she agrees to marry him. Kennedy, alas, is a narrow-minded, harsh husband who objects to Laura's spirit, and eventually she leaves him, a scandalous act in those days. Wilkie Collins sometimes focused more on plot and less on psychology than Trollope. In *The Woman in White,* Laura Fairlie is the pretty, blond, rich, biddable young lady beloved by Walter Hartright. (The last names leave little to the reader's imagination.) He is merely a drawing teacher, though, so Laura is married off to the sinister Sir Percival Glyde, who has her committed to an insane asylum in a plot to steal her money.

> *Laura was blooming still, had made the best*
> *Of time, and time return'd the compliment,*
> *And treated her genteelly, so that, dress'd,*
> *She look'd extremely well where'er she went;*
> *A pretty woman is a welcome guest.*
>
> —LORD BYRON, "BEPPO"

The French form of the name is **Laure,** and in Émile Zola's *The Earth,* Laure is the fortunate youngest sister of the Fouan family. She married into the family that runs the brothel in town. Zola stresses the fact that, in this world, sin *does* pay, for Laure and her daughter Estelle enjoy a material comfort and security that the rest of her work-hardened siblings never know. By the end of the book, Zola compares her to "a gentle old nun who has spent her life in cloistered seclusion."

> "*When Catherine is about seventeen,*" he said to himself, "*Lavinia will try and persuade her that some young man with a moustache is in love with her.*"
>
> —HENRY JAMES, *WASHINGTON SQUARE*

LAVINIA *(Latin mythology name)* According to Virgil, Lavinia is the daughter of Latinus, king of the Latins. It is Aeneas's destiny to found the Roman dynasty, and securing Lavinia's love is the first step in that direction. Latin warrior Turnus is in love with

Lavinia and starts a battle with Aeneas and the Trojans, with Lavinia as one of the causes. Aeneas, of course, triumphs. In Shakespeare's Roman bloodbath *Titus Andronicus*, Lavinia is the daughter of Titus. In the course of the play's mayhem she is raped and has her hands cut off and tongue cut out so that she cannot identify the culprits. Later, using her stumps, she writes their names in the dirt, and her father avenges her in an appalling fashion.

Dickens uses the name for a minor character in *Our Mutual Friend;* Lavinia Wilfer is the younger sister of Bella Wilfer, who marries hero John Harmon. Lavinia, tart and pert beyond the usual limits of ladylike behavior, is known to her family as "The Irrepressible." Catherine Sloper, the heroine of Henry James's *Washington Square,* lives with her father and her aunt Lavinia Penniman in New York. Aunt Lavinia is a silly woman with "a passion for little secrets and mysteries," and she encourages Catherine's ill-fated romance with Morris Townsend.

LEDA *(Greek mythology name)* A mortal woman whom Zeus loved and mated with in the form of a swan. She bore him two eggs, each of which held a pair of twins: Castor and Pollux, Helen and Clytemnestra. Dante places Leda in Paradise and refers to the constellation of Gemini as "Leda's lovely nest."

LEILA *(Arabic, "darkness, night")* Lord Byron's poetry owed some of its appeal to his resolutely exotic settings, which naturally carried through to the characters' names. **Leila,** as a pretty, pronounceable Arabic name, he used twice. In *Don Juan,* Leila is a ten-year-old Turkish orphan whom the hero rescues from Cossacks at the siege of Ismail, and makes his ward. In "The Giaour," a poem about a romantic Christian warrior in Turkey, Leila is the beautiful denizen of Hassan's harem who falls in love with the hero. "Her eye's dark charm 't were vain to tell,/But gaze on that of the Gazelle,/It will assist thy fancy well," says Byron, describing her.

LEMMA *(Greek, "profit, gain")* Thomas Love Peacock's *Crotchet Castle* is a satiric look at the social-climbing habits of the nouveaux riches in the early nineteenth century. Lemma Crotchet is the rich but otherwise undistinguished daughter of Squire Crotchet, the immensely wealthy owner of Crotchet Castle. Her potential in the marriage market is as vast as her dowry.

LENORE *(Variant of* **Eleanore;** *possibly Greek, "light")* A name greatly favored by Edgar Allan Poe in this and several other forms. She is often a lost love, as in the poems "Lenore" and "The Raven." A reader can possibly be excused, however, from wondering if the choice of the lost love's name in "The Raven" was not determined somewhat by the rhyme scheme. **Leonora** is a more elaborate form of the name, perfectly suitable for the Princess Halm-Eberstein, long-lost mother of Daniel Deronda in George Eliot's novel of that name. She came from a devoutly Jewish Italian family and married the husband chosen by her own father, but elected to become a renowned actress instead of a conventional mother. She asked an admirer to rear her son, and only meets Daniel late in her life, when she is mortally ill. Her great gift to him is the revelation of his Jewish background. A further elaboration of the name is the unusual **Léontine,** used by Balzac for Madame de Sérizy in *A Harlot High and Low.* A well-preserved flaxen beauty of forty-five, she is madly in love with the handsome poet Lucien Chardon de Rubempré and ignorant of his grand passion for the actress Esther Gobseck. Balzac paints Madame de Sérizy as a Parisian aristocrat of unusual power: "Her large fortune, her husband's fine position and that of her brother, the Marquis de Ronquerolles, had protected her from the mortifications with which any other woman would have been overwhelmed." Until Lucien comes along, that is.

> *Eagerly I wished the morrow;—vainly I had sought to borrow*
> *From my books surcease of sorrow—sorrow for the lost*
>   *Lenore—*
> *For the rare and radiant maiden whom the angels name*
>   *Lenore—*
>   *Nameless* here *forevermore.*
> —EDGAR ALLAN POE, "THE RAVEN"

LETO *(lee' toh; Greek mythology name)* The daughter of a Titan who caught Jupiter's eye. Juno persecuted her, forcing her to wander from one country to another until finally she found shelter on the Greek island of Delos and gave birth to the twins Apollo and Diana. In *Metamorphoses* Ovid tells how Niobe mocked Leto for the small size of her family, and was summarily punished for her pride. She was also known as **Latona,** and it was by this name that Dante placed her in Purgatory.

LIGEIA *(ligh jee' ah; Greek mythology name)* The name of one of the Sirens, beautiful monsters who enticed seafarers to their death by singing sweetly: Odysseus escaped them by filling his crew's ears with wax and having himself lashed to the mast of the ship as it sailed past the Sirens' rock. In Edgar Allan Poe's poem "Ligeia," the siren figure is the narrator's beautiful wife, who dies after a long illness. He marries again, a fair-haired woman named Rowena who does not resemble the dark-haired Ligeia. Yet he is haunted by Ligeia. When Rowena dies, in an opium dream the poet sees Ligeia rise from Rowena's coffin.

> *"Dear John, I wish for your sake it was otherwise. I will go home and I will write in my book, this very day, Lilian Dale, Old Maid. If ever I make that false, do you come and ask me for the page."*
> —ANTHONY TROLLOPE, *THE LAST CHRONICLE OF BARSET*

LILY *(English flower name)* Also occurs as **Lilly** or **Lillie.** Lily Dale (whose real name, **Lilian,** is seldom used in the book), is one of Anthony Trollope's best-loved characters. Pretty and ladylike, she also has a sardonic way with words. She is an outspoken, courageous young woman who falls hard for Adolphus Crosbie in *The Small House at Allington.* She loves Crosbie without caution, and is devastated when, within weeks of their engagement, he jilts her for a titled rival. She refuses to consider the affections of local boy Johnny Eames. In *The Last Chronicle of Barset,*

Adolphus Crosbie is a debt-ridden widower, John Eames has become a man of the world—and Lily is caught by her pride and loyalty and will wed neither. She was such a hit with Trollope's readers that two ships were named for her in the 1860s.

In Edith Wharton's *The House of Mirth* Lily Bart, though also a spinster, is not content to remain one. A ravishing and expensive "girl" of twenty-nine in turn-of-the-century New York society, she sees marriage to a rich man as her only option. She is like those biblical lilies that "toil not, neither do they spin." What makes Lily tragic is the intermittent self-awareness that makes her occasionally rebel against her plight.

> *Lily understood that beauty is only the raw material of conquest, and that to convert it into success, other arts are required.* —EDITH WHARTON, *THE HOUSE OF MIRTH*

LISA, LIZA, LIZZIE see ELIZABETH

LOGISTILLA *(Greek, "word, reason")* Ludovico Ariosto may have invented this name for the sorceress who represents logic in *Orlando Furioso*. She is the daughter of Uther, sister of Alcina and Morgana, and her teachings give power to the heroes Ruggiero and Astolfo.

> *Henrietta was perhaps the prettiest, Louisa had the higher spirits.* —JANE AUSTEN, *PERSUASION*

LOUISA *(German, "famous warrior")* Fanny Burney's *Evelina*, published in 1778, is an epistolary novel of manners, recounting Evelina Anville's adventures in polite society. The heroine, having been brought up by a minister in the country, has few worldly connections and little but her beautiful face and her manners to recommend to her suitors. Lady Louisa Larpent, by contrast, is the sister of the wealthy Lord Orville. But the noble Lady Louisa is proud, conceited, and narrow-minded, a contrast to the *truly* noble, if modest, Evelina. In Jane Austen's final novel, *Persuasion,* Louisa Musgrove is one of the two cheerful, slightly vulgar sisters with whom Anne Elliot visits Lyme Regis. Quiet, unassuming Anne believes that her long-ago suitor Captain Wentworth is attracted to Louisa's hearty sense of fun. When Louisa injures herself by jumping off the seawall at Lyme, Wentworth reproaches himself for encouraging her. The name was still well used in the middle of the nineteenth century, for Dickens employs it in *Hard Times.* Louisa Gradgrind is the daughter of the hard businessman Thomas Gradgrind. She marries equally hard Josiah Bounderby, a practically inhuman banker and factory owner. Her marriage is so miserable that she easily falls prey to a feckless aristocratic playboy. She is ruined when she leaves Bounderby for James Harthouse.

The usual French form of the name, **Louise,** is also used in anglophone countries. Molière, in *The Imaginary Invalid,* names a minor character **Louison,** which is a diminutive. Louison is an observant child whose analysis of her sister Angélique's courtship helps to move the plot along. Balzac's hero Lucien Chardon de Rubempré attracts many women in the course of his career, as narrated in *Lost Illusions* and *A Harlot High and Low.* Louise de Bargeton, known to everyone besides Lucien as Anaïs or Naïs, is Lucien's first important mistress. She is the grande dame of Angoulême, a slender woman of a certain age with intellectual pretensions and a melodramatic style: "She had palpitations, went into ecstasies, waxed enthusiastic over every occurrence." When handsome, romantic Lucien reads his poetry at one of her salons, she falls in love with him. The pair go to Paris, where Lucien measures her against the richer, prettier, Parisian aristocrats, and drops her. His Louise, however, is very well connected, and in revenge she manages to scuttle his social-climbing ambitions.

The proud and blue-blooded Nègrepelisse offered her beau-tiful angel the only one of her names which no one had used, and consented to be "Louise" for him alone.
—HONORÉ DE BALZAC, LOST ILLUSIONS

LUCY *(Latin, "light")* An early version of the name in English was **Lucia**, which is still the Italian form. Associations with light and also with the fourth-century virgin martyr Saint Lucy (whose own fiancé denounced her as a Christian, according to legend) have colored authors' use of the name. Alessandro Manzoni's *The Betrothed*, for example, concerns the radiant, pious peasant girl Lucia Mondella. Innocently betrothed to millworker Renzo, she is kidnapped by the evil Don Rodrigo who wants to seduce her as a virgin. Through all her adventures (captivity in a convent, capture by another nobleman, plague), she remains religious and faithful to Renzo. Shakespeare uses an elaboration of the name, **Luciana,** for one of a pair of sisters in *The Comedy of Errors.* Adriana is married to Antipholus of Ephesus. Luciana, unaware that her brother-in-law has an identical twin, urges the twin to reconcile himself with her sister. She is confused and the audience amused when he woos her instead.

Molière used two forms of the name (**Lucile** and **Lucinde**) in his plays, each time for the young and lovely daughter of a principal character. Lucile in *The Would-Be Gentleman* is frustrated in her romance because her father deems her boyfriend not a gentleman. In *Love's the Best Doctor,* Lucinde loves the wrong man, but a so-called doctor cures her of her folly. Lucinde in *The Doctor in Spite of Himself* shows a little more initiative: to frustrate her father's marital plans for her she pretends to lose her power of speech.

Lucinda is closely related to Lucinde, but the *a* ending is more typically Latin than French. Indeed, a minor character in Cervantes' *Don Quixote* is the fair young Lucinda, in love with Quixote's occasional companion Cardenio. By the mid-nineteenth century Lucinda was used in anglophone countries as well: Trol-

> *Lucilla, for her part, had the calmest and most profound conviction that, when she discussed her own doings and plans and clevernesses, she was bringing forward the subject most interesting to her audience as well as to herself.*
> —MARGARET OLIPHANT, *MISS MARJORIBANKS*

lope employs it for Lucinda Roanoke, a minor character in *The Eustace Diamonds*. She is a dark, handsome, somewhat intimidating American whom her aunt Mrs. Carbuncle is trolling around the hunting fields in the attempt to snare a husband. Lucinda is not entirely acquiescent and in fact goes mad rather than marry the dissipated Sir Griffin Tewett. Ariosto uses **Lucina** for a princess of Cyprus in *Orlando Furioso* (she has the ill luck to be captured by a monster and kept in a pen), and Goethe, in *Elective Affinities*, calls Charlotte's daughter **Luciane,** a name that reflects nothing of Goethe's German background. Thomas Hardy takes advantage of the faint exoticism of **Lucetta** in *The Mayor of Casterbridge*. Michael Henchard has an affair with Lucetta LeSueur. She comes from the Island of Jersey, in the English Channel, and her last name means "sweat" in French; Hardy thus labels her as a woman of the senses and very different from Henchard's stolid English wife Susan.

> *"Lucy is monstrous pretty and so good-humored and agreeable!"* —JANE AUSTEN, *SENSE AND SENSIBILITY*

Margaret Oliphant may have called the heroine of *Miss Marjoribanks* **Lucilla** after the paragon heroine of a Hannah More novel of 1809. Certainly Lucilla Marjoribanks, a strapping, confident young woman, considers herself to be peerless in her small town of Carlingford. Released from boarding school, she takes over the social engineering of Carlingford with zest and no evidence of self-doubt—nor any sense of humor. The majority of

Victorian writers, unlike Mrs. Oliphant, used the vernacular version of the name, **Lucy**, with the exception of Charles Dickens who used the French form, **Lucie**, in *A Tale of Two Cities*. Lucie Manette, however is half French; her father was imprisoned in the Bastille and becomes a hero of the Revolution. Blond, pretty, loving to her father and her husband, she is a classic Dickensian heroine.

> *Who shall tell stars as teaspoons? Who shall put down the charms of Lucy Tartan upon paper?*
>
> —HERMAN MELVILLE, *PIERRE*

The nineteenth-century characters named Lucy are not all so conventional, however. Jane Austen exercises her wit on Lucy Steele in *Sense and Sensibility*. Vulgar, clever, plausible Lucy is the niece of the man who tutored Edward Ferrars, and believes herself engaged to him. Charlotte Brontë's *Villette* is considered autobiographical, so the reader may suppose that intelligent, observant Lucy Snowe stands in for the author. A resourceful orphan, she has made her way first as a companion, then teaching at a boarding school in France. The reserve signaled by her last name prevents many of the characters from appreciating her passionate nature, and Lucy suffers agonies from unrequited love.

> *"It must not be Lucy any longer, Lord Lufton; I was madly foolish when I first allowed it."*
>
> —ANTHONY TROLLOPE, *FRAMLEY PARSONAGE*

Mid-nineteenth-century writing suggests that the name Lucy had connotations of refinement and modesty. Herman Melville's fantastic *Pierre* features pretty, blond Lucy Tartan as the prospective consort of the highstrung Pierre Glendinning. In George Eliot's *The Mill on the Floss*, Lucy Deane is Maggie Tulliver's angelic cousin. When Maggie visits Lucy, the latter's fiancé Stephen

Guest finds he prefers Maggie's spirit to Lucy's ladylike predictability—and Lucy forgives even this. Anthony Trollope created two important characters named Lucy, both of them quite conventional. Lizzie Eustace may be the most memorable woman in *The Eustace Diamonds* but Trollope never intended her for the heroine: that role is reserved for the sweet, modest governess Lucy Morris, whose contrast to Lizzie could not be more complete. Where Lizzie is grasping, Lucy wants nothing material. Where Lizzie is fickle, Lucy is endlessly loyal. Where Lizzie presents herself as a tragic figure, Lucy quietly suffers. No need to ask who ends up with handsome Frank Greystock. Lucy Robarts, in *Framley Parsonage,* is a clever, reserved young woman with a proud nature. She falls in love with a peer, Lord Lufton, but will not marry him because his mother considers her socially insignificant and hopes to match him up with a wealthy girl. Not until Lady Lufton relents will Lucy Robarts follow her heart. Mary Elizabeth Braddon, a contemporary of Trollope's, wrote in an entirely different vein, producing sensation fiction full of elaborate plotting and wicked characters. Her Lucy Graham, in *Lady Audley's Secret,* presents a surface similar to that of Lucy Robarts or Lucy Morris. She is even, at first, a governess, cheerful and bright, pretty and lovable—and only as the story progresses does the reader discover her dark secrets, which include bigamy and possibly even murder. The epitome of the angelic Lucy appears in Bram Stoker's *Dracula,* published at the very end of the nineteenth century. Lucy Westenra is blond, beautiful, and chaste, and irresistibly attractive to men—in one day she receives three proposals of marriage. Yet it is this ideal Victorian woman who becomes one of Dracula's victims, and it is all the more disturbing when she in turn becomes a vampire.

> *For you see Miss Lucy Graham was blessed with that magic power of fascination by which a woman can charm with a word or intoxicate with a smile. Every one loved, admired, and praised her.*
> —MARY ELIZABETH BRADDON, *LADY AUDLEY'S SECRET*

> *She seemed like a nightmare of Lucy as she lay there, the pointed teeth, the bloodstained, voluptuous mouth—which it made me shudder to see—the whole carnal and unspiritual appearance, seeming like a devilish mockery of Lucy's sweet purity.*
> —BRAM STOKER, *DRACULA*

LYDIA *(Greek, "from Lydia")* Richard Brinsley Sheridan's comedy *The Rivals* features the romantically minded Lydia Languish, who finds conventional matchmaking dull. Though her relatives want to wed her to the highly eligible Captain Absolute, she prefers Ensign Beverly, who presses her to elope. By 1813, when Jane Austen wrote *Pride and Prejudice,* a pointed last name like Languish would have intruded into the naturalistic comedy of manners. Lydia Bennet, however, does amuse with her hoydenish vulgarity and her irrepressible high spirits. At the age of sixteen, she runs off to be married to the scapegrace Wickham, and returns to her family delighted with herself. Anthony Trollope may have remembered her when he created the minor character of Lydia Fawn, the fifth of Lord Fawn's eight sisters in *The Eustace Diamonds.* Bluff, hearty, and tactless, Lydia has the personality of a friendly puppy. Lydia Glasher, in George Eliot's *Daniel Deronda,* is a different kind of woman altogether. She was once the beautiful Irishwoman who left her husband for Henleigh Grandcourt. She has borne Grandcourt four children, but he will not marry her. When she finds out that young, beautiful Gwendolen Harleth is engaged to Grandcourt, she desperately seeks out Gwendolen to warn her about Grandcourt's past. If Lydia Glasher is pathetic, Wilkie Collins's Lydia Gwilt is an alluring conundrum. In *Armadale,* she appears as a governess, but Collins gradually reveals her to be a brilliant conspirator with a sordid past whose goal is to marry the wealthy Allan Armadale. Lydia Touchett, in Henry James's *The Portrait of a Lady,* is by contrast a plainspoken American woman who has "her own way of doing all that she did." Though her husband lives in England, she prefers Florence, and visits her husband only for a month out of every year. In her decisive way, she brings her niece Isabel Archer to England, setting off the train of events that make up the novel.

The name is also used in France, as **Lydie,** and in Russia, as **Lidiya** or **Lida.** In Balzac's *A Harlot High and Low,* Lydie Peyrade is the modest, sheltered daughter of a police spy, whose quiet domestic life belies her father's degraded métier. In Chekhov's story "The House with an Attic," Lydia Volchaninov is one of two daughters of Yekaterina Volchaninov. The narrator falls in love with her sister Zhenya but Lydia, known at home as **Leda,** is a strict, severe, reform-minded teacher and the narrator fails to live up to her standards. The family closes ranks, and he is unable to see Zhenya any more.

> *"Ah," said Isabel slowly, "you must be our crazy Aunt Lydia!"*
> *"Is that what your father told you to call me? I'm your Aunt Lydia, but I'm not at all crazy: I haven't a delusion!"*
> —HENRY JAMES, THE PORTRAIT OF A LADY

LYNDALL *(English, "valley of linden trees")* Originally a place-name, and probably a last name after that. It may be unusual for a girl's name, but the style of Olive Schreiner's *The Story of an African Farm* is to present the reader with facts that are never quite explained. Lyndall is one of two girls who live on the farm in Africa. She is the cleverer, more magnetic of the two, very pretty, well read, and deeply cynical from a young age. She goes away to school, and comes back to the farm full of an unexplained anger that may have to do with her views about woman's unfulfilling lot in life. She may be a mouthpiece for the author's own views.

LYNETTE *(Welsh, "idol")* This is a French form of the Welsh name Eiluned, and not related at all to Lynn. The name came to prominence with the publication of Tennyson's *The Idylls of the*

King. One section of the epic poem is entitled "Gareth and Lynette." It tells the story of the fair and noble damsel who arrives at Arthur's court to beg a Round Table knight to rescue her sister Lyonors, who is besieged in the Castle Perilous. The modest former kitchen boy Gareth asks Arthur secretly to be permitted the rescue of Lyonors as his first knightly quest. However, since he has not yet revealed his noble birth, Lynette and the court think Arthur's assigning him the quest is an insult to Lynette. She is offended, even "petulant," but Gareth succeeds in rescuing Lyonors and marries Lynette. The source of the story is Malory's *Le Morte D'Arthur,* in which the name is spelled **Lynet,** and in which Gareth marries Lyonors.

LYONORS *(Origin unclear)* In Tennyson's version of the Arthurian legend the name is **Lyonors** and seems to be related to **Eleanor,** but in Malory's *Le Morte D'Arthur,* the character is called **Lyonesse** or **Liones,** which may be a version of Leo or other names that refer to lions. She is the sister of Lynette, besieged in the Castle Perilous and guarded by a variable number of knights according to the version of the tale. Sir Gareth, on his first quest, liberates her, and in Malory's version, marries her.

LYSISTRATA *(Greek, "she who disbands armies")* In Aristophanes' eponymous comedy, Lysistrata is the Athenian woman who organizes her fellow wives to end war in their country. The tactic is simple and effective: they will refuse to have sex with their husbands until a peace treaty is signed.

MABEL *(Latin, "lovable")* Natty Bumppo of James Fenimore Cooper's "Leatherstocking Tales" is the Noble Savage par excellence, and though several women find him alluring, only Mabel Dunham in *The Pathfinder* tickles his fancy. She is the strikingly refined daughter of a sergeant stationed at Fort Otsego in the New York State wilderness. Pretty, kindly, well-educated, she ultimately needs a man who can be more civilized than Natty.

MACARIA *(Greek, "blessed")* In Euripides' *The Children of Heracles,* the Greek hero is dead and his children are in flight from his cousin Eurystheus, who regards them as a threat to his throne. Macaria is Heracles' daughter, who is told by an oracle that she must sacrifice herself to Demeter, which she is prepared to do.

> *It was as infallible that Madeline should displease and irritate the women, as that she should charm and captivate the men.* —ANTHONY TROLLOPE, *BARCHESTER TOWERS*

MADELEINE *(Greek, "from Magdala")* There are many variants, including **Magdalene, Magdalen, Maddalena,** and **Madeline.** Saint Mary Magdalen was the fallen woman whose repentance Jesus accepted, despite her extravagant behavior and to the consternation of some of his followers. Most writers using the name have intended some allusion to the saint, but Madeline Bray, in

THE SAINTS OF GOD

The institution with the greatest impact on European naming patterns is probably the Christian church. Not only does the Bible provide dozens of names as inspiration, but the lives of the saints provide even more. In fact, the Calendar of Saints kept alive many names with ancient origins, like **Agnes** or **Felix.** It also provided a kind of grassroots cultural cross-pollination in days when the common man never traveled far from home. Thus a name like **Magdalen,** which originally pointed to a city in Asia Minor, traveled all over the world and was absorbed into different languages. The impact of saints on Russian naming patterns is even more direct. Throughout the nineteenth century, most Russians were named for a saint, and rather than celebrating the anniversary of the day they were born, they celebrated the feast day of the saint for whom they were named.

Charles Dickens's *Nicholas Nickleby,* is a simple sketch of the conventional sweet Victorian heroine. That she attracts the hero's attention is the most surprising thing about her. In "The Fall of the House of Usher" Edgar Allan Poe calls Roderick Usher's sister Madeline. She is wasting away from a mysterious disease, and the inexorable progress of her illness deepens the sense of doom at the Usher house. She is mistakenly buried alive, and fights her way out of her tomb to confront her brother and expire at his feet. Nothing so sinister ever happens in a Trollope novel, but in *Barchester Towers* Madeline Neroni is certainly frightening to the denizens of the cathedral close. She is the younger daughter of indolent cleric Vesey Stanhope, and was married unhappily to an Italian. She has been crippled (possibly by her dreadful husband) and takes great advantage of her inability to walk. She is, finally, beautiful and a terrible flirt—to the timid clergymen of Barchester, a Magdalen indeed! Wilkie Collins plays with the name more explicitly in *No Name,* a novel about two gently raised girls who, when their father dies, discover themselves to be illegitimate and destitute. The elder sister Norah, conventionally enough, finds work as a governess, but Magdalen becomes a professional actress and further uses her acting ability to achieve revenge on the cousin who inherits all of their father's money.

> *Magdalen was born with all the senses—except a sense of order.* —WILKIE COLLINS, NO NAME

The version of the name most commonly used in France is Madeleine, and in Balzac's hands, there is no connotation of the racy saint. Madeleine Vivet, by contrast, is the very proper ladies' maid in the house of the Baron Camusot de Marville. She has saved a reasonable dowry, and nurtured a sizable fund of resentment against the family she has served for many years, and she wants to marry the poor cousin Pons.

> *This Madeleine, in spite of, nay perhaps on the strength of, a pimpled complexion and a viper-like length of spine, had made up her mind that some day she would be Mme Pons. But in vain she dangled twenty thousand francs of savings before the old bachelor's eyes; Pons had declined happiness accompanied by so many pimples.*
> —HONORÉ DE BALZAC, COUSIN PONS

MAISIE *(Scottish diminutive of* **Margaret***)* Henry James wrote *What Maisie Knew* in 1896, filtering the story of a messily divorced couple through the consciousness of their precocious but stubbornly innocent daughter. The divorce decree provides for joint custody, but Maisie's parents are both more interested in their own romantic entanglements than in her. "It was to be the fate of this patient little girl," writes James, "to see much more than she at first understood, but also even at first to understand much more than any little girl, however patient, had perhaps ever understood before."

> *"Poor little monkey!" she at last exclaimed; and the words were an epitaph for the tomb of Maisie's childhood.*
> —HENRY JAMES, WHAT MAISIE KNEW

MAMIE (*Diminutive of* **Margaret** *or* **Mary**) A quintessentially American name used by Henry James for Mamie Pocock in *The Ambassadors*. She is brought to Paris from Woollett, Massachusetts, in part to lure Chad Newsome back to his native land and the textile mill that awaits his hereditary administration. She is thus one of the ambassadors from the New World to the Old. Tall, blond, and supremely confident, she fulfills her role to perfection.

> *Granted that a community might be best represented by a young lady of twenty-two, Mamie perfectly played the part, played it as if she were used to it, and looked and spoke and dressed the part.*
> —HENRY JAMES, THE AMBASSADORS

MANON (ma naw'; *French diminutive of* **Mary**) In 1731 a French priest, the Abbé Prévost, created an enduring portrait of a femme fatale in *Manon Lescaut*. Manon is a young woman of modest background but great beauty and charm. On her way to a convent, where she is to become a nun, she meets the young, handsome Chevalier des Grieux who is utterly smitten: "She seemed so lovely to me that then and there I was carried away by an overmastering passion." The pair abandon their plans and their families and set up housekeeping together, even though they are instantly relegated to the margins of society and must steal and cheat at cards to support themselves. Manon is chronically unfaithful to des Grieux, who makes every sacrifice for her, including serving jail time and becoming a priest. Ultimately the two go into exile in Louisiana, where des Grieux nearly kills the governor's son in a duel on Manon's behalf. She dies in his arms of exhaustion as the pair attempt to flee justice. This extravagant story has inspired two operas, Massenet's *Manon* and Puccini's *Manon Lescaut*.

> *I knew my Manon; experience had already taught me all too clearly that, however attached to me she might be when things went well, it was no use counting on her in hard times.*
> —ABBÉ PRÉVOST, *MANON LESCAUT*

MARCIA *(Latin, "warlike")* This name and its derivatives like **Marcella** and **Marceline** all ultimately come from **Mars,** the name of the Roman god of war. **Marcia** is the classic version and was actually used in the Roman era; Dante places Marcia the wife of Cato of Utica among the Virtuous Pagans in Canto 4 of the *Inferno* because of her submission to her husband. In William Dean Howells's *A Modern Instance,* Marcia Gaylord is anything but submissive to her oafish, degenerate mate, but that is largely the point of this 1882 novel that was one of the first to discuss divorce frankly. Certainly Marcia and her husband Bartley Hubbard are extremely poorly matched. He is vain and hot-tempered, she is impulsive and jealous. Thomas Hardy's *The Well-Beloved* is a meditation on the nature of romantic love; the protagonist, Jocelyn Pierston, spends the novel in search of the ideal woman and at twenty-year intervals falls in love with successive generations of the same family. Marcia Benbow provides the interludes. A tall, handsome woman—Hardy refers to her as "a very Juno"— she is dignified and self-sufficient, and she is the woman whom Pierston finally marries.

Marceline is a French version of the name, used by Beaumarchais in *The Barber of Seville* and *The Marriage of Figaro*. In the latter play she is the housekeeper to Count Almaviva. She wants to marry Figaro even though he is betrothed to Suzanne. She already has an illegitimate child by the music master Bazile. Part of what was so startling and revolutionary about Beaumarchais's plays was the intricate relationships among the servants that mirrored the intrigues among their aristocratic masters.

> *Margaret could not help her looks; but the short curled upper lip, the round, massive, upturned chin, the manner of carrying her head, her movements, full of a soft feminine defiance, always gave strangers the impression of haughtiness.* —ELIZABETH GASKELL, NORTH AND SOUTH

MARGARET (*Greek, "pearl"*) The eleventh-century queen Margaret of Scotland, wife of Malcolm III, was canonized, as was her son King David. Sir Walter Scott may have wanted to invoke this Catholic heritage when he named Lady Margaret Bellenden of *Old Mortality*. She is a semicomic character, constantly boring others with the tale of her life's high point—the evening King Charles II dined at her castle. In this historic novel about the religious struggles in eighteenth-century Scotland, Lady Margaret represents the aristocratic Catholic faction. The name bears no such baggage in Shakespeare's *Much Ado About Nothing,* where Margaret is merely Hero's lady in waiting.

Meg March, in Louisa May Alcott's *Little Women,* can be taken to represent the warm, maternal side of Victorian womanhood. The eldest of the four March girls, she has a taste for luxury and a very sweet nature. Not surprisingly, she is the first March daughter to marry and have children. Mrs. Gaskell's *North and South* contrasts the soft life of its heroine Margaret Hale when she lives comfortably in southern England with the harsh reality of a financially limited life in Milton, a city resembling Manchester. Pretty, slightly snobbish Margaret adjusts to this new world and finds interest and immediacy in the lives of her millworker neighbors—not to mention a romance with the owner of the mill.

Over the years **Margaret** has spawned many nicknames, among them **Meg, Maggie,** and **Marge.** Sir Walter Scott uses two of these for two unsavory characters in *The Heart of Midlothian.* Meg Murdockson is the truly wicked midwife who delivers Effie Deans's illegitimate baby and then spirits it away to be raised elsewhere. She is jealous of Effie because she knows that the father of Effie's baby also seduced her own daughter, Marge Wildfire. Marge, however, was driven completely insane by her seduction and abandonment. At the end of the book, Meg Murdockson is hanged as a witch. George Eliot's *The Mill on the Floss* is a portrait of a family of modest means and education; the heroine, Maggie Tulliver, is known to everyone by her informal nickname. Passionate, intelligent, and impetuous, tomboyish Maggie longs for a broader life and wider opportunities than those afforded by her life at Dorlcote Mill. She realizes, in the course of the novel, that her life can hold little but self-sacrifice and performance of her duties. Maggie Verver of Henry James's *The Golden Bowl* is a very different character. The daughter of an immensely wealthy widower, she has never had to fight for anything until she realizes that her deeply loved husband, the Italian prince Amerigo, is having an affair with her best friend Charlotte. What complicates the situation is that Charlotte has married Maggie's father. Though many of the characters consider Maggie an innocent, she finds sufficient duplicity and cunning to counter her friend's betrayal without alienating her husband.

The German form of Margaret is **Margarete** or **Margarethe,** often shortened to **Gretel, Gretl,** or **Gretchen.** In Goethe's version of *Faust,* Gretchen is a serving girl seduced by Faust with the help of a casket of jewels. She has a child by him and drowns it, then is jailed. Finally she turns to God and her soul is saved. In Gounod's famous opera she is known as **Marguérite,** the French form of the name. "The Girl with the Golden Eyes" is one of Balzac's most sensational tales, the kind of fiction that gave a bad name to French novels. **Margarita,** the Spanish version of Margaret, is the first name of the Marquise de San Real. Henri de Marsay, the illegitimate son of an English earl and a French countess, is a jaded dandy who finds the challenge he craves in Paquita, the girl of the title. She lives surrounded by luxury and carefully guarded, and de Marsay believes she is the mistress of the Marquis of San Real. He finds, however, once he has made his conquest, that she is technically a virgin. She is, however, infinitely experienced sexually, and de Marsay grasps to his horror that she is actually the sex slave of Margarita, the marquise. She has been in Margarita's control since the age of twelve and can neither read nor write. When the marquise realizes that Paquita has been seduced by a man, she kills her. To add yet another fiendish twist to the tale, de Marsay realizes that Margarita is his half sister.

MARTHA *(Hebrew, "mistress of the house")* In a New Testament story, Jesus visits a pair of sisters, Martha and Mary. While he teaches, Mary sits at his feet listening but Martha bustles about preparing food for the visitors. She gets huffy and appeals to Jesus to make Mary pull her weight, and is rebuked for her fussiness. Martha Garland in Thomas Hardy's *The Trumpet-Major* is a busy housewife in the classic Martha mold. The widow of a landscape painter, she has come down in the world, and lodges with the miller of a small village. Good-natured and somewhat silly, she eventually marries the miller even though such a marriage represents a social step down for her. Martha Dunstable first appears in Anthony Trollope's *Doctor Thorne* as an outspoken spinster of enormous wealth. She is something of a curiosity in Barsetshire because her money was made by her father's cosmetic company, which manufactured "Oil of Lebanon," a beauty aid. In *Framley Parsonage* she is presented as a potential mate for the bankrupt M.P. Nathaniel Sowerby, who needs a rich wife. She is far too astute, however, to be caught in this particular marital noose. At the end of this book the Barsetshire medic Dr. Thorne proposes to her, and she reappears in *The Last Chronicle of Barset* as a rich and immensely generous matron.

Mattie was a common nickname for Martha in the nineteenth century. Edith Wharton may be playing on the motif of housewifery when she names Mattie Silver in *Ethan Frome,* but she inverts it. Mattie is the cousin of Zeena, the sickly and self-absorbed Mrs. Frome, who takes the orphan in to help with the chores. But Mattie's gift to the household is vitality and high spirits rather than any ability in the kitchen—and even this gift is temporary.

The Russian form of the name is **Marfa,** used by Ivan Turgenev for Marfa Timofeyevna Pestov in *Home of the Gentry.* Like Martha Dunstable, Marfa Timofeyevna is independent and frank. She lives with her niece Marya Dmitriyevna Kalitin and manages to intimidate the much younger, wealthier woman.

> *Mattie had no natural turn for housekeeping, and her training had done nothing to remedy the defect. She was quick to learn, but forgetful and dreamy, and not disposed to take the matter seriously.* —EDITH WHARTON, *ETHAN FROME*

MARFISA *(Origin unclear)* In Ariosto's *Orlando Furioso* Marfisa is the warrior sister of the converted Christian hero Ruggiero. Known as "Marfisa the Fierce" and "Marfisa the Invincible," she is redoubtable in combat. In one episode she defeats ten knights single-handed.

MARTINE *(French, feminine of* **Martin:** *Latin, "warlike")* Molière's *The Doctor in Spite of Himself* is one of his broadest comedies, featuring Sganarelle as the crafty woodcutter who "diagnoses" the illness of the fair Lucinde. In the first scene Sganarelle beats his wife Martine for telling him that he is a gambler and a poor provider, but contentious Martine is well able to exact revenge.

MARY *(Hebrew, "bitter" or possibly "rebellious")* One of the most common names in the English language, with dozens of variants and derivative forms. Jane Austen used it for three characters, two of them irresistibly comical. Mary Bennet is the bluestocking sister in *Pride and Prejudice* who is always eager to air her knowledge and has never learned that this is not the way to become popular. Mary Musgrove in *Persuasion* is heroine Anne Elliot's youngest sister, a confirmed hypochondriac married to the socially inferior Charles Musgrove. *Mansfield Park* features the mercenary and socially ruthless Mary Crawford, who dumps Edmund Bertram when she realizes he sincerely desires to become a clergyman. The Brontë sisters also use the name for minor characters like Mary Millward in Anne's *The Tenant of Wildfell Hall*, the self-effacing vicar's daughter who runs the household efficiently. "She was trusted and valued by her father, loved and courted by all dogs, cats, children, and poor people, and slighted and neglected by everybody else," says the narrator.

> *Mary had neither genius nor taste; and though vanity had given her application, it had given her likewise a pedantic air and conceited manner.*
>
> —JANE AUSTEN, *PRIDE AND PREJUDICE*

George Eliot, whose real name was Mary Ann Evans, gave her own name to one of the most attractive characters in *Middlemarch*, the modest and practical Mary Garth. Mary takes care of the irascible invalid Peter Featherstone and attempts to guide unreliable Fred Vincy into a constructive occupation before she will marry him. Eliot may have identified with the brilliant Dorothea Brooke but she clearly has a great deal of affection for steadfast Mary. Mary Barton, in Elizabeth Gaskell's eponymous novel, can also be called steadfast. The book is set in a Manchester mill in the 1830s, and Mary is a seamstress in love with a workman, Jem Wilson. She is courted by the mill owner's son Harry, but resists him. When Jem is accused of Harry's murder, Mary manages single-handedly to clear Jem's name. In *Phineas Finn*, Anthony

Trollope uses Mary for the pretty Irish girl whom Phineas leaves behind him when he goes to London. Mary Flood Jones is a modest maiden who adores the glamorous Phineas and never reproaches him, even when tales reach Ireland of his London love affairs. At the end of the book, after Phineas returns to Ireland in disgrace, he marries Mary who has never wavered in her love. Trollope's heroines never do, of course. Mary Thorne, of *Doctor Thorne*, is cleverer than Mary Flood Jones. She is also better educated, and very proud. But she is equally tenacious in her love. She is, though she doesn't know it, the illegitimate daughter of a hat maker, brought up by her uncle the doctor. She loves Frank Gresham, the heir to a proud county family. Her unconventional birth would be anathema to them, but Trollope makes her the heir to an immense fortune. George Gissing's *The Odd Women*, written at the end of the nineteenth century, focuses on the plight of unmarried (or "odd," as in "not paired") women. Mary Barfoot is one of the luckiest of these, having some money of her own. She lives with a friend, Rhoda Nunn, and runs a school that teaches middle-class women secretarial skills that will make them employable. Handsome, cheerful, and tolerant, Mary is an appealing exemplar to other single women.

> *"You are so very kind to me,"* continued Mary, *"and it seems so cold to hear you call me Miss Thorne."*
>
> *"Well, Miss Thorne, I'm sure I'd call you anything else to please you. Only I didn't know whether you'd like it from me. Else I do think Mary is the prettiest name in all the language."*
> —ANTHONY TROLLOPE, DOCTOR THORNE

Though we may think of **Maria** as the Mediterranean form of the name and pronounce it *mah ree' ah,* it was well used in England through the nineteenth century, and most commonly pronounced *mah righ' ah.* In Shakespeare's *Twelfth Night*, Maria is the countess Olivia's maid, and responsible for discomfiting the

priggish Malvolio. She ends up married to loose-living Sir Toby
Belch. Jane Austen's *Mansfield Park* features two generations
of Maria Bertrams, mother and daughter. The mother is self-
indulgent and silly, the daughter elegant, cold, and calculating.
Worse, young Maria first marries a ninny and then runs off with
a wealthy rake, for which she is exiled from her family. Maria
Hale in Mrs. Gaskell's *North and South* might well be related to
the Bertram women, so foolish and vain is she. Having married a
young clergyman beneath her social class, she has suffered twenty-
odd years of genteel poverty—not especially gracefully. Her family's forced move to Milton (standing in for industrial Manchester)
effectively kills her. Wilkie Collins's sensational books sometimes
include sensational characters, and Maria Oldershaw of *Armadale*
is a deliciously deep-dyed Victorian villainess. The accomplice and
possibly foster mother of governess Lydia Gwilt, she is also a
blackmailer, an abortionist, and a procuress, known in London as
"Mother Jezebel." Henry James's Maria Gostrey in *The Ambassadors* is that unusual creature, an American Maria, but she is unusual in a number of ways. She serves, in the story, as a kind of
Virgil to the protagonist Lambert Strether: she is his guide to Europe as Virgil escorted Dante through the land of the damned.
Thirty-five years old, a single woman living in Paris, she grasps as
Strether cannot the social subtleties of what James might have
called "the European scene."

In France the name is **Marie,** and many French writers have
used it. Frédéric Moreau, the hero of Gustave Flaubert's *A Sentimental Education,* arrives in Paris from the provinces determined
to leave his mark as a romantic hero. The first step is conceiving
an unrequited passion for the married Marie Arnoux. When,
years later, she is widowed, she offers her love to Frédéric, but he
rejects her. Anglophone writers have also used Marie for characters with some French blood or French culture. In *Uncle Tom's
Cabin*, Marie St. Clare is a New Orleans matron, the self-centered
mother of saintly Eva. Harriet Beecher Stowe makes her a
hypochondriac and a constant complainer, though compared to
the slave characters, her life is one of the utmost ease and comfort. Marie de Vionnet does not appear until well over a hundred
pages into Henry James's *The Ambassadors,* but her character is

much discussed before the protagonist Lambert Strether and the reader finally meet her. She is the half English, half French wife of a reprobate French count, who has lived respectably separated from him for years. Charming, beautiful, and elusive, she is alluring and mysterious both to Strether and to young American Chad Newsome.

Trollope used Marie twice for important characters, each time for a woman who is specifically not English. *The Way We Live Now,* Trollope's most cynical novel, focuses on the social and financial shenanigans of the mysterious Augustus Melmotte who manages to cut a swathe in London. His daughter Marie is much courted for her putative dowry. Having read far too many romantic novels in her youth (Trollope's swipe at the moral influence of cheap fiction), she wants to be overwhelmed by a romantic suitor rather than the young nobleman her father has found for her. Marie Goesler is a far more attractive creation. She appears as a mysteriously wealthy widow in *Phineas Finn.* Dark-haired, slender, she is physically appealing and very charming. Phineas Finn flirts with her, but in the end he stays true to Mary Flood Jones. In *Phineas Redux,* she is greatly cherished by the elderly Duke of Omnium yet refuses his proposal of marriage, much to the relief of Lady Glencora Palliser. She appears once more in *The Duke's Children,* married to Phineas Finn and the confidante of the Duke of Omnium's daughter Mary. Throughout her appearances in the political novels, Madame Max (or Mrs. Finn) always maintains her dignity and her outsider's analytical view of London society.

> *As an old man he had taken the privilege of calling her Marie, and she had not forbidden it.*
> —ANTHONY TROLLOPE, *PHINEAS FINN*

Mary has been steadily used in Russia as well, both as **Marya** or **Mariya** and in the diminutive form **Masha.** Turgenev's *Home of the Gentry* concerns the wealthy Kalitin family, headed by

Marya Dmitrievna. She is a fifty-year-old widow, mercurial and slightly silly, and mother of the alluring Liza and Lena. Princess Marya Bolkonsky is a major character in Tolstoy's *War and Peace*. As a young unmarried woman she is subject to the selfish rules of her father, who wants her to continue to run his household. In Chekhov's drama *The Three Sisters*, Masha is the only married sister, but her dull husband provides her with little fulfillment and she embarks on an affair out of desperation. She always wears black, as a token of her depression. Masha Shamrayev in Chekov's *The Seagull*, though a young girl, also wears black because, she announces, "I am in mourning for my life."

A name as well used as Mary inevitably spawns variations. **Marian** or **Marion** originated as French diminutives, while **Mariette** or **Marietta** use a different ending. Stendhal's *The Charterhouse of Parma* introduces actress Marietta Valsera as one in a string of Fabrizio del Dongo's mistresses. George Gissing's *New Grub Street* is an exposé of late Victorian journalism. Bitter, disappointed Alfred Yule relies heavily on his daughter Marian to do his research for him. When he goes blind, she supports him. Marian Halcombe of Wilkie Collins's *The Woman in White* is similarly resourceful. The half sister of lovely Laura Fairlie, Marian is extremely ugly, with coarse black hair and a heavy jaw, but she is loving, loyal, and energetic. She is instrumental in freeing her sister from the clutches of the evil Sir Percival Glyde. Her looks and her assertiveness disqualify Marian Halcombe as a romantic partner by Victorian standards, and she ends up living with her sister when Laura marries. **Marionetta** is a name that combines two French endings in an extravagance of elaboration—and to make it worse, Marionetta O'Carroll of *Nightmare Abbey* is saddled with the middle name Celestina. But like all of the characters in this satire by Thomas Love Peacock, she is faintly ridiculous. The novel mocks the romantic passion for the gloomy, and Marionetta (castigated as "a dancing, laughing, singing, thoughtless, careless, merry-hearted thing") is considered too cheerful to be a suitable mate for Scythrop Glowrie.

Mary is often combined with other names, especially in Catholic families, which may name every daughter Mary, using different middle names to distinguish them. One of the most common combinations is Mary and **Ann,** the name of the saint who was Mary's mother. In France, the two names are joined to become **Marianne** or **Mariane.** Molière was so partial to the name that he used it for ingenue characters in *Tartuffe* and *The Miser.* In Émile Zola's *The Earth,* Marianne is the grandmother of the Fouan tribe of peasants; she is usually known simply as "*la grande.*" At the age of seventy she farms her land herself and is such a miser that she refuses to provide for her half-witted grandchildren. "Everyone went in deadly terror of her, and nobody would ever dare to disobey her." Jane Austen used this slightly exotic name for Marianne Dashwood, the highstrung sister of Elinor in *Sense and Sensibility.* Marianne seeks emotional sensation in everything, at the expense of decorum and comfort, and that is her downfall. As Austen says of her, "She was generous, amiable, interesting; she was everything but prudent."

Shakespeare uses a further elaboration, **Mariana,** in two plays. In *All's Well That Ends Well,* Mariana is a minor character, a friend of the widow whose daughter Diana is courted by Bertram. In *Measure for Measure* Angelo, deputized to rule over Vienna in Duke Vincentio's absence, enforces all of the city's laws very strictly. Yet he has abandoned Mariana, the woman to whom he was engaged, because her dowry has vanished. In 1830 Alfred, Lord Tennyson wrote a poem entitled "Mariana" whose epigraph was "Mariana at the moated grange." The refrain runs, "She only said, 'My life is dreary,/He cometh not,' she said;/She said, 'I am aweary, aweary,/I would that I were dead.'" Sir John Everett Millais later painted his interpretation of the dejected Mariana.

> *There, at the moated grange, resides this dejected Mariana.*
> —WILLIAM SHAKESPEARE, *MEASURE FOR MEASURE*

MATILDA (*Old German, "battle mighty"*) A young lady named **Matilda** is Dante's guide through *Purgatory* in that section of the

Divine Comedy. She represents the Active Life, and scholars suggest that she serves to prepare him for his vision of Beatrice. Anne Brontë includes a Matilda in her novel about a governess, *Agnes Grey.* Matilda Murray is an older daughter at one of the houses where Agnes is employed. A "strapping hoyden," she spends all her time in the stables and the kennels and seems at times barely civilized. Thomas Hardy, in *The Trumpet-Major,* portrays Matilda Johnson, a vulgar but enterprising camp follower who almost entraps Bob Loveday into marriage. Lady Matilda Carbury in Anthony Trollope's *The Way We Live Now* shares Matilda Johnson's energy, if not much else. The daughter of an aristocrat, she earns a living by writing, and hopes to become a successful popular novelist. She hounds newspaper editors, hoping to get her books reviewed, and finally ends up marrying one. Elizabeth Gaskell's most famous novel, *Cranford,* is a sketch of a village where men are absent or marginal, and women control the social scene. Miss Matilda Jenkyns, also called **Matty,** is one of a pair of sisters who form the nucleus of the community. Gentle, indecisive, and self-sacrificing, Matty has always deferred to her elder sister Deborah. In her fifties, she finds herself cut adrift upon Deborah's death, but her kindly friends ensure that she will thrive.

> *As an animal, Matilda was all right, full of life, vigour, and activity; as an intelligent being, she was barbarously ignorant, indocile, careless and irrational.*
>
> —ANNE BRONTË, *AGNES GREY*

Maud, surprisingly enough, was the old spoken form of Matilda. It was popular as a name during the Victorian era and given some prominence by Alfred, Lord Tennyson's long narrative poem "Maud," written in 1855. The somewhat cynical narrator tells the tale of his love for the young woman whose father ruined him. Ultimately he kills Maud's brother in a duel, she dies, and he is exiled from England. In *The Wings of the Dove,* Henry

James gives one of his heroines, Kate Croy, a brilliant and socially ambitious aunt, Maud Lowder. Aunt Maud wants Kate to marry well, and disapproves of journalist Merton Densher.

The French form of the name is **Mathilde,** used by Stendhal in *Scarlet and Black.* Mathilde de la Mole is a proud, intelligent, sophisticated, and bored young aristocrat whose comfortable life seems to her constrained by predictability. When handsome, ambitious Julien Sorel becomes her father's secretary, she is at first intrigued by his intelligence, then seduced. He gets her pregnant, and is prepared to marry her until his scandalous past catches up to him.

> *Come into the garden, Maud,*
> *For the black bat, night, has flown,*
> *Come into the garden, Maud,*
> *I am here at the gate alone.*
> —ALFRED, LORD TENNYSON, "MAUD"

MAY *(Origin unclear)* Some scholars suggest that **May** is a version of the medieval form of **Matthew.** It has also been used as a nickname for **Mary.** Queen Mary of England, for instance, George V's wife, was known through her youth as "Princess May." Month names like April weren't adapted as given names until the twentieth century. Thus when Geoffrey Chaucer calls a character May in *The Canterbury Tales* her name is clearly as symbolic as that of her husband, January. She is, naturally, a young wife, who cheats on her geriatric mate in "The Merchant's Tale." May Bartram in Henry James's tale "The Beast in the Jungle" is a well-bred and perceptive Englishwoman of thirty. The protagonist, John Marcher, is a single man whose whole life is marked by his conviction that he is to suffer some catastrophe. Having confided this secret only to May, he finds himself comfortably bound to her in a passionless way. May, for her part, is in love with Marcher and understands that his catastrophe will be to let life pass him by. May Welland, in Edith Wharton's *The Age of Innocence,* is the ideal consort for young New York bachelor Newland Archer—until Archer's perceptions of his world are altered by May's world-weary cousin Ellen Olenska. Virginal, conventional, and innocent, May seems to Archer as pure as the lilies of the valley he sends her daily. Her show of strength thus comes as a surprise to him.

> *There was no better match in New York than May Welland, look at the question from whatever point you chose.*
> —EDITH WHARTON, *THE AGE OF INNOCENCE*

MEDEA *(Greek, "ruling")* Medea's character and history appear in a number of forms, but perhaps Euripides' drama *Medea* treats them most completely. She is a sorceress, daughter of King Aeëtes of Colchis, and she falls in love with the hero Jason. She helps him steal the Golden Fleece and has several children by him. Later, the highly ambitious Jason discards her for the daughter of Creon of Corinth. A woman of Medea's stamp is not to be toyed with, however: she murders her children and Jason's new bride. Euripides portrays her as a woman driven to horrible deeds. Curiously enough, Chaucer ignores her bloodthirsty side and portrays her in "The Legend of Good Women" as a woman who gave all for her man.

> *Medea, a girl so sapient and fair*
> *That no man ever saw a lovelier . . .*
> —GEOFFREY CHAUCER, "THE LEGEND OF GOOD WOMEN"

MEDORA *(Greek, possibly "mother's gift")* Lord Byron created a number of dashing, charismatic protagonists and they tend to have suitable mates. In "The Corsair," the hero, Conrad, is married to a blond, beautiful, passionate, and phenomenally understanding woman named Medora who waits for him in his luxurious lair while he goes out on raids. He loves her obsessively and is devastated to return one day and find her dead.

MEDUSA *(Greek, meaning unknown)* One of the Gorgons, three monsters with golden wings and brass claws and snakes instead of hair. They were so terrifying that any creature who looked them in the face turned to stone. Medusa, the only mortal one of the three, was killed by the hero Perseus, who used Hermes' sword and watched her reflection in a shield loaned him by Athena. He then deployed Medusa's head to kill the sea monster that imprisoned Andromeda, and finally presented the head to Athena. The Greeks, Athena included, often used an image of Medusa on their shields and breastplates. The name was later given to a genus of jellyfish with snaky tentacles.

MEGAERA *(Greek, "full of envy")* The name of one of the Furies, also known as the "Erinyes," terrifying creatures with dogs' heads, bats' wings, snaky hair, and blood dripping from their eyes. They provide the punishment for Greeks who commit the worst crimes, like patricide—notably, they drive Oedipus mad after he kills his father Laius—until Athena tames them and turns them into fertility goddesses. From then on they are known as "the Kindly Ones."

MELINDA *(Greek, "honey")* The *inda* ending was very fashionable in the eighteenth century, when Tobias Smollett wrote *Roderick Random*. Melinda Goosetrap is a young heiress and "reigning toast" or great belle whom the hero Roderick Random courts. Her name is clearly emblematic—Roderick is the goose, trapped by the honey, for he plays cards with Melinda and she wins a large sum from him, possibly by cheating. Melinda Sprague in Horatio Alger, Jr.'s *Struggling Upward* is "a maiden lady, who took a profound interest in the affairs of her neighbors." In other words, the inquisitive spinster in the small town where the novel is set. Her nosiness and malice set up the events that prove the worth of the young hero, Luke.

MELISSA *(Greek, "bee")* A benevolent prophetess and sorceress in Ludovico Ariosto's *Orlando Furioso.* She lives in Merlin's cave and intervenes several times during the epic to help the Christian hero Ruggiero and the brave warrior maiden Bradamante.

MELPOMENE *(*mel poh' meh nee; *Greek, "the one who sings")* In Greek myth, as related in Hesiod's poem the *Theogony,* Melpomene is one of the nine Muses, daughters of Zeus and Mnemosyne. The mother was a Titan, the goddess of memory— our word "mnemonic" comes from her name. She shared her knowledge of the world's history with her daughters. Each one of the Muses inspired the artists and intellectuals who practiced her particular craft; Melpomene was the muse of tragedy, and is often pictured with a tragic mask.

MERCY *(English virtue name)* **Mercy** was used as a name in literature before it was adopted by parents for real-life use. It occurs first as an emblematic name, symbolizing the quality of forbearance extended to mankind by a powerful God. In Edmund Spenser's *The Faerie Queen,* Mercy is a matron in the House of Holiness where the Red Cross Knight is taken to be healed from his wounds in Book One. Spenser uses an elaboration, **Mercilla,** in Book Four. She represents the quality of mercy, of course, but is also another image of Queen Elizabeth I, Spenser's patron. Mercilla is attended by a court and dispenses justice. Another emblematic Mercy appears in the second part of John Bunyan's *The Pilgrim's Progress,* which follows the travels of Christian's wife to the Celestial City. Mercy is a comely young lady and marries the eldest son of Christian and Christiana.

In the seventeenth century, Puritans avoided the use of saints' names for their children and chose Old Testament names or names embodying the Christian virtues. Mercy is one of the most prominent of these, and Charles Dickens makes a little joke when he names the two Pecksniff sisters in *Martin Chuzzlewit* Mercy and Charity. (Not content with that, he makes their nicknames "Merry" and "Cherry.") Mercy is the younger, prettier sister who has the misfortune to marry sadistic, conniving Jonas Chuzzlewit. Elizabeth Stoddard's *The Morgesons* is set in small-town Massachusetts early in the nineteenth century, when names were still taken from the Bible or from the family headstones in a cemetery. Mercy Warren is the kindly, fussy aunt of the narrator Cassandra Morgeson. Unlike her niece, she is content in her limited life, possibly because she prefers her many plants to the human beings who surround her.

Mercédès is the Spanish version of the name, and may refer to one of the titles of the Virgin Mary, "Maria de las Mercedes," or "Mary of the Mercies." In Alexandre Dumas's *The Count of Monte Cristo*, Mercédès is the pretty young Marseillaise wench who is engaged to hardworking sailor Edmond Dantès. When Dantès is embroiled in a plot and imprisoned in the Château d'If, she marries wily Fernand Mondego, unaware that he is Edmond's enemy.

> *"That child,"* said my aunt Mercy, *looking at me with indigo-colored eyes, "is possessed."*
> —ELIZABETH STODDARD, *THE MORGESONS*

MERTILLA *(Italian, "myrtle")* Aphra Behn's *Love-Letters Between a Nobleman and His Sister* is the thinly disguised account of a love affair that scandalized the English court in the seventeenth century. Mertilla is the sister of Silvia, a virgin who was seduced by her brother-in-law—Mertilla's husband. Mertilla is in turn seduced by Cesario, who represents the Duke of Monmouth, Charles II's illegitimate son. Myrtle has significance dating back to Greek myth, when it was associated with Aphrodite, the goddess of love.

MILDRED *(Old English, "mild strength")* A name that was more popular in the United States than in England in the late nineteenth

THE MEDIEVAL REVIVAL

"Ethel is my cousin," replies little Newcome; "Aunt Ann's daughter. There's Ethel and Alice, and Aunt Ann wanted the baby to be called Boadicea, only uncle wouldn't; and there's Barnes and Egbert and little Alfred." William Thackeray set *The Newcomes* in the 1820s and '30s, though he wrote it in 1855. This artless confidence from young Clive Newcome describes a naming fashion of the nineteenth century whose effects still linger: the medieval or antiquarian revival.

Some scholars attribute the revival to Sir Walter Scott, whose historical novels like *Ivanhoe* were immensely popular. Scott's success may equally have been a symptom of a more widespread phenomenon, a fascination with the past that informed art and architecture in the Victorian era. The Houses of Parliament, designed in 1835–40 by Charles Barry and Augustus Pugin, are probably the most familiar examples of the English Gothic Revival.

But the names are familiar as well. **Ethel,** for instance, a very fashionable name until the 1930s, is a medieval revival. **Albert, Mildred,** and **Winifred** are, too. They may lack appeal to us today—these are the names of our grandparents and great-grandparents. They're old-fashioned, but not old enough to be charming. A hundred and fifty years ago, however, they were artifacts of the exotic Olden Time, and all the rage.

century; nicknames were **Milly** or **Millie.** Henry James uses it for the immensely wealthy Milly Theale in *The Wings of the Dove.* A young American girl traveling in England, she becomes friendly with Kate Croy and Merton Densher, who are secretly lovers. Kate is under pressure from her aunt to marry a rich man but Densher is merely a journalist. Kate manages to find out that Milly is mortally ill and hatches a plan for Merton to woo and marry Milly whose money he would inherit on her death. James makes Milly's name soft and mellifluous while Kate, the more active and aggressive character, has a very percussive name. James may have modeled Milly in part on a much-loved cousin of his, Minny Temple, who had died of tuberculosis in 1869.

> *Millicent, to hear her talk, only asked to keep her skirts clear and marry some respectable tea-merchant.*
> —HENRY JAMES, *THE PRINCESS CASAMASSIMA*

MILLICENT *(Old German, "noble force")* Also **Milicent.** In Anne Brontë's *The Tenant of Wildfell Hall,* Milicent Hargrave is a friend of the mysterious Helen Graham from her earlier life in London. This sweet, sensible woman's affection for Helen lends the tragic heroine some credibility. In Henry James's *The Princess Casamassima,* Millicent Henning also serves to provide context to a principal character. In this case, she is a beautiful, confident shop girl from Lomax Place, the working-class neighborhood where protagonist Hyacinth Robinson grows up. As he moves in more aristocratic circles, her friendly vulgarity marks the contrast between the two worlds he must bridge.

> *"Ah, that wonderful Madam Mina! She has man's brain—a brain that a man should have were he much gifted—and woman's heart."*
> —BRAM STOKER, *DRACULA*

MINA *(Diminutive of* **Wilhelmina:** *German, "will helmet")* A large portion of the narrative of Bram Stoker's *Dracula* is presented in the form of Mina Murray's diary. The fiancée of solicitor Jonathan Harker, she is at first a spectator of the vampire mystery, but as Jonathan gets drawn into the tale, she becomes a participant. She is attacked by Dracula and forced to drink some of his blood, so that he can call her. The vampire expert Van Helsing, who admires Mina immensely, hypnotizes her to find out more about her experience with the Undead.

MINERVA *(Latin mythology name)* The Roman name for the gray-eyed goddess of wisdom whom the Greeks called **Athena**. When an oracle told Jupiter that Metis would bear him a child who would rule the gods, he swallowed the woman whole. Minerva duly manifested herself as a crashing pain in her father's head. When Vulcan split Jupiter's head with an axe, Minerva sprang out, fully armed. She was the special protector of her city, Athens, and like Diana, the other cranky virgin of Mount Olympus, she was easily offended by mortals.

MINNEHAHA *(Native American, "laughing waters")* Henry Wadsworth Longfellow's long narrative about the Ojibway brave Hiawatha was written in 1855. Minnehaha, often referred to as "Laughing Water" in the poem, is his beautiful wife who has all of the virtuous attributes of Victorian womanhood.

> *Ferdinand:* I do beseech you—
>   Chiefly that I might set it in my prayers—
>   What is your name?
> *Miranda:*   Miranda.—O my father!
>   I have broke your hest to say so.
> *Ferdinand:*   Admir'd Miranda!
>   Indeed, the top of admiration; worth
>   What's dearest to the world!
>   —WILLIAM SHAKESPEARE, THE TEMPEST

MIRANDA *(Latin, "admirable")* Coined by Shakespeare for the heroine of his final play, *The Tempest*. Miranda is the daughter of Prospero, raised by him on his magic island, and when she sees

Ferdinand, the young Prince of Naples, is astonished and instantly loves him. This is, of course, precisely what her father has intended.

MIRIAM *(Hebrew, meaning disputed, possibly "sea of bitterness" or "rebellion")* In the Old Testament, Miriam is a prophet, the elder sister of Moses and Aaron. Nathaniel Hawthorne's *The Marble Faun,* written in 1860, is one of the first American novels to take up the issue (later so dear to Henry James) of how Americans interact with European culture. It concerns three young artists in Rome, a sculptor and two painters. Miriam is one of the latter, a beautiful young woman of mysterious antecedents who has attracted the allegiance of the young Italian Donatello. Some crime or sin lurks in her past and entangles all four of the characters, with grave results. Henry James later used the name for Miriam Rooth, the talented but farouche young actress in *The Tragic Muse.* Half English, half German Jewish, she is unskilled in her craft but focused, even "ruthless" in her pursuit of it.

The name is the root of **Mary** and also occurs as **Mirah.** In both Honoré de Balzac's *Cousin Bette* and George Eliot's *Daniel Deronda,* Mirah is a beautiful Jewish singer, but the resemblances end there. Balzac's story, characteristically, is one of cynicism and sexual obsession. His Mirah Josephs adopts the name **Josépha** and becomes the mistress first of the perfumer Crevel, then of Baron Hulot, whom she in turn leaves for the protection of the Duc d'Hérouville. Mirah Cohen in *Daniel Deronda* is by contrast an honest and scrupulously moral young girl who ran away from her father because he tried to force her into prostitution. Daniel Deronda saves her when she tries to commit suicide, and his search for the rest of her family illuminates his own growing affinity for Judaism.

> *The truth was, that nobody knew anything about Miriam, either for good or evil.*
> —NATHANIEL HAWTHORNE, *THE MARBLE FAUN*

MODESTY *(English virtue name)* Thomas Hardy clearly relished the unusual names used by farm workers in rural England, for not only did he call Tess of the D'Urberville's sister Modesty, he also alludes to minor characters in other novels with names like **Temperance** and **Soberness**. Charlotte Brontë seems to have taken some of the same pleasure in French names. In *Villette*, the head of the boarding school where heroine Lucy Snowe teaches is known by the French form, **Modeste**. (Her full name is Modeste Maria Beck, but of course she is generally known by her formal title, Madame Beck.) A cool, calm professional, she runs the school with great efficiency and resents Lucy's potentially disruptive romance with her kinsman Paul Emanuel.

> *"My name's Molly. It is an old-fashioned name, and I was christened Mary. But papa likes Molly."*
> *"That's right. Keep to the good old fashions, my dear."*
> *"Well, I must say I think Mary is prettier than Molly, and quite as old a name, too," said Mrs. Hamley.*
> —ELIZABETH GASKELL, *WIVES AND DAUGHTERS*

MOLLY *(Diminutive of **Mary**)* Daniel Defoe's *Moll Flanders* is the nominal autobiography of a woman who was born in prison and had an extraordinarily eventful life thereafter. Ambitious, good-looking, and resourceful, she is terrified of being poor. She marries five times (one of her husbands turns out to be her brother), is a prostitute for twelve years, and finally ends up as an owner of a Maryland plantation, rich, honest, and "penitent," as Defoe says. The personality that emerges from her narrative is kind-hearted and morally scrupulous. Not so Molly Seagrim, the gamekeeper's daughter in Henry Fielding's *Tom Jones*. She seduces innocent Tom and persuades him that he is the father of her unborn child, but he soon finds that he is not her only lover.

Molly Gibson in Elizabeth Gaskell's *Wives and Daughters* is one of the daughters of the title, the only child of the widowed Dr.

Gibson. When he remarries, his wife's daughter Cynthia joins the family. Molly is honest, brave, unpretentious, and grows into a very pretty girl in the course of the book. She is not pretty enough, however, to attract the attention of the squire's son Roger Hamley, whom she loves. He falls instead for the fascinating Cynthia.

MONA *(Irish Gaelic, "noble")* When Henry James chooses to be satiric at a character's expense, the result is often exquisitely comical. One of his funniest creations is the tall, handsome, vapid Mona Brigstock of *The Spoils of Poynton*. Adela Gereth has devoted much of her life to the refined beauty of the house called Poynton, and hopes that her son Owen will cherish it. But when Owen gets engaged to Mona, the doom of Poynton is plain. Not only was Mona reared in a vast Victorian monstrosity called "Waterbath," she is monumentally stupid. "Her expression would probably have been beautiful if she had had one," says James. Even Owen begins to have his doubts about her.

> *Mona met intense looks, however, with eyes that might have been blue beads.* —HENRY JAMES, *THE SPOILS OF POYNTON*

MONICA *(Origin unclear, possibly Latin "advisor")* The proud old Thorne family of Ullathorne plays a minor part in Anthony Trollope's Barsetshire novels. Remote cousins of Dr. Thorne (who is the protagonist of the eponymous novel), brother Wilfred and sister Monica Thorne pride themselves on their ancient ancestry and are among the most conservative denizens of the county. Miss Thorne even attempts to persuade her guests to play picturesque Elizabethan games at her annual garden party in *Barchester Towers*. Monica Madden in George Gissing's *The Odd Women* is the youngest sister of the unfortunate Alice and Celia Madden. Gentlewomen who were left orphaned without money or education, they are reduced to serving as companions to wealthier women. Monica, because she is young and pretty, "will marry," as her sisters predict. Her choice, however, does not provide her with a carefree existence, for she is wooed by reactionary Edmund Widdowson. He believes that he has the right to control his wife utterly and quashes Monica's attempts at independence.

MORGAN *(Welsh, "great and bright")* Also **Morgane** and **Morgana**. Morgan le Fay appears in the Arthurian legends as Arthur's sister or half sister, and a sorceress. In *Sir Gawain and the Green Knight* she is an ugly, wrinkled hag who has concocted the trial of Sir Gawain as a way to dishonor Camelot. She steals Excalibur in *Le Morte D'Arthur* and appears in Ariosto's *Orlando* epics as Fata Morgana. Even Mark Twain hews to the usual script—in *A Connecticut Yankee in King Arthur's Court* Morgan le Fay is a cruel sorceress who knifes a page reflexively because he jostles her—then continues on her way to Mass.

MORGIANA *(Meaning unknown)* The resourceful slave of Ali Baba in *Tales from the Thousand and One Nights*. It is quick-thinking Morgiana who immobilizes the forty thieves by pouring boiling oil on them as they lurk in Ali Baba's immense jars. Furthermore, she recognizes their captain dining with her master, and seizes the occasion of a dagger dance to stab him.

MYRA *(Origin unclear)* A literary name coined in the sixteenth century, possibly as a feminization of Myron, which means "scented oil" in Greek. It could also be construed as relating to Miranda (Latin, "admirable") and its use in William Hill Brown's *The Power of Sympathy* may support this theory. Brown's novel was one of the first published in the United States and deals with the seduction of the innocent young Harriot by Harrington, a young man of the gentry. Myra is Harrington's sister, more sophisticated that the unworldly Harriot. She is engaged to be married to Harrington's friend Worthy, which seems to be an attribute name rather than a naturalistic choice. Perhaps Myra is meant to be admired.

MYRRHA *(Greek from Hebrew, "bitter")* Myrrha, in Ovid's *Metamorphoses,* is the Greek king's daughter who is seized by an incestuous love for her father. With the help of her nurse, she tricks him into sleeping with her, and the child of this union is Adonis. In her penitence, she turns into a myrtle tree. (The aromatic, resinous substance known as myrrh is actually the sap of *Balsamodendron myrrha,* known as "Arabian myrtle.") Lord Byron reverts to this tale in his drama "Sardanapalus," about the Assyrian king who burned himself, his wife, and his possessions rather than surrender to his enemies in 880 B.C. Myrrha is an Ionian slave, his favorite, who urges him to courage and accompanies him to the pyre. There are hints that she has a similar history to that of Adonis's mother. Byron, of course, could not be as explicit as Ovid.

NADYA *(Russian, "hope")* Also **Nadia, Nadja.** Anton Chekhov's short story "The Fiancée" concerns Nadya, a restless young woman who is about to be married to the son of a nearby priest. Attendant at the festivities is a remote cousin, Sasha, who is poor but cultured. He talks earnestly to Nadya, opening her eyes to possibilities she had not considered. A longer form of the name, **Nadezhda,** appears in another Chekhov story, "With Friends." The protagonist Podgorin renews contact with a group of old friends. One of them, Nadezhda, is even supposed to be his fiancée. He stays with Nadezhda's married sister Tatyana and discovers that his friends pick his brains for financial advice and borrow money from him. He concludes that he is "very fond of them, but more in memory than in actuality, it seemed."

NANCY *(Diminutive of **Anne:** Hebrew, "grace")* Also **Nan.** In the nineteenth century, names and styles of address were clear markers of social class, and it was the lot of those lowest on the ladder to endure familiarity from their social superiors. Thus a name like Nancy was relegated to the lower classes. In Anne Brontë's *Agnes Grey,* the earnest governess heroine visits humble Nancy Brown in her cottage on the estate. And in Charles Dickens's *Oliver Twist,* terrifying Bill Sikes has a girlfriend named Nancy. She loves Bill and tolerates his violence but he ultimately beats her to death. In France the equivalent of Nancy might be considered **Nanon,** which Honoré de Balzac uses for a servant in *Eugénie Grandet.* She is known as "Big Nanon" because she looms over her five-feet-tall master Félix Grandet by eight inches. She even matches him in his capacity for avarice.

Nana is more of an endearment than Nanon, and it is the name of one of Émile Zola's most memorable characters. Nana, called Anna at her birth, is the daughter of Gervaise in *L'Assommoir.* When the reader meets her in *Nana,* she has become a stage phenomenon. Her vitality and her looks make her immensely alluring to men, and her appearance in any theatrical piece guarantees a certain kind of risqué success. Nana's sense of self-preservation is not very highly developed, however, and she makes poor choices of "protectors." She takes up with an actor who beats her, loses her appeal to the audience, and ends up in squalor.

NARCISSA *(Feminization of* **Narcissus:** *Greek, "daffodil")* Tobias Smollett's *Roderick Random* is the story of a scapegrace young Scot in search of a fortune. While serving as a footman in an English house he meets beautiful, dark-haired Narcissa and falls madly in love with her. The joke is that he talks of her nobility and amiable character, when it is obvious he simply lusts after the girl. The mythological Greek youth Narcissus was also memorably good-looking.

> *I led a pretty easy and comfortable life, drinking daily intoxicating draughts of love from the charms of Narcissa, which brightened on my contemplation every day more and more.*
> —TOBIAS SMOLLETT, *RODERICK RANDOM*

NASTASYA *(Russian, "resurrection")* Also spelled **Nastasia;** a longer version is **Anastasia.** Nikolai Gogol's *Dead Souls* is a sardonic novel about Pavel Chichikov, a man who travels the Russian countryside buying up the names of landowners' dead serfs in a complex and shady financial scheme. One of the landowners he encounters is Nastasya Petrovna Korobochka, a dim-witted widow who complains endlessly about her poor crops and cannot begin to comprehend Chichikov's scheme. Rather than dead serfs, she persists in trying to sell him honey, hemp, and other products of her farm, none of which he wants. Fyodor Dostoyevsky chose names for his characters with great attention to meaning and connotation. What could he mean, then, by naming the femme fatale of *The Idiot* Nastasya? She is not resurrected or redeemed in any obvious way in the novel. A strikingly lovely woman of twenty-five, she was raised by Prince Totsky to be his mistress, but she is irresistible to several of the other characters in the book. She even becomes engaged to the "idiot" of the title, Prince Leo Myshkin.

NATASHA *(Russian, "birthday")* In other words, the birthday of Jesus, or Christmas Day. The given name in Russian is ordinarily **Natalya** or **Natalia**, though it was sometimes turned into the French **Natalie**. Natasha Rostov is one of the most compelling characters in the vast tapestry of Leo Tolstoy's *War and Peace*. She goes from a self-willed, naive young girl to the powerful matriarch of a complex Russian household. Throughout, Tolstoy stresses her warmth and enthusiasm and passion for life. The simplicity that led her to betray her fiancé Prince Andrei Bolkonsky for the decadence of Anatoly Kuragin is tempered by her experience of the war. She nurses the wounded Andrei in the final days of his life and in her chastened, mature new guise, attracts the love of Pierre Bezuhov. In Chekhov's play *The Three Sisters*, Natasha Prozorov is the sister-in-law. Married to Andrei Prozorov, she is the crude, selfish provincial girl who blights the hopes of the entire Prozorov family. She is blatantly unfaithful to her husband but has the sheer force of will to dictate the terms on which he and his sisters continue to live together—in stagnant misery.

NAUSICAA *(*naw si' kay a; *Greek mythology name)* In *The Odyssey*, Nausicaa is the beautiful daughter of King Alcinous of Phaeacia. When she and her handmaidens are washing their clothes at the beach, they find the naked Odysseus washed up from a shipwreck. Quick-thinking Nausicaa, who finds Odysseus very appealing, thinks of the cleverest way to present the newcomer to her father. She falls in love with him, but Odysseus wants only to reach his home in Ithaka.

NELL *(Diminutive of* **Helen** *and* **Eleanor***)* Like **Nancy, Nell** (and the elaborated forms, **Nelly** and **Nellie**) is an informal name indicating modest social status. In Emily Brontë's *Wuthering Heights,* Nelly Dean is the housekeeper of the Heathcliff clan, and much of their story is told through her eyes. She is very loyal to the family without being blind to their faults. Nell Trent of *The Old Curiosity Shop* is one of Dickens's most sentimental creations. A fresh young girl, she lives with her grandfather in the shop of the title. When the shop is sold to satisfy his gambling debts, he and Nell must take to the roads as beggars. The novel was serialized in England for several months and readers became very fond of Little Nell, who was sweet and pure and kind. As she became ill, they would plead with Dickens to let the character live, but he felt the story required her death. He was, however, an emotional wreck after he had written her touching deathbed scene.

> *She was dead. Dear, gentle, patient, noble Nell, was dead. Her little bird—a poor slight thing the pressure of a finger would have crushed—was stirring nimbly in its cage; and the strong heart of its child-mistress was mute and motionless forever.* —CHARLES DICKENS, THE OLD CURIOSITY SHOP

NERISSA *(Greek, "sea nymph")* A fanciful name used by Shakespeare for Portia's maid in *The Merchant of Venice.*

NICOLE *(French feminization of* **Nicholas***: Greek, "victory people")* In Molière's *The Would-Be Gentleman,* Nicole is the pert maid. This is a stock character in Molière's comedies, the only character who sees through the pretensions and follies of her employers and social superiors. The name also occurs in anglophone countries as **Nicola** or **Nichola,** the form that Thomas Hardy uses in *The Well-Beloved.* This novel is a mediation on one man's search for the Ideal in women—and how that quest prevents his ever finding domestic happiness. Nichola Pine-Avon is, by any standard, an attractive and eligible mate for protagonist Jocelyn Pierston. She is a wealthy, pretty, aristocratic widow who finds him appealing. For a brief moment he believes that she has the capacity to be "the Well-Beloved," but a coldness of manner discourages him and he rejects her. He feels justified when he meets her years later, after she has married a friend of his and had several children, and she seems appallingly ordinary.

NINA *(Spanish, "girl")* Not a name that was widely used in anglophone countries. Anthony Trollope set up a joke in *The Eustace Diamonds* when he gave the timid Lord Fawn eight sisters, all of whose names end with *a*. Nina is the youngest and her name may be something of a stretch in plausibility. On the other hand the name is quite common in Russia, where it is considered a diminutive of **Anna**. Nina Zarechnaia is one of the principal characters in Chekhov's drama *The Seagull*. She is a young neighbor of the landowner Sorin, and has ambitions to be an actress. When Sorin entertains his sister Irena Arkadina and Arkadina's lover Trigorin, Nina is drawn into their circle. She is the "seagull" referred to in the title, full of aspiration but liable at any time to be brought down in her flight. Trigorin seduces her and she bears his child, who later dies, but she does succeed in her ambition to become an actress.

Charles Dickens plays with the name in *Nicholas Nickleby*. Ninetta Crummles is the youngest member of the Crummles's theatrical troupe, and she is commonly known as "the Infant Phenomenon." In fact, in the five years Nicholas stays with the Crummles, she never gets a year older. **Ninetta** is an elaboration of a name that means "child," and stresses the character's youth.

NIOBE *(nigh oh' bee; Greek mythology name)* Ovid's *Metamorphoses* tells the story of Niobe, a descendant of the gods. She brags about her numerous children (seven sons and seven daughters), her illustrious ancestors, her beauty, and her stature as queen of Thebes, contrasting all of these attributes to the mere twins that Leto has borne. "I am beyond the reach of Fortune's blows," she claims. This, of course, is the kind of statement the

Greeks called hubris, and sure enough, Niobe is amply punished by Apollo and Diana, Leto's scorned twins. She loses every one of her children and her husband, then turns to stone—but her petrified face perpetually weeps. She was a subject much loved by Victorian sculptors. There is a metal in the Table of Elements named for her. Niobium is closely related to tantalum—so-called for its inability to absorb acid. (Tantalus, Niobe's father, was punished for *his* hubris by having to stand in the middle of a lake, suffering eternal thirst yet unable to reach the water.)

NOÉMIE *(noh ay mee'; French for* Naomi: *Hebrew, "delight, pleasantness") The American* is one of the novels in which Henry James explicitly contrasts American and European cultures. Christopher Newman is an American in Paris who cannot distinguish among the various segments of French society. He meets Noémie Nioche at the Louvre, where she is copying paintings. She sells him a canvas for a ludicrously inflated price, a point he does not grasp until later in the book. She also flirts with him, which he finds exciting. It is only with growing sophistication that he apprehends her place in the demimonde, rather than the world of Paris's aristocrats that he finds much more attractive.

NOKOMIS *(Native American, "daughter of the moon")* Henry Wadsworth Longfellow's long narrative poem about the Ojibway brave Hiawatha was written in 1855. He is raised by his grandmother Nokomis, a woman of great wisdom, who lives with him even after he marries Minnehaha.

NORA *(Diminutive of* **Eleanor**: *Greek, "light")* Also spelled **Norah,** as in Wilkie Collins's *No Name.* Norah Vanstone is the elder of two sisters who are revealed as illegitimate upon their father's death. Norah is gentle, reserved, and staid, in contrast to her more resourceful and ruthless sister Magdalen. To support herself, Norah becomes a governess, the conventional choice for a genteel but poverty-stricken young lady. Nora Rowley in Trollope's *He Knew He Was Right* is the somewhat spoiled younger sister of Emily Trevelyan. Pretty, charming, and fond of a luxurious life, Nora is expected to do her best to attract a wealthy husband so that she can, in turn, find rich men for her numerous sisters to marry. Alas, Nora's heart refuses to be guided by financial concerns. The novel sheds a discouraging light on the limited options for women in Trollope's day. Victorian mores also bind Nora Helmer, the heroine of Henrik Ibsen's *A Doll's House*—as the play opens, at least. She is the highstrung, immature wife of sober, controlling Torvald. He sees her as little more than a plaything, a pretty creature who is supposed to reflect his views, but in the course of the play Nora begins to understand that his protection is also repression.

> *"Nora is such a singular girl—so firm, so headstrong, so good, and so self-reliant that she will do as well with a poor man as she would have done with a rich."*
> —ANTHONY TROLLOPE, *HE KNEW HE WAS RIGHT*

OLGA *(Russian, "holy")* This was a favorite name of Anton Chekhov even before he married actress Olga Knipper in 1901. The principal character of his story "The Grasshopper," for instance, is Olga Dymov, a doctor's wife who is perpetually drawn to pretentious artists who tend to treat her badly. She seeks a great man to admire, but not until her husband dies does she realize that he was that great man. "The Party" concerns Olga Mikhaylovna who is entertaining for her husband Peter's name day. The weather is stiflingly hot and in the course of the festivities her snobbish, intolerant husband flirts with several other women and picks a fight with Olga. She ends up having a miscarriage. Olga Plemyannikov of "The Darling" is the kind of woman who "was always in love with someone and could not live without it." The story tells of her attachments to a lumber merchant, a man who runs an amusement park, and a veterinarian, and her sadness when she is unattached. Olga Prozorov in *The Three Sisters* could be named for Chekhov's wife since the play was written in the year he married. Olga is the eldest of the three sisters who live unhappily in a provincial town and dream of moving to Moscow. At twenty-eight she has given up all hope of marriage and teaches at a girls' high school. The best she can hope for is to become headmistress, and the prospect embitters her.

OLIMPIA *(Greek, "from Mount Olympus")* Olympus is the home of the gods. The name occurs as **Olympia** as well, but **Olimpia** is the Italian version. In Ariosto's *Orlando Furioso*, Olimpia is a noble young beauty with romance problems. The daughter of the count of Holland, she loves Bireno, the duke of

Selandia. Her love is not requited, however. The hero Orlando intervenes, at one point she is held captive by brigands and threatened by a sea monster, then ultimately she is married off to the king of Ireland. **Olympe** (*oh lahmp'*), the French form of the name, is used by Émile Zola in *The Earth*. Set in the deepest countryside, this novel takes an unromantic look at the brutal life of the rural peasantry. Olympe, for all the grandiosity of her name, is a poor, unkempt tomboy known to the village as "the brat." She keeps a flock of geese, and has neither father nor mother to care for her.

> *Our second child, a girl, I intended to call after her aunt Grissel but my wife, who during her pregnancy had been reading romances, insisted on her being called Olivia.*
> —OLIVER GOLDSMITH, THE VICAR OF WAKEFIELD

OLIVIA *(Latin, "olive tree")* In ancient Greece the olive was a symbol of Athena as well as a token of peace and of fertility, and olive wreaths were awarded to the winners at the Olympic games. Shakespeare's *Twelfth Night* is set in Illyria, which is now the Croatian coast of the Adriatic. It was long under Italian domination, and many characters in the play have Italian names. Olivia is the countess beloved by the duke of Illyria, Orsino. She, however, ignores him to mourn her dead brother. Only the appearance in Illyria of the shipwrecked Cesario is enough to end her mourning—but Cesario, as the audience knows but Olivia does not, is actually a woman, Viola. In Oliver Goldsmith's charming *The Vicar of Wakefield,* the narrator, kindly cleric Dr. Primrose, has a large family of whom Olivia is the eldest girl. A charming coquette, she is as happy to flirt with a farmer as with a young squire. She is actually seduced by the latter and her reputation is ruined until it transpires that he has legally married her. The frankness with which Goldsmith can discuss these events is an artifact of the eighteenth century and would scandalize later readers.

The name also appears without the softening *ia* ending, as

Olive, and it is thus that Henry James employs it in *The Bostonians*. Olive Chancellor is a well-to-do Boston bourgeoise with a passion for social reform. She is especially interested in the nascent cause of feminism, and the beautiful young orator Verena Tarrant sparks a new passion. Olive becomes Verena's patroness and would like to protect the girl from men, but Mississippi attorney Basil Ransom may prove too much for her.

> *There are women who are unmarried by accident, and others who are unmarried by option; but Olive Chancellor was unmarried by every implication of her being. She was a spinster as Shelley was a lyric poet, or as the month of August is sultry.* —HENRY JAMES, *THE BOSTONIANS*

OPHELIA *(Greek, "help" or "innocence")* Most famously, the daughter of Polonius in Shakespeare's *Hamlet*. Young, virginal, and beautiful, Ophelia is a potential wife for Hamlet until, in his deepening paranoia, he kills her father. She then goes spectacularly mad and kills herself. Harriet Beecher Stowe seems to care little about this precedent in *Uncle Tom's Cabin,* for Ophelia St. Clare is a bracing, practical Vermonter. A cousin of New Orleans slave owner Augustine St. Clare, she is horrified by slavery. Augustine buys the slave Topsy for her to see if she can teach Topsy right from wrong.

OPORA *(Greek, "harvest")* Aristophanes' play *The Peace* concerns the long-drawn-out wars between Athens and Sparta. Opora is the symbolically named wife of Trygaeus, whose name means "crop grower."

OTTILIE *(French from Old German, "battle prosperous")* Johann Wolfgang von Goethe's *Elective Affinities* is a study of irresistible attraction among two men and two women. Ottilie is the foster daughter of Charlotte, who is happily married to Baron Eduard. Yet when Ottilie comes to stay at the Baron's castle, he falls madly in love with her. Her attractions are not obvious: she is reserved, even something of a cipher. Furthermore she finds Eduard's attentions appalling, and stops eating in a kind of oblique protest.

PALMYRE *(pahl meer'; French from Hebrew, "city of palms")* **Palmyra** is a form that occurs occasionally. The original source is probably the ancient Roman city in Syria whose ruins were discovered by Europeans toward the end of the seventeenth century. Why, then, would a French peasant have the name? In Émile Zola's *The Earth*, Palmyre is the granddaughter of the Fouan matriarch. Because she also has to labor to support her feebleminded younger brother Hilarion, she is "exhausted and broken-down by excessive toil," looking fifty instead of thirty. Zola proffers no explanation for the pretentious names of this pair, though they are outstanding in a village of Mariannes and Jeans and Françoises. In George Washington Cable's *The Grandissimes*, Palmyre la Philosophe is a New Orleans octoroon who practices voodoo. She is in love with a white man, but his mulatto half brother loves her.

PAMELA *(Greek, "all honey")* *Pamela*, written in 1740 by Samuel Richardson, is widely considered the first modern English novel. It is the tale of modest country girl Pamela Andrews and her earnest attempt to maintain her chastity. She works as a maid to a wealthy woman. When her mistress dies, the woman's son attempts to seduce Pamela. He even kidnaps her, but is ultimately shamed by her virtue, and marries her. Henry Fielding's *Joseph Andrews*, written two years later, is a comical retort to *Pamela*— Joseph is supposed to be Pamela's brother. Pamela herself, as Mrs. Booby, even appears briefly.

PANSY *(English flower name)* The name of the flower comes from the French *pensée*, or "thought," possibly because its blossom is thought to resemble a human face. Another old English name for the pansy is "heartsease," a point Henry James may have remembered when he named Pansy Osmond in *The Portrait of a Lady*. Pansy is the lovely, sheltered daughter of Gilbert Osmond, the aesthete whom Isabel Archer marries. Osmond has had the girl raised in a Roman convent and regards her as a project: he wishes to turn her out as the very flower of innocent girlhood, and to marry her off to an English lord. Isabel, disillusioned by her husband, is horrified to find that his great friend Madame Merle is actually Pansy's mother. She considers leaving Osmond but returns to him partly to take Pansy's side in the girl's quest for independence. Her sacrifice for Pansy's sake may possibly ease her heart.

PAQUITA *(Spanish, "Easter")* The full name is probably **Pasqualita** or **Pascualita**. Paquita Valdes is the young lady mentioned in the title of Balzac's novella "The Girl with the Golden Eyes." An ash-blond, fine-boned, sensual-looking beauty, she has eyes "yellow as a tiger's, a golden, gleaming yellow." Though carefully guarded by a fierce Spanish duenna, she makes overtures to Parisian dandy Henri de Marsay, who becomes obsessed with her. He manages, with elaborate subterfuge, to launch an affair with her though she is clearly kept by a grandee of some sort. Curiously, she is also a physical virgin, though knowing about sex. In fact, she is the sex slave of de Marsay's half sister, who ends by killing her in a jealous rage.

PATIENCE *(English virtue name)* In Anthony Trollope's *The Eustace Diamonds*, Patience Crabstick is a function more than a character, though Trollope does endow her with a few traits other than her comical name. She is Lizzie Eustace's maid, one of the characters whom Lizzie is never able to sweet-talk, and she steals the famous Eustace diamonds.

PATRICIA *(Latin, "noble, patrician")* Patty Cornbury, formally Mrs. Butler Cornbury, is the grandest lady in the neighborhood in Anthony Trollope's novel *Rachel Ray*. Yet as Trollope's use of her nickname suggests, she is warm and approachable.

PURITAN VIRTUE NAMES

When Puritanism swept England in the seventeenth century, saints' names were jettisoned. Men were often named after biblical characters, but men considerably outnumber women in the Old and New Testaments. The Puritans also turned to the virtues to name their daughters. **Faith, Hope, Charity, Patience, Temperance, Justice,** and **Fortitude** appeared, as well as other desirable traits like **Prudence, Silence,** and **Modesty.** Other abstract concepts occurred as names for boys, like **Desire**—which meant desire for a savior, certainly not *lust.* The eminent Mathers, preachers in Massachusetts, counted a son named **Increase,** referring to the Holy Spirit. And early New York history notes a man named **Preserved** whose surname, unfortunately, was Fish.

PAULA (*Latin, "small"*) Paula Power, in Thomas Hardy's *A Laodicean,* is a young lady uncomfortably straddling the present and the past. She lives in Stancy Castle and wishes to renovate it to a "romantic and historical" form. Yet she is a very modern woman, independent, self-determined, addicted to modern conveniences like the telegraph. Her architect, George Somerset, thinks much more clearly on the conflict between preservation and modernity and is able to set her straight, as well as to romance her. His name is pointedly redolent of English history, while hers, especially the last name, seems a construct of the Industrial Revolution.

Paulina and **Pauline** are more elaborate forms of the name, and somewhat more common until the modern era. Shakespeare used Paulina for the strong-minded friend of Queen Hermoine in *The Winter's Tale.* In Honoré de Balzac's fantastic novel *The Wild Ass's Skin,* Pauline de Gaudin is the intelligent, beautiful daughter of protagonist Raphaël de Valentin's landlady. Raphaël, a handsome but destitute young marquis, was on the verge of suicide until he found the enchanted skin of the wild ass. It can grant any wish, but shrinks each time it does so, and Raphaël intuits that when it vanishes he will die. He first uses the skin to improve his financial situation, to provide himself with a beautiful house and financial security. He is surprised to meet Pauline in his new social circle, but her father, long lost in the Napoleonic Wars, has come back with a fortune and she is now a suitable fiancée for him. He falls in love with her, but realizes that he cannot marry her, for every time he feels sexual desire for her, he shortens his life. The Russian form of the name is **Polina,** and Anton Chekhov uses it in his tale "Three Years." Alexei Laptev is the shy and undistinguished man who falls in love with the daughter of his sister's doctor. Polina Rassudin is Laptev's old flame and confidante, an eccentric musician who believes that he has married badly.

> *"May I call you Paula?" asked he.*
> *"Yes, occasionally," she murmured.*
> *"Dear Paula!—may I call you that?"*
> *"Oh no—not yet."* —THOMAS HARDY, *A LAODICEAN*

PEARL *(English jewel name)* Nathaniel Hawthorne's use of **Pearl** predates the Victorian popularity of jewel names by at least ten years. What's more, though *The Scarlet Letter* was written in 1850, it was set in the mid-seventeenth century when names were ordinarily drawn from the Old Testament. But Pearl, the offspring of Hester Prynne by the minister Arthur Dimmesdale, is a symbolic creature. Elfin and clever, she is more a sprite than a child. The very circumstances of her parentage set her outside all social control; she is "a born outcast of the infantile world."

> *But she named the infant "Pearl" as being of great price—*
> *purchased with all she had,—her mother's only treasure!*
> —NATHANIEL HAWTHORNE, *THE SCARLET LETTER*

PEGGY *(Diminutive of* **Margaret:** *Greek, "pearl")* In William Thackeray's *Vanity Fair,* Peggy O'Dowd is an almost cartoonishly Irish character. Her husband, Major Michael O'Dowd, is the regimental commander of George Osborn and William Dobbin. She is especially kind to Amelia Sedley Osborne, downtrodden wife of the rakish George.

PENELOPE *(Greek, "bobbin")* In *The Odyssey,* Penelope is Odysseus's wife, left behind for twenty years, besieged by suitors who demand her hospitality. Homer portrays her as "wary and reserved." She tells the suitors that she will not marry until she has finished weaving a shroud for her father-in-law, but at night, she unravels her work. (Hence the bobbin of her name.) When Odysseus finally comes back she does not accept him right away, testing him instead to see if he possesses information that only her husband would know. Jane Austen uses the name for one of the least attractive characters in *Persuasion,* a vulgar, pushy widow who has set her cap at Sir Walter Elliot. Penelope Clay is the daughter of the Elliot solicitor and has displaced daughter Anne in Sir Walter's affections. Almost more damning than her pushy manners are her buck teeth and thick wrists—Penelope Clay is clearly no lady.

In Wilkie Collins's *The Moonstone,* Penelope Betteredge is a minor character, the pretty daughter of household steward Gabriel Betteredge, and Rachel Verinder's personal maid. She is strong-minded and affectionate, and is able to shed some light on the mystery of the Moonstone—she could even be said to have "unraveled" a portion of the conundrum. William Dean Howells's *The Rise of Silas Lapham* is the story of a nouveau riche paint manufacturer trying to make his way in the Boston society of the late nineteenth century. Silas and Persis Lapham have two daughters with Greek names, Penelope and Irene. Tom Corey, a Boston Brahmin, has been dangling after the Lapham daughters and it is assumed he wants to marry the prettier Irene. But it is outspoken Penelope he prefers.

PERDITA *(Latin, "lost")* Like **Miranda,** a Shakespearean coinage. In *The Winter's Tale,* the wronged Queen Hermione, imprisoned by her jealous husband, bears a daughter. The king refuses to acknowledge the baby and orders it to be abandoned. A shepherd finds and raises the infant Perdita to be a virtuous young woman who catches the eye of Prince Florizel of Bohemia. In a 1779 production of the play, Perdita was played by the young actress Mary Robinson, who caught the eye of the seventeen-year-old Prince of Wales. In a correspondence that somehow became quite public the prince, calling himself "Prince Florizel," negotiated with the actress to become his mistress. She was supporting a debt-ridden husband and a child at the time, and eventually succumbed to the royal proposal. Though the affair lasted only a year, she became an eighteenth-century celebrity. She was painted by Gainsborough and never escaped the nickname of Perdita.

> "... and, for the babe
> Is counted lost for ever, Perdita,
> I prithee, call't. ..."
> —WILLIAM SHAKESPEARE, THE WINTER'S TALE

PERSEPHONE see **PROSERPINE**

PERSIS *(Latin, "from Persia")* One of the principal impediments to Silas Lapham's social climbing (see **Penelope,** above) is his hopelessly provincial wife Persis. Ultimately, however, she is a staunch support to him when his business speculations fail and he must go back to Vermont to sell high-quality paint—the "Persis Brand."

PETRA *(Feminization of* **Peter:** *Greek, "rock")* Thomas Stockmann in Henrik Ibsen's *A Public Enemy* is the brother of a small town's mayor. He discovers that the public baths, the town's source of prosperity, are making people sick. It is his proposal that the baths be closed down that makes him a public enemy, and his daughter Petra, a schoolteacher, supports him in his crusade, though she is fired from her job.

PHAEDRA *(Greek mythology name)* In Greek myth, Phaedra is the sister of Ariadne, Minos of Crete's daughter. It was Ariadne who gave Theseus thread to help him return from the labyrinth after killing the Minotaur. It was also Ariadne whom Theseus first intended to marry. But on the homeward-bound ship, his preference shifted to her sister Phaedra. He left Ariadne on the island of Naxos, carrying Phaedra home to Athens. Euripides' drama *Hippolytus* focuses on the aftermath of this choice. Phaedra falls madly in love with her young and handsome stepson Hippolytus. (Aphrodite's meddling prompts this affection.) She wastes away, and when Hippolytus scorns her, she commits suicide, leaving a note for Theseus that accuses the young man of rape. Theseus is horrified and calls upon Poseidon to destroy Hippolytus. In the seventeenth century, Jean Racine adapted the story in his tragedy *Phaedra,* making the Cretan a victim of overwhelming passion rather than (as in Euripides' version) the whims of the gods.

PHILOMELA *(Greek, "lover of song")* In *Metamorphoses* Ovid tells the story of Philomela, the sister of Procne, who is married to Tereus, king of Thrace. Escorting Philomela on a visit to her sister, Tereus rapes her and then cuts out her tongue so that she can never betray him. But Philomela weaves a tapestry that depicts the whole story and sends it to Procne. In revenge, Procne kills Tereus's son and feeds him to his father. Procne, Tereus, and Philomela are all turned into birds, but it is Philomela, robbed of speech, who becomes a nightingale, with a beautiful song. Both Matthew Arnold and Samuel Taylor Coleridge wrote poems based on the tale.

PHOEBE *(Greek, "bright, shining")* Also **Phebe.** In Shakespeare's *As You Like It,* Phebe is one of the rustic denizens of the forest of Eden, but she and her male counterpart Silvius (whose name means "woods") are parodies of rustic swains rather than the genuine article. They speak in polished verse and have no practical relationship with the forest. Phebe falls in love with "Ganymede," who is Rosalind in male garb. Nathaniel Hawthorne takes great advantage of the name's associations in *The House of* *the Seven Gables.* It is derived from the Greek word *phoibos,* which means "brightness" and was another name for Apollo. In addition, a phoebe is a tuneful American bird, and a kind of primitive oil lamp shaped like a bird. Thus Phoebe Pyncheon is not exactly subtly named. She is the fresh, cheerful young girl who comes to live with her elderly cousin Hepzibah at the House of the Seven Gables. Energetic, optimistic, and musical, she brings new light and comfort to the ancient house and its owner simply by moving a chair, opening a shutter, or bringing a jug of daffodils indoors. By the late nineteenth century the name Phoebe was not fashionable among the upper classes, but had a modest, old-fashioned ring. In Mary Elizabeth Braddon's *Lady Audley's Secret,* Phoebe Marks is Lady Audley's heartless, scheming maid, a match for every bit of ambitious plotting her mistress can think up. Phoebe Browning, in Elizabeth Gaskell's *Wives and Daughters,* is one of the humble Browning sisters in the small town of Hollingford. Lower in class than Doctor Gibson, they are nevertheless very fond of his daughter Molly. When Lady Harriet Cumnor mocks them, Molly Gibson hotly defends them.

> *Little Phoebe was one of those persons who possess, as their exclusive patrimony, the gift of practical arrangement.*
> —NATHANIEL HAWTHORNE, *THE HOUSE OF THE SEVEN GABLES*

PHYLLIS *(Greek, "leafy branch")* The Greek word fragment *phyll* means leaf, as in "chlorophyll." In his poem "The Legend of Good Women" Geoffrey Chaucer unites the stories of women wronged in love. One of them is Phyllis (or **Phillis**), the queen of Rhodope. On his way home from Troy the warrior Demophon lands on her island and requests her aid, which she willingly gives. He seduces her, promises marriage, then sails away. This pattern of seduction and abandonment appears repeatedly in "The Legend of Good Women."

PICOTEE *(Origin unclear)* In Thomas Hardy's *The Hand of Ethelberta,* the butler Chickerel and his wife have ten children, and selected their names by a system: "The choice of the girls' names became [their mother's] prerogative, and that of the boys' her husband's, who limited his field to strict historical precedent as a set-off to Mrs. Chickerel's tendency to stray into the regions of romance." Thus Ethelberta, as well as Gwendoline, Emmeline, Georgina, Cornelia, and Myrtle. Picotee, however, is of mysterious origin. It is a term used to describe the narrow colored border of a flower's petal, as in a white carnation with red picotee edging. Hardy does not explain Mrs. Chickerel's choice, but Picotee is a young lady of substance. Bright, pretty, and susceptible to romance, she is training to be a teacher but is distracted by falling in love with musician Christopher Julian. She has none of her sister Ethelberta's driving ambition, but a much sweeter nature. Hardy calls her "an April-natured, pink-cheeked girl."

POLLY *(Nickname, usually for* **Mary** *via* **Molly***)* Fanny Burney makes clear that this is a lower-class name when she introduces Polly Branghton in *Evelina.* She and her elder sister Biddy are cousins of Evelina's, and distinctly not an asset in the polite world. Evelina has been raised as a lady and introduced to the world of fashion, which was very formal in 1778. The familiarity of her cousins, their constant talk of money and pushy behavior with her acquaintances, makes Evelina miserable. For her part, Polly thinks Evelina is a snob. Polly Home in Charlotte Brontë's *Villette* is a small, fiercely loyal young girl who seems much older than her age. She has little time for the heroine Lucy Snowe, devoting herself instead to John Graham Bretton. Years pass and she reappears as Paulina de Bassompierre, a sophisticated young lady but otherwise little changed. She serves as a foil to the unregarded heroine Lucy Snowe, for Lucy cannot compete with Paulina's cleverness and her worldly poise. Tom Sawyer, in Mark Twain's eponymous novel, lives with his Aunt Polly whom he dominates in important ways. Though she provides him with a strong background of affection she is incapable of disciplining him, and he is too crafty ever to submit to her demands for maturity or responsibility. It was, after all, Aunt Polly who wanted Tom Sawyer to paint her fence.

POLYHYMNIA *(Greek, "many hymns")* In Greek myth, the Muse of sacred song, frequently portrayed with a garland of roses. She and her eight sister Muses inspired artists and intellectuals in their respective crafts.

POMONA *(Latin mythology name)* The Latin word particle *pom* refers to fruit. Ovid's *Metamorphoses* tells the story of the skittish wood nymph Pomona who was very fond of trees, especially apple trees. She was courted by satyrs and humans but avoided them. One man named Vertumnus, however, figured out how to win her love by dressing as an old woman and helping her prune and care for her beloved trees. Thus disguised, he gave Pomona frequent and sensible advice to marry Vertumnus, pointing out Vertumnus's charms and adding, "Besides, you like the same things." His suit was successful.

PORTIA *(Latin clan name)* The clever heroine of Shakespeare's *The Merchant of Venice*. An heiress, engaged to the young aristocrat Bassanio, she sees her chance for married bliss evaporating when Bassanio's friend Antonio's debt to the usurer Shylock comes due. Shylock has required a pound of Antonio's flesh to back the loan. Though Bassanio can repay the funds, Shylock insists that Antonio honor the original agreement. The case is taken to court and Portia, disguised as a (male) Doctor of Law, successfully argues against Shylock. The courtroom drama includes Portia's famous speech that starts, "The quality of mercy is not strain'd,/It droppeth as the gentle rain from heaven . . ."

PRASKOYA *(Russian, "preparation," as for the Sabbath)* Leo Tolstoy's story "The Death of Ivan Ilyich" offers a searing look at a man's last days. As Ivan Ilyich grows more ill his superficial relationships fall away. But his wife Praskoya, with whom he has had an unsatisfying marriage, appears weeping tears of genuine grief as he nears death. Her name may point to some preparation for redemption in her husband's last days.

PRISCILLA *(Latin, "ancient, primitive")* In *The Blithedale Romance*, Nathaniel Hawthorne sets up a distinction between a pair of half sisters, the passionate Zenobia and the passive Priscilla. The latter is a very young, demure, ethereal creature who says of herself, "I never have any free will." She is manipulated by several of the characters in the novel.

PROSERPINE *(Latin mythology name)* Known in Greek myth as **Persephone**, and in Roman myth also as **Proserpina**. She is the daughter, by Jupiter, of the queen of the harvest (Ceres to the Romans, Demeter to the Greeks). Pluto (Hades) spies her picking flowers one days and whisks her off to the Underworld to be his queen. Ceres petitions Jupiter to have Proserpine returned to her, but there is a condition laid down by the Fates: if food or drink has passed her lips she will have to stay with Pluto forever. Alas, Proserpine ingested six pomegranate seeds. Jupiter decreed that she would spend six months of the year with Ceres and six with Pluto. The six months when Proserpine is with her mother are the six fertile months, when the goddess of the harvest allows crops to grow. For the other six she is in mourning: winter. Proserpine briefly appears in both Dante's *Inferno* and in Spenser's *The Faërie Queen*.

PRUDENCE *(English virtue name)* Part of Dante's *Purgatory* is devoted to the Pageant of the Sacrament, and four of the characters in it are played by the "Cardinal Virtues," dressed in purple. Prudence is distinguished by her three eyes, the third of which is Wisdom. Virtue names of this sort are much less common in France than in England, but there is a kind of sinister suitability to Balzac's use of it for Prudence Servien in *A Harlot High and Low*. She is one of a pair of servants hired by the Abbé Vautrin for Esther Gobseck—servants and bodyguards. They are known as Europe and Asie, but Europe, née Prudence, is really an ex-convict from Valenciennes who owes her life to Vautrin. She resembles a weasel, small and twitchy and "full of evil."

PSYCHE *(sy' kee; Greek, "life, soul, self")* The Greek myth of Psyche concerns a beautiful maiden who was visited every night by Eros, but never knew his identity. Ignoring his warnings, one night she lit a lamp while he was sleeping. A drop of the lamp oil wakened him and he fled forever. Edgar Allan Poe refers to this tale in his poem "Ulalume." He is walking with his "soul," Psyche, in a forbidding landscape, and comes across the tomb of his beloved Ulalume on the anniversary of her death.

> *Thus I pacified Psyche and kissed her,*
> *And tempted her out of her gloom—*
> *And conquered her scruples and gloom;*
> *And we passed to the end of the vista,*
> *But were stopped by the door of a tomb—*
> —EDGAR ALLAN POE, "ULALUME"

PYRRHA *(Greek, "red" or "tawny")* In the classical version of the flood myth, Pyrrha is the wife of Deucalion, the only man left after Jupiter floods the world. He and Pyrrha were chosen to survive because of their reverence for the gods. Following the directions of an oracle, they seed the earth with stones, and humans spring up to replace those killed in the flood.

RACHEL *(Hebrew, "ewe")* In the Old Testament, Rachel is the wife of Jacob. He wanted to marry her but had to labor seven years under her father to wed her—and was then tricked into marrying her sister Leah. After another seven years of hard work he was finally permitted to marry Rachel, who bore him Joseph and Benjamin. She is referred to in the *Inferno* as "ancestral Rachel," and Dante suggests that she was released from Limbo during the Harrowing of Hell. Dickens uses the alternate spelling, **Rachael,** for a millhand in *Hard Times* who is the patient, selfless woman loved by heroic Stephen Blackpool. Unfortunately for the lovers, Blackpool is already married to an alcoholic so his Rachael is clearly going to have to wait, as her biblical namesake did. There is also a good deal of waiting involved in Lady Castlewood's affection for Henry Esmond, in Thackeray's *The History*

of Henry Esmond. She is the stepmother of narrator Henry, only eight years older than he, and Thackeray manages to indicate that she always takes a more than warm interest in him.

> "*Rachel's best friend and Rachel's worst enemy are, one and the other—Rachel herself.*"
> —WILKIE COLLINS, *THE MOONSTONE*

In Louisa May Alcott's *Work,* the character named Rachel is as much an idea as a person. She is a quiet, refined young woman whom heroine Christie Devon meets in a sewing workroom, and who loses her job once her mistress discovers that she is a "fallen woman." Alcott and her heroine both find this treatment deeply unjust. Anthony Trollope's *Rachel Ray* falls into neither the Barchester nor the Palliser series of novels. Rather, it is the story of a genteel young girl named Rachel Ray and her anxiety-fraught romance with the jejune young heir to a brewery. Rachel is tall, pretty, blond, and steadfast—in short, virtually interchangeable with any number of Trollope's heroines. Not so Rachel Verinder, the heroine of Wilkie Collins's *The Moonstone.* Some critics suggest that, unlike most Victorian novelists, Collins wrote three-dimensional and convincing female characters because his own love life was very complex. Rachel Verinder is certainly no demure miss. A dark-haired, pretty eighteen-year-old, she is headstrong and immensely stubborn. This willfulness causes her distress when she suspects her cousin Franklin Blake of having stolen the Moonstone, an immense diamond, from her. She won't confide her suspicions but she can't ignore them either, and makes herself truly miserable.

REBECCA *(Hebrew, meaning unsure, possibly "noose" or "joined")* Another Old Testament name. The biblical Rebecca (or **Rebekah,** as the name is sometimes spelled) was the mother of Jacob and Esau. Dante places her in Paradise, enthroned among the "women of the Hebrew race." Sir Walter Scott uses the name in *Ivanhoe* for Rebecca of York, the brilliant, beautiful, and resourceful daughter of the moneylender Isaac of York. She has all the rich exoticism then attributed to Jews by Victorian English culture, and she is in love with Wilfred of Ivanhoe. He, however, must marry a Saxon girl, so Rebecca clears the field for Rowena. There is nothing exotic about William Thackeray's masterpiece of amorality, Rebecca Sharp, heroine of *Vanity Fair*. (She is generally known by the nickname **Becky**.) She is small, sandy-haired, and slender, even childish-looking. But she is a cunning, grasping, selfish, manipulative creature who manages to fool many of the characters in the book. She is both exasperating and fascinating, for the reader always wonders what Becky is going to get away with next.

> *Downstairs, then, they went, Joseph very red and blushing, Rebecca very modest, and holding her green eyes downwards. She was dressed in white, with bare shoulders as white as snow—the picture of youth, unprotected innocence, and humble virgin simplicity. "I must be very quiet," thought Rebecca, "and very much interested in India."*
> —WILLIAM THACKERAY, *VANITY FAIR*

REGAN *(Irish, "the little king")* One of the two heartless daughters in Shakespeare's *King Lear*. While Goneril, the eldest, is weak and mean, Regan is truly sadistic. It is she who plucks out one character's eyes onstage—and relishes the act.

REGINA *(Latin, "queen")* Henrik Ibsen's use of the name in his drama *Ghosts* may be ironic, for Regina Engstrand is anything but a queen. In the course of the play she discovers how little control she has over her fate. She is the maid in the Alving household, beautiful and headstrong. She would like to marry the dissolute Osvald Alving, but learns that she is his half sister. This discovery arouses her fury that she was not raised as a lady, but adopted by a carpenter who married her housekeeper mother. At the end of the play she elects to go work in the brothel that her father has established.

REMARKABLE *(English adjective as name)* A bit of local color in James Fenimore Cooper's *The Pioneers,* the first of his "Leatherstocking Tales." Cooper is writing about upstate New York in the mid-eighteenth century, stressing the extreme isolation of the European characters in the wilderness. Miss Remarkable Pettibone is the snuff-taking, nearly toothless housekeeper who runs the Temple household, a virtually feudal outpost of civilization. Her name is reminiscent of the odder Puritan names.

> *She presided over the female part of the domestic arrangements, in the capacity of a housekeeper; was a spinster, and bore the name of Remarkable Pettibone.*
> —JAMES FENIMORE COOPER, THE PIONEERS

RHODA *(Greek, "rose")* Rhoda Nunn is one of the spinsters alluded to in the title of George Gissing's *The Odd Women.* Her last name suggests a kind of cloistered existence that is threatening to Everard Barfoot, who courts her. Rhoda, however, is quite a fierce feminist, and though she falls in love with Everard, refuses to marry him, aware that as his wife, she would sacrifice her independence.

ROMOLA *(Italian, "belonging to Rome")* *Romola* is the novel in which George Eliot strays farthest from home, for it is set in fifteenth-century Florence, in the era of Savonarola. Her heroine is Romola de Bardi, the beautiful and brilliant daughter of a proud blind scholar. Though fiercely intelligent and extremely well educated, she is nevertheless limited by her feminine frailty. Her father reproaches her for the shortcomings of her scholarship, and she falls in love with the wrong man. Handsome, charming, plausible Tito Melema is clever enough to satisfy her father and alluring enough to earn her love, but he is morally weak, and ultimately Romola bears the brunt of his weakness.

> *Romola was laboring, as a loving woman must, to subdue her nature to her husband's.* —GEORGE ELIOT, *ROMOLA*

ROSE *(English flower name)* The Victorian fashion for flower names points up how decorative and demure the ideal Victorian woman was. In fact, **Rose** and its variant **Rosa** were used almost indiscriminately by Charles Dickens, among other writers, for pretty, mild-mannered, submissive women. Rosa Bud (known inevitably as "Rosebud") in *The Mystery of Edwin Drood* and Rose Maylie in *Oliver Twist* are two examples of Dickens's occasionally vapid heroines. Rosa Dartle, in *David Copperfield,* is a different story, the seduced and abandoned cousin of the rakish James Steerforth. Bitter and vindictive, she brings a whiff of melodrama to the plot. So does the Rosa in Catharine Maria Sedgwick's *Hope Leslie.* She is the illegitimate daughter of an English nobleman, who has traveled to the New World with the dissolute Sir Philip Gardiner, disguised as his page. Though she loves him to distraction, she recognizes his evil, and warns Hope Leslie against him.

> *As for Rose, she was a little gentlewoman born, and had a horror unspeakable of her sister's bad manners.*
> —MARGARET OLIPHANT, *MISS MAJORIBANKS*

A more conventional maiden is found in Sir Walter Scott's *Waverley.* Though the novel as a whole is the tale of Edward Waverley's adventures among Highland Jacobites in 1745, and although

FLOWER NAMES

Every era has its fashions in naming, and one of the striking vogues of the Victorian era was for flower names. Anthony Trollope created Violet Effingham and Lily Dale, Henry James is responsible for Daisy Miller and Pansy Osmond, Elizabeth Gaskell invented Hyacinth Clare, and the name **Rose** pervades Victorian literature. This was actually a reflection of truth: Victorian girls were also named **Myrtle, Ivy,** and (in Gilbert and Sullivan, at least) **Buttercup.** Curiously, a nearly contemporary vogue for jewel names (**Ruby, Beryl, Coral, Garnet**) did not transfer from life to fiction.

there is even a bright-eyed, passionate woman among them, Waverley ends up marrying the predictably pretty and bland Rose Brawardine. Even *Miss Majoribanks,* a High Victorian comedy of manners by Margaret Oliphant, features an eligible, ladylike Rose. In this case, Oliphant allows herself a little joke: Rose Lake is the daughter of a drawing master, and "rose lake" is the name of a color, a dark reddish orange. The character is a sweet, modest young lady who takes her Art very seriously. Henry James, usually unswayed by sentiment, also created a ladylike Rose in *The Princess Casamassima.* She is Rose Muniment, the invalid sister of revolutionary Paul Muniment. She runs a kind of salon from her bedside, entertaining aristocrats and anarchists in her extremely modest lodgings.

Variations on the name are numerous and various. Though scholars trace both **Rosalind** (or **Rosalynde**) and **Rosamond** (also seen as **Rosamund** and **Rosamunde**) back to German roots meaning "horse" or "fame," they have been associated with **Rose** for hundreds of years. **Rosalind** may have been invented by Edmund Spenser as a near anagram of Rosa Daniel, his mistress. Shakespeare took it up for the principal female character in *As You Like It,* one of his best-loved heroines. Rosalind, the aristocrat's daughter banished to the Forest of Arden, is quick-thinking, witty, and (of course) beautiful. She turns her exile to good account, disguising herself as a youth and subjecting her suitor Orlando to a "love cure" that demonstrates how enraptured by her he really is. In William Thackeray's *The Newcomes*, Rosalind Mackenzie, better known as **Rosey** or **Rosa**, is the pretty, blond, and somewhat insipid girl who is married off to Clive Newcome by her mother's strenuous efforts. Rosamund Oliver is a minor character in Charlotte Brontë's *Jane Eyre*, a rich girl whom Jane's fatuous cousin St. John Rivers decides not to marry because she doesn't have enough stamina and mettle to be an effective missionary. Rosamond Vincy, in George Eliot's *Middlemarch*, is also a beautiful and wealthy girl, but she has none of Rosamund Oliver's innate kindness. Eliot makes Rosamond Vincy empty-headed, vain, and selfish. She fascinates the physician Tertius Lydgate into marrying her, then cannot live within his means. Her extravagance puts his whole career at risk.

Other variations on **Rose** are simple elaborations. **Rosine,** for instance, adds the French diminutive *ine* ending. In Beaumarchais's play *The Barber of Seville,* Rosine is the beautiful young ward of Bartholo who is courted by the Count Almaviva. Plucky, clever, and sardonic, she is reluctant to let Bartholo dictate her marital fate. She appears again in *The Marriage of Figaro* as the count's wife, but marriage has not been kind to her, as her husband neglects her for other women. **Rosalie** is an elaboration with a Continental air, used by Anne Brontë in her governess novel, *Agnes Grey*. Rosalie Murray is one of the most fully described of heroine Agnes's charges—a pretty, spoiled flirt. "Her temper being naturally good, she was never violent or morose," says the narrator, "but from constant indulgence, and habitual scorn of reason, she was often testy and capricious." Even when she is engaged to a local baronet, the great catch of the neighborhood, she cannot resist meddling with other men. **Rosanna** is a combination of **Rose** and **Anna,** used by Wilkie Collins for the sinister Rosanna Spearman in *The Moonstone*. She is the unhappy ex-convict hired by Lady Verinder to be a housemaid. Silent, reserved, and mistrustful, she is a natural object of suspicion once the gigantic Moonstone goes missing.

> *Celia:* Why, cousin! why, Rosalind! Cupid have mercy! Not
> a word?
> *Rosalind:* Not one to throw at a dog.
> —WILLIAM SHAKESPEARE, AS YOU LIKE IT

ROSWITHA *(Old German, possibly "white horse")* Roswitha was a German nun of the late tenth century, a Benedictine scholar who dramatized the lives of a number of virgin saints. In Theodor Fontane's *Effi Briest,* she is the loyal maid of the female protagonist Effi. There is something saintly indeed about Roswitha's unswerving warmth and loyalty as naive young Effi commits adultery, is disgraced, and loses contact with her daughter.

ROWENA *(Invented name)* Sir Walter Scott may have based this name on the Welsh **Rhonwen** (possibly meaning "slender and fair"). He used it in *Ivanhoe,* his immensely popular novel about the struggle between the Saxons and Normans for control of England. Rowena is a proud and beautiful young princess who has been raised by her distant relative Cedric. He wants to marry her off to the powerful Athelstane but his own (disgraced) son Wilfred of Ivanhoe is in love with her. Naturally the younger, handsomer hero ultimately prevails, after proving his mettle against boorish Norman knights. No less romantic than Sir Walter Scott is Edgar Allan Poe, who wrote his tale "Ligeia" almost twenty years after *Ivanhoe* was published. Ligeia is the ravishing, darkhaired, passionate wife of the narrator—who dies. The narrator takes as his second wife the fair-haired aristocrat Lady Rowena Trevanion, but never loves her. When Rowena dies at a young age, her corpse appears, to the opium-addled narrator, to turn into the much-mourned and irreplaceable Ligeia.

ROXANA *(Persian, "daybreak")* Daniel Defoe's *Roxana,* written in 1724, is one of several eighteenth-century novels that focus on the issue of a woman's chastity. In *Pamela* and *Clarissa,* the heroines struggle to maintain their virtue but Roxana, driven by practicality, surrenders hers. Having married a fool and lost her children and every hope of supporting herself, she allows herself to be supported by a "gentleman." From there it is a short step to a life as a kept woman. She tells the story in retrospect, full of regret. In Mark Twain's *Pudd'nhead Wilson,* Roxana is a slave descended from Virginia planters. She switches her son with the son of her master so that her child will never be sold.

> *"How singular it is," said he, "that the name of Ruth is so seldom chosen by those good people who go to the Bible before they christen their children. It is a very pretty name, I think."*
> —ELIZABETH GASKELL, *RUTH*

RUTH *(Hebrew, "companion")* The biblical story of Ruth was particularly dear to the Victorians. She was the Moabite woman who, when widowed, stayed with her Hebrew mother-in-law Naomi. In the Book of Ruth she says to Naomi, "Whither thou goest, I will go." John Keats's "Ode to a Nightingale" refers to Ruth "when, sick for home,/She stood in tears amid the alien corn." The name thus has associations with womanly duty, familial affection, and tragedy. Fanny Fern may have sought to play on these in her autobiographical *Ruth Hall,* a best-seller in the 1850s. It tells the story of a middle-class girl who is mistreated first by her father and later by fate when she loses her daughter and then her husband. Even her parents-in-law refuse to help her and her two remaining daughters, so she must write to support her family—ultimately successfully. Elizabeth Gaskell's *Ruth,* written in 1850, tells a somewhat similar story of a woman beaten down by circumstances. Ruth is a beautiful and naive orphan of sixteen who is apprenticed to a dressmaker in a country town. She is seduced by a wealthy young man, barely knowing that she has done wrong, but when she becomes pregnant she is acutely aware of her shame. She is taken in by a minister and his sister but eventually the facts about her circumstances leak out, and she is shunned in their small town. *Ruth* is an attempt to portray the plight of fallen women in sympathetic terms, so the heroine is honest, hard-working, religious, long-suffering, and slightly unbelievable.

SABINE *(sah been'; French, "a Sabine")* This name, which also occurs as **Sabina,** probably endured because of a Sabina who used to be on the Calendar of Saints. In Émile Zola's *Nana,* Sabine Muffat de Beuville is a young countess whose life illustrates the two moral poles of Parisian high society. The daughter of a debauched marquis, she was married off at an utterly innocent seventeen to a count. Having spent seventeen further years immured in a dark provincial house rearing her family, she has emerged to scout husband material for her own utterly innocent seventeen-year-old daughter. Both her husband and her father are caught in the spell of the great courtesan Nana, and Sabine herself is beginning to waken to the power of sex under the influence of her husband's cousin.

SARAH *(Hebrew, "princess")* Also **Sara.** The biblical Sarah was the wife of Abraham who, at the age of ninety, bore him a son, Isaac, from whom the Hebrew people were descended. Sarah is a forthright, outspoken woman who, when the angel told her she would bear a child, laughed out loud. Something of her matter-of-fact air clings to the name, as in Henry James's Sarah Pocock. She is the sister of Chad Newsome in *The Ambassadors,* but while Chad has tasted the delights of Europe and been overwhelmed, Sarah—emphatic, stately, "inclined to the massive"—never swerves from the American point of view. She *embodies* Woollett, Massachusetts. One of Dickens's most enduring comic creations is Sarah Gamp, more commonly known as "Sairey" for that is how she pronounces her own name. She is nominally the nurse to old Martin Chuzzlewit in the novel of that title, but her nursing skills are nonexistent. In fact, she is deeply preoccupied with death and cannot resist prematurely "laying out" her patients to see how they will look as corpses. With her vast umbrella, her constant guzzling of tea, and her insistent references to her (possibly non-existent) friend "Mrs. 'Arris," she is really nothing more, as a character, than a bundle of eccentricities. But only Charles Dickens could have assembled them.

A common nickname for **Sarah** is **Sally**, most likely to be used in literature before the twentieth century as a name for a servant. Elizabeth Gaskell's *Ruth* features a no-nonsense, somewhat rough and ready housemaid named Sally. She has been with minister Thurstan Benson and his sister Faith for her whole life, and is fiercely loyal to them. When they bring the pregnant, unmarried Ruth into their house, she disapproves deeply. Yet her acquiescence in their scheme to pass Ruth off as a widow becomes clear when she insists on shearing off Ruth's red-gold hair, according to the custom for widows. If the aim of *Ruth* is to humanize the face of the fallen woman, Sally, with her stern religion, is the acid test. Her principles are tested by Ruth's presence in the Bensons' house, but she is won over by the goodness and humility of Ruth herself.

SASHA *(Russian, usually diminutive of* **Alexandra**: *Greek, "defender of mankind")* Chekhov's drama *Ivanov* focuses on the plight of the earnest, intelligent, reform-minded landowner Nikolai Ivanov. He is beset on all sides—bankrupt, discouraged, exhausted by his wife's gradual death of tuberculosis. Sasha Lyebedev is the daughter of a neighbor, and she is his opposite: young, energetic, modern, brilliant. She finds Ivanov's very passivity alluring, and makes an effort to attract him.

SCYLLA (sih′ lah; *Greek mythology name*) Though many readers are familiar with the monster called Scylla that Odysseus had to steer his ship past in *The Odyssey*, Ovid's *Metamorphoses* tells the story of a human Scylla. She is the daughter of King Nisus of Megara, who fell in love with her father's sworn enemy Minos of Crete. Her father has a lock of purple hair that guarantees him victory and she cuts it off to give it to Minos—who is horrified by her betrayal of her family and her city. After Megara's defeat she is turned into a bird called "Ciris" or "Shearer."

SELINA (*Greek, "moon"*) Much of Wilkie Collins's *The Moonstone* is narrated by the Verinder family butler, Gabriel Betteredge. Though she is dead, his wife Selina's presence hovers over the narrative at times. He married her because he felt it would be cheaper to keep a wife than to pay a housekeeper, and he was repaid for his calculating attitude by the way she bullied him during her lifetime.

SEMELE (*sem' eh lee; Greek mythology name*) In classical myth, Semele is the daughter of Cadmus, the founder of Thebes. She is pregnant by a lover who has identified himself to her as Jupiter. Juno, disguising herself as Semele's old nurse, persuades the girl to insist that Jupiter reveal himself to her in all his glory. She is burned to ashes by his brilliance and the child she was carrying is sewn into Jupiter's thigh. When the fetus has reached its full growth it is cut out—hence his Greek name, Dionysos, which means "twice born."

SEMIRAMIS (*Meaning unknown*) Semiramis is the legendary wife of Ninus of Babylon, around 2000 B.C. She is said to have charmed her husband into letting her reign for five days, during which time she had him killed. After his death she constructed the city of Babylon and founded the kingdom of Nineveh. Her brilliant reign continued for forty-two years, and on her death she turned into a dove. Dante disapproves of her, placing her in Hell with the Lustful, but Chaucer feels otherwise, and tells her story in "The Legend of Good Women." Voltaire wrote a tragedy based on her life, and Rossini's opera *Semiramide* also recounts her story.

SERENA (*Latin, "calm"*) In Edmund Spenser's *The Faerie Queen* this name, like so many others, is symbolic. Serena is a damsel who, wandering away from her protector to pick flowers, exposes herself to attack by the Blatant Beast, who represents slander. The point is how vigilant a lady must be to safeguard her reputation. Henry James may have been aware of this precedent, for Serena Merle in *The Portrait of a Lady* has gone to extraordinary lengths to protect her good name. She first appears as a friend of Gilbert Osmond's who rapidly becomes intimately friendly with Isabel Archer. Extraordinarily cultured and sophisticated, she seems to represent civilization and control taken to their highest level.

SHAHRAZAD (*Persian, "city dweller"*) Also **Scheherezade, Sheherezade, Sheherazad,** etc. The young woman who tells all the stories in *Tales from the Thousand and One Nights*. Her father is a vizier at the court of King Shahriyar. The king, having been betrayed by his wife, resolves never to undergo such an indignity again and marries a new virgin each day. Each new wife is then executed in the morning. Shahrazad witnesses these proceedings with indignation and insists that her father wed her to Shahriyar so that she may put a stop to this nonsense. The first night, she embarks on a story but cannot finish it before daylight, so Shahriyar lets her live on to finish it the next night. She continues thus for a thousand and one nights, and Shahriyar finally relents and lets her live, proclaiming her the liberator of her sex.

> *Shahrazad possessed many accomplishments and was versed in the wisdom of the poets and the legends of ancient kings.* —*Tales from the Thousand and One Nights*

SHIRLEY (*Old English, "bright clearing"*) When Charlotte Brontë wrote *Shirley* in 1849, this was a last name, rarely used as a first name. The novel's heroine Shirley Keeldar was expected to be a boy, hence the name (which was not taken up widely for girls until much later). It suits the character, however, for she is as unusual and independent as it might indicate. Rich and beautiful, Shirley does not need to marry to secure her survival, as so many nineteenth-century women had to. She is courted by several men and turns them all down either because she doesn't love them, or feels that they don't really love her.

SIBYL *(Greek mythology name)* In the ancient world a sibyl was a woman who delivered the wisdom of an oracle; some sources say there were ten, geographically scattered. Ovid tells how the Sibyl of Cumae became a seer. She was a beautiful maiden whom Apollo loved. When he offered her anything if she would yield to him, she asked for as many birthdays as motes of dust in a broom pile. Her mistake was to forget to request eternal youth as well. For eternity, she will continue to shrink and get older and older— "but still, the fates will leave me my voice, and by my voice I shall be known." In Oscar Wilde's *The Picture of Dorian Gray*, Sibyl Vane is an actress who attracts Dorian's attention because of her immense talent. They embark on a love affair but she neglects her art for her love of him.

SILVIA see **SYLVIA**

SOBERNESS *(English virtue name)* A bit of local color in Thomas Hardy's *Far from the Madding Crowd*. As she is paying her laborers, Bathsheba Everdene reads the list and says, "Temperance Miller—oh, here's another, Soberness—both women, I suppose?" These old-fashioned virtue names were more commonly given to women than to men.

SOPHIA *(Greek, "wisdom")* Wisdom is actually the least important attribute of Sophia Western, the love interest in Henry Fielding's *Tom Jones*. She is beautiful, warm, well-born, clever, and beyond Tom's reach, and that is enough to drive the plot along. In Oliver Goldsmith's *The Vicar of Wakefield*, Sophia is the younger Primrose daughter. Like her sister Olivia she was intended to be called Griselda, but her father was overruled because a rich relation named Sophia wanted to be the godmother. Less of a scandalous flirt than her sister, she is still awake to the charms of the male gender, and ends up on promising terms with Sir William

Thornhill, the family's benefactor. The name was clearly in style in the late eighteenth century, possibly because George I and George III of England married, respectively, Sophia Dorothea of Brunswick and Sophia Charlotte of Mecklenburg-Strelitz. In Jane Austen's last novel, *Persuasion,* Anne Elliot is somewhat hopelessly in love with naval man Frederick Wentworth. His sister Sophia, married to Admiral Croft, rents the Elliot family home of Kellynch Hall. Mrs. Croft is a bluff, outspoken, sensible woman who has lived as much on her husband's naval craft as she has on the land. She is quietly influential in reuniting her brother and Anne. **Sophie** is the French form of the name and both it and **Sophy** are used as nicknames. In *The Mill on the Floss,* Maggie Tulliver's aunt Sophy Pullet is the pleasantest of Mrs. Tulliver's three sisters. Neither snobbish nor miserly nor given to complaining, she nevertheless has a morbid imagination, which George Eliot exploits to comic effect. Sophy Viner is the resourceful young woman who innocently derails George Darrow's plans in Edith Wharton's *The Reef.* Darrow, a diplomat, is on the verge of proposing to his old flame Anna Leath when he is sidetracked by Sophy. At first he is entranced by her vitality but soon finds her limited: "The mere fact of not having to listen to her any longer added immensely to her charm." Their brief affair has repercussions on both of their futures.

Sofia (or **Sofya**) is also a popular name in Russia, where the diminutives are **Sonia** or **Sonya** and even **Sonetka**. In Chekhov's *Uncle Vania* Sofia Serebriakov is the daughter of Alexandr Serebriakov, owner of the estate that Uncle Vania manages. Sonia lives on the estate and helps to manage it. She is practical and self-sacrificing, in marked contrast to both her father and her beautiful young stepmother. Chekhov uses the name again in the story "Misfortune" for Sophia Petrovna Lubyantsev—possibly ironically. Sophia is the beautiful young wife of a notary, and she feels unappreciated. Knowing that she is making a mistake, she fails to fend off the approaches of another man, and ultimately agrees to run away with him without really wanting to. Sonya Rostov is a minor character in Tolstoy's *War and Peace,* the poor cousin of the Rostov family who was raised as a companion for Natasha.

She and Nikolai Rostov have a youthful boy-and-girl romance. Dostoyevsky, who freighted his names with meaning, used **Sonya/Sofya** twice. In *The Brothers Karamazov*, Sofya Karamazov is the mother of two of the brothers, Ivan and Aleksey (also known as Alyosha). Beautiful and innocent when she married their father, she did not long survive his cruel treatment of her, which included having orgies in her presence. In *Crime and Punishment*, Sonya Marmeladov is the classic whore with a heart of gold. She has turned to prostitution to support her reprehensible drunken father, but this pragmatic response to necessity does not prevent her from being a devout Christian. She even serves as Raskolnikov's confessor of sorts, and represents the notion that suffering has a redemptive power. Nikolai Leskov's "Lady Macbeth of Mtsensk" proposes no such notion; its Sonya (**Sonetka,** in this case) is a victim, and not an attractive one. She is one of the convicts accompanying Katerina, the Lady Macbeth figure, to exile in Siberia. She casually sleeps with Katerina's lover Sergey and teases Katerina about it.

> *"I wish young ladies had not such a number of fine christian names. I should never be out, if they were all Sophys, or something of that sort."*
>
> —JANE AUSTEN, *PERSUASION*

SPERANZA *(Latin, "hope")* In Book One of Edmund Spenser's *The Faerie Queen* the Red Cross Knight finally enters the House of Holiness where he meets the three daughters of Coelia. They are Fidelia, Speranza, and Charissa, or faith, hope, and charity. Speranza carries an anchor, a symbol of her special virtue.

STELLA *(Latin, "star")* See also **Estella** and **Esther.** Thomas Love Peacock's *Nightmare Abbey,* published in 1818, is a satiric look at the wave of romanticism sweeping England at the time. More particularly, it skewers some of the era's leading romantic poets like Byron, Coleridge, and Shelley. Stella Toobad, with her dark hair and her gloomy, melodramatic attitude, is thought to be based on Mary Godwin, who in real life married Shelley. Stella makes a mystery of her very presence at Nightmare Abbey and insists on behaving unconventionally: assignations must be at midnight, letters must be read in secret, and so forth.

> *"What is a name?" said the lady; "any name will serve the purpose of distinction. Call me Stella."*
> —THOMAS LOVE PEACOCK, *NIGHTMARE ABBEY*

STEPANIDA *(Russian, "crown")* An example of the unwesternized Russian names found among peasants and rural people in the literature of the nineteenth century. In Chekhov's story "The New Villa," Stepanida is the wife of the village blacksmith Rodion—and is also a blacksmith herself. Her competence contrasts with the helplessness of Yelena, the engineer's wife who has moved into the new villa.

SUSAN *(Hebrew, "lily")* In *The Mill on the Floss,* George Eliot makes one of Maggie Tulliver's aunts a Susan—she is aunt Deane, "the thinnest and sallowest of all the Miss Dodsons." She is also the one who married best, from a material point of view. Anthony Trollope uses the name for Susan Harding Grantly in *Barchester Towers* and the following Barsetshire books, but Mrs. Grantly is rarely known by her first name. The elder daughter of Mr. Harding and sister of Eleanor Bold, she is already married to Archdeacon Grantly by the time we meet her. She is extremely sensible and manages her volatile husband with great tact. In Thomas Hardy's *The Mayor of Casterbridge,* Susan Henchard is the wife whom Michael Henchard sells at a fair at the beginning of the novel. Bought by a sailor, Susan passes out of Henchard's life for twenty years. She reappears, however, when he has become the mayor of Casterbridge. The sailor who bought her has been lost at sea and she has no one else to turn to. Henchard remarries her out of a sense of guilt and duty. She is a simple rural woman with low expectations of life. Not so Sue Bridehead, the heroine of Hardy's *Jude the Obscure*. Cousin to the protagonist Jude Fawley, she is an extraordinary figure. Hardy says, "She was so vibrant that everything she did seemed to have its source in feeling." Sensitive, intellectual, imaginative, she proves fatally attractive to Jude. Their tangled, unhappy relationship also involves their respective spouses and children with heart-rending results.

Susan is actually a shortening of **Susanna** or **Susannah,** which comes closer to the Hebrew original of the name. Thomas Love Peacock's *Crotchet Castle,* written in 1831, combines a satire on romance with some sharply pointed mockery of nouveau riche social climbing. Susannah Touchandgo is the pretty, resourceful daughter of a banker who has absconded with his bank's profits. Originally intended as the wealthy bride for the young squire of Crotchet Castle, she is canny enough to disappear when her dowry has vanished. Anthony Trollope's *The Eustace Diamonds,* while more naturalistic than *Crotchet Castle,* is equally satiric and full of comical characters. One of the most entertaining is the elderly Lady Linlithgow—Trollope calls her "worldly, covetous, and not unfrequently cruel." Both mild-mannered Lucy Morris and conniving Lizzie Eustace must spend certain spells of time living with Lady Linlithgow because they are very remotely related to her and have nowhere else to go. Trollope's joke is to name her Susanna. His biblically literate readers would remember the story of Susanna and the elders. She is the beautiful young wife of a righteous man, and she attracts the attentions of two elders of the community. They watch her bathe in the garden one day—a scene much beloved by Renaissance artists, and irresistibly funny when coupled with the cranky Lady Linlithgow.

The French version of the name is **Suzanne,** and one memorable Suzanne in French literature is the maid in Beaumarchais's play *The Marriage of Figaro.* Figaro himself calls her "for ever laughing, blooming, full of gaiety and wit, loving and wholly delightful! And yet prudent." Unfortunately, Figaro's master Count Almaviva feels the same way and the plot turns around his attempt to bed Suzanne before her husband does. The story is probably most familiar from Mozart's opera based on the play. Beaumarchais's comedies were considered revolutionary in the way they dramatized and gave validity to the emotional lives of servants: Denis Diderot's novel *The Nun* went further in upsetting the status quo. Written in 1760 but not published until 1796, it is an exposé of cloistered life. Diderot's heroine, Suzanne Simonin, is sent to a convent because her family has no money for a dowry for her. She knows she has no religious vocation, and strenuously resists subsiding into communal life. Her experiences in several convents include a number of humiliations and a virtual seduction by a Mother Superior.

> *Who is Silvia? What is she,*
> *That all our swains commend her?*
> *Holy, fair, and wise is she;*
> *The heaven such grace did lend her,*
> *That she might admired be.*
> —WILLIAM SHAKESPEARE,
> THE TWO GENTLEMEN OF VERONA

SYLVIA *(Latin, "woods")* The earlier form of the name is **Silvia,** which was used by Shakespeare for one of the two heroines of *The Two Gentlemen of Verona.* She is the fair daughter of the Duke of Milan, courted by the two characters of the title as well as a third man. Engaged against her will to one, she undertakes to elope with the other, but misadventure strands her in a forest with a gang of ruffians. Aphra Behn also used the name in her shocking roman à clef *Love-Letters Between a Nobleman and His Sister.* In the early 1680s Lady Henrietta Berkeley, a virgin, was seduced by her brother-in-law Lord Grey. Behn calls her Silvia in the novel, and gives her enough initiative to begin using her sexuality to achieve her goals in life. Elizabeth Gaskell's *Sylvia's Lovers,* though written in 1863, is set on the coast of Yorkshire during the Napoleonic Wars. It is very much a novel of local color, and Sylvia, the strong-willed heroine, has limited choices available to her. In fact, her only future is her husband, and the selection she makes will haunt her.

This, then, was the beautiful little cousin about whom Philip had talked to her mother, as sadly spoilt, and shamefully ignorant; a lovely little dunce, and so forth. Hester had pictured Sylvia Robson, somehow, as very different from what she was: younger, more stupid, not half so bright and charming (for, though she was now both pouting and cross, it was evident that this was not her accustomed mood).

—ELIZABETH GASKELL, SYLVIA'S LOVERS

TAMORA (*Possibly a variant of* Tamar: *Hebrew, "date palm"*) Shakespeare's *Titus Andronicus* concerns the enmity between the Romans and the Goths; Tamora is the Gothic queen, brought to Rome as a prisoner by Titus Andronicus. Titus kills one of her sons to avenge the deaths in his family. Tamora is married off to the emperor of Rome, and plots revenge with the help of her slave/lover Aaron. She is ruthless and unswerving in her quest.

TANAQUILL (*English, meaning unknown*) Also **Tanaquil**. The first name of the fairy who was later known as Gloriana, the Faerie Queen. She is the daughter of Oberon in Edmund Spenser's allegory.

> *Tatyana was her name . . . I own it,*
> *Self-willed it may be just the same;*
> *But it's the first time you'll have known it,*
> *A novel graced with such a name.*
> *What of it? It's euphonious, pleasant,*
> *And yet inseparably present,*
> *I know it, in the thoughts of all,*
> *Are old times, and the servants' hall.*
> —ALEXANDER PUSHKIN, *EUGENE ONEGIN*

TATYANA (*Russian, origin murky*) This name (and its other familiar form, **Tatiana**) seems to have migrated into Russian use from an ancient Italian name. A Saint Tatiana, a virgin martyr of the third century A.D., is venerated in the Eastern Rite churches. It was considered sufficiently Russian so that one of Tsar Nicholas II's daughters was named Tatiana. In Alexander Pushkin's *Eugene Onegin,* Tatyana Larin is a rustic beauty who falls victim to Onegin's considerable charms. Though he sees her only as a clumsy child, her passion for him is genuine (albeit possibly fueled by her avid reading of romantic fiction). Onegin rejects Tatyana crudely and she marries another man. Several years later, when Onegin returns to Moscow, he finds Tatyana a changed woman, poised and dignified, and he attempts to rekindle their romance. Though Tatyana admits she still loves him, she realizes that her value to him is that of novelty and excitement, and she resolves to remain true to her husband. Fyodor Dostoyevsky considered Tatyana Larin "the apotheosis of the Russian woman." Pushkin's little apologia for the name suggests that before 1830, when he wrote *Eugene Onegin,* Tatyana was not a name used by educated Russians. If so, his use of it may have popularized it. In Anton Chekhov's tale "With Friends," Tatyana Losev (also called **Tanya**) is a much less imposing figure than her literary predecessor. The story explores an old friendship that cannot survive the stress of revival, from the point of view of the narrator Podgorin. He visits Tatyana at the estate that her husband Sergey has badly mismanaged, and discovers that the relationships he remembers so warmly from his student days are worth little.

> *As for Tatyana, already a beautiful mature girl then, she could think of nothing but love.*
> —ANTON CHEKHOV, "WITH FRIENDS"

TEMPERANCE *(English virtue name)* Temperance is one of what were known as the "Cardinal Virtues," along with Justice, Prudence, and Fortitude. The name was used in pockets of rural England into the nineteenth century (see **Soberness**). New England, with its strong Puritan heritage, also saw these names lingering for several hundred years. In Elizabeth Stoddard's *The Morgesons* (a novel packed full of unusually named characters), Temperance Tinkham is the Morgeson family "help," a spinster of thirty who cooks for the Morgesons and lives with them on a quasi-familial basis. Brisk, warm, and practical, she provides a refreshing counterweight to the emotional extravagances of Cassandra and Veronica Morgeson.

> *"Temperance is as good a cook as ever,"* said one; *"she is a prize isn't she, Miss Morgeson?"*
> —ELIZABETH STODDARD, THE MORGESONS

TERESA *(Greek, "harvest")* The name, which is also commonly spelled **Theresa**, may be rooted in a Greek place-name. Spanish mystic Saint Teresa of Avila is much revered in the Catholic Church, which may explain why her name has been used more readily on the Continent than in Protestant England, with the great exception of *Tess of the D'Urbervilles*. Tess's full name is Teresa, and perhaps Hardy intends association with the ecstasies of Saint Teresa, whose heart was pierced, so she said, with a spear of divine love. Tess's ecstasies, however, are limited to the physical, and not especially happily. She is the naive and passionate daughter of a laborer, who comes under the sway of the domineering Alec D'Urberville. Her history is dominated by her enormous physical allure for men and her intense aspirations and longings. In George Eliot's *Romola*, the Italian form of the name, **Tessa,** is used for another simple girl led astray by her social and intellectual superiors. Romola's husband, Tito Melema, meets Tessa when she is but a sixteen-year-old contadina selling milk in the city of Florence. He carelessly seduces her and she believes she is married to him. When Tito dies, Romola finds Tessa and her children and takes them into her household.

> *Tess Durbeyfield at this time of her life was a mere vessel of emotion untinctured by experience.*
> —THOMAS HARDY, *TESS OF THE D'URBERVILLES*

The French form of the name, **Thérèse**, appears in Dickens's *A Tale of Two Cities* attached to a character who hardly seems to deserve a first name. Madame Defarge, however, the sinister, ever-knitting tavern keeper, was named Thérèse by her family in a long-ago childhood. Émile Zola's *Thérèse Raquin* was one of his earliest novels, and addressed sexuality with a frankness that was shocking at the time. Thérèse is the orphaned cousin who grows up with Camille Raquin and is groomed from her early childhood as his wife. Camille, however, is very much under the influence of his mother, and the marriage is never consummated. When Thérèse meets Camille's old acquaintance, the virile Laurent, he seduces her and the two become utterly obsessed by their sexual life. Laurent kills Camille to free Thérèse, but the memory of the dead man haunts the pair and they have no satisfaction.

> *Thérèse grew up sharing Camille's bed and her aunt's tender affection. She had an iron constitution but was coddled like an ailing child.*
> —ÉMILE ZOLA, *THÉRÈSE RAQUIN*

TERPSICHORE (turp sih' koer ee; *Greek, "rejoicing in dance"*) One of the best-known of the nine Muses, the daughters of Zeus and the Titaness Mnemosyne. Their function was to inspire artists and intellectuals, and Terpsichore's realm was the dance; she is often depicted holding a lyre. She was the mother of the Sirens.

THALIA (*Greek, "festive"*) Like **Terpsichore** above, one of the nine Muses. Thalia, whose identifying accessory was a laughing mask, inspired comedy.

THEA (*Greek, "goddess"*) In *Hedda Gabler,* Thea Elvsted represents the choices that Hedda has not made. A friend of Hedda's since childhood, she has made peace of sorts with her unhappy marriage, and it is under her calming influence that Ejlert Lovberg, once in love with Hedda, has been able to publish a book. Thea is less brilliant than Hedda and expects less from life, which may be the key to her contentment.

THETIS (*Greek mythology name*) In classical myth, Thetis is the mother of Achilles. Ovid's *Metamorphoses* tells how the goddess of the waters came to produce the great Greek hero. She is loved by Jupiter, but an oracle predicts that any child she bears will eclipse his father in might and glory. Jupiter thus marries her off to the heroic but mortal Peleus. (It was at their wedding that the goddess Eris tossed a golden apple inscribed "for the fairest" onto the ground. Juno, Venus, and Diana fought over it.) When Achilles is born, Thetis dips him in the river Styx to immortalize him.

THISBE (*Meaning unknown*) (Another version of the name is **Tisbe**.) The mythical character of Thisbe is best known from the play-within-a-play in Shakespeare's *A Midsummer Night's Dream,* but Chaucer also refers to her in "The Legend of Good Women." In his view, Thisbe is one of "Cupid's saints," women who persist in loving men who treat them badly. Thisbe is a Babylonian princess who falls in love with the prince next door. Though the parents are opposed to the romance, the pair court through a crack in the wall dividing the two properties. They agree to elope, and plan to meet at a well outside of town. Thisbe gets there first, only to find a lion prowling around, so she hides in a nearby cave. Pyramus, on arriving, finds Thisbe's veil and bloody footprints from the lion's earlier kill. He assumes the lion has devoured Thisbe and kills himself in grief. When Thisbe emerges from her cave, she follows suit.

> *Upon the one side of the wall stood he,*
> *And on the other side stood fair Thisbe,*
> *Each there the other's sweet words to receive.*
> —GEOFFREY CHAUCER, "THE LEGEND OF GOOD WOMEN"

THOMASIN *(Hebrew, "twin")* A feminine version of **Thomas** that also occurs as **Thomasina** and **Tamsin.** In Thomas Hardy's *The Return of the Native,* Thomasin Yeobright is sometimes called Tamsin. She is the young girl in Egdon who loves lady-killer Damon Wildeve. A day before their wedding, he jilts her. Throughout the book Thomasin's charms and claims to loyalty take second place to Eustacia Vye's bewitching sexuality; when Damon does ultimately marry Tamsin, he insists that they name their daughter Eustacia.

THORA *(Scandinavian, "Thor's battle")* Thor is the thunder god in the Scandinavian pantheon. *Egil's Saga,* probably written around A.D. 1230, recounts events of the ninth and tenth centuries in Norway and Iceland. Thora Lace-Cuff is a young woman who is abducted by the impulsive young Norwegian Bjorn.

TISHY see **LAETITIA**

TISIPHONE (tih sih' foe nee; *Greek, "she avenges the murdered")* The name of one of the Furies, also known as the "Erinyes," terrifying creatures with dogs' heads, bats' wings, snaky hair, and blood dripping from their eyes. They provide the punishment for Greeks who commit the worst crimes, like patricide—notably, they drive Oedipus mad after he kills his father Laius—until Athena tames them and they turn into fertility goddesses. Thenceforward they are called "the Kindly Ones."

TITA *(Diminutive of various names)* Martita is one of the more likely sources for a name like **Tita,** but its Spanish origin is unex-

GOOD GODDESS, BAD GODDESS

Greek myth is full of sister acts, from the Pleiades to the Muses, but among the most famous were a pair of three-somes: the three Graces and the three Furies. The Graces were minor deities, sometimes known as the the Charities, and their names were **Aglaia, Thalia,** and **Euphrosyne,** or "brilliance," "flowering," and "joy." Their fame, however, pales compared to the fame of the Furies, with their snaky hair and eyes that oozed blood. In some depictions they even have the wings of bats and heads of dogs. They lived in the underground realm of Hades, and emerged upon earth to torment the perpetrators of such crimes as patri-cide. Their names are **Tisiphone** ("she avenges murder"), **Alecto** ("the unresting one"), and **Megaera** ("full of jeal-ousy").

pected for Miss Tita Bordereau of Henry James's novella *The Aspern Papers.* Her aunt, Miss Juliana Bordereau, was once the beloved of famous poet Jeffrey Aspern. The narrator wants desperately to see the letters he feels sure Aspern has written to Juliana. After much careful plotting and manipulation he finds that Miss Juliana is too clever for him—her price for revealing the papers is that he marry her silly, ignorant, elderly niece Tita.

> *Miss Tita (for such the name of this high tremulous spinster proved somewhat incongruously to be) . . .*
> —HENRY JAMES, *THE ASPERN PAPERS*

TITANIA *(Greek mythology name)* Titania is the Queen of the Fairies in Shakespeare's *A Midsummer Night's Dream.* It seems likely that her name comes from the Titans, the race of earth giants who preceded the Olympian gods. (Their name is also the source for the adjective "titanic" and the element titanium.) Though she is not large in size, Titania is powerful, and part of the comedy of the play is the subversion of her power when, influenced by a potion, she falls in love with the donkey-headed Bottom.

TOINETTE see **ANTONIA**

TOPSY *(English invented name)* One of the issues behind the antislavery movement in the mid-nineteenth century was the question of whether or not African Americans had a moral sense. In *Uncle Tom's Cabin,* the benevolent (but benighted) slave owner Augustine St. Clare has a tart Yankee cousin, Ophelia. Augustine gives Ophelia a slave, Topsy, to see if Ophelia can teach Topsy the difference between right and wrong. At first, Topsy is bright and energetic and utterly ignorant. Asked who had made her, she famously answers, "I 'spect I growed. Don't think nobody never made me." (In the Victorian worldview, the correct response is "God made me.") Ophelia reads the Bible to Topsy and shows her the light.

TRILBY *(Invented name)* George du Maurier's 1894 novel *Trilby* was an immense success, inspiring a stage version and giving its name to a soft felt hat. The character of Trilby O'Ferrall is a half-Irish, half-French laundry maid who poses for a set of English art students in Paris. "She was out of the common clever, simple, humorous, honest, brave and kind," and the most perceptive of the artists falls in love with her. She supports her young brother Jeannot with her hard work but turns to the hypnotist Svengali to cure her of crippling headaches. He manages to make her into an extraordinary singer who becomes famous throughout Europe, but she can only sing under his hypnotic spell. Svengali's control of Trilby is complete, and has tragic consequences.

UMA *(Meaning unknown)* Robert Louis Stevenson's "The Beach at Falesa" has its origins in Stevenson's travels in the South Pacific. The very ordinary English narrator, John, enters into a "marriage" with the slender, sober, beautiful native girl Uma. The bonds of this relationship, and his solicitude for their children, awaken him to the moral ambiguity of colonialism.

UNA *(Latin, "one")* In Edmund Spenser's allegory *The Faerie Queen,* Una represents the One True Church—the Church of England. Spenser was writing under Elizabeth I, whose predecessor Mary had been Catholic. Establishing the legitimacy of the Church of England was one of Elizabeth's important tasks and Spenser did his part. Una wears black for mourning over her white dress, which represents purity. Throughout Book One of *The Faerie Queen* Una is powerless. She must rely on the protection of various partisans like the Red Cross Knight, and she is ever prey to deception.

> *"Undine Spragg—how can you?"*
> —EDITH WHARTON, *THE CUSTOM OF THE COUNTRY*

UNDINE *(French, "wave")* The protagonist of Edith Wharton's satirical *The Custom of the Country* is the beautiful, headstrong, and selfish Midwestern girl Undine Spragg, named after "a hair-waver her father put on the market the week she was born."

Undine's beauty and force of character propel her to the heights of New York and then Paris society, yet her limited imagination ultimately limits her happiness.

URANIA *(Greek, "of the heavens")* The Muses, nine daughters of Zeus and the Titaness Mnemosyne, inspired the artists and intellectuals of Greece as well as performing for the gods on Mount Olympus. Each Muse had a specialty—Urania's concern was astronomy, and she used the stars to tell fortunes.

URSULA *(Latin, "bear")* One of Hero's ladies-in-waiting in William Shakespeare's *Much Ado About Nothing*. The French form of the name is **Ursule**. *Ursule Mirouet* is one of Honoré de Balzac's novels depicting life in the provinces. Balzac himself referred to Ursule as "Eugénie Grandet's happy sister." The martyrdom of the virgin Saint Ursula casts no shadow over the story of the pious, sweet, well-educated young Mlle Mirouet. Balzac refers to her "divine artlessness," which is enough to attract the affections of her aristocratic but spendthrift neighbor, Savinien de Portenduère. Ursule uses her substantial inheritance to pay off Savinien's debts and finance the start of his political career, so that finally even the proud Madame de Portenduère is won over.

VALÉRIE *(Latin, "to be strong")* Balzac's *Cousin Bette* is one of the most cynical of his novels depicting "the human comedy." The marriage of the Baron and Baroness Hulot is one of the relationships that Balzac skewers. While the Baroness Adeline is faithful to her beloved Hector, he betrays her right and left, both with courtesans and with the bourgeoise Valérie Marneffe. Madame Marneffe is the more dangerous, because her husband (who connives at the affair) must be placated. In fact, the amoral Valérie encourages Hulot, recognizing from the start of his interest in her that he can be pressured into providing a new job for her husband.

VARVARA see **BARBARA**

VENUS *(Latin mythology name)* Ovid's *Metamorphoses* provides the most thorough character sketch of the love goddess of Mount Olympus. Known in Greek as **Aphrodite,** she emerged from the ocean and was carried to land on the island of Cythera, hence her other name of **Cytherea.** The secret of her enduring allure is the girdle she wears, which causes all men to fall in love with the wearer. She has at least ten children (including Aeneas) by various men, but does not favor her husband Vulcan in the least. With her constant jealousies and plots she is almost as much of a menace to mankind as fellow goddess Juno.

VERA *(Russian, "faith")* In the sprawling cast of Leo Tolstoy's *War and Peace,* Vera Rostov is the elder sister of warm, natural Natasha and may represent Tolstoy's notions of repression and formality borrowed from Western Europe. Vera marries a strict, correct army officer of German descent, whose rigidity, combined with hers, leads to strained relations with the rest of the family. In Mikhail Lermontov's *A Hero of Our Time,* Vera is one of the victims of the remorseless hero Grigory Pechorin. Lermontov may have based his portrait of Vera on one of his own mistresses, Varya Lopukhina. Vera is a former mistress of Pechorin's who married a dull elderly man when Pechorin ended their affair. When she meets Pechorin again, she does not hesitate to resume the affair, for she has never stopped loving him. Even her husband's knowledge of her adultery does not deter her.

VERENA *(Latin, "true")* Verena Tarrant is the beautiful red-haired orator at the center of Henry James's *The Bostonians*. She attracts the attention of both Boston reformer Olive Chancellor and southern lawyer Basil Ransom. (The names in this book appear to have been chosen with garden imagery in mind.) Verena's most successful subject is women's rights, a notion dear to Olive and repellent to Basil.

VERONICA *(Latin, "true image," or Greek, "bringer of victory")* According to legend, Veronica is the woman who wiped Jesus' brow as he carried his cross up Calvary. His image appeared afterward on the cloth she had used. The name would be unusual in New England, and adds to the general air of disjunction in Elizabeth Stoddard's *The Morgesons*. Veronica is Cassandra Morgeson's frail, incalculable sister. She suffers from fits, and presents an extremely reserved front to the world.

> *Veronica was an elfish creature, nine years old, diminutive and pale. . . . She was too strange-looking for ordinary people to call her pretty, and so odd in her behavior, so full of tricks, that I did not love her.*
>
> —ELIZABETH STODDARD, *THE MORGESONS*

VICTORINE *(Latin, "victory")* A French form of **Victoria.** Victorine de Taillefer is one of the boarders at the Maison Vauquer in Balzac's *Old Goriot.* The hardened criminal Vautrin promotes a scheme whereby Eugène de Rastignac, the handsome provincial, takes up with Victorine who is the illegitimate daughter of a wealthy man who has not acknowledged her. To Vautrin, she represents an opportunity that Eugène should grasp: by securing her affection and approaching her father, he could secure a fortune. Victorine, in all innocence, loves Rastignac, but he fails to return her interest.

VIOLET *(Latin, "purple")* The late nineteenth century saw a fashion for flower names but Violet Effingham, in Trollope's *Phineas Finn,* is anything but a shy, shrinking bloom. Though small and demure-looking she is both fierce and stubborn, and determined to have her way in her romantic life. "She is exactly the girl to remain unmarried if she takes it into her head that the man she likes is in any way unfitted for her," suggests one character. Phineas Finn, in his ambitious way, makes a try for her but ultimately she marries the unpredictable Lord Chiltern, whom she loves deeply. **Viola** is the Italian version of the name and Shakespeare uses it for the heroine of *Twelfth Night.* The fair, well-born victim of a shipwreck in Illyria, she disguises herself as Cesario to safeguard her virtue in this strange country. Unfortunately she makes an exceedingly beautiful young man, and attracts romantic interest from the Countess Olivia, while she falls in love with Duke Orsino. She is one of Shakespeare's most appealing characters, being resourceful, intelligent, and generous as well as good-looking. In *All's Well That Ends Well,* Shakespeare uses another variant, **Violeta,** for a minor character. She is a neighbor of the widow whose daughter Bertram attempts to seduce.

> *Violet Effingham was an orphan, an heiress, and a beauty.*
> —ANTHONY TROLLOPE, *PHINEAS FINN*

VIRGINIA *(Latin, "virgin")* This name was used first as an attribute name, denoting a chaste woman—in "The Physician's Tale," for instance, of Chaucer's *Canterbury Tales*. Virginia is a pure and honorable woman. An evil judge tells her that she must die or submit to him sexually, and she calmly chooses death. Virginia Madden is one of the spinsters referred to in the title of George Gissing's *The Odd Women*. Raised as gentlewomen with no skills and no knowledge of money, Virginia and Alice Madden have worked as governesses and companions because they can do nothing else to support themselves. Virginia, out of work and in near despair, considers taking an unpaid job merely to be fed and housed. She also drinks, secretly, to dull her dread of the future.

VIVIAN *(Latin, "full of life," or may descend from a clan name of uncertain meaning)* Also **Vivien**. Many of the Arthurian legends include mention of the fay Vivian who enchants Merlin, ultimately keeping him captive in a cave or a tower. She is additionally known as the Lady of the Lake. In Matthew Arnold's "Tristram and Iseult," Iseult of Brittany, Tristram's legitimate wife, tells her children the story of Merlin and Vivian.

WALLACHIA *(Invented name)* Anthony Trollope wrote *He Knew He Was Right* in 1867, and while he was working on it, the ruler of Romania was deposed. Eight years before, Moldavia and Wallachia had been combined to form Romania, so names of the two former provinces were much in the news. Trollope sometimes adopted words as names, and since Wallachia Petrie is an American, he may have felt that he had extra latitude with her name. English observers often found American names (especially the more elaborate ones) perfectly outlandish. Wallachia, finally, is a comical character, a crusading feminist, so her silly name works. Trollope used his friendship with several American women as a basis for Wallachia, and one of them, Kate Field, objected. Trollope, in a letter to Miss Field, wrote, "I never said you were like W. Petrie. I said that that young woman did not entertain a single opinion on public matters which you could repudiate, and that she was only absurd in her mode of expressing them."

WENONAH *(Sioux Native American, "firstborn daughter")* Also **Winona** and **Wenona**. In Henry Wadsworth Longfellow's narrative poem "Hiawatha," Wenonah is the mother of Hiawatha.

WILHELMINA see **MINA**

WINIFRED *(Welsh, "blessed peacemaking")* *The Way We Live Now* was Anthony Trollope's thirty-second novel, and one of his most cynical. Set mostly in London, it depicts a society given over to the pursuit of money. One of the minor characters, Winifred Hurtle, is not pursuing money so much as a husband, which Trollope may have regarded as equally unseemly. She is an American widow of murky antecedents and her relationship with pleasant young Paul Montague is closer than it should be. Mrs. Hurtle wants to marry Paul. He in turn needs to get over the hurdle of the pushy widow in order to marry his far more conventional English sweetheart.

XIMENA *(hee may′ nah; Spanish, origin unclear)* Also **Jimena.** The legend of El Cid goes back to the twelfth century and has been handled by many Spanish poets. French dramatist Pierre Corneille compressed elements of the story into a tragedy called *Le Cid* in 1637. He stresses the conflict between passion and the quest for honor. Don Rodrigo is a great soldier of Castile and Ximena is his highborn fiancée. When her father insults his father, Rodrigo must exact avenge. He kills Ximena's father and goes off to fight the Moors as a penance. (He is so brave that he earns from them the title of *Sidi* or "Lord"—hence "le Cid.") Ximena, however, is not content with Rodrigo's restitution and recruits another champion to battle Don Rodrigo for her. All this time, she loves Don Rodrigo, but values honor more highly than her romantic impulses.

> *Ximena's noble, and although in love,*
> *She cannot tolerate a craven thought.*
> —PIERRE CORNEILLE, *LE CID*

ZARINA *(Persian, "golden")* Lord Byron borrowed this name from a historical source—apparently Zarina was the chieftain of an Asian tribe. Byron transformed her into the wife of the despot Sardanapalus in the eponymous drama. Gentle, kind, and forbearing, she does not reproach Sardanapalus even though he is flagrantly unkind to her.

ZÉLIE *(Probably French, "solemn")* Balzac's *Ursule Mirouet* is set in the provincial town of Nemours, where the postmaster, Minoret-Levrault, is a man of consequence. In fact, it is his wife Zélie who provides the brains and efficiency in the family, promoting both her husband and her son to a level of status and material well-being that they could not reach without her.

ZENOBIA *(Greek, "power of Zeus")* Zeus is not invoked lightly in novels set in nineteenth-century Massachusetts. Where the strict Protestant heritage of the Puritans lingered, the pagan set off alarm bells. Zenobia Moodie (the last name is also a give-away) is one of the most colorful characters in Nathaniel Hawthorne's *The Blithedale Romance*. Dark-haired, passionate, mysterious, she is full of life force and not particularly amenable to control by any of the novel's main characters. She is a journalist and a feminist who lives in the experimental community of Blithedale, and she falls in love with the reformer Hollingsworth. He, alas, prefers the more conventional version of femininity as embodied in her half sister Priscilla. Zenobia Frome, better known as **Zeena,** is another denizen of rural Massachusetts in Edith Wharton's *Ethan Frome*. Her sensitive but taciturn husband Ethan attempts to escape her sickly, selfish domination of him with her lively young cousin Mattie, and tragedy results.

ZERBINETTA *(French, invented name)* In Molière's *That Scoundrel Scapin*, Zerbinetta is the daughter of Argante, one of the old fogey fathers in the play. She is the typical Molière tart soubrette, in love with Léandre and frustrated by her father's stupidity about the merits of her loved one.

ZHENYA *(zhen' yah; Greek, "welcoming")* Anton Chekhov's tale "The House with an Attic" recounts the narrator's obsession with a young girl named Zhenya Volchaninov. Slender, pretty, and frail, she is no more than eighteen: "She was not as yet considered grown up by the family, who still called her by her pet name of Missie, because that was what she had called her English governess when she was a little girl." Once her elder sister Lydia perceives the narrator's feelings about Zhenya, the family closes ranks around her and he is not allowed to see her again.

ZINAIDA *(Russian, "belonging to Zeus")* Turgenev's novel *First Love* is narrated by a sixteen-year-old boy, Vladimir Petrovich. Dreamy, given to writing poetry, he is excited when "Princess" Zasyekin moves into his family's gatehouse with her pretty gray-eyed daughter Zinaida. He is instantly fascinated by Zinaida, who treats him with a mocking, manipulative mixture of affection and scorn. Only gradually does he realize that his rivals for her affection (and possibly her favors) include his father.

> *I was like soft wax in the hands of Zinaida.*
> —IVAN TURGENEV, *FIRST LOVE*

ZOE *(zoh' ee; Greek, "life")* Haidée, the Greek smuggler's daughter in Byron's *Don Juan*, has a maidservant named Zoe, and so does Émile Zola's Nana, the great courtesan and center of the eponymous novel. The Russian variation on the name is **Zoya.** In Turgenev's *On the Eve*, Zoya is a "nice-looking Russian-German girl, blonde and plump, with a slight cast, a tiny 'dimple' at the tip of her nose, and tiny red lips." She was engaged by the Stahov family to serve as a companion to their daughter, Elena. The dilettante sculptor Pavel Shubin, frustrated in his love for Elena, flirts with Zoya.

> *I remember I was very much amused when I first heard her Christian name; it was Zoraïde—Mademoiselle Zoraïde Reuter. But the Continental nations do allow themselves vagaries in the choice of names, such as we sober English never run into. I think, indeed, we have too limited a list to choose from.* —CHARLOTTE BRONTË, *THE PROFESSOR*

ZORAÏDE *(zoe righ eed'; French from Arabic, "captivating woman")* Another one of Charlotte Brontë's exotic French names. In *The Professor*, Mademoiselle Zoraïde Reuter is the proprietor of the girls' school next door to the one where the protagonist William Crimsworth teaches. Crimsworth is attracted to her but she ultimately marries Crimsworth's boss, the proprietor of the Pension Pelet—a better financial bet. Charlotte Brontë may

CHARLOTTE BRONTË'S FRENCH NAMES

Charlotte Brontë paid close attention to names. Look at the characters in *Jane Eyre:* besides Jane herself and Mr. Rochester (Edward, to his intimates), we have Rochester's ward Adele Veran, his would-be fiancée, Blanche Ingram, and Jane's clerical cousin, stuffy St. John Rivers. Each name is perfectly appropriate for its character's position in life, cultural background, even personality. It is hardly surprising, then, that Brontë came back from her stint teaching in Belgium with a collection of French names that she later worked into her fiction. *The Professor,* in particular, includes a wonderful selection. Among William Crimsworth's students are Eulalie, Hortense, Sylvie, and Léonie. His fellow teachers include Mademoiselles Suzette, Zéphyrine, and Pélagie. And Madame Reuter, who runs the Pensionnat, rejoices in the name of Zoraïde.

have picked up the name **Zoraida** from Cervantes's *Don Quixote,* and she evidently regarded it as an exotic one, since characters named **Zorayde** appear in two of her earliest stories.

ZULEIKA *(Arabic, "fair")* "The Bride of Abydos" is another one of Byron's narrative poems with an exotic setting. Zuleika is the daughter of a Turkish pasha. Her father wants to marry her off to a powerful ally, but she is in love with her cousin Selim. The pair elope, the father kills Selim, and Zuleika dies of a broken heart. Eugène Delacroix, a great aficionado of things Turkish, painted *The Bride of Abydos* in 1857.

INDEX

INTRODUCTION
TO THE INDEX

But where is . . . ? But what about . . . ? Has she forgotten . . . ?

Not every familiar name occurs in the Penguin Classics. Dionysos appears, but not Dennis. Nathaniel, but not Nathan. What's more, the canon of the Penguin Classics themselves is mutable. Works that were on the list when I began have been dropped, while some significant additions have been made since I finished the manuscript. Milton's *Paradise Lost,* for instance, is a new entry, just brimming with classic names that I couldn't get into this book. Certain works of Shakespeare are published as Penguin Classics while others, strictly speaking, are Pelicans. The works of Edith Wharton are published as Twentieth-Century Classics but have been included here. What's more, I have often put in even minor characters in the books included (especially if they had unusual names), while certain books I didn't get to at all. I hope the reader will forgive my lapses, and I suggest that William Rose Benét's classic *The Reader's Encyclopedia* is a good place to follow up any queries.

This apologia is necessary because the Index exposes the book's shortcomings. It is intended, though, to be helpful to the reader who wants to browse through a favorite author's characters for inspiration. This is where you will find all of Jane Austen's heroines in one place. Names in brackets indicate the entry under which you'll find reference to a given book. Thus, "Marianne" is listed in the Index under *Sense and Sensibility*, but the bracketed reference [**Mary**] indicates where that character is discussed.

INDEX

Aeschylus

AGAMEMNON
- Cassandra
- Clytemnestra
- Orestes

THE EUMENIDES
- Alecto
- Apollo
- Megaera
- Orestes
- Tisiphone

THE LIBATION BEARERS
- Electra
- Orestes

THE PERSIANS
- Darius

PROMETHEUS BOUND
- Helen
- Prometheus

SEVEN AGAINST THEBES
- Eteocles
- Laius

THE SUPPLIANTS
- Danaos

Alas, Leopoldo

LA REGENTA
- Alvaro
- Ana [Anne]
- Fermin
- Victor

Alcott, Louisa May

LITTLE WOMEN
- Amy
- Beth [Elizabeth]
- Friedrich [Frederick]
- Josephine
- Margaret
- Theodore

THE INHERITANCE
- Amy
- Edith
- Ida

WORK: A STUDY OF EXPERIENCE
- Christie [Christina]
- Hepsey [Hepzibah]
- Rachel

Alger, Horatio, Jr.

RAGGED DICK
- Dick [Richard]
- Frank [Francis]
- Johnny [John]
- Roderick

STRUGGLING UPWARD
- Florence [Flora]
- Luke
- Melinda
- Prince
- Randolph

anonymous

ARTHUR LEGENDS
- Arthur
- Bedivere
- Bors
- Galahad
- Gareth
- Gawain
- Guinevere
- Igraine
- Iseult
- Kay
- Lamorack
- Lancelot
- Lynette
- Lyonors
- Merlin
- Mordred
- Morgan
- Percival

Index

Index

Index

Index

Index